The Clandestine History
of the
Kovno Jewish Ghetto Police

The Clandestine History
of the
Kovno Jewish Ghetto Police

By anonymous members
of the
Kovno Jewish Ghetto Police

—m—

Translated and edited by Samuel Schalkowsky
Introduction by Samuel D. Kassow

Published in association with the
United States Holocaust Memorial Museum,
Washington, D. C.

INDIANA UNIVERSITY PRESS
Bloomington and Indianapolis

This book is a publication of

INDIANA UNIVERSITY PRESS
Office of Scholarly Publishing
Herman B Wells Library 350
1320 East 10th Street
Bloomington, Indiana 47405 USA

iupress.indiana.edu

Telephone 800-842-6796
Fax 812-855-7931

⊖ The paper used in this publication meets the minimum requirements of the American National Standard for Information Sciences—Permanence of Paper for Printed Library Materials, ANSI Z39.48–1992.

Manufactured in the United States of America

Library of Congress
Cataloging-in-Publication Data

The clandestine history of the Kovno Jewish ghetto police / anonymous members of the Kovno Jewish ghetto police ; translated and edited by Samuel Schalkowsky ; Introduction by Samuel D. Kassow.
    p. cm.
    Includes bibliographical references and index.
    ISBN 978-0-253-01283-8 (cloth) — ISBN 978-0-253-01297-5 (ebook)
    1. Jews—Persecutions—Lithuania—Kaunas. 2. Jews—Lithuania—Kaunas—History—20th century. 3. Jewish police officers—Lithuania—Kaunas—History—20th century. 4. Holocaust, Jewish (1939-1945)—Lithuania—Kaunas. 5. Kaunas (Lithuania)—Ethnic relations. 6. Lithuania—History—German occupation, 1941-1944. I. Schalkowsky, Samuel editor, translator. II. Kassow, Samuel D., author of added text.
    DS135.L52K3829 2014
    940.53'184793—dc23
                        2013042348

1 2 3 4 5   19 18 17 16 15 14

CONTENTS

DEC   2014

Contents

PREFACE

Geschichte fuhn der viliampoler yiddisher geto-politsei (History of the Viliam-pole[1] [Kovno] Jewish Ghetto Police, referred to hereinafter as "the history") is a 253-page document written in Yiddish by members of the Jewish police in the Kovno ghetto during 1942 and 1943. It covers events from the start of the German attack on Soviet Russia, on June 22, 1941, through most of 1942.

The history itself is a part of a large collection of documents, secretly assembled by the Jewish ghetto police, containing over 30,000 pages in over 900 files. When the liquidation of the ghetto became imminent, these documents were placed into a wooden crate covered with tin and buried.

The burial of the police documents in the Kovno ghetto, in itself, was not unique. For example, Avraham Tory, secretary of the Kovno ghetto Elder Council, maintained a detailed diary and buried it before the destruction of the ghetto. Rabbi Ephraim Oshry, who addressed halachik issues associated with ghetto life, buried a collection of his written responsa. The Kovno ghetto was totally destroyed and burned to the ground by the retreating Nazis in July 1944. In August 1944, when Kovno was liberated by the Soviet army, Tory and Rabbi Oshri, both of whom had survived in Kovno, searched and found their buried material. But the crate buried by the Jewish ghetto police remained buried for twenty years. Apparently, no one who knew of its existence and location survived to attempt to retrieve it.

The crate was accidentally found in 1964 during the bulldozing of the former ghetto area. It was turned over to the Soviet authorities, who did not allow publication of these (or any other) Jewish documents. The documents remained unavailable for an additional twenty-five years, until after Lithuania achieved its independence.[2] A microfilm copy of the entire collection was obtained by the United States Holocaust Memorial Museum (USHMM) in 1998.

In 2000, having recently retired, I began working as a volunteer in the archives of the USHMM. Since I was born and raised in Kovno and was an inmate of the Kovno ghetto, I was assigned to work with the Kovno ghetto police document collection. My task was to create a finding aid for future researchers, an inventory of the files in the collection, including a brief description of their contents.

I came across the History of the Viliampole Jewish Ghetto Police and was captivated by it. It had been written—actually typewritten—in the ghetto by Jewish ghetto policemen, describing events within about a year or less of their actual occurrence, and it covered the entire time that I was there.[3] It illuminated my experiences and provided background and details of which I either had not been aware or, perhaps, had preferred to forget.

Some of the documents had a personal connection. For example, internal ghetto correspondence written by or about Michael Bramson, the initial deputy chief of the Jewish ghetto police and later chief of its criminal division, resonated with me, because Bramson had been my high school teacher during the year preceding the war. I could therefore associate a face and a voice with the words. I could wonder about how he was transformed from an individual who had been concerned only a few months earlier with the academic progress of his students into an enforcer of Nazi orders.

In February 1942, Jewish policemen had forcibly seized my mother and me on a ghetto street and brought us to the square, where many other inmates were assembled. We were told we were being transported to the Riga ghetto. But we didn't believe it, as all others included in previous selections ended up being killed at the Ninth Fort.

Bramson was in charge of the Jewish police detail guarding the assembled inmates. Didn't he remember me as one of his students? (I had had extracurricular contacts with him.) Shouldn't he therefore have helped? He didn't, and I held it against him for a long time. The history provided a different, more realistic perspective.

I have been puzzled by the fact that of all the languages that I knew before the war, only Lithuanian was—selectively and completely—wiped from my memory: after the war, I could no longer understand any written or spoken Lithuanian, and I certainly could not speak it. What was it in my wartime experience that brought this about? Chapter 2 of the history, describing the initial seven-week period of Lithuanian atrocities against the Kovno Jews, provides a possible explanation.

Visual images and words tend to run together in my memory. (For example, to remember someone's name, it helps me to associate an image with it.) To effectively repress—to block out—memories of traumatic experiences, it seems necessary to remove the associated words, in order to contain the emotions of fear, extreme anxiety, and the sense of impending doom connected to them. But if this is so, then why did I not only retain but even increase my knowledge of the German language as a result of my ghetto and concentration camp experiences? The memories of many of these experiences were also repressed, but the German language associated with them was not. What is the difference?

One explanation is that being able to communicate with the Germans in concentration camps was essential to my survival. But knowing Lithuanian was, at least for me, not relevant to my survival efforts. (I was not, for example, involved in trading with Lithuanians for food.) Indeed, my well-being, my very survival, required that I avoid Lithuanians whenever possible.

Chapter 2 brings back memories of hearing the Lithuanian "partisans" shouting on the street outside our house, and of the fear of being dragged out by them and taken to a painful death. Hiding in the house, I didn't see them—there are no visual memories, only the shouting in Lithuanian. The trauma of this seven-week period preceding the establishment of the ghetto is therefore predominantly connected to words spoken in Lithuanian. (I suspect that our small, unassuming dwelling at the end of the street was passed over by the Lithuanians because their interest was in plundering Jewish property and our house didn't look promising.) Added to this, the abruptness of the stark change from a normal existence to being engulfed by the Lithuanian orgy of brutality, humiliation, and slaughter so well described in chapter 2 makes my complete repression of the Lithuanian language seem understandable.[4]

The history manuscript is a work in progress. If one assumes that its introduction was written at the outset of the project, it represents a statement of purpose, not necessarily of accomplishment. The author or authors recognized that writing so close to the events to be described made "objective reporting" impossible. The introduction nevertheless asserts the intention of the author(s) to "try with all their might to preserve objectivity, to convey all experiences and events in their true light, as they actually occurred, without exaggerating or diminishing them." Regardless of how close they may or may not have come to achieving their objective, how did they go about trying to reach it?

As more fully described in the appendix, "Evolution of the Manuscript," the police history project was very likely initiated by the police leadership during the last quarter of 1942. This was a time when life in the ghetto had changed for the better and the police undertook a number of internally directed activities, including an oath taken by all policemen to devote themselves to the well-being of the Jewish community. They also organized a police association "to educate and develop the police staff," which became a venue for weekend music concerts. Inasmuch as their other actions evidence that the police leadership was intent on providing a record of Nazi crimes against the Kovno Jews, creation of the police history manuscript, which, as the introduction stated, is "also the history of the entire Kovno ghetto," exactly corresponds with the environment and the spirit of the time.

The police history was authored by a lead author and at least two additional contributing authors whose material was most likely integrated by the lead author. The 76 manuscript pages of text of chapters 1, 2, and 3, as well as the 54 manuscript pages of chapters 9, 10, and 11 can be attributed to the lead author. The 19 manuscript pages of chapter 5, dealing with the interrelationships of the principal ghetto institutions and the ghetto population, were very likely written by a high-ranking official of the Jewish police. The 100 manuscript pages of chapters 4, 6, 7, and 8 were written by a different contributor; they were composed as continuous text, and the different sections were then assigned chapter numbers and integrated into the text by the lead author.

Additional individual policemen were involved in the project. Some critiqued the written material—at least of chapter 3—and provided handwritten notes in the margin. Others provided inputs to the authors as witnesses or participants in the events being described. The authors clearly had complete access to police files and archives, as evidenced by the numerous data tables incorporated in the text and inclusion of Elder Council orders and instructions transmitted to the police by the Nazi rulers.

The manuscript material was hastily arranged in its final order during the last quarter of 1943 (the last time-marker, deriving from the last pages of the manuscript, is November 1943). The Kovno ghetto was then well along on the path to liquidation: the ghetto was declared to be a concentration camp; its operations, as well as the functions of the Elder Council, were taken over by the SS; and deportations to nearby work camps, to Estonia, and to Auschwitz had taken place.

The police history is thus clearly a product of the ghetto police as an institution, rather than of an individual author working independently.

Earlier English translations of chapters 6 and 11, an excerpt from chapter 3, and the table of contents of the history have been published in *Yad Vashem Studies* 29 (2001): 203–40. They accompany an article by Dov Levin, entitled "How the Jewish Police in the Kovno Ghetto Saw Itself" (ibid., 183–202).[5] Levin selected chapters 6 and 11 because "the information and statistical data in these chapters provide comprehensive, as well as clear and systematic details about the structure of the police and its activities to a greater extent than in other chapters" (ibid., 200).

For fear that the document might fall into the hands of the Nazis, the history carefully avoids any reference to the collaboration and active participation in ghetto resistance activities by some policemen—including some of the police leadership.[6] An excerpt from chapter 3, which deals with rescue attempts by the Jewish police during the Great Action of October 28–29, 1941—"the blackest day in the history of the ghetto"—was published by Dov Levin as an introduction to "the nature of the relationship between the Jewish police and the anti-Nazi underground movement."

Herein is a complete and unabridged English translation of the entire manuscript of the history. It is hoped that ordinary readers, as well as historians and social scientists, will gain further valuable understanding from the additional chapters translated here for the first time. My principal concern in translating the Yiddish text has been to provide a faithful rendition of both the factual content and the emotional overtones of the original text. I approached this by preserving the sentence order of the original to the extent possible while adapting the sentence structure for the English-speaking reader. However, in some instances, the sentence order of an entire (long) paragraph was rearranged in order to convey the information and mood of the original. On other occasions, a number of short consecutive paragraphs dealing with the same topic were combined into one paragraph, when their separation in the original text disrupted the continuity of the narrative. Readers will note that text and maps sometimes use variant spellings for the same feature; that is occasioned by the fact that some references are in Yiddish and others in Lithuanian. Additionally, where ellipses appear in the translated text, these reflect actual ellipses points that appear in the Yiddish original.

The history was written in an environment of ongoing persecution. To some extent it is therefore a "history in progress." The past and present tense can therefore be encountered side by side, when past events were related to, or overflowed into, conditions at the time of the writing.

It may indeed be, as Dov Levin wrote, that "in the nature of things, since the Holocaust, this body [the Kovno Jewish ghetto police] has been practically synonymous with collaboration with the occupying forces" (ibid., 183). But such judgment is best made on an individual basis, from one's own personal perspective, particularly concerning the moral dilemmas faced by them. It is important therefore that the original source material be accessible, including the entire history, not only because it was written by policemen during the Holocaust—"in the storm of events"—but also because it describes police activities from their own perspective, in the context of what was happening at the time to the ghetto population.

The diary kept by Avraham Tory, secretary of the Elder Council during the ghetto years, provides an invaluable record of events in the ghetto.[7] The book by Leib Garfunkel, vice-chairman of the Elder Council and an activist in the Kovno Jewish community before the war, although published fourteen years after the end of the war, adds greatly to our understanding of events.[8] Both provide the unique perspective of active participants in these events, from the vantage point of the Elder Council and its direct dealings with the Nazi rulers of the ghetto. But the history adds another dimension: not only does it offer a firsthand account of the Jewish ghetto police, by the police themselves, it also describes the impact of events on the lives of ordinary ghetto inmates. Policemen were more directly involved with the population than was the Elder Council. Theirs was a "hands-on" experience, and their description of events and their effect on ordinary ghetto Jews reflects it.

The following quotation is from the text of the history, following the description of the small-ghetto action, which included the burning of the ghetto hospital with doctors, nurses, patients, and resident orphans locked inside: "The threat of death and annihilation hovers like a specter over our heads to this day. . . . If we should not survive, then perhaps the document we are writing here will fall into the hands of Jews, who will read and be astonished by what was done to us in the gloomy ghetto." They did not survive.

On March 27, 1944, the same day that the German command launched an action against the ghetto's children and elderly inmates, the entire Jewish ghetto police force of about 150 was taken to the Ninth Fort, the killing grounds of Kovno ghetto Jews. The Germans brutally tortured the police leadership, seeking to have ghetto hiding places disclosed to them. All of the about forty ranking policemen bravely refused to divulge any information useful to the Germans, and they were all murdered, including the then chief of the ghetto police, Moshe Levin, his two principal lieutenants, Yehuda Zupovitz and Ika Grinberg, and essentially the entire current police leadership.[9] Michael Bramson, the initial deputy chief of the ghetto police and later chief of its criminal division, died later in a Dachau labor camp.[10] Michael (Moshe) Kopelman, chief of the Jewish ghetto police and a member of the Elder Council from the inception of the ghetto until the end of December 1943 (when he resigned for health reasons and was replaced by Moshe Levin), escaped from the ghetto when it was being liquidated in July 1944, but was arrested by Soviet authorities in September 1944, tried for "collaboration" with the Germans in the ghetto, and sentenced to fifteen years of hard labor. He died in September 1945 in a Soviet hard-labor camp in the Irkutsk region.[11]

It seems appropriate to facilitate the wish of the authors of the history by making their document "fall into the hands" of a wider English-speaking audience, so that more people will be able to read about—and perhaps be astonished by—"what was done to us in the gloomy ghetto."

Acknowledgments

Being a writer as well as knowing Yiddish made Ellen Cassedy particularly helpful in her detailed editing of the entire translation. She sought to remove deficiencies in the use of the English language and generally raise the quality of the final product while adhering to the letter as well as the spirit of the Yiddish original. This project was also greatly facilitated and moved forward over a number of years by my wife, Ellen Schalkowsky, who provided constant encouragement, discussion of problem areas, and, when necessary, prodding.

Dedicated to the memory of my mother Chaya Kupershmit Shalkovsky, who perished by means unknown to me, in the Stutthof concentration camp after nearly four years of Nazi persecution.

Samuel Schalkowsky

Notes

1. Vilijampole, which appears on the map of the ghetto in this volume, is the Lithuanian spelling.

2. See Foreword by Esther Mayerowitch-Schwarz to "The History of the Kovno Jewish Ghetto Police (Excerpts)," in *YIVO Bleter*, new series, 3 (1997): 206–207 (Yiddish).

3. I was born in Kovno, Lithuania, in 1925 and was an inmate of the Kovno ghetto until February 1942, when I was transferred to the ghetto in Riga, Latvia. In August 1943, when the Riga ghetto was liquidated, I was taken to the Kaiserwald concentration camp outside Riga. In September 1944 I was shipped (by boat and barge) to the Stutthof concentration camp. From November 1944 until my liberation in April 1945 I was in a slave labor camp in Magdeburg.

4. Another Kovno survivor writes: "I was so deeply and lastingly shocked by the inhumane, almost animalistic conduct of the Lithuanians that a short time after the war I discovered I was no longer fluent in Lithuanian. Suddenly I could no longer utter sentences in this language that I had spoken as well as my mother tongue. Worried that there was something very wrong with my brain, I went to a doctor who determined that I had suffered such a shock from my observations outside the ghetto that a mental block now paralyzed my memory, preventing me from recalling this language." Memoir by Zev Birger, *No Time for Patience: My Road from Kaunas to Jerusalem* (New York: Newmarket Press, 1999), 59.

5. For a critique of some aspects of Dov Levin's article and his response, see Letter to the Editor by Samuel Schalkowsky in *Yad Vashem Studies* 31 (2003): 433–437.

6. See, for example, Alex Faitelson, *Heroism and Bravery in Lithuania 1941–1945* (Jerusalem: Gefen Publishing House, 1996).

7. Avraham Tory, *Surviving the Holocaust: The Kovno Ghetto Diary* (Cambridge, Mass.: Harvard University Press), 1990.

8. Leib Garfunkel, *The Destruction of Kovno's Jewry* (Hebrew) (Jerusalem: Yad Vashem, 1959).

9. Ibid., 176–184.

10. Josef Gar, *The Destruction of Jewish Kovno* (Yiddish) (Munich: Association of Lithuanian Jews in the American Zone in Germany), 1948.

11. Personal communication from Henry Kopleman, grandson of Michael Kopelman, 2004.

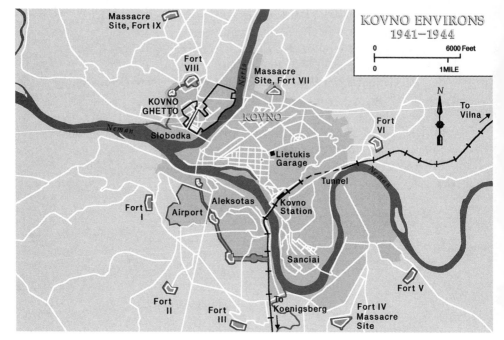

Map of the Kovno area (*above*) and detail of the Kovno ghetto (*facing*), marking the locations of significant events mentioned in the text. The River Neris is locally known also as the Vilija River. *Both maps courtesy of the United States Holocaust Memorial Museum.*

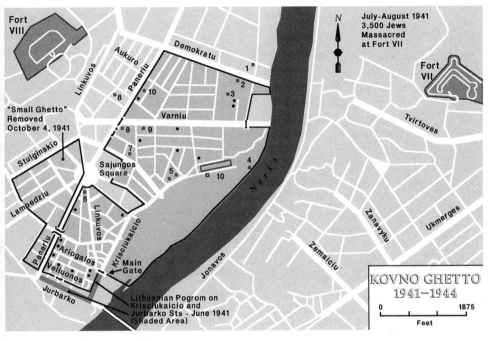

⋈ Footbridge
— Ghetto Surrounded with Barbed-Wire Fence
• Underground Hiding Places
— Gates
■ Select Features

1. Hiding Place for Books
2. Clandestine Arms Training
3. Ammunition Hiding Place
4. Clandestine Meeting Place
5. Clandestine School and Arms Training
6. Young Zionists
7. Pharmacy (Clandestine Radio)
8. Safe House
9. Jewish Council Building (Judenrat)
10. Workshop

The Clandestine History
of the
Kovno Jewish Ghetto Police

Inside the Kovno Ghetto

SAMUEL D. KASSOW

ON MARCH 26, 1944, SS-Hauptsturmführer (Captain) Wilhelm Goecke told the commanders of the Jewish police in the Kovno (Kaunas) ghetto to assemble the entire force the next morning for an air raid drill. Goecke wanted to see all the police clean-shaven, with boots shined and uniforms pressed. The next morning 140 policemen, led by commander Moshe Levin and his two immediate subordinates, Yehuda Zupovitz and Ika Grinberg, lined up in perfect order. To their great surprise, an order suddenly rang out for all the police to sit down on the ground. After the seven policemen in the ghetto orchestra were separated from the rest of the group, armed Germans and Ukrainians suddenly surrounded the police and ordered them to board buses. The vehicles took them to the nearby Ninth Fort, where many thousands of Kovno Jews had been killed some time before. Two policemen who tried to jump from the buses were shot dead, and the others were locked into three large cells after they arrived at the fort.[1]

The Germans summoned the police commander for an interrogation. A short time later Levin returned, badly beaten and covered in blood. SS-Oberscharführer (Sergeant First Class) Bruno Kittel, the main interrogator,

1

demanded that Levin disclose how the police had helped Kovno Jews leave the ghetto to join the partisans. He also wanted information about the whereabouts of hideouts that Jews had been building in the ghetto. Levin told the Germans that they would get nothing out of him. Kittel then summoned Levin again, and he never returned.

A short time later the Germans came for Yehuda Zupovitz, the deputy police commander, and Ika Grinberg, the police inspector. Like Levin, Zupovitz and Grinberg had been closely involved in the effort to smuggle Jewish fighters out of the ghetto and into partisan units. Recent veterans of the Lithuanian army, both of them had trained ghetto Jews in the use of weapons. Now Zupovitz and Grinberg suffered brutal torture, and when they returned to their cells the other policemen could barely recognize them. According to one account, the Germans gouged out Zupovitz's eye after he spit in the face of one of the interrogators.[2] Neither Zupovitz nor Grinberg divulged any information.[3]

The Germans went from cell to cell and promised to release any policeman who would lead them to ghetto hideouts. Hirsh Neuberger recalled that Kittel told the police in his cell that many of their comrades already had agreed to collaborate and had left the fort. He gave them fifteen minutes to think it over. At that point Ika Grinberg, who was in great pain, told his comrades to stand fast. Under no circumstances should they give the Germans the satisfaction of seeing them break down. They had to conquer their fear of death. All the policemen in the cell made a promise to stay silent. Some hours passed. Their nerves were strained to the breaking point. Kittel then came again and called out names. Thirty-three policemen, including the entire leadership of the force, were shot.[4] The rest, much to their surprise, were later allowed to return to the ghetto.

Indeed, a few policemen in another cell broke down and agreed to point out hideouts in order to save their lives. What they could not know was what was happening in the ghetto that very day: the notorious Kinderaktion, the "children's action." Moments after the trucks hauled the police off to the Ninth Fort on March 27, German autos with mounted loudspeakers ordered all ghetto inhabitants to stay in their homes. Anyone found on the street would be shot. Groups of Germans and Ukrainians, using dogs and axes, went house to house. They were looking for children and the elderly. All the victims were hustled onto buses with whitewashed windows. To drown out the crying and screams of frantic parents and the panicked children in the buses, the Germans set up a loudspeaker that blared out jazz tunes. Perhaps the policemen who went into the ghetto to lead the Germans to hideouts did not know that those places already were full of frightened Jews, including, in some cases, their own wives and children.

Horrible scenes took place. Distraught mothers fought to keep their children, even as the Germans ordered vicious dogs to attack them. Parents hustled their children into hideouts, shoved them under bundles of clothing, gave them heavy doses of sedatives. The first day the Germans found 1,000 victims, who were sent to the gas chambers of Auschwitz. The second day, helped by the policemen who had agreed to divulge the location of bunkers, the Germans found 800 more, who were shot in the Ninth Fort.

The murder of the police leadership meant the end of the Kovno ghetto police as it had been. To be sure, the occupation authorities set up a new force, but it was led by characters whom the Jews in the ghetto despised.

It was only when word had spread of the heroic behavior of Levin, Grinberg, and Zupovitz and other police commanders that many Jews in the Kovno ghetto began to realize that the story of the Kovno ghetto police was more complicated than they had believed. The police had not enjoyed a favorable reputation in the ghetto. Their faults were quite apparent. The police rounded up Jews for daily labor service. When the Germans demanded a contingent for deportation to distant labor camps, it was the police who produced the required number of deportees. Some policemen earned notoriety for their brutal behavior. Ghetto Jews envied the police because they and their families seemed safe from roundups and deportation. What was not so apparent, however, was the fact that the ghetto police played a major role in facilitating armed resistance by helping Jews escape to the partisans. The police helped smuggle in food and weapons and smuggle out children. The leaders of the Kovno ghetto police were individuals of courage and integrity. Levin, Grinberg, and Zupovitz were staunch Zionists, but that did not stop them from working closely with the communists to give young Jews military training and lead them safely to partisan units in the forests.

The story of the Jewish police is complex and nuanced. The police themselves were all too aware that they had to serve two masters: the Germans and the Jews in the ghetto. They had to walk a fine line, even as they found themselves in a very delicate situation. How would they be remembered? It was a question that was clearly on the minds of the police leadership. And therefore they decided—exactly who it was remains unclear—to leave a police chronicle to record the history of the ghetto police and of Kovno Jewry under German occupation. (The chronicle, along with the police archive, was hidden in the home of Ika Grinberg.) Of all the Jewish institutions in the ghetto, it was the police who had the most ongoing day-to-day contact with the ghetto population. As the chronicle noted, "all phases, events, and shocks are reflected in the activities of the police as if in a ribbon of film."

—⚬⚬⚬—

Generally speaking, the history of Kovno Jewry under the Nazi occupation falls into three rather distinct periods. The first, from June 22 until late October 1941, was a time of violence, terror, and mass executions that decimated Kovno Jewry and left few Jews alive in the Lithuanian provinces. The vicious behavior of much of the Lithuanian population toward the Jews underscored a feeling of total isolation and helplessness. In June 1941, just before the invasion, there were about 35,000 Jews in the city. By the end of October 1941 only about half of the Kovno Jews were alive, and women heavily outnumbered men. Yet, compared to those in the Lithuanian provinces, Kovno Jews were fortunate. Town after town experienced massacres of all or virtually all of its Jews in the summer and autumn of 1941. In the course of 1941 the Germans and their eager Lithuanian helpers murdered more than three-quarters of Lithuanian Jewry.

The second period, the "stable time," was from November 1941 into October 1943. This period, which is the focus of much of the police chronicle, saw no major massacres, although there were several deportations to work camps and to Riga. Individual executions of Jews also were a common occurrence; as a rule when the Gestapo decided to kill a Jew they also murdered his entire family. During this time the Jewish ghetto leadership, the Ältestenrat, or Elder Council, established the ghetto's major institutions, enforced German demands for Jewish labor, and avidly bribed and cultivated local German officials in order to protect the ghetto's inhabitants. It also had to deal with various crises that threatened the security of the ghetto. The Germans granted the Jews a temporary reprieve because they needed their labor. The Jews hoped that work would buy them time and perhaps a chance of survival. Indeed, only the Łódź ghetto, liquidated in August 1944, lasted longer than the one in Kovno.

The third period—"the breakup of the ghetto"—lasted from October 1943 until July 1944. As a result of Himmler's June 21, 1943, order to wind up the remaining ghettos of the Ostland and turn them into concentration camps, the SS assumed direct control of the Kovno ghetto. Under the new command of SS Captain Goecke, the ghetto was progressively dismantled into smaller work camps around Kovno, and many Jews were deported to more distant labor camps. These deportations traumatized the ghetto inhabitants. The ghetto suffered a major blow in October 1943 when Goecke asked the Elder Council to prepare lists for a routine transfer to a nearby labor camp. In fact the able-bodied Jews on the list were sent to Estonia while elderly, children, and those unfit for work were sent to Auschwitz.

During this period close ties developed among the ghetto resistance movement, the Elder Council, and the police force. The major goal of the Jewish resistance in the Kovno ghetto was to send Jews to partisan groups in the forests, not to start an uprising in the ghetto. As has been stated by Dov Levin, a former Kovno partisan and the leading historian of Lithuanian Jewry, without the active help of the Elder Council and the Jewish police this flight of armed fighters to the forests could not have happened.

A few days after the murder of the police leadership and the Kinderaktion, the Germans disbanded what was left of the Elder Council. On April 4, 1944, Goecke ordered the Elder Council to report the next day. Chairman Elchanan Elkes handed out poison to the members of the council in case they had to face German torture. The next day the Germans took the entire Elder Council, with the exception of Dr. Elkes, to the Ninth Fort. Like the police leadership, they too were interrogated about links to the partisans. Most were soon released, but Leib Garfunkel was kept behind and subjected to extended beatings. Finally, he too was allowed to return to the ghetto. But the effective authority of the Elder Council had ended.

The ghetto was finally liquidated in July 1944. When the Soviets liberated the city in early August 1944, they found 90 Jews alive. About 2,500–3,000 Kovno Jews survived the war in Nazi camps; another 500 had remained alive with the partisans or were hidden by Christians.[5]

—ɯ—

The Holocaust began in Lithuania. The Germans attacked the Soviet Union on June 22, 1941, and occupied most of that southernmost of the former Baltic republics within five days. When the invasion began, there were more than 220,000 Jews in Lithuania, including the Vilna region. By the end of 1941, only 40,000 still were alive, concentrated in four ghettos: Kovno, Vilna, Shavli, and Swiencian. The vast majority of Lithuanian Jews were murdered by Lithuanians affiliated with various police and paramilitary units who, for the most part but not always, acted under German direction and at German instigation. And, especially at the very beginning of the German occupation, many Jews were killed by their Lithuanian neighbors in acts of ugly, spontaneous, and random violence.

The suddenness and viciousness of the onslaught stunned Lithuanian Jewry. Adding to the shock was the fact that, by East European standards, relations between Lithuanians and Jews had been relatively peaceful. As waves of pogroms swept through the southwestern provinces of the Russian Empire during 1881–1882 and 1905–1906, Lithuania had remained, with some exceptions, largely quiet. During World War I and its aftermath, Lithuanian-Jewish relations were quite good—in stark contrast to Jewish relations with the Poles. Jews welcomed the Lithuanian fight for independence, and in the struggle between Poles and Lithuanians over Vilnius—a contest that the Lithuanians lost—most Jews supported Lithuania.

Inside the new borders of independent Lithuania in 1923 there were 155,095 Jews, constituting 7.6 percent of the country's population. Approximately 25,000 Jews lived in Kaunas. In 1939, 32,000 Jews lived in Kaunas; they were approximately one-quarter of the city's population. As was the case in neighboring Poland, the occupational structure of Lithuanian Jewry was markedly different from that of the largely agricultural non-Jewish population. Most Lithuanian Jews were employed in commerce, in handicrafts, and in small industrial enterprises.

In the hope that world Jewry would help them retain their independence and wrest their historic capital, Vilnius, from Polish control after World War I, the leaders of the newly formed Lithuanian state made far-reaching concessions to the Jews. The government granted Jews more autonomy than they enjoyed anywhere else in Europe. Jewish communities could collect taxes to support educational and communal institutions. Yiddish and Hebrew were recognized as official languages, and Jewish schools received funding from the state. The state established a ministry of Jewish affairs. Lithuanian Jewry elected a national representative body. In 1920 a Conference of Jewish Communities elected a National Council to deal with schooling, culture, and social welfare issues.

The honeymoon did not last. Unable to avert the Polish takeover of Vilnius, Lithuanians now had less need to court Jewish support. Lithuanian nationalists resented what they called Jewish domination of the economy and the free professions, and they demanded the dismantling of the "state within a state," the network of Jewish autonomy. By 1924 the Ministry of Jewish Affairs had been eliminated, as well as the taxing power of the Jewish communities.

In December 1926 a coup d'état that put Antanas Smetona in power curtailed liberal democracy and set the stage for the authoritarian rule that would remain in force until the Soviets took over in June 1940. This period saw a steady growth of anti-Jewish feeling. Newspapers such as *Verslas* launched the slogan "Lithuania for Lithuanians," which garnered increasing support from small business owners, craftsmen, university students, and professionals. In the 1930s the state took over key economic segments in which Jews had played leading roles. New cooperatives in the flax industry and the trade in meat and other food products largely eliminated Jewish employees. The civil service and municipal government saw an almost complete purge of Jews, and the number of Jewish university students dropped from 1,206 in 1932 to 500 in 1939.

Yet, despite the growing antisemitism, Lithuanian Jews were much better off than their brethren in Poland or Romania. There were no pogroms. By and large, the Smetona government, even as it carried through an ongoing "Lithuanianization" of the economy, cracked down on antisemitic violence. Here and there Jews were beaten up, signs on Jewish-owned stores were smeared with tar, but Jews still were relatively secure.

Despite political setbacks, Lithuanian Jewry remained a community suffused with Jewish national pride, cultural vitality, and a deep sense of communal responsibility. Its greatest single achievement was a superb network of schools, attended by between 80 and 90 percent of all Jewish children, as distinct from fewer than 40 percent in neighboring Poland. This network included Zionist, religious, and Yiddishist secular schools. Unlike Poland, the Lithuanian state continued to fund most of the school budgets.

No Jewish community in Europe was less assimilated—and less acculturated—than Lithuanian Jewry. In neighboring Poland, more and more Jews were speaking Polish as their first language, and a majority of Jewish children in the 1930s were receiving their primary education in the Polish language. But Lithuanian culture, relatively young and undeveloped, still held little attraction for Jews. Russian, widely popular with the Jewish bourgeoisie and intelligentsia before 1914, was no longer politically acceptable. Therefore in independent Lithuania the vast majority of Jews, including the middle and professional classes, used Yiddish as their first language. In no other Jewish community in the world was Yiddish used as widely as in Lithuania. In the late 1930s there were several daily Yiddish newspapers and journals, along with theaters and libraries. Furthermore, in no other Diaspora community did so high a proportion of Jews have as thorough a knowledge of Hebrew.

After World War I, Kovno Jewry found itself thrust into a new position of leadership and responsibility. The lands of the "Litvaks"—the Jews of Lithuania proper, Belorussia, and parts of eastern Poland, northern Ukraine, and Latvia—no longer were a part of the old Russian Empire but now were divided among new, mutually hostile states. The Polish-Lithuanian border was closed; there no longer was easy contact with other Litvak centers such as Vilna, Minsk, or Bialystok. Kovno Jewry now was on its own, called on to provide direction and guidance to the Jews in the new Lithuanian state. This it did with distinction, and in the process new cadres of Jewish professionals, businessmen, and intellectuals received valuable experience in communal leadership. It was from these cadres that the Jews would draw their leadership in the Kovno ghetto.

Lithuanian Jewry built a solid network of hospitals, credit societies, and economic organizations. The Jewish hospital in Kovno was one of the best in the country and boasted a large staff of dedicated doctors and nurses, including many physicians who would play a major leadership role in the Kovno ghetto. The Jewish People's Bank helped hard-pressed Jews secure credit and counter economic antisemitism.

To be sure, Lithuanian Jewry was, like other Jewish communities, riven by political factionalism. The strongest political trend was Zionism, with its youth movements, Hebrew cultural activities, and its own various factions. Lithuanian Jewry probably was the most fervently Zionist community in the Diaspora, despite a certain drop in support in the late 1930s. Zionist youth movements were particularly important, and they too would play a major role in the ghetto. Much of the key leadership of the Jewish police, including Moshe Levin and Yehuda Zupovitz, was recruited from the ranks of the Revisionists, the nationalistic followers of Ze'ev Jabotinsky, although other elements, such as the leftist Hashomer Hatzair, also were represented.

The second most popular movement was religious Orthodoxy, the Akhdus, led by eminent Torah sages such as Rabbis Duber Shapiro and Yosef Kahanemann. Lithuanian Orthodoxy boasted world-renowned Torah academies in Slobodka, Panevezhys, and Telshe. Even most secular Jews felt a residual respect for the leading rabbis. In a time of great crisis, in October 1941, the Elder Council would turn to Rabbi Shapiro for guidance and advice.

The third major political and cultural trend, somewhat less popular than the first two, was secular Yiddishism and populism, based on the idea of *Doikeit* (hereness) (pronounced: Doh'-i-kayt). As opposed to Zionism, Doikeit stressed that the Jews' future lay in the land in and with which they lived, and with the language, Yiddish, that they spoke. Whereas in Poland the primary exponent of Doikeit was the Bund, in Lithuania the Bund was quite weak. The major political movement of the secular Yiddishists was the People's Party (Folkspartei). However, with the rise of antisemitism in Lithuania, pro-communist sympathies increased within this Yiddishist sector. Young communists would be quite active in the Kovno ghetto, especially in the establishment of a partisan movement in the forests.

In the late 1930s Lithuania suffered serious setbacks at the hands of its more powerful neighbors. In 1938 Poland presented Lithuania with a humiliating ultimatum that forced the smaller country to renounce its claim to Vilna and to resume diplomatic relations. In early 1939 Germany forced Lithuania to cede the Memel region, which contained the country's only port. These setbacks strengthened right-wing nationalist groups and their calls for a fascist regime that would protect Lithuanian interests.

On September 1, 1939, Germany invaded Poland, and seventeen days later the Red Army attacked Poland from the east. In October 1939, Lithuania received a "gift" from the Soviets: the long-cherished Vilna region. But the Soviet largesse came with many strings. Lithuania was forced to allow the Red Army military bases.

The return of the Vilna region greatly increased the Lithuanian Jewish population, who now numbered more than 250,000, 10 percent of the entire population. The outbreak of the war also saw an influx of 15,000 Jewish refugees from Poland into Lithuania. They received decent treatment from the Lithuanian government.

Suddenly, on June 16, 1940, the Red Army occupied Lithuania and the other two Baltic states and a short time later annexed them after rigged elections designed to prove that the Baltic peoples wanted nothing more than to acquire the privilege of Soviet citizenship. Lithuanians could not resist the Soviet assault on their independence. They suffered in silence and looked to the country that seemed to be their only possible source of salvation, Nazi Germany.

Few issues are more critical to an understanding of the Holocaust in Lithuania than Lithuanian charges that the Jews betrayed their country to the Soviets. Accusations of Jewish treachery to Lithuania went hand-in-hand with stories of how Jewish members of the Soviet secret police supervised the deportations of thousands of Lithuanians to Siberia. To this day one hears the notion of the "Double Holocaust," which posits an equivalence between the Nazi killing of the Jews and the purported Soviet genocide perpetrated on the Lithuanians. For many Lithuanians, even today, an implicit corollary of the "Double Holocaust" was that alleged "Jewish complicity" in Soviet crimes against their Lithuanian countrymen counterbalanced whatever guilt certain Lithuanians incurred by their killing of Jews in 1941.

However, a careful study of the facts undercuts these charges of Jewish collaboration with the communists. It simply was not true that Jews gave massive support to the Communist Party of Lithuania and to the Soviet occupation in 1940 and 1941. At the end of 1939 the Lithuanian Communist Party had only 1,407 members. Of these, 54 percent were ethnic Lithuanians and 35 percent were Jewish. In other words, out of 220,000 Jews fewer than 500 were party members.[6] A somewhat greater number belonged to fellow-traveling organizations such as MOPR (Mezhdunarodnaia Organizatsiia Pomoshchi Revoliutsioneram—International Red Aid), a group to aid political prisoners. To be sure, this Jewish percentage in the Communist Party far exceeded the Jewish percentage of the overall population. But these Jewish communists comprised a minuscule proportion of Lithuanian Jewry, which was overwhelmingly Zionist, Orthodox, or Yiddishist.

The Jewish community suffered greatly from the Soviet suppression of religious, political, and cultural freedom. The communists closed down the flourishing Yiddish press, and only one Yiddish newspaper was allowed to appear. The Soviets destroyed the thriving network of Hebrew schools and religious academies; only Yiddish schools were now allowed, and they had to follow the party line. Soviet economic policy also dealt a body blow to many Jews. Owners of medium-sized shops, factories, and real-estate holdings lost their property to the state. By far it was the Jews who paid the heaviest price for the Soviet confiscation of business enterprises.

One of the most damning and damnable charges used by Lithuanians to explain the massacres of Jews that followed the German invasion was the accusation that it was mainly Jewish secret police officers who arrested and deported Lithuanians. But here, too, figures show a different story. Jews were somewhat overrepresented in the ranks of the Soviet secret police in Lithuania, but they still were a pronounced minority. Christoph Dieckmann shows that most of the leadership of the secret police came from the Soviet Union and that the proportion of Jews in the staff of the NKVD was 16.8 percent in June 1941.[7] Furthermore, many of those arrested and deported were themselves Jewish. Records document that 1,660 Jews were deported to the interior of the Soviet Union—13.5 percent of the total. An additional 385 Jews were sent to the Gulag, 9.8 percent of those arrested.[8]

Of course it would be absurd to deny basic differences in the attitudes of the Jews and the Lithuanians toward the Soviet takeover. The Lithuanian population hated the Soviets, and as has been noted, looked to the Germans as the only force that could liberate them. Jews, on the other hand, understandably preferred the Soviets to the Germans. They had no choice but to support the Soviets as the lesser evil. As one Jewish leader said, this was like a choice between life imprisonment and a death sentence.[9]

To be sure, many Jews benefited from the Soviet occupation. In independent Lithuania, Jews had been virtually eliminated from state employment. After the Soviet takeover, however, many Jews served in the state ministries, as judges in the courts, as directors of industrial enterprises. Jewish students now had easier access to higher education. The poorest Jews saw their economic and social status improve. On the one hand, they, like everyone else, were badly affected by new shortages of consumer goods. But their relative status often rose with guaranteed employment and opportunities to fill various lower-level posts. Lithuanians were not used to seeing Jews serve in public positions. They saw this influx of Jews as proof that all of Lithuanian Jewry had jumped onto the communist bandwagon. Analogous feelings surfaced among Poles in the Soviet-occupied parts of Poland.

About a week before the German invasion, on June 14, the Soviet secret police began to carry out large-scale arrests and deportations. Widespread rumors that Jewish officials supervised the arrests further inflamed Lithuanian anger, which reached a fever pitch just when the Germans attacked the Soviet Union.

Jews feared the growing rift between themselves and their Lithuanian neighbors. But even the greatest pessimists did not realize just how terrible the rift had become or foresee what the consequences would be.

—⁓—

Germany invaded the Soviet Union on Sunday, June 22, 1941. The first German units appeared in Kovno on Tuesday night, June 24. Thousands of Jews tried to flee Kovno and Lithuania with the retreating Red Army, but relatively few could outrace the onrushing German panzers.

As soon as the Germans attacked, Lithuanian nationalists rose up against the Red Army. The major Lithuanian nationalist organization, the Lithuanian Activist Front (LAF) had been formed in Berlin in November 1940 and maintained secret contacts with underground nationalist organizations in the homeland.[10] On March 24, 1941, the LAF issued so-called Instructions for the Liberation of Lithuania. These maintained that since the Jews had "betrayed" Lithuania, they no longer had a future in the country.[11] As soon as the Germans invaded, the LAF called on Lithuanian partisans to attack retreating Soviet units.

These many groups of partisans, who sprang up to attack the Red Army on the first day of the war, also lost no time in assaulting Jews. Even before the Germans arrived, the LAF commander in Kovno, Colonel Jurgis Bobelis, warned on the radio that Jews had been reported firing on German soldiers. For every German soldier killed, he declared, 100 Jews would be shot. In his account of the destruction of Jewish Kovno, Yosef Gar wrote that even before the entry of the first German troops, Lithuanian activists collected a group of twenty-five Jews on Jonava Street and forced them to dance and sing Soviet songs. They then ordered the Jews to kneel down, and the nationalists shot them in the middle of the street.[12]

Anxious to confront the Germans with the fait accompli of an established Lithuanian authority, Lithuanian leaders already in the country proclaimed a provisional government on June 25. This provisional government was led by Juozas Ambrazevičius-Brazaitis and included representatives of most of the major political groupings.

On Wednesday, June 25, Lithuanian partisans in Kovno, under the command of Algirdas Klimaitis, attacked the poor Jewish Quarter of Viliampole (Vilijampole or Slobodka in Lithuanian), known for its renowned yeshiva, and in that one night killed between 800 and 1,000 Jews. They killed their victims with incredible violence and brutality. They butchered every Jew they saw and seemed to take special delight in sawing people in half. The Zionist activist Mordecai Yatkonski was decapitated, and the body of his wife was found lying next to him with her breasts cut off. According to the testimony of Rabbi Ephraim Oshry, the Lithuanians tied up Rabbi Zalman Ossovski, put his head over a volume of the Talmud, and chopped it off. They also murdered his mother and son. Only Esther, the rabbi's five-year-old daughter, survived, by hiding under a bed. A survivor of the Kovno ghetto wrote that the rioters placed the heads of murdered Jews in the display windows of stores. On one wall a Jew wrote in Yiddish in his own blood: NEKOME (revenge).[13] The events in Slobodka, coming just one day after the Germans took over the city, certainly did nothing to raise the Jews' opinion of their Lithuanian neighbors. One survivor recalled that some Jews naively hoped that perhaps the Germans might be able to protect them.[14]

On Friday, June 27, a gruesome massacre of Jews took place at the Lietukis garage in central Kovno. Jews were seized on the street by Lithuanian partisans. The Lithuanians dragged their victims into the courtyard of the garage, where "partisans" smashed their skulls with tire irons and sledgehammers. Many Jews suffered terrible torture. The partisans forced high-pressure water hoses down the throats of some and into the rectums of others. Years later the writer and Lithuanian Sejm member Vytautas Petkevicius recalled what he saw that day. He was a child and happened to be at the garage because the father of one of his friends worked as a truck driver there.

At around one in the afternoon after several dozen Jews had been assembled in the yard, the Lithuanians set upon them with clubs and iron bars. They battered them until they were senseless and then, as the victims lay prostrate on the ground they set upon them with hosepipes (usually used to wash cars) which they forced up their rectums and then turned the water on and left it on until the victims' bowels burst under the pressure. I stood at the side of the yard and watched it all together with my friend Ricardas. I will never forget what I saw for as long as I live.

As sixty-eight Jews were killed, nearby German soldiers took photographs, many of which have survived. A Lithuanian climbed atop dead bodies, pulled out his harmonica, and played the Lithuanian national anthem.[15] The large crowd of onlookers sang along.

The terrible massacres in Slobodka and the Lietukis garage were only a prelude to the killings that began that week. Worse was yet to come. Starting with the first week of the German occupation, Lithuanian partisans arrested thousands of Jewish men, women, and children and sent them to the Seventh Fort and to the central prison.[16] Conditions at both places were horrible. The partisans attacked and raped many Jewish women and took sadistic pleasure in torturing their victims. Years later, William Mishell, a survivor of the Kovno ghetto, recounted what his neighbor, who miraculously survived the Seventh Fort, told him:

> Under heavy blows with the butts of rifles, we were chased down the slopes into the large hole. The entire area was full of humanity. The women and small children, we found out, were locked up in the underground barracks. Here we were now kept for days without even a piece of bread or a drink of water. On top of the slopes were hundreds of Lithuanian partisans with machine guns. Escape was totally impossible. We received strict orders to sit on the ground and not to talk. When somebody moved or was caught talking the partisans opened automatic fire into the crowd . . . the mid July sun was hot and merciless and the people were fainting for a drop of water. [17]

A few days later the Lithuanians released the women and the children, as well as about 70 Jewish men who had fought for Lithuanian independence between 1917 and 1922. The rest, about 5,000 men, were shot in the Seventh Fort.[18] Among the victims was the world-famous rabbinical scholar Elchanan Wasserman.

The massive avalanche of vicious violence that descended on Lithuanian Jewry has touched off some debate among historians about exactly how much of the killing was due to behind-the-scenes German instigation and how much was due to Lithuanian initiative. The Israeli historian Dov Levin cites more than forty localities where Lithuanians began to kill Jews before the Germans arrived. Christoph Dieckmann agrees that Lithuanians began killing Jews before the arrival of the Wehrmacht, but he emphasizes that Germans played the critical instigating role even at the very beginning of the occupation. The pace of the killings, Dieckmann notes, sharply increased after June 25, when SS-Brigadeführer (Brigadier General) Dr. Franz Walther Stahlecker, the head of Einsatzgruppe A, arrived in Kaunas. Stahlecker quickly established contact with Algirdas Klimaitis, who led the rampage in Slobodka the night of June 25, the day after the Germans arrived in the city. German units also were present at the mass shootings in the Seventh Fort, even though most of the killers were Lithuanians. It should be added that some Wehrmacht members stationed in Kovno were appalled by how the Lithuanians carried out the mass shootings at the Seventh Fort, not so much because Jews were being murdered, but because the bodies lay unburied in the hot sun and because the Lithuanians did not finish off wounded Jews with a final shot.[19] After July 7 the German security police began to tighten its control over and supervision of the mass killings.

Defenders of the Lithuanian provisional government have tried to argue that it did not instigate the mass murders of the Jews and that in any event the Germans had no intention of granting the Lithuanians even a vestige of independence. They also point out that Klimaitis and his followers were acting under German instigation and were considered a "rogue" group. Indeed, by the end of June the provisional government had been superseded by German administration, first military and then, after July, a civilian administration that would be part of the Reichskommissariat Ostland. Lithuanians were retained as advisors and councilors, but real power rested in German hands. The controversy about the direct responsibility of the Lithuanian provisional government in the killings of Jews intensified in 2012 when the Lithuanian government, in a solemn ceremony, reinterred the remains of Juozas Ambrazevičius-Brazaitis, who headed the Provisional Government in June 1941. Brazaitis was hailed as a great patriot, a symbol of the Lithuanian people's determination to fight for their independence.

Critics of this decision pointed out that the Provisional Government had to bear a heavy share of responsibility for the murders. As previously noted, even before the German invasion, the LAF propaganda broadcasts intensified anti-Jewish hatred. Because all major parties except the communists were in the Provisional Government, that "authority" enjoyed the respect of the Lithuanian population, if not of the Germans. Therefore, had that body taken a forthright stand against massacres of Jews it might have carried some weight.

With the onset of the war, the Provisional Government organized the Tautino Darbo Apsaugos, or TDA (Battalions to Defend National Work), units whose ostensible goals were to coordinate the activities of the various partisan organizations fighting the Soviets and to protect vital bridges and power stations from destruction by the retreating Red Army. But as many historians have pointed out, it did not take long for the Germans to co-opt the TDA and to reorganize them as the cadre for auxiliary police units who would kill hundreds of thousands of Jews, not only in Lithuania but in Belorussia.

As soon as the German invasion began, major Jewish dignitaries approached Lithuanian leaders whom they had known for decades, pleading for them to condemn the nationalists' atrocities and to call upon their people to stop the killing. Yakov Goldberg had been a fighter for Lithuanian independence and the long-time chairman of the Association of Jewish Soldiers in the Lithuanian Army. He also had been arrested by the Soviets: no one could accuse him of being a communist. Goldberg approached Jonas Vileisis, a former mayor of Kovno and a long-time leader of the People's Party; Vileisis waved away his appeals for help. "What's the big deal?" Vileisis replied to Goldberg. "Our young people will let off some steam and then everything will quiet down." Another acquaintance, Jonas Matulionis, also rebuffed Goldberg's pleas for help. Matulionis, who was the finance minister in the Provisional Government, told Goldberg that Jews and Lithuanians had no future together; the wrath of the Lithuanian people was too great. Perhaps when the Jews moved into a ghetto, things might settle down.[20] Other Jewish leaders tried to persuade Catholic Bishop Vincentas Brizgys to issue a public statement. Brizgys expressed sympathy with the Jews' plight but responded that he could do nothing.[21]

While the protocols of the Provisional Government show that some members felt some unease at the mass killings of Jews, no move was made to use radio broadcasts or newspapers to condemn the anti-Jewish violence. No minister made a public protest. Furthermore, the Provisional Government issued edicts that confiscated Jewish property and underscored that the Jewish presence in Lithuania was to end. One of the most damning charges that weighed on the reputation of the Provisional Government was the fact that it organized and supervised the concentration camp for Jews at the Seventh Fort, the scene of the mass executions in early July.

The anti-Jewish onslaught continued. Jews were to wear a yellow star on the front and back of their clothing. They no longer could use the sidewalks or parks and were allowed to shop for food for only a few hours a day, after virtually everything had disappeared from the shelves.

On July 7, SS-Standartenführer (Colonel) Karl Jäger summoned some Jewish leaders and told them that by August 15 all Kovno Jews were to move into a ghetto in Viliampole (Slobodka). The Lithuanians, he said, refused to live together with Jews any longer. Once the ghetto was in place, Jäger assured them, Jews would be safe from the wrath of their Lithuanian neighbors.[22]

Viliampole was one of the poorer parts of the city. It lacked a sewer system, and few buildings had running water. More than 30,000 Jews now would have to crowd into an area that previously had housed 7,000 people. The Lithuanian municipal authorities in Kovno were so hostile to the Jews that they deliberately dismantled infrastructure improvements that had begun in Viliampole before the war. Jewish leaders tried to persuade Jäger that Slobodka was an inadequate place for a ghetto. In view of its primitive sanitary facilities, crowding so many people into its ramshackle wooden dwellings could lead to serious epidemics. They pleaded for the ghetto to be established in the Old City, where many Jews lived and where most Jewish institutions were located. Jäger rebuffed this request.

Resigning themselves to the inevitable, the Jews formed a Committee for Jewish Resettlement to Slobodka. Totally isolated, terrified, and shocked by the violent assaults of their Lithuanian neighbors, more and more Kovno Jews actually began to see a ghetto as a lesser evil. Perhaps there, they reasoned, they might at least be safe from the constant manhunts and arrests.

Beginning in mid-July, Kovno Jews began to prepare for the move to the ghetto. Wealthier Jews made deals with Lithuanians living in Slobodka to exchange their spacious apartments for the poorer homes in the future ghetto; this was a practice that the committee deeply resented. Such actions, the committee charged, undercut from the very beginning the first attempt by Kovno Jewish leaders to impose some kind of moral authority that would be accepted by everyone.[23]

Poorer Jews besieged the Committee for Jewish Resettlement for help in finding a place to live. The committee could not cope with the impossible task of finding space for thousands of people. Crowds of desperate Jews stormed the committee offices, overturned chairs, and loudly complained. The mood was ugly; poor Jews charged the committee with favoring friends, relatives, and the well-connected.[24] This class resentment would become a familiar theme of life in the Kovno ghetto.

As the time approached to complete the community's move into the ghetto, the Germans demanded the establishment of a Jewish Council and the appointment of a "Head Jew" (Oberjude) to relay German orders and to represent the Jewish population. On August 4 a somber and desperate meeting of prominent Kovno Jews took place in the former Jewish primary school on Daukshios Street. A long-time community leader, Dr. Gregory Wolf, tried to lift people's spirits by reminding them that the Jewish people had faced other disasters in their history and had survived. One after another, various candidates refused to be considered for the post of Oberjude. But one person in particular stood out: Dr. Elchanan Elkes. Dr. Elkes was one of the most respected figures of Lithuanian Jewry. In addition to his medical training, he was the son of a rabbi and had extensive Jewish learning. Before the war he had a successful medical practice; he had treated Lithuanian ministers and diplomats as well as members of the local German colony. Thus he enjoyed the respect not only of his fellow Jews but also had valuable contacts with the Lithuanian elite. At first Elkes refused. At this point Rabbi Yakov Moshe Shmukler rose and faced Elkes. He reminded him that the community was engulfed in a disaster: "Jews! The German authorities insist that we appoint an Oberjude, but what we need is a 'head of the community,' a trustworthy public servant. The man most fitting for this position at this tragic moment is Dr. Elkes. We therefore turn to you and say: Dr. Elkes you may be our Oberjude for whomever wants to regard you as such, but for us you will be our community leader."

Everyone knew, Rabbi Shmukler continued, that the road ahead would be terribly hard. But, he told Elkes, "with your Jewish faith you will lead us and take us out of the ghetto, this exile within exile, to our holy land."[25]

An eyewitness, Yakov Goldberg, recalled that Rabbi Shmukler's words made a powerful impact. Many participants began to sob. One by one, the Jews in the room approached Elkes and asked him to take the post. "Deeply moved and stunned, Dr. Elkes did not utter a sound."[26] Finally he agreed to head the council. The meeting closed with the singing of "Hatikva," the Zionist hymn that would become the national anthem of Israel. Dr. Elkes would remain the leader of the Kovno Jews until the final liquidation of the ghetto in 1944.

The new Committee of Elders that he headed also included Yakov Goldberg, Leib Garfunkel, who served as deputy chairman, Rabbi Shmuel-Abba Snieg, Dr. Ephraim Rabinowitz, and Michael Kopelman.[27] There also would be "unofficial" members of the council, among them Hersh Levin and Chaim Nakhman Shapiro.

Around this time, the first steps were taken to organize a Jewish police force. The council appointed Michael Kopelman to serve as chief of police. Kopelman was a well-respected businessman who had run the Lithuanian branch of Lloyd's insurance before the war. He spoke fluent German and had extensive contacts outside the ghetto.

On the other hand Kopelman had no experience in police work. Michael Bramson, an army veteran and a former teacher in a Kovno Jewish high school, was chosen as the deputy chief of police, and the day-to-day running of the police force was placed in his hands. He had already organized a group of young men to watch over the unruly crowds who were besieging the housing office. At first, because few answered the initial call for volunteers for the police force, Kopelman and Bramson "mobilized" a number of young men who were army veterans or who were members of a well-known Jewish sporting club, Maccabi. These included Ika Grinberg and Yehuda Zupovitz, who would rapidly rise to prominence in the force. Both men were graduates of a leading Kovno Hebrew high school and were veterans of the Lithuanian army.

The Jewish ghetto police began its formal operations on August 15 with about sixty men. According to the chronicle, this was the time that the police force was at its best, before a certain degree of corruption set in. There was a spirit of idealism, and Kopelman and Bramson tried to recruit policemen from all segments of the ghetto population in the hope that ordinary Jews would be less likely to regard the police as a bastion of the middle class and the well educated.[28] By September 1941 the force, formally known in German as the Jüdische Ghetto-Polizei in Wiliampole, counted 270 members. Subsequent cutbacks reduced its size to 150 by November 1942, a number that remained stable until March 1944.[29]

If Jews hoped that the announcement of the ghetto would provide some relief, they were quickly shocked by new disasters. In early August the Germans shot 26 Jews who had been caught buying food from Lithuanian peasants on the roads leading into the city. On August 7, "Bloody Thursday," Lithuanian partisans grabbed 1,000 Jewish men off the streets and killed them.

On August 18, three days after the ghetto was closed, the German civil administration—through its Lithuanian liaison, Mikas Kaminskas—told the council that it required 500 educated Jews to report for work in the state archives. Kaminskas gave personal assurances to Jews who had been long-time acquaintances that this was a legitimate project. Many Jews eagerly volunteered, hoping for work that would not be physically taxing and for food rations. In the event, 534 men left for "work in the archives." All of them were murdered. A few weeks later SA-Sturmhauptführer (Captain) Fritz Jordan, the new head of Jewish matters in the Kovno civil administration, told Elkes that fifty sacks of sugar had been sabotaged, probably by Jews. Therefore, Jordan said, it was only fair that ten Jews had been killed for each sack of sugar.[30]

Meanwhile Germans and Lithuanians made incessant incursions into the ghetto to look for valuables. In the process they casually murdered Jews. In early September the Germans told the council that Jews had to surrender all their valuables. If the Germans happened to find *hidden* valuables, they would not only kill the guilty party but also murder all the neighbors who lived nearby. On September 3 the Elder Council posted an appeal that told Jews that they had a moral and national responsibility to hand over everything. Long lines appeared at the collection centers as the Germans scooped up buckets of gold coins, foreign currency, watches, and jewelry. But many refused to heed the call and instead hid their valuables. Jews spied on each other, gripped by the fear that their neighbor's refusal to relinquish assets would spell their own doom. Again, ugly rumors began to circulate, this time aimed mainly at the newly established Jewish police. The police, many charged, pocketed much of the property for themselves. As the police chronicle admits, some of these charges were in fact true.

No sooner had the Germans robbed the Jews of most of their wealth than the authorities confronted the Elder Council with a new moral dilemma. On September 15 Jordan entered the council offices with 5,000 certificates to be distributed to skilled craftsmen and their families. The council immediately suspected a deception. What would happen to the Jews who did not get a certificate? Was this a prelude to the selection and murder of the rest of Kovno Jewry? News already had reached the ghetto about the mass killings of Jews in the Lithuanian provinces. By this time the council had come to know Jordan as an extraordinarily vicious Jew-hater, who kicked in doors, yelled at council members, and took real pleasure in shooting Jews on the street.

As the council debated what to do about the certificates, it realized that the Germans now had put them in a terrible position in which the Jewish leadership became arbiters of life and death. Should they simply hand out the certificates to artisans and craftsmen? Should they set some aside for other worthy Jews, such as intellectuals or writers? And of course there was a great temptation for members of the council and those with access to the certificates to set some aside for their own families and for their own friends. As rumors spread through the ghetto that the Germans had given the council a quota of "life certificates" to hand out, an enraged mob attacked the council offices, accosting officials and overturning chairs and tables. Craftsmen demanded certificates for themselves and for their families. That's what the Germans wanted, they cried, and the council had no business handing over the certificates to anyone else.[31]

The chronicle describes how the Germans had forced the council into a no-win position. When life or death rested on a piece of paper, what should the council do? Any decision it would take would spark outrage, anger, and accusations of favoritism and corruption. The chronicle gave an unsparing account of the hatred that many Jews had for the council. The chronicle also described the dilemmas faced by the council members themselves. If they distributed the certificates only to craftsmen, and if the Germans killed everyone else, what kind of Jewish community would be left? But if they were to decide to give the certificates to other Jews as well, who should decide who would live and who would die?

There was no respite from the unceasing assault of terror and murder. Outside Kovno, Lithuanian Jewry was being obliterated. In August the systematic killing of all Jewish men, women, and children began. The SS organized a Rollkommando (mobile killing squad), under the command of Joachim Hamann, that fanned out through Lithuania and killed the entire Jewish population town by town. While the commanders were German, most of the actual killers were Lithuanians. The TDA units, now reorganized, were particularly active in carrying out the German murder plan.

While Jews in the provinces were being murdered, the noose also tightened around the Jews of Kovno. On September 17 the Germans surrounded that ghetto, checked the Jordan certificates, began a fateful selection—and then suddenly called off the operation. This reprieve did not last long. On October 3 the Germans surrounded the "small ghetto," the streets east of Paneriu. They carried out a selection and sent 1,000 Jews to be shot in the Ninth Fort. They also barged into the children's home and loaded 114 children, along with their caregivers, onto trucks that took them to their deaths. Many infants lay on the ground in their swaddling clothes. German police kicked them as they lay there.

On October 4 the Germans surrounded the ghetto hospital. They locked all the doctors and nurses in the hospital, along with the patients, and then set the entire building afire. According to the chronicle, a Jewish informer had told the Germans that some patients in the hospital had leprosy. After that day the remaining Jewish doctors in the Kovno ghetto made heroic efforts to conceal any cases of typhus and other contagious diseases.

On October 24 two members of the Gestapo, Captain Heinrich Schmitz and Master Sergeant Helmut Rauca, drove into the ghetto. The Elder Council instructed the Jewish police to follow them. The Germans seemed to be reconnoitering large spaces in the ghetto. The next day Rauca told the Elder Council to order the entire ghetto population to assemble at six o'clock in the morning on October 28 at Demokratu Square. Everyone was obliged to appear, including infants and the very sick. Anyone remaining at home would be shot on the spot. Rauca reassured the frightened Elder Council that this was purely a routine selection to separate the productive workers from the rest of the Jews and to ensure that the workers would get better rations.

The council members were frightened. What was the meaning of the roll call? What were the Germans planning? Rather than announce the measure themselves, why were the Germans insisting that the Elder Council publish the order to assemble?

The council members argued bitterly about whether they should obey the German order. Did they have a moral right to order Jews to go to their deaths? Some council members felt that, no matter the consequences, the council had to refuse to publish the order. If the Germans were going to make a selection, they should tell the Jews themselves. Others argued that if they did not comply the Germans would destroy the entire ghetto.[32] The council sought more information from Josef Caspi-Serebrovitz, a Jew who worked with the Gestapo. But Caspi said he had no idea what was about to happen. The council met again with Rauca. Elkes pleaded with him to tell the truth, but Rauca expressed amazement that the Jews should be so worried. This was merely about reclassifying workers, he insisted. Meanwhile news reached the council that the Germans were digging large new pits at the Ninth Fort.

Because the council was deadlocked about whether to publish the German order, it finally decided to seek the advice of Rabbi Duber Shapiro. The elderly rabbi was the most respected religious authority in the ghetto. At eleven o'clock at night on Sunday, October 26, Dr. Elkes, Garfunkel, Goldberg, and Levin went to the rabbi's house and asked him to rule on whether they should issue the decree. Terribly upset, Shapiro asked them to return at six in the morning the next day. When they arrived, the rabbi, still poring over his books, asked for more time. Finally at eleven that morning the rabbi announced his decision: "When an evil edict had imperiled an entire Jewish community and, by a certain act, a part of the community could be saved, communal leaders were bound to summon their courage, take the responsibility and save as many lives as possible. According to this principle it was incumbent on the Council to publish the decree."[33]

Taking leave of Rabbi Shapiro, the council called a special meeting at which the decision was taken to publish the decree. It called on "all inmates of the ghetto, without exception, including children and the sick" to assemble at six o'clock the following morning, Tuesday, October 28.

The night before the selection no one in the ghetto slept. Some ate and drank, consuming their entire stocks of food; others prayed. Single people sought a "spouse," preferably someone with a Jordan certificate or proof of a secure job elsewhere. People adopted orphans, while the many widows in the ghetto, whose husbands had died in the previous two months, sought a new mate who might ease their way through the selection.

The morning of October 28 was chilly and damp, and a thin layer of snow covered the ground. From all over the ghetto people left their homes in the dark and assembled on the square. The Jews were lined up in columns, according to place of work. At nine o'clock Gestapo sergeant Rauca appeared, along with Fritz Jordan, Heinrich Schmitz, Captain Alfred Tornbaum, and many German police and Lithuanian partisans.

Rauca found a mound on which to sit, munched on a sandwich, and began the selection. The Elder Council and the Jewish police were sent to the left, and soon it became clear that the "left" was the "good side." But, apparently to confuse the Jews, Rauca would motion people to the left, and then shift them to the right. Jordan certificates were no longer a guarantee of safety. Rauca would shoot a quick glance at his victim, size up his physical appearance, and send him to the right—regardless of his or her documents. The fate of Jews who had just returned from an entire night of hard labor at the German airfield was especially painful. The Jews had believed that these airfield workers were safe. But as they shuffled onto the square, filthy, hungry, and tired from a night working in knee-deep mud, Rauca ordered many of them to the right.

Every so often Rauca would ask for a count of those on the "right." By nightfall, about 10,000 Jews had been sent to the bad side and were escorted by Lithuanian and German police to the small ghetto. Rauca gave Elkes permission to go to the small ghetto and take up to 100 Jews back with him. As soon as he arrived, he was besieged by a crowd of desperate people who implored Elkes to save them. In the tumult, a Lithuanian policeman slammed Elkes on the head with a rifle butt. Unconscious, the leader of the Elder Council was carried back into the main ghetto.[34]

The next day all 10,000 Jews who had been held in the small ghetto were marched to the Ninth Fort and shot. Survivors in the main ghetto watched the slow procession that marched past the ghetto fence on Paneriu Street, on their way to the prepared shooting pits at the fort. People looked on helplessly as their loved ones went to their doom. Throughout the day and well into the night, Jews could hear bursts of machine gun fire coming from the direction of the fort. A few days later a small boy who survived the shooting returned to the ghetto and related the gruesome details of the mass killings. People had been badly beaten before they were killed. Jews who were wounded but not dead were crushed under the next group of victims. Children were buried alive.

The chronicle emphasized that during the Great Action the police did all they could to save Jews. As the selection progressed, police circulated among the crowd. They told large families to break up into smaller groups, and when they could, tried to divert the attention of the Germans as they hustled someone to the "good side." After the 10,000 victims were marched out of the small ghetto, the Jewish police were ordered to search the abandoned buildings. The searchers brought extra police hats and armbands, which they gave to Jews whom they had discovered hiding in the empty buildings. Marching these "policemen" back into the ghetto, they thus saved about twenty people.

Immediately after the Great Action the entire ghetto fell into a deep depression. All illusions about how work might save Jews from death now collapsed. There seemed to be no rhyme or reason to the selection. Airfield workers were sent to their death, along with holders of Jordan certificates.

On November 1, a few days after the mass slaughter, Fritz Jordan told the Elder Council that there would be no more killings, and that the ghetto could rest easy if the Jews conscientiously met their labor obligations. To back up his reassuring words, he brought a large sum of money to enable the council to pay Jews working at the airfield.[35]

In fact Jordan's promises of a respite reflected an important change in German policy toward the Lithuanian Jews who still were alive. The blitzkrieg had stalled before Moscow, and the Wehrmacht now feared a longer war. High-level arguments were taking place among the Reichscommissariat for the East (RKO—Reichskommissariat Ostland), the Wehrmacht, and the SS about whether to complete the annihilation of Lithuanian Jewry or to leave alive some Jews who would serve as skilled workers and laborers. While the SS wanted to kill all the Jews, the Wehrmacht and some civilian administrators objected. In November 1941 Friedrich Trampedach, who headed the political department of the RKO, circulated a memorandum calling for a halt to the killing of Jewish workers. This included not only Jewish workers who were directly employed in military enterprises but also "Jewish skilled workers in factories that do not serve the Wehrmacht directly but perform important tasks for the war economy."[36]

Despite grumbling by the SS, it was decided to halt, for the time being, the mass killings in Lithuania. In his notorious report of December 1, 1941, which summarized how many Jews had been killed in Lithuania, SS-Standartenführer Karl Jäger stated that "there are no longer any Jews in Lithuania except for the working Jews and their families, which total 4,500 in [Shavli], 15,000 in [Kovno], and 15,000 in [Vilna]. I intended to kill off these working Jews and their families too but met with the strongest protest from the civil administration (Reichskommissar) and from the Wehrmacht, and I received an order prohibiting the murder of the Jews and their families."

While the Lithuanian Jews still alive had obtained a reprieve, the mass killings in the Ninth Fort did not stop. In November and December about 5,000 Jews from the Reich were murdered there.[37]

Between August 15 and December 31, 1941, a total of 13,421 inhabitants of the Kovno ghetto had been killed. After the Great Action on October 28, only 17,400 Jews remained in the Kovno Ghetto.[38]

—⁊⁊⁊—

In November 1941, after Jordan's "reassurances," the Elder Council began to organize a basic network of ghetto institutions. Besides the Jewish police, the council established labor, social welfare, health, food, finance, and technical departments, a housing bureau, and, for the time being, a ghetto court. Later a school department, a fire department, and a control commission also were organized, although they functioned for only a limited period.[39]

The council knew that it was entering uncharted territory. As was the case in other ghettos, the Jewish Council now had to assume responsibility for functions that previously had been the domain of the regular municipal government. Could it find a way to fulfill German demands without betraying the Jews in the ghetto? Could the council walk the fine line that separated forced cooperation and collaboration? What would happen if and when the Germans called for another selection? Or if they demanded a transport of Jewish workers to some camp outside the ghetto? How could the council know that they were not about to send Jews to their death, as had happened in August when the Germans demanded Jews to work in the "archives."

Everything in the ghetto was in short supply. There was little food or housing. Winter had set in, and the Germans had not allowed any firewood for heating and for cooking. How would the council cope?

In December 1941 the council discussed its own future and that of the ghetto.[40] Leib Garfunkel said what everyone knew: the last six months had brought unprecedented suffering. Everything that the council had tried to achieve had collapsed in failure. But now, Garfunkel declared, despair was not an option. The council had to keep working on the principle of "as if": as if the council were facing normal conditions, as if its members were paid professionals, as if it could take a long-term view of its work, as if it would be able to develop stable sources of income.[41]

One of the most pressing problems that the council had to face was finding food to feed the ghetto. The official rations issued by the Germans came to 710 calories a day, which included 200 grams of bread a day, and weekly allocations of barley and wheat flour. There was no provision for potatoes or vegetables. In practice the German rarely allowed delivery of even the official allotments to which they had entitled the Jews. And over time, the quality of the bread ration deteriorated.

The Elder Council did its best to overcome the crisis. Compared to other ghettos, Kovno had a relatively large amount of open space, and the council ordered the extensive planting of vegetable gardens. The chronicle records that at first hungry Jews would storm the gardens and devour the vegetables that had not yet ripened. They initially resisted police efforts to protect the gardens, but in time the council mobilized a group of young people who, backed up by the police, were able to keep some order.

A critical problem faced by the ghetto during the entire time of its existence was that the Jews depended on smuggled food in order to survive. The Germans officially forbade smuggling and, quite often, Germans guards would randomly shoot Jews they caught buying food or trying to smuggle it in. But the Jews had no choice, and the Jewish police played a key role in ensuring that the smugglers got through the ghetto gate. It also was vital to smuggle in firewood, without which cooking was impossible.

Jews who worked in the city in various labor formations contacted Lithuanian acquaintances and traded clothing or valuables for food. Jews who did not work in the city enlisted Jews who did as intermediaries.

What made smuggling possible was the venality of the Germans and Lithuanians, from the top levels of the city administration down to the guard details at the ghetto gate. It was critically important to know which Germans and Lithuanians would be watching the gate on a particular day. Surprises meant serious trouble.

As the chronicle shows, the Jewish police were the key link in the cat-and-mouse game played out every day at the ghetto gate. As Jews returning from the city lined up to be searched before returning to their homes, they depended on the Jewish police to signal whether the guards that day were letting things through. At other times the Jewish police distracted the guards so Jews could pass through the gate without a search.

Highlighting the critical importance of the gate, the chronicle devoted much attention to the various German and Lithuanian guard units and their commanders. The Jewish police quickly learned that greed often trumped antisemitism; entire units sent to guard the gate could be bribed. But disaster could strike at any moment. Once a new set of guards unexpectedly appeared and intercepted an entire truckload of grain—650 kilograms—at the ghetto gate. Three Jewish policemen involved in the smuggling of that grain were shot, along with their families.[42]

The food situation took another turn for the worse in August 1942, when the Germans warned that they would institute a moneyless economy in the ghetto and ruthlessly crack down on smuggling. If any worker was found with food, his whole brigade would be punished. A terrible panic set in at the ghetto gate as frantic Jews scrambled to go to the city to smuggle in some food before the announced deadline.[43] But after a while the panic subsided. Yet another new group of Lithuanian guards appeared at the ghetto gate, and they proved to be as corrupt as their predecessors.

The Elder Council in the Kovno ghetto and the other Jewish bodies, including the police, understood that the lull in the killing campaign would last only as long as the Germans needed Jewish labor. Where the Germans in Kovno needed that labor most was at the nearby airfield at Aleksotas, which the Luftwaffe wanted to improve and expand. During the entire existence of the ghetto the Elder Council's single great concern was to meet German demands for Jewish labor at the airfield. In late 1941 and in the early part of 1942 the Germans demanded 3,000 people a day.

The council issued several appeals, laced with threats, to the ghetto population not to shirk its work obligations, especially at the airfield. For example, in January 1942 an appeal warned that this was a matter of life or death and that the council might find itself forced to hand over persistent shirkers to the Germans. (In fact this never happened.)

Working closely with the ghetto Labor Office and the Jewish police, the council tightened its control over the ghetto workforce. Men and women faced a compulsory labor obligation that became ever more stringent. The burden of enforcement fell on the Jewish police. In 1942 the Labor Office and the police issued identification papers and labor books that recorded the daily labor of each ghetto inhabitant. As of July 1 of that year, all ghetto inhabitants had to carry a new identity card issued by the police. Shirkers were put into the ghetto jail. Often neighbors informed on those who ducked work. Perpetual shirkers faced the danger of being included on one of the dreaded lists that the council drew up when the Germans demanded Jews for outside labor camps.

In theory the ghetto Jews agreed with the council's ceaseless reminders that the fate of the entire ghetto depended on providing a steady stream of airfield workers. In practice, however, many Jews did all they could to avoid going there, and for good reason. First, workers had to rise at four o'clock every morning to join the brigades that would make the three-mile trek to the worksite. The Germans did not provide suitable clothing or footwear, and Jews ruined their shoes and clothes in the daily march. Most of the work at the airfield was outdoors, and it took place in all sorts of weather—from -30°C (-22°F) degrees in the winter to searing heat in the summer. Many workers suffered frostbite or heat exhaustion. While some of the German overseers were "decent," many of them were sadistic brutes who ceaselessly beat the Jewish workers. The work itself was exceptionally difficult. Jews had to carry heavy sacks of cement, or dig deep drainage ditches for the long runways that the Luftwaffe required.

After a while the Germans began day and night shifts so work could proceed around the clock. The day shift was not allowed to return to the ghetto until the night shift arrived. Each shift served as a hostage for the next one. It often happened that when a shift arrived short of workers, the Germans would force the previous shift to remain. In that case Jews had to work twenty-four hours without a rest.

As if the physical labor itself were not enough, musters and roll calls before and after shifts often forced the exhausted workers to stand in formation for many extra hours. The German and Lithuanian guards who escorted the Jews to and from the ghetto often made them run the entire distance.

In addition to the exhausting trek and terrible work conditions, the Jews at the airfield, unlike Jews who worked in other places, had no opportunity to buy food from Lithuanians in exchange for clothing and household items.[44]

While the airfield was the most critical employer of Jewish labor, other sources of employment also opened up for the ghetto Jews. Some Lithuanians were less eager to work for the Germans now that the Nazis had rebuffed their bid for independence. German demands for Jewish workers steadily escalated, and women were conscripted into the work force. The German Labor Office expanded its cooperation with the Elder Council and opened many new sites that employed Jewish workers outside the ghetto.

In the weeks immediately following the Great Action, the Elder Council entrusted Moshe Segalson, a respected businessman before the war, with the task of setting up workshops in the ghetto. The council was worried that too many Jews still were unemployed, and this well could tempt the Germans to organize another massacre. Many Jews simply lacked the physical stamina to go to the airfield. The ghetto also needed a way to mend clothing, and to provide airfield workers with wooden shoes. In time, two basic categories of workshops developed. The "small workshops" worked for the needs of the ghetto, while the "large workshops," managed by Segalson, produced items for "export."

Segalson set up the first ghetto workshops in January 1942. They included departments of tailoring, glove making, shoe repair, and brush making, and a laundry. Segalson was a brilliant organizer and manager who steadily expanded the scope of the workshops. By May 1942, there were 650 workers, including 500 women. Eventually the workshops came to employ 4,500 workers in forty-four different departments. They also had a special contingent of Jewish police assigned to them.

The workshops became critically important for many reasons. Not only did they employ Jews who were too weak for taxing physical labor, but they also enabled the Elder Council and the Labor Office to foster close relationships with local German officials. Both the ghetto workshops and the Jewish labor brigades that worked in the city offered ample opportunities to bribe Germans who were eager to receive jewelry, gold, furs, and various other items to take home to their families in the Reich. It goes without saying that the Germans received these articles as "gifts." Over time the Jews and the local Germans discovered a common interest in protecting the workshops. The Jews needed to buy time. The Germans preferred their comfortable billets in Kovno to the dangers of the front. Both Jews and Germans pilfered various items, and after a time, Germans helped Jewish accountants fix the books to cover up evidence of theft and thereby satisfy visiting commissions and auditors from the Reich. Furthermore, some German officials treated the Jews humanely and did their best to help them.[45]

In time the workshops became vital to the ghetto for other reasons as well. Material "stolen" by the Jewish administration of the workshops was used to produce much-needed clothing and footwear for the ghetto inhabitants. When groups of Jewish fighters left the ghetto to join the partisans, the workshops, acting on the direct order of Elkes and the Elder Council, supplied them with warm clothing, boots, and other equipment. The workshops used supply wagons going into and out of the ghetto to smuggle out Jewish children, especially in the second half of 1943 and in 1944. And during the Children's Action on March 26–27, 1944, when the Germans deported more than 1,800 children and old people, more than 200 children found shelter in the workshops, where they were hidden under mounds of clothing.[46]

The workshops, and the proliferation of worksites in the city, underscored the ongoing development of a veritable caste system that heightened tensions within the ghetto and caused growing resentment. The basic problem was the unfair way that the labor burden was distributed.

The lowest caste was the airfield workers, or the *aerodromshchikes;* they had the worst working conditions and found it difficult to buy food. In a very short time it became easy to tell an aerodromshchik by his or her physical appearance.

By contrast, many Jews had found comparatively good jobs in warm, indoor sites where they could get away to meet Lithuanians and barter for food. Unlike the airfield workers, they did not have to walk miles to work.

The unfair allocation of labor began in the ghetto Labor Office, which decided who worked where. The officials in charge of making up the lists of airfield workers had a particularly unenviable reputation. While the Labor Office determined who would work at the dreaded airfield and who would get a comparatively easy post, it was the Jewish police who had to enforce these unpopular decisions, rousting people out of bed at four o'clock, hustling them off to trudge to the airfield.

In theory it would have been relatively simple to spread out the burden more equally. There was much talk about rotating assignments so that airfield workers and workers in better posts would alternate. But in fact there was little real improvement, and caste divisions hardened. Jews who had easy jobs strove fiercely to keep them. Anyone with connections in the Labor Office used them to protect his position. It soon became clear that to leave the airfield one had to have what the ghetto called vitamin P (*protektsia*), or influence. Members of political parties, friends of people in the Elder Council or other ghetto institutions, and Jews from prominent families were protected, more or less. But if a Jew was unfortunate enough to work at the airfield and did not have powerful friends, he was stuck there.

The sense of discrimination deepened after the SS takeover of the ghetto. As Captain Wilhelm Goecke ordered the transfer of large numbers of Jews to new camps, the Elder Council established a "Camp Commission" to draw up lists of the unlucky deportees. Here too the unconnected, the poor, and Jews who were single found themselves out of luck. One perceptive veteran of the Kovno ghetto emphasized the particular problems faced by ghetto inmates who were not Kovno natives.[47] German Jews and Polish Jews found themselves at a major disadvantage in the ongoing struggle for privileges. Seven hundred Jews from the nearby Zezmer labor camp were rescued from probable execution in the summer of 1943 by the valiant efforts of the Elder Council. These were settled in the Kovno ghetto. But after their arrival they found themselves on the bottom of the class ladder; they were the first to go when the council needed to draw up lists for transfer to labor camps.

In fairness, the Elder Council and the Labor Office were not entirely blind to the problems of the unprivileged. The Elder Council secured extra food rations for the workers at the airfield and the small workshops in the ghetto tried to keep their clothes in decent repair. In addition, airfield workers and Jews in what were considered other bad work places occasionally could secure day passes to join a good brigade and go into the city, making it possible to meet Lithuanian acquaintances and procure food. In the second half of 1943 these passes became critically important for Jews who were trying to persuade Lithuanians to hide their children.

The folklore of the Kovno ghetto is full of songs and proverbs that reflect the resentment at the unfair way in which Jews treated each other.[48] Privileged Jews, such as members of the Elder Council, their friends, and heads of good work brigades were called *yalehs* (or sometimes *yaalehs*), from the Hebrew word "to ascend." These people were seen by most ordinary Jews as a caste who were so efficient at protecting themselves that an outsider had no chance at improving his lot. One song also underscored the special resentment that many ghetto Jews felt toward the police:

> *Every yaaleh has his girlfriend*
> *And every policeman has two.*[49]

Jews working at the airfield employed the term "yaleh" with a variant meaning, to warn of the approach of a supervisor or guard. Although quite aware of the inequities of the caste system, the council clearly made a decision to concentrate on "high politics": relations with the Germans and dealing with the life-threatening crises that often seemed likely to engulf the ghetto. Faced with charges of favoritism and inequality, the council tended to take a fatalistic attitude. This was a ghetto, things were not perfect, what could one expect? The council faced enough problems, and it could deal with only so many at once. Shmuel Gringauz, who actually gave a lecture in the ghetto on this very problem of inequality, recalled that a high-ranking Jewish functionary told him that "one could not make a straight shoe fit a crooked foot." This attitude was understandable, but it was one that many Jews found hard to forgive.

The council certainly had ample cause to worry about the security of the ghetto, even during the "quiet period." As already has been mentioned, every now and then crises flared up, threatening to destroy the fragile stability of the ghetto. Twice the Germans demanded that the Elder Council draw up lists of Jews for transfer from the Kovno ghetto to Riga. The nasty job of catching the unlucky deportees and guarding them fell to the Jewish police. Indeed, Elkes sent that force a letter thanking them for their cooperation in rounding up 300 Jews for transport to Riga in October 1942. "The police," Elkes noted, "carried out its duties, however difficult and unpleasant, in a disciplined and dignified manner. I expect the same dedication and discipline from the police in the future."[50] It was not every ghetto where the Jewish leadership was so confident of its control over the Jewish police.

The "Meck Affair," in November 1942, for a short time threatened the ghetto with a major disaster. On the night of November 15, 1942, Noah [Nahum] Meck and two friends tried to sneak out of the ghetto through the fence. Meck got caught on the barbed wire and was noticed by a German named Fleischmann. When Fleischmann approached, Meck pulled out a pistol and fired. He was immediately apprehended, but his two associates managed to escape.

As the chronicle points out, when the ghetto populace learned that a Jew had fired on a German, they expected terrible reprisals. The Gestapo entered the ghetto, arrested almost the entire Elder Council, and also ordered the police to prepare a list of twenty Jews to be shot. Although this put the police in a terrible position, the chronicle also asserted that it was better for Jews to make the decision. The Germans would have chosen young people and heads of families. The police selected Jews from the insane asylum, some very elderly, and some very sick Jews who were on the brink of death.[51] Then to the great relief of the ghetto, matters suddenly took a turn for the better. Some heavy bribes arranged by the Elder Council helped persuade the Gestapo to relent. Fleischmann declared that Meck had fired into the air, not at him directly. The Germans released the Elder Council and even the hostages. They were content to order the public hanging of Meck and the shooting of his family.

In 1943, as the Jews inwardly celebrated the news of the German defeat at Stalingrad, the local Gestapo vented its frustration by murdering forty-five Jews who had been detained for minor offenses. In April more horrifying news arrived. The Germans had told the Elder Council to prepare room for 5,000 Jews from small towns near Vilna; these internees were to be transferred from the Vilna ghetto. Most were young and healthy. But instead of taking the Jews to the Kovno ghetto, the train stopped at the killing site of Ponar. After desperate resistance, all the Jews were murdered. The fact that the Germans could murder 5,000 Jews even when they badly needed workers placed a large question mark over the hope that labor might save the remaining Jews from death.

Although the chronicle itself does not discuss the resistance, the fact remains that the leadership of the Kovno ghetto police played a major and even indispensable role in the resistance movement.[52] Unlike the nearby Vilna ghetto, where Commandant Jacob Gens had a fraught relationship with the leaders of the FPO (Fareinigte Partizaner Organizatsiye), the main ghetto resistance organization, Elchanan Elkes, and the Elder Council took forthright steps to support the plans to send Jews into the partisans.[53]

The Elder Council was profoundly moved by the two visits of a Polish gentile courier, Irena Adamowicz, in the summer of 1942. Adamowicz, who had close ties to the Zionist youth groups and Dror, brought news from the Warsaw and the Vilna ghettos.[54] The council members also were affected by news of the Warsaw ghetto uprising. In 1941 and 1942 there had been talk, especially in the youth movements, of a battle in the ghetto or a flight to the forests. Neither option, however, seemed practical then. A fight in the ghetto was tantamount to collective suicide and flew in the face of the Elder Council's fundamental policy: to buy time. And until late 1943 there was no Soviet partisan movement in any forests near Kovno.

Things changed in late 1943 when, for the first time, Kovno Jews established contact between Soviet partisans and the ghetto. The main pillar of the resistance movement in the Kovno ghetto was the communists, led by the resourceful and brilliant Yiddish writer Chaim Yellin, supported by Dima (Dmitry) Galperin and others. One reason that the communists played such a prominent role in the Kovno ghetto was the obvious fact that the only partisan units that would accept Jews were Soviet units and the Red Army offered the only hope of liberation. It was also true, by all accounts, that Yellin was an extraordinary leader. However, the communists in the ghetto depended on the cooperation of the mostly Zionist Elder Council and police leadership to implement their agenda and get Jews out of the ghetto and into the forests. Despite tensions and some mutual suspicion, the communists managed to establish a good working relationship with Matzok, the Zionist umbrella organization in the ghetto, with the leftist youth group Hashomer

Hatzair, and with the right-wing Revisionists, who, as has been mentioned, were well represented in the leadership of the ghetto police.

In December 1943 Michael Kopelman stepped down as commander of the police force and was succeeded by Moshe Levin. Levin was energetic, abrasive, and a committed Revisionist. He was ready to cooperate with his political archenemies, the communists, in order to resist the Germans. Another prominent police commander, Yehuda Zupovitz, had many clandestine meetings with Chaim Yellin. Although Zupovitz was also a Revisionist, he too recognized that the communists offered the only realistic option for resistance.[55]

After some false starts and disasters that cost many lives, the resistance found a way to move fighters by truck from the ghetto to the Rudniki forest. Thanks to daring and successful reconnaissance by Chaim Yellin, the first group left for that forest in November 1943. Not only fighters left the ghetto, but also weapons, which had been smuggled in and repaired in various workshops.

As Dov Levin points out, the entire operation depended on the help of the Elder Council, the Labor Office, and the police. The flight to the forest coincided with the period of the SS-ordered *kasernierung* (sending of Jews into camps); a Jewish "Camp Commission," thoroughly detested by many ghetto inmates, drew up the lists of those to be shipped out. The commission made sure that members of the underground would not be sent to those camps. To meet the quotas, however, others were shipped off in their place. Elkes directed Moshe Segalson, who ran the big workshops, to equip all the partisans leaving the ghetto; these were to have warm clothing and mess kits. The police watched the ghetto gates and helped procure trucks. By the end of 1943, as Dov Levin points out, very close ties indeed had developed between the police at the gate and the German guards. The police detachment at the gate easily hoodwinked the Germans when weapons came in or fighters left. Between November 23, 1943, and March 31, 1944, eight organized partisan groups, including about 170 fighters, left the ghetto for the forest, taking with them many weapons, including submachine guns and rifles. In April 1944 disaster struck, when the Germans apprehended and killed Chaim Yellin. Nonetheless, according to Dov Levin a total of about 250 Jews from the Kovno ghetto fought as partisans, mostly in the Rudniki forest south of Vilna. Approximately 100 of these were killed in action or died of their wounds.[56]

—⚭—

The chronicle was compiled in a Jewish community that had been shattered and traumatized by the sudden disaster that had befallen Lithuanian Jewry in 1941. When the Germans invaded Lithuania in June 1941, the "Holocaust" had not yet begun. Few if any of the potential victims had any notion that the Nazis would undertake to annihilate European Jewry. Indeed, the Germans themselves did not take that decision until some time in late 1941.[57] The Kovno Jews had no reason to suspect that their Lithuanian neighbors would descend on them in an orgy of cold-blooded and ruthless violence. Yet within ten days thousands of Kovno Jews had been murdered. Former friends had turned into betrayers. Within a few months most of Lithuanian Jewry would be dead—even before the Final Solution had really begun elsewhere. The Kovno Jews were isolated, traumatized, forlorn, bereft of any hope of a helping hand. How would they survive? How would they be able somehow to bring into their new lives in the ghetto some semblance of order, discipline, and solidarity? To a large extent the chronicle reflects the difficult attempt to build some modicum of stability in a ghetto exposed to the constant threat of total annihilation. Unlike Jews elsewhere in Europe, the Jews of Kovno already had seen the mass killing firsthand, and they had no illusions about what the Germans and their Lithuanian neighbors were capable of doing.

For whom and why was the chronicle written? One might ask the same question about other diaries and archives left by Jews who did not survive the Holocaust. The authors did not know whether they would survive, but they were confident that the Germans would lose the war. And then, if their writings reached the hands of sympathetic readers, perhaps they might in some way help others remember who they were and what they had faced.

It also is quite possible that the chronicle was part of a larger effort to document ghetto life and institutions. The writers of the chronicle enjoyed access to official department records, and they used a typewriter, not easily available to people who were not employed in some official capacity. We know that the Elder Council in the Kovno ghetto was very mindful of the importance of leaving a documentary account. It asked Avraham Golub (Tory) and Abba Balosher and others to keep a historical record. Balosher's chronicle was lost, but large remnants of Tory's diary, Esther Lurie's drawings, and George Kadish's photographs survived and are examples of the imperative felt by many ghetto inmates to document what they experienced and saw. Was the police chronicle part of a documentation effort sanctioned by the Elder Council? If so, why didn't Leib Garfunkel mention the document in his valuable memoirs? Garfunkel not only was the second-highest-ranking official on the Elder Council, but also had direct responsibility for the police.[58] Still, this does not rule out the possibility that Garfunkel and the Elder Council encouraged the compilation of the chronicle.

The chronicle underscores the fact that the Jewish police in the Kovno ghetto differed from police forces in other major ghettos in some significant ways. First, and most important, unlike the Jewish police in Warsaw, or Vilna, or Łódź, the Kovno Jewish police remained firmly under the authority of the Kovno Judenrat, or the Elder Council, as it was called.[59] As distinct from the Jewish police in most other ghettos, the establishment of the Kovno ghetto police was largely the result of Jewish initiative.[60] The police did not act independently but by and large followed the orders of the Elder Council. Indeed, one of the major complaints registered in the chronicle was that far too often the police suffered the odium of enforcing decisions made elsewhere: by the Elder Council or the ghetto Labor Office. Significantly, the Kovno ghetto police consisted almost entirely of Kovno natives, with few if any outsiders.

A second major difference was that the record of the Kovno ghetto police was more complex than that of police forces in other major ghettos. On the one hand, as has been mentioned, there was ample evidence of heroism.

But there was another side to the story. As the Kovno ghetto's first historian, Yosef Gar, wrote, most Jews in the ghetto did not like the police.[61] Certain individual policemen, as the chronicle readily admits, became brutal and vicious.[62] They beat fellow Jews, took bribes, and helped their friends stay off the deportation trains, even if that meant putting other Jews in their place. In the words of one ghetto survivor:

> I heard later that some of those in the Jewish police were involved in
> the resistance movement and helped the council shield others who were

wanted by the Gestapo. This may be true. We didn't know any of this at the time. All we knew was that we didn't want anything to do with members of the Jewish police. . . . To meet up with one of them could mean only trouble. We suffered from the blows and kicks of the police and being dragged out of our homes into one work brigade or another, not knowing if we would return. This is why we felt so bitter as we watched the Jewish police living well while we did the backbreaking work and went begging for food. We saw them working hand-in-hand with the Germans. What the Germans said, the police would carry out to the letter.[63]

The chronicle does not tell the complete history of the ghetto or of its police force, nor is it merely a self-serving apology. It often hurls harsh criticism at the police, and its barbed comments do not spare the Elder Council, the Jewish Labor Office, and indeed the behavior of ordinary ghetto Jews as well.

The authors were careful not to put incriminating evidence on paper, lest the manuscript fall into German hands. There is nothing about how the police helped the resistance, how it executed collaborators and informants, how it helped smuggle weapons and children. The chronicle breaks off sometime in late 1943. There were good reasons to call a halt. The SS was slowly dismantling the ghetto as it sent Jews out to smaller camps. Sudden deportations were becoming more and more frequent, and the authors of the chronicle could not know from day to day where they would be or what might happen to their document. We do not read about the Jewish Sonderkommando organized by the Germans to burn the bodies in the Ninth Fort, their amazing escape on Christmas Eve 1943, and how the police and the Elder Council helped some of them make their way to the forest.[64] Nor is there mention of how the Germans murdered the Jewish police high command in March 1944. It is striking that in the chronicle there is hardly any mention of the notorious Benno Lipzer; a Jew and a Gestapo agent, he tried, without success, to muscle his way into the leadership of the force. Clearly the authors of the chronicle believed that the less said about Lipzer the better, especially if the manuscript fell into the wrong hands.

The chronicle offers a rare glimpse into the complexities and difficulties faced by the Kovno ghetto leadership and a Jewish police force that found itself caught between the demands of the Germans and the anger and frustrations of their own people, the Jews in the ghetto. Without denying police corruption and failings, the chronicle tried to explain the difficult position in which the police found themselves. The very survival of the ghetto depended on Jewish labor. If Jews didn't report for work, somebody had to force them to do so. If the ghetto's inhabitants wanted to avoid epidemics, which might bring down savage German reactions, somebody had to force the residents of overcrowded buildings to clean up garbage and waste. When Jews jostled and shoved each other at the ghetto gate, Lithuanians and Germans were quick to fire randomly into the crowd. Was it not better for the Jewish police to enforce order, even if that meant dealing out a few blows? When the Germans demanded 500 Jews to go to Riga, who else would collect them? And if they refused to do so, then what?

In Kovno both the Elder Council and the police drew a fine line. When the Germans asked them to send Jews to labor camps they complied. After the searing experience of the Great Action in October 1941, however, there was an implicit understanding that they would not knowingly send Jews to a certain death. While Jewish leaders in other ghettos had to grapple with German demands to furnish victims, the Jewish leadership and police in Kovno were spared having to make such choices—if one does not count the call to assemble on the square in October 1941. The October 1943 order to send Jews to labor camps claimed many victims, but the council and the police did not know in advance that the Germans would in fact carry out a selection that would send many children and older people to Auschwitz.

The authors of the chronicle had a complicated story to tell; like everyone else in the ghetto, they found themselves in uncharted territory even as they tried to make sense of the "choiceless choices" that they faced every day. The authors simultaneously defend the police force and criticize it. On one page the chronicle explains why sometimes the police had no choice but to use force in order to control crowds, compel Jews to work, enforce unfair work rules that protected the privileged and oppressed ordinary Jews, and instill discipline to avoid worse from the German reprisals. But often, even on the next page, the same authors excoriate the corruption of the force and the brutalization by some policemen. It also is obvious that whoever the chroniclers were, the authors were not writing a paean to the police leadership. Many of the chronicle's judgments of major police leaders are blunt, and the document does not hesitate to point out the faults of those individuals. One constant complaint was that a stronger, more assertive and politically deft leadership would have spared the police force some of the moral opprobrium that caused it to be disliked by so many Jews in the ghetto.

One basic problem that the police faced from the very beginning was how to impose their authority on recalcitrant Jews. Before the war there had been no such thing as a Jewish policeman. The same Jews who would tremble in fear before a gentile, the chronicle pointedly noted, treated the Jewish policeman in the ghetto with wry contempt. In the early days of the ghetto, police who tried to stop Jews from pilfering gardens suffered humiliating beatings from the hungry crowds. Police were pummeled, too, by the poorer Jews who crowded into the refugee centers in August 1941. The establishment of a ghetto jail was just one step that imbued the police with more authority. Another curious attempt to assert authority was the decision, eventually rescinded, to use Lithuanian rather than Yiddish as the official language of command. Yiddish was somehow too familiar and did not instill the same deference.

Another major step that strengthened the authority of the police and increased its effectiveness was the establishment of a system of precincts; this gave the police an opportunity to get to know the Jews in their particular area. After the Great Action in October 1941 there were three precincts, and two after a large section of the ghetto was ordered cleared in January 1944.

In order to maneuver in the tangled world of the ghetto, caught as they were between the Germans and their own people, the Jewish police needed good leadership, policemen with a conscience, and the formal guidelines of rules, statutes, organizational charts, and strict definitions of where and when authority began and ended.

Today a reader might express surprise at the amount of space that the chronicle devotes to organizational and procedural issues. But, in the conditions of the ghetto, the police clearly needed a sense of where they stood and what they could do, what punishments they could and could not levy, what physical force they were allowed to use, and what was their exact relationship to the Elder Council or to the ghetto Labor Office. The fact that many policemen violated their own rules almost every day does not mean that this search for guidance in a chaotic and treacherous situation was unimportant. It reflected an ongoing conflict within the police, a realization that precisely because ghetto conditions made it possible to turn individuals into corrupt brutes, it was all the more important to try to preserve some basic norms of proper conduct. Like their counterparts in other ghettos, the Kovno ghetto police were barely paid. But to make up for this, the police were safe from deportations to the labor camps, and they were in an ideal position to pocket bribes in exchange for favors. How then could the leadership of the police keep the force from becoming entirely demoralized?

This search for a moral compass is perhaps one reason for the solemn oath that the police force took on November 1, 1942, which constitutes one of the most moving and impressive passages in the chronicle. Yehuda Zupovitz proposed a formal ceremony in the Slobodka Yeshiva, an important symbol of Lithuanian Jewry, where generations of Jews had received a Talmudic education.

The choice of the Slobodka Yeshiva also underscored that these were Lithuanian Jews, filled with pride at being part of a community that long had been seen as a cultural vanguard of Ashkenazi Jewry. National pride and honor served not only to prop up morale. They also were important markers of individual conscience, reminders to a policeman not to abuse his power.[65] The chronicle was written by policemen who were very conscious of their pedigree and heritage.

In front of the Elder Council and other invited guests, Zupovitz barked out the orders of the day in clear, fluent Hebrew. The text of the oath was read from a scroll in Hebrew and in Yiddish, and the assembled police repeated the oath word for word. The use of a scroll, a clear reminder of religious texts such as the Torah, underscored the seriousness of the promises that they were making. The oath obligated the police

> to conscientiously and unconditionally carry out all assignments and orders without regard to time, personal considerations, or danger;
>
> to fulfill all duties without regard to personal benefits, kinship, friendship or acquaintance;
>
> to rigorously guard all service-related secrets and information.

Furthermore each policeman had to promise to devote all his "strength and experience to the well-being of the Jewish community in the ghetto."

As historian Dina Porat points out, the oath, which was written at least in part by Elder Council secretary Avraham Golub (later Tory), referred to the Jewish policeman as a *be'amter,* a civil servant. A policeman accepted his subordination to the Elder Council even as he promised to do his job without bias.[66]

After the policemen took the oath the orchestra played the march "B'shuv adonai," Psalm 126: "When the Lord brings the captives of Zion home, we will be as dreamers, yet our mouths will fill with laughter, our lips with song." The entire audience joined in singing that psalm.

While the chronicle touches on many aspects of ghetto life, a few basic themes may be singled out. First, the chronicle registers dissatisfaction with the Elder Council and its relationship to the police. The writers of the chronicle certainly respected the members of the Elder Council, but they also believed that these members of the Jewish professional elite, among them doctors and lawyers, lacked a "common touch," an ability to find a common language with the ordinary ghetto Jew. The situation in the Shavli ghetto, the authors of the chronicle believed, was much better. There the council was made up of businessmen, less cultured perhaps, but people still cut from the same cloth as the ordinary Jew and able to communicate with him. The Elder Council in Kovno did not take seriously enough the need to do something about the ghetto caste system and the unfair allocation of labor. More specifically, the chronicle bitterly complained that the council worked too closely with the ghetto Labor Office and did not show enough support for the ghetto police. In this regard the chronicle also criticized the by-now veteran police chief, Michael Kopelman, for not showing enough verve and energy in defending the interests of the force.

Moshe Levin replaced Kopelman in December 1943, a change of command that happened after the chronicle broke off.[67] The chroniclers had immense respect for Levin but noted that he was so energetic, conscientious, and diligent that he clashed frequently with his colleagues. Here again the chroniclers did not spare their own leaders from forthright criticism.

The chronicle underscored the importance of developing and enforcing an up-to-date system of records and documentation for the inhabitants of the ghetto, as many records and documents had been lost in 1941. This caused many difficulties. For instance, the women who had lost their husbands in 1941 needed to document their widowed status. Otherwise, according to Jewish law, they could not remarry. Furthermore, only proper records gave the police the means to control the ghetto population and to catch shirkers.

The chronicle sheds some important light on the role of Jewish collaborators in the ghetto. Two prominent Jewish Gestapo agents in the ghetto were Josef Caspi-Serebrovitz, a colorful and unstable character, and Benno Lipzer.[68] Caspi and Lipzer insinuated themselves into ghetto affairs and tried to interfere with the work of the Elder Council, the Labor Office, and the police. On more than one occasion Lipzer successfully vetoed Elder Council efforts to dismiss troublesome ghetto officials. The leadership of the police handled Lipzer carefully. He was occasionally present at what he thought were important meetings of the police leadership, but the important business was handled behind his back.

How to deal with these collaborators was one of the most difficult issues that faced the Elder Council. For obvious reasons, because of their backing, the two men could not be insulted or ignored. To complicate matters further, on many occasions the council actively enlisted the help of Lipzer or Caspi to overcome specific crises in its relations with the Germans. Caspi took special interest in the affairs of the Jewish police, and as the chronicle makes clear, the police at times tried to use him, even as they continued to regard him as an unstable and unpredictable schemer.

The chronicle does not shrink from mentioning some blots on the record of the police force. Besides corruption and bribery, the chronicle noted the shameful fact that some policemen treated their fellow Jews brutally. As has been mentioned, one of the major problems that faced the police every day was keeping order at the ghetto gate. Thousands of Jews crowded the gate, and hundreds would try to move from one brigade to another that promised easier work. Police had to keep order, and ensure a proper count, knowing full well that the German or Lithuanian guards could randomly open fire at any moment, especially if people were missing from the undesirable brigades.

What was the fine line between necessary and gratuitous force? This was not exactly clear, but the chronicle implicitly agreed that such a line did exist. It singles out one of the policemen, Tankhum Arnshtam, in charge of the gate detail, as someone who crossed that line too often. Michael Kopelman told his NKVD interrogators in September 1944 that Arnshtam frequently used excessive force against ghetto inmates. Kopelman tried to have him dismissed but was ordered by the Elder Council to reinstate him.[69] Clearly neither the council nor the police leadership had total freedom to hire and fire members of the force.

The chronicle also sheds light on another important aspect of police activity—the ghetto court. From the very beginning of the ghetto the Elder Council realized the need for a court system.[70]

In a normally functioning society the police and the courts were two separate institutions, but after July 1942 both enforcement and the courts actually were in the hands of the police.[71] Offenses in the Kovno ghetto ranged from the most serious to the routine, but even routine transgressions could have unforeseen consequences. Given the unexpected role of the police as the major adjudicator of disputes, the chronicle noted how extensively the police were involved in practically every aspect of ghetto life. Council secretary Avraham Tory asserted, in a memorandum written very shortly after the war, that despite terrible difficulties the court helped maintain a basic standard of morality in the ghetto.[72]

What were some of the cases handled by the police? One of the most common infractions was avoidance of labor service. It was up to the police to find the offenders and, if necessary, jail them.[73] Hunting down Jews who avoided labor was made easier by an ever more elaborate registration and documentation system, which the chronicle described in detail.

Another common offense was theft. An individual might accept an item from another Jew to sell it in the city and later assert that he had lost the item in a search. Courts had to ascertain whether he was telling the truth. Neighbors would accuse each other of pilfering property. Ascertaining true ownership of the possessions of those murdered in 1941 also provided an endless source of conflict.

The crowded housing conditions kept the courts busy. Neighbors fought with each other and tried to claim extra living space. As the Germans often shrank the size of the ghetto during the period 1941–1943, the police had the thankless job of forcing Jews to take in new residents who had just lost their homes.

When the Germans burned the ghetto hospital in October 1941, after locking inside all the patients, nurses, and doctors, the Elder Council recognized the danger that any epidemic would pose to the entire ghetto. Strict enforcement of sanitary regulations then became another important police function.

Crimes of a more serious nature also occurred. In 1943 and 1944 the police command worked closely with the Elder Council and the leaders of the resistance to catch and kill Jews who were informing to the Gestapo.[74] Naturally this was not reflected in the pages of the chronicle. There was also a case in which a gang of five Jews burst into a residence and demanded money, ostensibly to buy weapons for the resistance. During the course of the robbery three Jews were killed. The Jewish police apprehended the gang after a gun battle. On the orders of the Elder Council all of the offenders were executed.[75]

The chronicle of the Kovno ghetto police serves as caution not to rush to blanket judgments of the Jewish police—or of Jewish ghetto leadership. Each ghetto had its own context and circumstances. To be sure, the general image of the Jewish police in the ghettos of Eastern Europe has been extremely negative. In the Warsaw ghetto, Jews despised them for their corruption and, above all, for their readiness to hunt down Jews for deportation in order to save their own skins. In the Łódź ghetto, Jewish police, whose own children were safe from deportation, helped collect other parents' children for the transports to Chełmno during the notorious roundup in September 1942. But there were other ghettos in which the Jewish police risked their lives to save fellow Jews. And even in the case of the much-hated police in the Warsaw ghetto, some contemporary memoirs written by former policemen argue for a more nuanced and balanced judgment.[76] We have very few chronicles or memoirs written by Jewish police during the war, making this chronicle all the more significant.

The chronicle underscored that, for all their travails and sufferings, the Kovno Jews were lucky to be in a ghetto, not in a concentration camp.[77] The possibility of the Germans transforming the ghetto into a camp was never far from the minds of the Kovno Jews, and when the SS took control of the ghetto in October 1943 that is exactly what it set out to do—with terrible consequences.

In the Kovno ghetto most Jews still lived in family units, not in segregated barracks. Even in the shadow of German terror and the fear of death, the Jews in the Kovno ghetto were not an atomized collection of prisoners. They remained a society, a community that still drew on the energy, vitality, and sense of solidarity and mutual responsibility that marked prewar Lithuanian Jewry. The ghetto organized cultural events, underground schooling, and welfare assistance, and provided for a modicum of religious activity.[78] The Kovno ghetto, although much smaller than some other ghettos, could draw on the experience of a community that had proven its ability to care for itself, look after its poor, fight antisemitism, and maintain its brilliant cultural traditions. In the Kovno ghetto there were, of course, enormous disparities: in wealth, in access to better work, in quality of housing. As the folklore of the ghetto shows, these disparities caused sharp resentment. But one might venture to guess that precisely because of the shared sense of belonging to Lithuanian Jewry, with its high expectations of public conduct and leadership, the failings of the Elder Council and the police were judged by even harsher standards.

In an important postwar essay, Samuel (Shmuel) Gringauz, survivor of the Kovno ghetto, stressed that morally and ethically, the Kovno ghetto was a case of the glass being half-full, not half-empty. Given the terrible conditions the Jews suffered, egotism and corruption were to be expected. But, Gringauz stressed, the criminal and deviant elements in the ghetto had already been involved in such activity before the war. What stood out, Gringauz emphasized, was the ability of the ghetto to protect a basic modicum of morality and solidarity.[79]

In the Kovno ghetto there was a common language—Yiddish—shared by the middle classes and the masses, by the privileged and the poor. This was a marked contrast to ghettos such as Warsaw, with its large number of Polish-speaking Jews and its sharper cultural disparities. By the same token, in a ghetto such as Warsaw's, there was a greater chasm between the largely Polish-speaking Jewish police and the Jewish masses struggling to survive. The head of the Jewish police in Warsaw, Josef Szerynski, was a convert who had absolutely no connection to the Jewish masses and was thoroughly despised. The Jewish Fighting Organization tried to assassinate him, and it did manage to kill one of his leading deputies, Jakob Lejkin.

It is instructive to compare the hated Jewish police leadership in the Warsaw ghetto with the chiefs of the Kovno Jewish Police, Michael Kopelman and Moshe Levin. Levin's bravery already has been mentioned. As for Kopelman, when the Soviets arrested him after they retook Kovno in 1944, more than seventy Jewish survivors courageously signed a petition that defended his conduct and pleaded for leniency.[80] Kopelman himself, the petitioners noted (perhaps with some exaggeration), did not benefit from special privileges and in the final analysis was in the same position as any other Jew. He could not even save his own mother.

One of the major differences between Kovno and other ghettos was that the Jewish leadership of the ghetto—the Elder Council, the police, the Labor Office—was chosen by Jews, not imposed by the Germans. It was composed of people who had enjoyed the respect of the community before the war. This was a matter of luck and happenstance. In nearby Vilna, the proud "Jerusalem of Lithuania," matters turned out quite differently. Vilna Jewry saw what was left of its communal leadership devastated in the summer of 1941, when most of the members of the first Judenrat were murdered. The second Judenrat included few first-rate, respected figures, and by 1942 it had lost power to Jacob Gens, the commandant of the Jewish police, who was appointed by the Germans. Gens and many other Jewish leaders in the Vilna Ghetto were outsiders. In Kovno the Jewish leadership consisted of Kovno natives.

Jews in the Kovno ghetto would complain about many aspects of Elder Council behavior, but almost everyone agreed that its top leaders—Elchanan Elkes, Leib Garfunkel, and Yakov Goldberg—were people of great personal integrity who did not take advantage of the ghetto tragedy to enrich themselves or enjoy the material trappings of power. They were faulted for not doing enough to fight favoritism and corruption. They were bitterly attacked for having called on Jews to assemble for the notorious selection in October 1941, and for having compiled lists of Jews for deportation to Riga and to labor camps, but no one accused them of personally benefiting from the sufferings of their fellow Jews.

Indeed, it is instructive to cite some survivor testimony about the Elder Council. One of the harshest assessments comes from Dr. Lazar Goldstein, who bitterly criticized the council's decision to call on the ghetto population to assemble on Demokratu Square in October 1941. The council, he averred, should have flatly refused to do this and it should also have warned the Jewish population of the danger that awaited them.[81]

In his introduction to Goldstein's memoirs, historian and Kovno ghetto survivor Dov Levin criticizes what he sees as a tendency by many historians to cast the activities of the Kovno ghetto Elder Council in too positive a light and to ignore its many moral failings.[82] Levin and Goldstein also criticize the memoirs of Elder Council former members such as Yakov Goldberg and Leib Garfunkel.

Aryeh Segalson, the nephew of Moshe Segalson, is also critical of the council's actions just before the Great Action. Even the decision to consult Rabbi Shapiro in October 1941, he believes, was a sign of weak leadership. Segalson, like the police chroniclers, explains the council's action by the fact that its members were upstanding professionals but were not born leaders. In no circumstances, in Segalson's view, should they have made lists of Jews for transport to Riga. There was no escaping the fact, he writes, that, in the final analysis, the council was a tool in the hands of the Germans.[83] That said, Segalson does not suggest what else the council could have done.

Yosef Gar, in 1948, took a more measured approach. In assessing the actions of the council and the Jewish police in the Kovno ghetto, Gar laid out both the positive and the negative sides of the record. Samuel Gringauz criticized the council's failure to deal with inequality in the ghetto but concluded that there was no alternative to the council's basic strategy of buying time.

The most eloquent defense of the Elder Council and by implication of the ghetto police was made by Leib Garfunkel, who stressed that, despite their carping and criticism, the Jews of the Kovno ghetto ultimately supported the council because they understood the need for discipline and because they knew that the council was acting in the best interests of the ghetto population as a whole.[84] Garfunkel's assertion is buttressed by the 1944 petition that asked the NKVD to show leniency to Michael Kopelman. The signers of the petition stressed that the entire Jewish leadership of the Kovno ghetto had done its best and that matters would have been far worse had the ghetto leadership abandoned its post and let the Germans run things.

Sara Ginaite-Rubinson, another survivor of the ghetto and a partisan fighter in the forests, tried to arrive at a balanced assessment of both the police and the Elder Council. "The police," she wrote, "struggled to find a balance between their forced service to the Nazis and their readiness to help and support the [Kovno] Ghetto community." As for the Elder Council, while it

> did everything possible to preserve life in the ghetto, this was often done at the expense of certain groups in the community. . . .
>
> There is no question that members of the Jewish administration cooperated with the Nazis in the matters of property, delivery of people to slave labor, and deportation. On the other hand, both the members of the Elder Council and the ghetto police did everything in their power to help the ghetto community survive.[85]

In her 1963 book *Eichmann in Jerusalem,* Hannah Arendt simplistically criticized the Jewish councils and the Jewish police for their alleged complicity in the Final Solution. They drew up inventories of Jewish-owned property and lists of deportees, transmitted German orders, and lulled Jews into obeying instructions that led them to their doom. Had the Jews refused to establish Jewish councils, Arendt asserted, had they simply scattered, many would have died, but far fewer than the six million murdered by the Germans. "To a Jew," Arendt wrote, "this role of the Jewish leaders in the destruction of their own people is undoubtedly the darkest chapter in the whole dark story."

The appearance of Isaiah Trunk's magisterial *Judenrat* in 1972 undercut Arendt's generalizations about the Jewish councils. Unlike Arendt, Trunk worked with Yiddish and Hebrew sources, and his painstaking research stressed the critical difference between collaboration and cooperation as well as the importance of understanding local conditions and the context in which Judenrat heads and Jewish police had to act and make decisions.

As the research of Trunk and of Israeli scholar Aharon Weiss shows, there also were wide variations in the organization of the Jewish police and in their relations with the Judenräte.

Trunk's study pointed the way for further research on the Jewish councils and the Jewish police. It underscored the need for detailed local studies that would take into account German policy, local German decision makers, specific economic circumstances, and the context that defined the freedom of action open to Jewish leaders. Since the publication of Trunk's

Judenrat, many such studies have indeed appeared, most of them by Israeli scholars.

While no comprehensive history of the Kovno ghetto has yet been written, this chronicle makes a major contribution to our understanding of the Jewish police. It also gives us important insight into the struggle of Kovno Jewry during the Nazi occupation. For those who prefer clear and unambiguous judgments of Jewish behavior under the Nazis, the example of the Kovno ghetto offers an instructive note of caution. Few individuals or institutions had flawless records. They had to function within a zone of choiceless choices, to borrow a phrase from Lawrence Langer. All institutions and individuals walked a very fine line. Often the need to buy time exacted a heavy price.

In the spring of 1944 the noose tightened around the Jews of Kovno. As the Red Army began its spring offensive in June 1944, the inhabitants of the Kovno ghetto were torn between the hope of liberation and the dreadful realization that the Germans would do everything in their power to ensure that the Jews would never live to see freedom.

After the Red Army liberated nearby Vilna, Elchanan Elkes requested a meeting with Goecke. Goecke and Elkes had held certain previous conversations that were, to say the least, somewhat bizarre. After the Children's Action Goecke had told Elkes that he certainly did not want to deport the children. He was a parent himself and had tried to delay the action for as long as possible. But, he sighed, orders were orders. He also assured Elkes that now that the action was over, he would not go to great lengths to find the children whom the Jews had managed to hide.

Now that the ghetto's fate was sealed and the Jews of Kovno had been told to prepare for deportation in the face of the oncoming Red Army, Elkes apparently felt that he had nothing more to lose. He told Goecke that Germany had lost the war. Elkes asked him to let the Jews stay in Kovno unharmed. If he did so, the Jews would know how to repay him. Goecke struggled to keep his self-control. He was a SS officer, he told Elkes. He would obey orders, come what may.[86] Elkes would die in Dachau that fall.

The final deportation of the Kovno Jews began in July. Another selection sent to Auschwitz surviving children and individuals too weak to work. Most of the remaining Jews found themselves in German concentration camps, mainly Stutthof, Kaufering, and Dachau. Two thousand Jews ignored the deportation order and tried to survive in hideouts specially constructed beneath the houses of the ghetto. The Germans systematically set fire to almost every building in the ghetto, and all but ninety of the Jews who had hoped to survive to see the liberation perished just a couple of days before the arrival of the Red Army.

Notes

1. All these details are taken from the testimony of Hirsh Neuberger. See Hirsh Neuberger, Yalkut Moreshet Archive, No. A.571. A slightly altered published version can be found in Tzvi Neuberger, "Be-geto Kovno," *Yalkut Moreshet* 18 (1974): 158–62.

2. Aryeh Segalson, *Be-lev ha-ofel: Kilyonah shel Kovna ha-Yehudit* (Jerusalem: Yad Vashem, 2003), 291.

3. In the unpublished version of Neuberger's testimony, in addition to information about ghetto hideouts and details on police involvement with the partisans, the Germans also wanted to know about hidden archives and chronicles.

4. Neuberger mentions thirty-three. According to Dov Levin "forty or so" police were murdered. See Dov Levin, "How the Kovno Ghetto Police Saw Itself," http://yadvashem.org/odot_pdf/Microsoft%20Word%20-%202020.pdf.

5. Dov Levin, "Kaunas," in *The YIVO Encyclopedia of Jews in Eastern Europe*, ed. Gershon David Hundert (New Haven, Conn.: Yale University Press, 2008), 1:879.

6. Christoph Dieckmann, *Deutsche Besatzungspolitik in Litauen 1941–1944* (Göttingen: Wallstein, 2011), 1:164.

7. Ibid., 170–71.

8. Ibid., 153. Deportees and those arrested were two separate categories, although in many cases their ultimate fate was equally grim.

9. Dov Levin, *The Lesser of Two Evils: Eastern European Jewry under Soviet Rule, 1939–1941* (Philadelphia: Jewish Publication Society, 1995), 294.

10. As Christoph Dieckmann points out, the LAF, which included all Lithuanian parties except the Communists, was headed by Kazys Skirpa, who had been the Lithuanian ambassador to Berlin and who wanted a future Lithuania to be run along fascist lines.

11. Christoph Dieckmann, "The German Invasion and the Kaunas Pogrom," in *Shared Memory-Divided Memory: Jews and Others in Soviet-Occupied Poland, 1939–1941*, ed. Elazar Barkan, Elizabeth Cole, and Kai Struve (Leipzig: Leipziger Universitätsverlag, 2007), 373.

12. Yosef Gar, *Umkum fun der Yidisher Kovne* (Munich: Farband fun Litvishe Yidn in der Amerikaner Zone in Daytshland, 1948), 37.

13. Alfonsas Eidintas, *Jews Lithuanians and the Holocaust* (Vilnius: Versus Aureus, 2003), 179–80. It should be noted that Klimaitis lived out his days undisturbed in Hamburg, Germany, where he died in 1988.

14. Shmuel Gringauz, "Kurbn Kovne," *Fun letztn khurbn*, no. 7 (1948): 11.

15. Dieckmann, *Deutsche Besatzungspolitik*, 323. A few onlookers did register their disgust at the scene.

16. The Seventh Fort, completed in 1888, was one of the military fortifications that the Russians built and improved between 1882 and 1915. These installations ringed the city. Most Jews later would be murdered in the Ninth Fort; some would be killed in the Fourth Fort.

17. William W. Mishell, *Kaddish for Kovno: Life and Death in a Lithuanian Ghetto, 1941–1945* (Chicago: Chicago Review Press, 1988), 38.

18. Dieckmann, "The German Invasion and the Kaunas Pogrom," in *Shared Memory-Divided Memory*, 373. In his summary of the activities of Einsatzkommando 3, Karl Jäger reports a total of 2,977 Jewish men and women killed in the Seventh Fort on July 6 and 7. According to several Jewish sources, including the Jewish ghetto police chronicle, members of a Lithuanian basketball team were allowed to go to that fort to help shoot Jews. This was their reward for a victory against a Wehrmacht team. Aryeh Segalson, *Be-lev ha-ofel*, 36. According to Segalson, the name of the team was Perkūnas.

19. Dieckmann, *Deutsche Besatzungspolitk*, 1:334.

20. Yakov Goldberg, "Bletlekh fun Kovner Eltestenrat," *Fun letztn khurbn*, no. 7 (1948): 32.

21. Ibid. Goldberg also received some expressions of private sympathy from Gen. Stasys Rastikas, but no willingness to intervene. According to Dieckmann, in September, after the Germans already had disbanded the Provisional Government, Ambrazevičius-Brazaitis and some other members of the former cabinet approached Catholic Archbishop Juozapas Skvireckas and asked him if he would be willing to sign a letter protesting the killings of the Jews. Skvireckas declined. He did not want to complicate his relations with the Germans. He did try to intervene, however, for Catholics of Jewish origin. Dieckmann, *Deutsche Besatzungspolitk*, 321.

22. This meeting is described in detail by Goldberg, "Bletlekh," 33–34.

23. On this see the very important memoir by Leib Garfunkel, *Kovna ha-yehudit be-hurbana* (Jerusalem: Yad Vashem, 1959), 45.

24. Ibid.

25. Quoted in Avraham Tory, *Surviving the Holocaust: The Kovno Ghetto Diary* (Cambridge, Mass.: Harvard University Press, 1990), 28.

26. See the account of the meeting in Goldberg's memoirs of the ghetto. Goldberg, "Bletlekh," 39–40.

27. Attorney Leib Garfunkel, who was the council member with direct authority over the Jewish police, was one of the most important leaders of pre-war Lithuanian Jewry. He had been the general secretary of the Jewish National Council and an editor of major Jewish newspapers, and he also had served as a member of the Lithuanian parliament. He was a leading Labor Zionist. Attorney Yakov Goldberg, who oversaw the ghetto Labor Office, was a leader of the major Jewish veterans organizations in Lithuania and also was well connected with Lithuanian political figures. Rabbi Snieg had been the chief rabbi of the Lithuanian army before the war. Dr. Rabinowitz was a respected gynecologist.

28. Gar, *Umkum,* 301.

29. Dov Levin, "How the Kovno Ghetto Police Saw Itself."

30. Garfunkel, *Kovna ha-yehudit,* 58.

31. Gar, *Umkum,* 61–62; Garfunkel, *Kovna ha-yehudit,* 64–66.

32. Goldberg, "Bletlekh," 55.

33. Tory, *Surviving the Holocaust,* 47.

34. After the war Rauca lived a comfortable life in a Toronto suburb, where he managed a motel. In 1983 he was finally extradited to Germany but died before he could stand trial.

35. Garfunkel, *Kovna ha-yehudit,* 83–84.

36. See Dieckmann, *Deutsche Besatzungspolit*k, 2:1008–11.

37. The chronicle mentioned a much higher figure.

38. Dov Levin, ed., *Pinkas Ha-kehillot: Lita* (Jerusalem: Yad Vashem, 1996), 548.

39. A insightful discussion of the various ghetto institutions is contained in Gar, *Umkum,* passim.

40. This closely follows Dieckmann's description in *Deutsche Besatzungspolitik,* 2:1057. Dieckmann is basing his description on the Elder Council meeting protocols contained in the Central Lithuanian State Archive in Vilnius, R-973.

41. Dieckmann, *Deutsche Besatzungspolitik,* 2:1057.

42. Ibid., 2:1064.

43. There is a good description of this panic in the August 26, 1942, entry in Ilya Gerber's unpublished diary. This diary, written in Yiddish, is in the Central Lithuanian State Archives, R-139-1-144. I am grateful to Professor Solon Beinfeld for lending me a copy that is in his possession.

44. There are many sources on the dreaded worksites at the airfield. Typical is Israel Kaplan, "Di aerodrom arbet in Kovner Geto," *Fun letztn khurbn,* no. 8 (1948): 3–27.

45. Particularly important in this regard is Gustav Hörmann, who headed the German Labor Office in Kovno. In the ghetto the Elder Council established a

German Labor Office branch headed by Yitzhak Rabinowitz. Until the takeover of the ghetto by the SS, Hörmann worked closely with Rabinowitz and had excellent relations with the Elder Council. He did a great deal to help Jews in the ghetto. See Yitzhak Rabinowitz, "Lishkat ha'avodah ha-germanit ba'geto," in *Yahadut Lita* (Tel Aviv: Mutual Assistance Association of Former Residents of Lithuania in Israel, 1984), 4:105–106. Gar, on the other hand, took a more cynical view of Hörmann and his motives.

46. The best source on the workshops are Moshe Segalson's own memoirs. See "Mayne Zikhroynes" (unpublished). A copy is in the United States Memorial Holocaust Museum. I am grateful to Michlean Amir for sending me a copy. See also Moshe Segalson, "Di groyse varshtatn in Kovner Geto," *Fun letztn khurbn,* no. 8 (1948): 50–58.

47. Samuel Gringauz, "The Ghetto as an Experiment of Jewish Social Organization," *Jewish Social Studies* 11 (January 1949): 18.

48. A collection of these ghetto songs can be found in Garfunkel, *Kovna ha-yehudit,* 266–319.

49. Levin, "How the Jewish Police Saw Itself," 13.

50. Central State Archive of Lithuania, R-973, Letter of Elchanan Elkes, October 26, 1942

51. Garfunkel recalls that the list included criminals and Jews of low moral character. This version obviously is different from that given in the police chronicle.

52. The best succinct summary is contained in Dov Levin, "Tnuat hameri viha-partizanim shel yehudei Kovna b'milkhemet ha'olam ha'shniya," in *Yahadut Lita,* 159–77.

53. A gripping firsthand account of the Elder Council's direct orders to help the partisans is contained in Moshe Segalson's unpublished memoirs, Moshe Segalson, "Mayne Zikhroynes," 5–8.

54. Tory, *Surviving the Holocaust,* 108.

55. See the account of Zupovitz's wife: Dita Zupovitz-Sperling, "Gvure hot a sakh penimer," in *60 AKO: Nisht vi shof tsu der shkhite,* ed. Tzvi Hersh Smoliakov (Tel Aviv: Y. L. Peretz, 2001), 139.

56. Dov Levin, "Tnuat ha-meri," 170.

57. The exact timing is a matter of scholarly debate.

58. The chronicle and the very large police archive were hidden in the home of Ika Grinberg. Immediately after they were taken to the Ninth Fort, Azriel Levy, Meir Lampert, and Mishka Levin were told to remove the documents and hide them in a secure place. (See September 21, 1991, Yad Vashem Hebrew-language interview with Levy available at U.S. Holocaust Memorial Museum Archives, RG-50. 120*0088, and accessible online at http://collections.ushmm. org/search/catalog/irn502763. They showed the hiding place to the wife of

Yehuda Zupovitz, but it is striking that two surviving members of the Elder Council, Garfunkel and Yakov Goldberg, seemed to have no knowledge of the cache. Dita Zupovitz-Sperling told the author of this introduction that Zupovitz cared a great deal about leaving a documentary record. He also encouraged George Kadish to take as many photographs as he could.

59. Various documents from the archive of the ghetto police show the degree of this control. In March 1943 the Elder Council sternly warned the police not to take wood that was assigned to the council. In another document the Elder Council told the police that a group of high-level Nazis was about to visit and that it was important to have a full contingent of workers at the airfield. Therefore the police were directed to provide forty-five men to work at the airfield. See Central State Archive of Lithuania, R-973.

60. Aharon Weiss asserts that "the Jewish police was a totally new phenomenon, previously unknown in Jewish communal life. Indeed, in all of the communities, the Jewish police was established by specific orders of the Germans. One can not point to a single community in which Jewish internal initiative led to the establishment of a Jewish police." See Aharon Weiss, "Relations between the Judenrat and the Jewish Police," in *Patterns of Jewish Leadership in Nazi Europe 1933–1945*, ed. Yisrael Gutman and Cynthia J. Haft (Jerusalem: Yad Vashem, 1979), 202. It seems here that Kovno was an exception to the pattern.

61. Gar, *Umkum*, 304.

62. Tankhum Arnshtam had a particularly unpleasant reputation. But Sara Ginaite-Rubinson recalled that even Arnshtam could be helpful. Once, as she was entering the ghetto gate with a concealed weapon, she told Arnshtam that she was "treyf" (i.e., carrying contraband). Arnshtam let her through. See Sara Ginaite-Rubinson, *Resistance and Survival: The Jewish Community in Kaunas, 1941–1944* (Oakville, Ont.: Mosaic Press, 2005), 97. See also the Protocol of the NKVD interrogation of Tankhum (Tanchum) Arnshtam, conducted on August 16, 1944. USMHM Archives RG 26.004M-War Crimes and Investigation Trial Records from the Former Lithuanian KG-B Archives, 1944–1990 (Lithuanian Special Archives, File #B11236-3, vols. 1–3). Dita Zupovitz-Sperling told the author on June 3, 2013, that Arnshtam was also secretly working for the resistance. However, it is a fact that most accounts of his behavior are quite negative.

63. Harry Gordon, *The Shadow of Death: The Holocaust in Lithuania* (Lexington: University Press of Kentucky, 1992), 74.

64. In late 1943 the Germans established a special brigade of Jews to burn the thousands of bodies buried in the Ninth Fort. On Christmas Eve 1943 the Sonderkommando made an amazing escape. See Gar, *Umkum*, 180–85. For a gripping firsthand account by a survivor see Alex Faitelson, *The Truth and Nothing but the Truth* (Jerusalem: Gefen, 2006).

65. A similar ceremony took place in the Bialystok ghetto, after a purge of criminal elements from the police. In the Warsaw Ghetto there were serious concerns from within the police force about corruption and about how to deal with it. See Stanislaw Adler, *In the Warsaw Ghetto, 1940–1943: An Account of a Witness* (Jerusalem: Yad Vashem, 1982).

66. Dina Porat, "The Justice System and Courts of Law in the Ghettos of Lithuania," *Holocaust and Genocide Studies* 12, no. 1 (Spring 1998): 56.

67. According to the NKVD interrogation protocol of September 1944 (see note 62 above), Kopelman stepped down for reasons of health.

68. Benno Lipzer was especially dangerous. Lipzer's protector, the Kovno Gestapo, was in a bitter rivalry with the SA officers who dominated the civil administration and who controlled the ghetto until late 1943. More than once these intra-German rivalries put Jewish leaders in a dangerous situation, and they had good reason to fear Lipzer's intrigues. Moshe Segalson recounts how he incurred Lipzer's hatred because of Segalson's determination to keep Lipzer out of the ghetto workshops. Had he gained a foothold there, the massive help given the resistance by the workshops could not have happened. Segalson found himself caught up in the Gestapo-SA rivalry and once suffered a severe beating at the hands of SS Master Sergeant Schtitz, whose main purpose was to taunt Segalson's German patrons in the civil administration. See Moshe Segalson, "Di groyse varshtatn in Kovner Geto; also, "Mayne Zikhroynes."

69. See Protocol of Interrogation of Michael Kopelman, September 4, 1944. USHMM archives. See note 62 above.

70. When Dr. Elkes addressed the members of the first ghetto court, in December 1941, he told them to remember "the dangers which lie in wait for the population of the ghetto every day, and lay stress on the mutual obligation of the council and the court of law to preserve Jewish morality and the collective responsibility for those imprisoned in the ghetto." Citing the Hebrew edition of Tory's diary, 478, Porat, "The Justice System," 58.

71. In the summer of 1942 the Germans ordered the shutdown of the existing ghetto court. As Tory noted in his diary entry of July 20, 1942, the Jewish police took over the prerogatives of the ghetto court. See Tory, *Surviving the Holocaust,* 113.

72. Ibid., 424–25.

73. The archives of the police are replete with such cases. In June 1942 a policeman making his rounds was amazed to see a virtually nude woman sunbathing in the middle of the day, while everyone was supposed to be working. When he asked her for documents she unleashed a stream of vulgar oaths. Her case was referred to the ghetto court. See Central State Archive of Lithuania, R-973.

74. See "Kamfs bavegung in Kovner Geto," *Fun letztn khurbn*, no. 10 (1948): 6–8. See also Shmuel Gringauz, "Khurbn Kovne," 27–28. Gringauz wrote of a total of nine executions carried out by the police in consultation with the resistance and the Elder Council. See also Garfunkel, *Kovna ha-Yehudit*, 174–75.

75. "Kamfs bavegung in Kovner Geto," 6–8. The five were a group of daring and resourceful smugglers. The Elder Council wanted them out of the ghetto because their activities were likely to cause trouble with the Germans. The resistance decided that their particular skills might be useful in the partisans and gave each of them a pistol. Thus armed, the group of five then committed the robbery.

76. See, for example, the important memoirs of two Jewish police officials in the Warsaw Ghetto: Stanisław Gombiński (Jan Mawult), *Wspomnienia Policjanta z Warszawskiego Getta*. (Warsaw: Stowarzyszenie Centrum Badań nad Zagładą Żydów, 2010); Adler, *In the Warsaw Ghetto*.

77. Samuel (Shmuel) Gringauz, a survivor of the Kovno ghetto and Dachau and an active figure in the community, wrote shortly after the end of the war that it was very important to distinguish between a ghetto and a concentration camp. "While the concentration camp period was the most intensive from the standpoint of physical suffering, moral corruption and social disintegration, the ghetto was the more interesting period for sociological study. The concentration camp was an individual regime, the ghetto was a social regime. In the concentration camps the inmates were placed as individuals into the specific circumstances of life and death. Sociologically these were not too dissimilar from prisons, convict camps, and penal colonies. The ghetto, however, was basically different. It developed its own social life and formed a social community. From the standpoint of Jewish sociology it was a form of Jewish national and autonomous concentration." Samuel Gringauz, "The Ghetto as an Experiment of Jewish Social Organization," 5.

78. On the cultural life of the ghetto see Shmuel Gringauz, "Dos Kulturlebn in Kovner Geto," in *Lite*, ed. Mendel Sudarsky (New York: Kultur-Gezelschaft fun Litvische Yidn, 1951), 1:1743–57.

79. Samuel Gringauz, "The Ghetto as an Experiment of Jewish Social Organization."

80. I have a facsimile of the petition, sent to me by Michlean Amir of the USHMM.

81. Although Goldstein admits the personal integrity of the council members, he levels very harsh personal accusations against the council's secretary, Avraham Tory Golub. See Lazar Goldstein-Golden, *Fun Kovner Geto biz Dachau* (New York: E. Goldstein, 1985), 31–45.

82. Ibid., 20–25.

83. Aryeh Segalson, *Be-lev ha-ofel,* 55, 86, 172.

84. Garfunkel, *Kovna ha-yehudit,* 260–62.

85. Ginaite-Rubinson, *Resistance and Survival,* 50–51.

86. The most thorough account of this conversation is in Moshe Segalson, "Mayne Zikhroynes." Segalson, too, was present at the meeting.

HISTORY OF THE VILIAMPOLE [KOVNO] JEWISH GHETTO POLICE

Introduction

1

THE HISTORY OF THE Jewish ghetto police is, at the same time, also the history of the entire Kovno ghetto. All the shocks and grim experiences, the persecutions and bloody murders—the entire chapter of blood, pain, and tears—form the horrible background of the evolution of the Jewish ghetto police, from its first moment of creation to this day.

It is impossible at this time to sum up, to achieve what might amount to a comprehensive description of life in the Kovno ghetto, or to provide a summary of the activities of the ghetto institutions. First, to this day, we are still, regrettably, in the midst of "activity," in the storm of events. The history of the Kovno ghetto is not yet complete; new pages are added daily, drenched in tears and blood. The future fate of the few Lithuanian Jews in general, and of the surviving remnants in Kovno in particular, is not yet known. There cannot as yet be any talk of summarizing. Second, too many events are still too close, too fresh, to allow for objective reporting of the behavior of this or that person, of this or that institution. We are too deeply immersed in the ghetto to rise high above it, as would be necessary to be able to objectively judge people and events.

The creators of this history are themselves policemen; they will, of necessity, look, so to speak, through policemen's glasses. They will, however, try with all their might to preserve objectivity, to convey all experiences and events in their true light, as they actually occurred, without exaggerating or diminishing them. The time has not as yet come to make it possible to accurately investigate everything. Certain inaccuracies are therefore possible in some places, but they will not be significant. In any event, the future historian will find here sufficient verified material of the history of the Kovno Jews in the gruesome years of 1941, 1942, . . . and this is the most important objective of the lines that follow.

The Prehistory of the Kovno Ghetto

2

The First Weeks

June 22, 1941, the day when the two giants—the National Socialist Germany and the Bolshevik Soviet Union—collided, is the turning point in the history of the world war, which will determine the fate of all the nations and of all the continents for centuries to come. June 22 is also a fateful day for Lithuanian Jewry—in the months to follow the destiny of eight- to nine-tenths of Lithuania's Jews will forever be sealed.

On Sunday, June 22, on the very first day of the war, as soon as it became clear that the Soviet army was retreating and that the principal institutions were being evacuated from Kovno in a strange haste, a terrible turmoil began among the Jews of Kovno. As early as Sunday night, increasingly on Monday, and even into Tuesday, the Jews of Kovno began to flee the city. They traveled by train, by truck, by wagon, by bicycle, and on foot. They left behind and abandoned all their worldly possessions, taking along a bundle of necessities, a suitcase, and headed to the train station or directly to the highway that leads through Vilkomir to Dvinsk. Jews were trying to escape the black fate that had more than once descended upon them like a dark cloud. They knew that with the arrival of the Germans a terrible time awaited them. When we, the Jews of Kovno, attempted to look ahead, to make even a crude prediction as to what awaited us, we shuddered from the blackness and envisaged terrible things. Even so, the reality greatly exceeded in blackness and dreadful events anything the greatest pessimist could have imagined.

The Jews of Kovno ran, but they did not get far. The trains were bombarded from the air, the rail lines destroyed. On the highway, motorized military units caught up with and overran the Jewish refugees. The small group of Jews who managed to reach the Russian front line (to the extent that it is known in the ghetto), were not allowed in for fear that they might be spies. And so thousands of Jews began the return trip, which ended in prisons, at the Seventh Fort (in Kovno),[1] in villages, or in ghettos (for example, in Vilkomir). Here they were "annihilated" along with tens of thousands of other Jews. An indeterminate number of the refugees did manage to sneak back into Kovno, but most were unable to reenter their homes: Germans and Lithuanians had already occupied them, or had, at least, taken all their valuable belongings.

Immediately, in the first days of the war, Lithuanian partisans[2] began to grab Jews in the streets, to brutally drag men and women from their homes, and to take them to prisons and to the forts. At first it was thought that this was a passing event. Increasingly it became clear that the slaughters were organized and orchestrated from one place and carried out in pogrom style.

Before there was even a trace of Germans in Kovno, Lithuanian partisans were already raging and planning their bloody treat. Monday, June 23, around noon, there was an announcement on the Kovno radio station, which had already been captured by the Lithuanian partisans, that there were incidents of Jews firing from windows on Lithuanian "freedom fighters"; that for each

1. The seventh of nine fortifications constructed by Tsarist Russia for the defense of Kovno. Each included embankments, artillery placements, and underground storage rooms for munitions. Used between the two world wars as prisons and execution places of political and criminal prisoners.

2. Armed bands of Lithuanian "freedom fighters," who referred to themselves as "partisans." Organized with the support of Nazi Germany shortly before June 22, 1941, they emerged into the open to attack the retreating Soviet Army, but mostly to engage in the slaughter of Lithuania's Jews.

such shot, 100 Jews would be shot. Numerous provocations started after this announcement. Lithuanian partisans would run into a house and announce that shots had been fired from this house, and the Jews from such a house would immediately be taken to prison or to the fort, or, in some cases, shot on the spot. Partisans would come looking for weapons, which might have been planted—a box of cartridges would be sufficient—and again, prison, fort, or finished on the spot. The original threat—"a hundred Jews for one shot"—was transformed into "hundreds of Jews—for nothing."

The "yellow prison" (the large Kovno prison), which emptied out early Monday—during the interregnum—when everyone ran away, filled up again. Shortly afterwards (as reported by the newly baked Lithuanian newspaper *Freedom*) a "Concentration Camp for Jews" was established—the infamous Seventh Fort. To this place were transferred all the men, women, and children from the yellow prison, as well as families from the city, and the escaping Jewish families who were captured on the roads leading to Kovno.

The Seventh Fort! One shudders when hearing from the dozens of eyewitnesses, who by miracle or chance had returned from the fort, the horrifying descriptions of the murders that took place there. They tell of the four to five thousand Jews held there in 30-degree [87 degrees Fahrenheit] heat without water or bread, of the hundreds of women who were raped and then brutally murdered by the scoundrels. They tell of the four to five thousand young men—among them the best, most talented and intelligent that Jewish Kovno possessed—who perished there at the hands of the Lithuanian partisans in horrible ways.

The Seventh Fort was a "Concentration Camp for Jews" in name only; in truth it was a place where Jews were murdered. Jews would be led in groups to a pit at the fort and shot. Following one group, a second group would have to cover them, dig their own graves, and themselves be shot. One member of the last group would bring back the shovels.

The picture of the Seventh Fort is unimaginably horrible. Hundreds and thousands of people languishing on the ground, some of them having lost consciousness. Standing up is not allowed; those who disobey are beaten or shot on the spot. Those nearby are jealous of the few "fortunate ones" who have a bottle of water. All lie beaten and battered like whipped dogs, without energy or will power. No one even thinks about escape. A kind of instinctive apathy overcomes the people: When will this finally end?

To shoot Jews was a sport and an honor. A basketball match took place during the first few days of the war between a select Lithuanian team and a German team. After the match, the winners—the Lithuanians—were honored by being allowed to shoot a group of a few dozen Jews.

Even more vicious than the heroics at the fort was the story of the garage on Vitautas Prospect opposite the Polish gymnasium. Many Jews were assembled there, but they were not shot—that would be too easy a death for Jews. Instead they were beaten with auto repair tools until they fainted, then revived with a bucket of cold water and beaten again until they were dead.

A similar scene also played out in the "Lietukis garage." There the Jews were also beaten to death with tools, and the few who had not yet expired had to smear a rag in the blood of the dead and dance around the "red flag," as the partisans called it. Partisans sat down on a pile of the dead and played Soviet melodies on a harmonica. We heard of a case in the "Lietukis garage" of a hose being pushed into the mouth of a Jew and the water allowed to gush until he suffocated.

The partisans sought to outdo each other in their cruelty to the Jews. To be ordered to clean the filth from the street with one hand, while holding a broom in the other hand, but not being allowed to use it—such tortures were heard of. But to be forced to lie on one's stomach and clear the manure from the street by shuffling with the face on the ground—that was a new, apparently Lithuanian, invention.

Jews who by chance did not end up in the fort or in the garages, or in similar places, sat for weeks in their dwellings, afraid to stick their noses out into the street because of the ever-present danger of death.

When the capture of Jews on the streets became too meager, the "clearing" of the houses began. A number of them would surround a building, having previously contrived with the building superintendent that shots had been fired from within the building, and bring out the Jews. The *storuzes*[3] played a decisive role in these events: if they interceded for the building, then all went well (some wardens would flatly deny that Jews lived in their building); if not—then the end result came quickly. Other wardens wanted to share in the material goods acquired by the Lithuanians—here, again, the

3. Gentile warden, building superintendent.

fate of the building was sealed. The planting of weapons in these cases was widely practiced.

On Thursday, June 26, occurred the terrible, organized pogrom of the Jews in Slobodka. The Kovno suburb of Slobodka, particularly the old section, is—as is known—largely inhabited by Jews.

Organized groups of Lithuanian partisans, with the concurrence and blessing of the German authorities, went from house to house, particularly in the densely populated streets (Jurburker, Velianos, Synagogos, Mesininku, and others) and "searched for communists." They stabbed and slaughtered in the most brutal ways, men and women, old people and small children, without distinction. With terrible sadism they struck heads with hatchets, stabbed and shot. The partisans went into the houses and chased the people out of their beds into the yards, where they lined them up against a wall and shot them. Or they would assemble a few dozen people in one room and blindly shoot them; those who remained alive they stood up against a wall and shot them (for example, in the dwelling of the well-known Jewish sportsman Mishelski, Mesininku 9).

The slaughter continued throughout all of Wednesday night. On Thursday morning the slaughter and shooting stopped. The partisans decided to make a public spectacle. They grabbed Jews—mainly men—on the streets of Slobodka, brought them to the "house of the shooters" (shaulists) on Raudondvario Street, and from there transported them over the Slobodka bridge to the bank of the Vilia (on the Kovno side), where a pit had already been prepared. They captured about thirty men, some from the bridge itself (they took Doctor Minz off the Red Cross motor vehicle and brought him to the pit). Altogether they assembled thirty-four men, gray-haired and young Jews alike. One rabbi was standing in prayer with talith [prayer shawl] and tfilin [phylacteries] just as the murderers entered. They dragged him, "the communist," to the execution place at the river. There they were all shot and buried in the presence of an audience of Lithuanians who cheered and applauded.

The same day, Thursday, the partisans went around sealing the doors of all dwellings that contained dead bodies. Refuse carts were mobilized on Friday to carry the murdered people to graves that had been dug to the left of the bridge on the Slobodka side, and to the right—near the meadow.

The situation of the Jews in the first weeks after the Germans marched in can be quite simply characterized as follows: we, our life and our belongings, became *hefker:*[4] Any non-Jew could do with us as he pleased. We were plundered, beaten, raped, shot, slaughtered. The most disgusting and shameful deeds were done to us in the suburbs of Kovno and in the center of the city (not to mention the entire province), and there was no one to raise his voice on our behalf. Dark powers assumed authority, the slumbering demon awoke. Many heinous deeds were done only to rob, to delight in Jewish possessions. Many murders crying out to heaven happened only out of sadism.

It would seem that there had been so many friends of the Jews among the Lithuanians. Where were they all? Did they all crawl into holes out of fear? Or did a substantial number of them secretly delight in the plight of the Jews? We observed on the part of many intelligent, previously quite decent Lithuanians such lack of understanding of the situation of the Jews, such lack of empathy, such lack of desire to help, such willingness to justify the Lithuanian's "rage" toward the Jews, that the entire Jewish attitude toward the Lithuanian nation was shaken.

Transfer to the Ghetto

When it was announced on July 2 that Jews would be required to leave the city by August 15 and settle in Slobodka, in the ghetto, many of us felt a certain "relief," because we had already put up with a great deal from our dear neighbors, the Lithuanians; the ground under our feet was too hot. We wanted to live apart, to be by ourselves, with and among Jews, so as not to see anymore the murderous faces that looked at us with malicious glee and greedy plunderer-eyes. Jews thought that the pogrom had ended and now the Jewish question would be justly regulated in this or that manner. In these new circumstances, good or bad, one wanted to be among Jews.

Around July 7 the order came to create a Jewish committee; its assignment was to be the resettlement of all the Jews of Kovno into Slobodka.

On July 10 it was ordered that, as of July 12, all Jews must wear a yellow patch on their heart. This had, so to speak, "legalized" the existence of the

---

4. Like abandoned property; wanton.

Jews as such, and more people started to show up on the streets. The ruling also enabled the committee to develop a wider range of activity. A secretariat, a judicial department, a transport department, and a finance department were established, located in the Rotush building. A week later the committee moved to 24 Daukshios Street, into the public school building.

Initially, the plan was to evacuate the Jews street by street, from the train station to the old city, and to provide everyone with a means of transportation. However, later, because of the large crowds and congestion, the "impatience" of the Germans and Lithuanians, and the disorder and chaos in the Housing Office, these plans fell through. The principal cause of the congestion was the fact that long before the deadline Germans and Lithuanians evicted Jews from their dwellings; Germans and Lithuanians would go around the homes, and if they liked a Jewish apartment, they would throw the Jews out. The evicted Jews made up a large number of the people who besieged the committee. Those who still remained in their apartments were afraid of eviction and wanted to acquire housing right away. It was assumed that everyone would be assigned living space with square footage consistent with the number of members in the family. In a short time, however, the chaos became so great that most of the population started to look for dwellings on their own initiative and only later came to the Housing Office to secure a permit.

A general meeting of community leaders took place on July 24; an order had been received from the Germans to select from among us an "Ober-Jude" [Head-Jew], to represent us. There were no volunteers for this post. The choice fell upon the renowned-in-Kovno Dr. Ch. Elkes, who accepted the post with a heavy heart. At the same meeting, a chief of the Jewish ghetto police was also elected in anticipation of the need for such an official in the ghetto. Kopelman was elected since, at the time, he was the only one with contacts with Germans because of his knowledge of the language and business relationships with Germans; a weak and meaningless connection, but still—a contact.

The Work Assignment Bureau was also created at the same time—the seed of the later Labor Office.

As is well known, as soon as the German military forces marched in, in accordance with a general order, all Jews were dismissed from whatever positions they had held in all offices and enterprises. Jews were grabbed in the streets, or dragged from their homes, to clean toilets or to do other dirty work. The persecutions, maliciousness, and violence that Jews seized from the streets had to endure from their "employers" in most instances cannot be described. Jews were ordered to clean toilets with their bare hands; they were ordered to stand half-naked for hours in the sun, in terrible heat, using the shirts from their backs to clean the German tanks and trucks. Jews were ordered to carry heavy loads to the fourth floor, being allowed for each "trip" a limit of ten minutes. Increasingly, there were dozens and hundreds of instances of cruel sadism, some of which are not even known to us because the seized Jews did not come back: in "payment" for their work, they were taken to the fort or the prison, never to return.

Any German or Lithuanian with a rifle, who so desired, could go and grab from the street any Jew, at will, and drag him to work. The Jewish committee intervened with the German authorities, asking them to call upon the Jewish committee when workers were needed, so that they could provide the required number of people. After a number of conversations the committee was promised that people would no longer be grabbed from the streets and that requests would be made directly to the Jewish committee. (On assurances from the Germans one cannot rely much; afterwards, instances of Jews being grabbed from the street continued—albeit considerably less frequently.)

From then on the Work Assignment Bureau would receive demands for workers directly. One would then know how many people were required and where they would work. Treatment in the workplaces became more-or-less bearable, to the extent that for some assignments there were many volunteers, because at some places food was provided and others would issue certificates verifying their place of work—and a piece of paper with a German stamp was desirable: Lithuanians had great respect for German papers, and Jews could use them to avoid many troubles and pain, suffered especially at the hands of the Lithuanians.

During the same time period the speed of the evacuation was greatly accelerated. At first it was expected that the deadline of August 15 would be extended. But then the famous order No.1 of Stadts Kommissar SA Brigadeführer Leader Kramer was published, which put an end to this illusion. The order stated that Jews had to wear two patches, one on the heart, the second on the back; that they were not allowed to be on the sidewalk, but must walk in the street, near the sidewalk—in the gutter; that they must not buy from or sell anything to gentiles; and that they must be in the ghetto by August 15, at the latest. Following this order, a chaotic mass-rush began to Slobodka. Tens, hundreds of wagons and thousands of people on foot stretched in an endless stream from the city to the ghetto.

One burning issue stood out on the day's agenda: housing, a roof over the head. All of the work of the committee consisted entirely of providing housing.

Already around June 25 [*sic*—July?] the Jewish Housing Office and the Work Assignment Bureau had moved their work in part to the ghetto. The Housing Office had not grown sufficiently to carry out the extraordinary assignment of providing everyone with housing. From the very first day on, a system of "protection" [preferential treatment] began, which later became well known in the ghetto under the name of Vitamin P. Whoever had Vitamin P (protection), received a housing permit faster, better quarters, without lining up; those without protection had to find housing on their own and then come to the Housing Office for a permit. Those unsuccessful in their search would be homeless for weeks, with small children, almost on the street, in public quarters that were hastily arranged in the ghetto, in attics, in stalls, in one place during the day, in another place at night. There were many instances of small families taking spacious housing, the square footage allotted not being consistent with the number of family members.

Because of the disorder in the Housing Office, there were also instances when several permits were issued for one and the same dwelling. This led to disputes and fights that did not do us honor, only causing much bad blood.

As a consequence, the Housing Office, and the committee in general, and anything that whiffed of committees and "committeeing," was hated by the population. Even though people would run to the committee for the slightest reason, in their hearts they despised the committee members for the problems they caused.

A Conflict Commission was even created, intended to resolve disputes over dwellings between applicants and the Housing Office, or between individual applicants, but the commission had no effect on solving the housing problems.

In addition to housing, the problem of food became increasingly more pressing, even before the ghetto was sealed. It was anticipated that after the closing of the ghetto, food would become the most urgent problem.

Even while the Jews were still living in the city, it had become increasingly difficult to obtain food products. Most of the small, private food stores were owned by Jews. Needless to say, they were no longer active. Most of their owners were languishing in the forts, their stores plundered. But, aside from that, there were very few private stores remaining; most had been nationalized during the year of Soviet occupation. Of these, only a small number remained open after the arrival of the Germans. Huge lines formed at these stores. It was very dangerous for a Jew to stand in such a line. Lithuanians would walk around these lines, remove the Jews from them, and take them away. It saved them the trouble of going to houses; the lines were a more convenient "collection point" for the easy assembly of a large number of Jews. At best, the Lithuanians would expel the Jews from the lines. Somewhat later, when the Jews started to wear patches, there remained in all of Kovno only two or three stores that would sell to Jews.

Clearly, these few stores were unable to fulfill the Jews' need for food. Jews therefore started to look for other sources—seeking to buy food directly from the farmers who brought products from their villages to the city markets. Even this was dangerous. But the farmers willingly sold their products to the Jews—for money, or trading for clothing—not because they loved us, or had pity for us, but simply because we would pay a higher price. Thus, these farmers found ways to reach the Jews and sell their products to them.

By that time, the trading of clothing for food had begun. The farmers would acquire valuable Jewish items for a little flour, a small bag of potatoes, or a kilogram of butter. To this day, trading is the sole source of nourishment for the Jews of the ghetto.

Slobodka was located only 3–4 kilometers from surrounding villages. The farmers, traveling to the city with their products, passed through the Magistral Street, and Paneriu Street, in the center of the ghetto. Because at that time the ghetto was not yet fenced in, the Jews still retained a certain freedom of movement: thus one could still reach the source of food—the village farmer.

Granted, the law forbidding Jews to buy from or trade with gentiles was already in force, but no one was as yet caught committing this "sin" and there was as yet no punishment precedent. Then the first casualties in this category fell, victims of the need to secure something to eat.

On August 6 a few dozen Jews went to Paneriu Street to buy food products from the passing farmers. Suddenly, a truck with Germans drove in and detained twenty-six Jews, who were taken to the Ninth Fort and immediately shot. Afterward, a German came to the committee and ordered it to warn the population that Jews were not allowed to buy from non-Jews. He gleefully emphasized that Jews had already received the first lesson; in the future it should not happen again.

Against the background of the general dire situation, the mood on that day was very depressing. But, life goes on, those who survive must and need to live, eat, find shelter, adjust.

With clenched fists and gnashed teeth we must continue on our blood-spattered road.

As we noted, August 15 was the final deadline for the evacuation of the city. But by the first days of August 90 percent of the Kovno Jews were already in Slobodka. At first, it was not known what the borders and shape of the ghetto would be. Earlier it had been rumored that Jews would be able to move between the ghetto and the city at all hours of the day, but would have to return to the ghetto at night. But this was not to be. By the end of July the area specified for the Jews began to be fenced in with barbed wire. In the beginning of August, when many Jews had already relocated, the Work Assignment Bureau sent men to the homes to sign up people for the work of building the fence.

A bitter irony of fate: Jews go from house to house to sign up Jews to make for themselves a barbed wire fence, to build for themselves a camp, a prison.

In addition to the fence, Jews also had to build a tunnel under Jurburker Street. This street was specified to remain outside the ghetto, but the houses on either side belonged within the ghetto; thus, the tunnel had to connect the two parts of the ghetto separated by Jurburker Street. But the building of the tunnel was never completed; a sudden order was received to fill it up again because the borders of the ghetto were changed.

A bridge was also built over Paneriu Street, which also remained outside the ghetto, separating the main part of the ghetto from the so-called small ghetto. The high bridge over Paneriu street was thus the only connection between the small ghetto—a row of streets in which Jews lived until October 4—and the rest of the ghetto.

The work of building the fence, the tunnel, and bridge proceeded at full speed. We were warned that if the work was not completed by six o'clock on the evening of August 14, there would be shooting in the open streets.

Until the last day before the closing of the ghetto Jews were still free to go over the Slobodka bridge to the city. Many went, risking their lives to obtain food products (in spite of the fact that the experience of August 6 was well remembered). Mostly women went, because although it was not illegal to go to the city, for men it was more dangerous. Upon meeting a Jew on the street, Germans and Lithuanians would frequently murderously beat him. Until the last day, many did not completely sever their connections to their old dwellings in the city and to their neighbors. They would still go to bring back their belongings or to liquidate their possessions. There were a few dozen Jews, mostly professional specialists, who remained in their places of work until August 15.

Thursday, August 14, the Kovno Jewish community again made a large sacrifice: many Jews who were in the city on that day were arrested on the streets and taken to the prison, where the same fate as that of earlier victims awaited them.

These were the last casualties before the closing of the ghetto.

On August 15 the ghetto was sealed.

The Gruesome Period from the Beginning of the Ghetto to the Great Action

3

The First Days; Establishment of the Jewish Ghetto Police

The fast pace of the evacuation, and the approach of the deadline when ghetto life would begin, required the rapid development and expansion of committee activities. To bring order to the life of the Kovno Jewish community, which had been suddenly uprooted and transplanted into the cramped, fenced-in area of the Slobodka ghetto, required the speedy establishment of various municipal offices.

From the very beginning of the ghetto, the first and most urgent task was to create and maintain order in the ghetto. The Jewish ghetto police started its work on the first day.

As early as July 9, while the committee was still in Rotushke, besieged by thousands of people in connection with the forthcoming evacuation, the pressing need to create an entity for maintaining order in the offices of the committee had become clear. The reserve officer M. Bramson was assigned to organize a group of young men for this purpose. The same group maintained order in the committee on Daukshios Street, in the Housing Office and in the refuge.[1]

At the previously mentioned wide-ranging meeting on July 24, the idea arose that, following the model of other ghettos, a Jewish police force should be created here (in Poland, we heard, this was also the case). Based on this model, and with the concurrence of the authorities, Kopelman was elected as the chief of the police, to serve as the second representative, after the "Ober-Jude" [Head-Jew], and contact to the outside world.

On August 6, community leaders, meeting in Slobodka, began to discuss the organization of the Jewish police. In addition to Bramson, a whole line of younger activists—almost all of whom were reserve officers, war veterans [of the 1918–1920 war of independence] or athletes—participated in the deliberations.

On August 10 it became known through the committee—already referred to as the Ältestenrat [Elder Council]—that men were being accepted into the police force, priority being given to those who had served in the military. Twenty-six applications had been received, of which ten were accepted.

The rank and file of the young people did not, in general, wish to join the police. It is also of interest that some in this group, who participated in the almost daily meetings and consultations concerning the organization of the police, were willing to help organize and structure the police force, but were not willing to join it themselves.

The reasons for this attitude were as follows:

First, as noted, our future was clouded and veiled. We had no contacts with the authorities, except for those instances when demands were received for workers, or if we happened to hear instructions concerning a new evil decree. We were completely in the dark as to the intentions of the authorities concerning us, not only with regard to general questions affecting the entire community, but also as to their preferences

1. Garfunkel (*Kovna ha-yehudit be-hurbana*, 105) explains: "There was no other solution to the [housing] situation, except to place people in buildings which were not at all suitable to serve the needs of dwelling there, and were never intended for this purpose. They had no kitchens or the most elementary conveniences—these were synagogues, movie houses and schools. In these 'reservats' [refuges] (that's how these dwelling places were referred to)—16 all told—were crowded in 3,500 people."

concerning the establishment of the administrative life of the ghetto and the shape and duties of the offices. It was therefore feared that, outside the direct duties of the police to maintain peace and order in the ghetto, the force would be given other work and become a tool of the Gestapo, and that all of our police officials would have to serve as their functionaries.

Second, there was fear of the external administrative aspects, which could make each policeman individually responsible for any misunderstanding, any trivial matter.

Third, the very creation of a Jewish police was big news in the life of our community: we know from experience that Jews have difficulty getting along with Jews; that a Jew hates to obey a Jewish *chinovnik* [functionary]. The members of the organizing group figured—with all due respect, but rightly so—that Jews would not obey, that there would be quarrels with everyone, such that the task would be difficult— indeed, thankless.

Because of all of the reasons listed above, the organizing group refrained from joining the police. But life goes on and the demands and needs that arise take no account of sentiments or personal motivation. It was desirable and necessary for the police to be created so as to regulate and maintain order over that which was within our domain.

On August 11 a conference of the organizing group took place, where it was decided to elect a deputy chief of police, because, as noted, it was expected that the elected chief, Kopelman, would be a representative to the external world, to maintain contacts with the outside. The deputy chief would be the technical chief, who would oversee the operation of the police force and maintain order within the ghetto. There was no exact picture of the future nature of the police, but one thing was understood, that it must be an organization ruled by a strict, military discipline.

The deputy chief was elected at the above meeting, which took place during the day and evening of August 12. A number of candidates were proposed: Dr. Segal, attorney Goldberg, and Captain Bramson. Initially, all declined. Finally, Bramson was elected, who had to accept the election result, and the first organizational activities began.

As noted, it had been announced on August 10 that men were being accepted into the police. Since there were few applications, it was decided to mobilize men with previous military service, sportsmen, members of Maccabi,[2] and war veterans. The mobilization was planned so as to recruit men from all classes and quarters of the population, without consideration of party affiliation, position, or social standing, so that neither this nor that tendency or group would have a monopoly in the police, so that it would be the protector and advocate of the entire ghetto.

And indeed, the attitude of those who either volunteered or were mobilized into the police during those first days was idealistic—to work for the good of the people, in contrast to the later times, beginning with the gold action, when everything became so cheap and gray and very far from any kind of idealism. Initially, people worked day and night unselfishly, for the well-being of the ghetto. These first weeks were the cleanest period for the police. Whether these good intentions had any practical significance is a separate question.

The police force went into operation on August 15. The twelve men of the organizing group who had volunteered formed the nucleus of the police from the beginning.

From the very first day, the police force was drawn into the whirlwind of events and immediately started to play an important role in the life of the ghetto. In the first days, the borders of the ghetto were in flux. A number of streets that had been planned as Jewish dwelling quarters, where Jews had already moved, were separated from the ghetto at the last minute, and an order was suddenly received to vacate these streets: these included Tilzhes, Raudondvario, and Degtuku Streets, among others.

On the morning of August 15, an order was suddenly received to completely vacate Jurburker Street, as well as the houses extending to Velianos Street. This had to be accomplished by six o'clock in the evening. (As already mentioned, this deadline also applied to the construction of the tunnel under Jurburker Street.)

As noted, the housing problem was already difficult, and, clearly, vacating such a large street very much exacerbated the problem. The basic evacuation of the street, the manner of evicting people from the dwellings, was

2. A Jewish sports organization.

replete with cruelty and sadism; the infamous bloodhounds—the partisans—arrived immediately, robbing belongings from the loaded carts and off people's backs, beating and terrorizing in the most ugly manner. One Jew who had the impudence to step onto the sidewalk was immediately gunned down.

A number of police officers were sent to the area in order to maintain as much order as possible among the Jews, to guard their belongings, and, in general, to help with the evacuation. The partisans ordered the police to bury right there the Jew who had been shot. The police officer Greenberg put him into a grave there. Later that evening, he returned to the ghetto and went to the hall where his fellow policemen had assembled, completely stained with the blood of the innocent victim.

The next day, August 16, all of those who had volunteered or had been mobilized—all together about sixty men—assembled in a bungalow near the blocks,[3] at 32 Varniu Street. They were at once assigned to carry out a variety of tasks at different posts. The work assignments on this day already contained nearly all the elements of later police activity.

Work assignments consisted then of the following: watch at the 107 Krishchiukaichio Street refuge, maintaining order in the lines at the food stores, and fifteen to twenty men at the disposition of the Labor Office.

The refuge was full, packed with all kinds of people who had no housing, the majority from the very low classes, people among whom disputes, quarrels, and fights were persistent occurrences even in normal times. Clearly, therefore, scores of quarrels and fighting occurred daily in the ghetto, particularly because of the great congestion, the severe crowding.

In addition, the Housing Office moved into a set of buildings in the refuge. The pressure on the office was very great, with long lines, tumult, and quarrels a daily occurrence. To the people already without housing were added those evicted from Jurburker Street, who seemed to be receiving housing slots without standing in line; needless to say, the others raised an outcry of protest as if the sky had opened up.

3. Workers' apartments built by the Lithuanian government and, later, by Soviet authorities.

The police had a very difficult task containing such a crowd of people. No matter how many policemen were sent, it was never enough—there was always more than enough work for every one of them.

The job of the police was all the more difficult on account of the fact that residents of the refuge did not obey—they would be confrontational, and there were instances of physical force against the police; they would simply beat up the policemen. From the first days on, it was felt that if the police force was to maintain order, its prestige must be held high in the eyes of the people so that it would be obeyed, and there must be a penalty for those who did not obey. It was immediately felt that it was necessary to establish some kind of house of detention.

As will be seen later, on August 17 the Elder Council gave the police leadership the assignment of developing a plan for the establishment of a house of detention for inhabitants who did not comply with regulations.

The second most important task was to maintain order in the lines in the food stores. Only two or three food distribution points were allowed in the first days. Clearly, for a population of 26,000, the congestion was very great and the lines stretched for tens of meters. The policemen had the difficult task of maintaining order in the lines near the stores as well as inside the distribution points.

The third and most important assignment was that of the policemen in the work-distribution bureau, which was by then known as the Labor Office. Demands for workers were received from the city every day. These people had to be assembled, order had to be maintained at the assembly point, and then they had to be brought to the gate. Later, the same policemen were most frequently assigned to the Labor Office, as they had become acquainted with the Germans who came to collect the workers as well as with the workplaces themselves. They knew which people were more suitable for this or that workplace, how to maintain order in the column lines, and so forth. From this group later evolved the so-called gate guard, on which we will dwell more particularly later.

The police had to handle various other, smaller assignments, as, for example, it was forbidden to go near the fence, or to walk in the ghetto on the sidewalk (this was later rescinded; Jews were, "thank God," allowed to walk on the sidewalk in the ghetto, but when meeting a German or Lithuanian official of the ghetto guard, or other such official, had to step down from the sidewalk and greet him by removing the hat); or to keep one's hands in one's pockets; or to assemble in the streets; or to go without a hat. The police maintained patrols at all the important intersections and on the larger streets, and went from house to house to inform all residents of all these decrees, whose common purpose was to make our lives miserable. Unable to do anything about it, we had to submit to the brutal power, to the bloody fist, because as punishment for not obeying any one of these decrees, one could be shot on the spot. Later, such occurrences did indeed happen, and the police had to be alert to inform everyone about what to do in order to avoid sorrowful consequences.

The Elder Council and the police made an effort to have the outward appearance of the ghetto make a good impression on the Germans. The police therefore went from house to house telling everyone to maintain cleanliness in the yards and dwellings, to black out the lights, not to go out into the street—not even to assemble in the yard—after eight o'clock, not to speak Russian publicly in the evening, not to assemble in the streets, to greet the Germans by removing the hat in accordance with their orders, and so on.

Those were the activities of the police force in the first days of its organization. It is to be noted that, from the very first day, almost the entire burden of producing the work details rested exclusively on the shoulders of the police. True, early on, when going to work in the city was new, many volunteers could be found. But immediately after the episode of the 500 men, it became very difficult to drag men to work: people trembled to go somewhere without being sure they would come back, because the 500 men had been requisitioned for one day's work and to this day have not returned to their parents, wives, and children.

A demand came to the Elder Council on August 15 to provide by seven o'clock on the morning of August 18 500 young men of good appearance. We were told they would work in the city, arranging archives. The Labor Office sent out people to go from house to house registering men to come to the assembly point on Monday, August 18, and to march from there to work in the city. Many volunteers signed up, because their conscience dictated that when the Jews were required to provide workers, they should not stand on the sidelines, but help with the yoke of slavery with which all were burdened.

On the morning of August 18, Germans and Lithuanian partisans came to take away the people. It turned out, however, that the quota had not been fulfilled; only _____ [blank space—no number] came to the assembly point. The police were ordered to supply the missing men. Policemen went to take men from the street and from houses and deliver them to the assembly point, clearly not having the slightest notion that they were sending their own brothers to their deaths.

The entire affair was cleverly disguised by the Germans, no one having the slightest suspicion that the people were going to be taken somewhere else, not just to work in the city; unfortunately, to this day, the men have not come back.

Their exact fate has not become known to us, much as with all the other gruesome acts against us that still remain unknown to us. From the little, sparse information that has happened to reach us from this or that Lithuanian, the men were taken to the Fourth Fort near the Kovno suburb of Palemon, and have never returned. About a year later, Jews who happened to be working at the Fourth Fort found documents scattered on the ground belonging to members of the 500.

The various rumors circulating in the ghetto that they were resettled as workers in the west have, regrettably, not been confirmed to date.

And so, through their assistance, the police have perhaps helped to deliver 500 Jews to their death, although, as they saw it, they acted with the best of intentions and with a clear conscience—in the belief that their work and what they did was for the well-being of the ghetto.

Those were the duties and assignments of the police during the first days after the formation of the organization.

As noted, from the very beginning, the police force was in a way the center of attention, the place that everyone turned to for information and news. Circumstances were such that the police had to include in their field of activities matters that normally are not considered police functions—for example, personal civil disputes, various investigations, etc.—that in a functioning administrative apparatus properly belong to a court or other administrative organs. Since we had no such organs, everything was brought to the police.

The police force was also the first officially organized body—and the largest—with endless assignments.

The internal apparatus slowly began to develop during the first few days of the ghetto. Plans were made to broaden the work and to organize the developing apparatus and to extend its reach.

But events occurred that temporarily slowed the pace of development and the organizational work of the police.

Those were the infamous house searches, which began the 19th of August and lasted, together with their culmination—the gold action—until the 10th of September.

The Personal Effects and Gold "Actions"

On August 19, around seven o'clock in the morning, a large contingent of Germans and Lithuanians arrived in a number of trucks, encircled an entire street, and went from house to house conducting "house searches." These consisted of looting from the Jewish homes whatever they liked: the best and nicest items, collected over the years, were plundered in a few hours by the rampaging "heroes." These were not ordinary plunderers—people who came to steal from the Jews on their own initiative, but SA men[4] with soldiers and officers from the 3rd Company,[5] following a direct order from above, "officially and legally" robbing Jewish belongings from each and every one of the houses.

The house searches began in the blocks where they believed the wealthy Jews to be living; then, each day, a different street would be encircled and the "operation" carried out again. The work proceeded with German order and punctuality, with full official authorization.

The abuse, beatings, and cruelty endured during these "house searches"— as they were labeled in ghetto terminology—were very great; the plunderers would search and ransack the cellars and attics, yards and stalls, frequently beating people in an effort to find out where the gold and silver was hidden.

But this was not all. At the same time, systematic shootings began. Before the house searches, a few Jews had been shot—for example, on August 16

---

4. *Sturmabteilung*—Storm Detachment, storm troopers.
5. Part of the German 11th Police Battalion, patrolling the ghetto fence.

at the fence in the small ghetto, and on August 29 at the gate—in incidents portrayed as "accidental." For the house searches, on the other hand, they were carried out in a planned, systematic fashion.

As can be seen now from the police archive, where accurate numbers, dates, and circumstances are recorded, the shootings proceeded as if the number of Jews to be shot daily had been specified. This was apparently due to the fact that the plunderers were not satisfied with the results of the house searches. The offices in question apparently had not received enough—the searchers themselves having stolen many of the valuables. Orders were therefore issued to shoot a certain number of Jews every day in order to scare the survivors into coming forward voluntarily with everything that they had hidden.

The shootings started on September 1 with the first six victims. They would enter a house, take out the first Jew they encountered, order him to carry out packs and suitcases, mock him, beat him, and then shoot him.

The streets were so full of such plunderers that a bullet could come from any direction. Such was the case with Rabbi Fakelnishky: he happened to be walking on Paneriu Street when several Germans came up to him, asked him why he had not greeted them, and immediately shot him on the spot in the yard.

The next day, September 2, six more victims were killed, some of them in their sleep. It was half past six in the morning when they shot them in their beds; one was too old, the second too young, the third looked too Jewish— they always provided a "reason" for their gruesome deeds.

On September 3 there were "only" three victims and on the 4th also three.

The fear and panic were very great, the tension and confusion unbearable. People would thank God if they got off with only losing their belongings. Some dragged things from their houses and distributed them to anyone who wanted them—so that when the plunderers came they would not find too much. There were instances when in the course of the house search the plunderers would find wine or liquor from the good old days and would get drunk, killing and beating.

As noted, the house searches started on August 19. Two weeks of terror passed without an end in sight; we would have given anything in the world to bring an end to these bloody visits.

Everything was conducted and arranged by the Germans with trickery. Having created a mood of panic, fear, and terror, they then informed the Elder Council that they would stop the house searches and shootings on the condition that the Jews themselves deliver up all the valuables they owned. The proposal seemed at the moment to be a "reprieve"; we would give away everything in order to be relieved of the shootings and terror.

On the September 3, in accordance with the orders of the authorities, the following announcements of the Elder Council appeared, word-for-word as follows:

All the inhabitants of the Ghetto are obligated to appear before the Elder Council by six o'clock in the evening of September 4, for the purpose of turning over to the authorities the following items:

A.

1) All monies, Russian or German, retaining only 100 rubles per family.
2) All foreign currencies, gold, silver and all other precious metals and their manufactured products.
3) Securities and deposit receipts.
4) Valuable paintings, fur products and furs, good rugs and pianos.
5) Typewriters.
6) All electric appliances, including those used for medical and professional applications.
7) Good suit and coat material.
8) Cows and poultry.
9) Horses with wagons and harness.
10) Postage-stamp collections.

These were—as they were then jokingly referred to—the "ten commandments" of the order.

B. From this day forward it is forbidden for ghetto inhabitants to slaughter poultry and cattle.

C. All ghetto inhabitants are required to conscientiously carry out the delivery of the required items because the fate and destiny of the ghetto depends on it. Lack of conscientious or timely delivery of all the listed items threatens the life of not only the individual involved, but also of all the inhabitants of the same house and even of the entire street.

The authorities are aware that many of the objects demanded are
hidden or buried.

Taking this into account, the hiding of such objects is a great threat to
everyone's life; the hidden and buried items must be retrieved and
delivered.

All the enumerated objects must be delivered to the collection points
by six o'clock in the evening on the 4th.

The time for delivery of cows, horses, and poultry will be announced
separately.

Signed—The Elder Council

It was also announced that stringent random checks would be made,
sometimes with dogs. Where forbidden items were found, all inhabitants of
the yard or of the entire quarter were to be shot.

As said before, the terror and mood of panic during the house searches
was very great. The order appeared Wednesday, the evening of September
2, and by seven o'clock on Thursday morning, thousands of people were
standing at the collection points with millions worth of items in their hands
and pockets, brought for delivery to the committee; they were pushing and
shoving to give everything away as soon as possible and be rid of it.

Millions worth of rubles and other paper bank-notes were burned in
flames so the Germans would not get them. People dug up their treasures
from the ground, where no one would ever have found them; one trembled
to have in the house one kopeck more than one hundred rubles. Things were
brought to the committee that were not even listed in the order, in case the
Germans should forbid Jews to own them. For example, people delivered
thousands of watches and fountain pens. One listened to all rumors, however wild they seemed, and obeyed them out of panic and fear. For example,
a rumor spread that leather and leather goods were forbidden. Immediately
people delivered hundreds of leather coats, shoe soles, briefcases, etc.

Everything was carried with fear and trembling in hopes that the shooting of innocent people would come to an end.

On the first day, that is September 4, the shootings did not stop. As
noted, three Jews were shot on that day; the despair was great.

But the Germans recognized that their methods had worked, that they
were spared the work of going and searching, that deliveries were being

made on their own, so they extended the date by one more day, and the next day the shootings did stop.

Notwithstanding the prevailing mood, there were some Jews who did not want to deliver their money and gold to the committee. In spite of the order made by the authorities to the Elder Council via the SA Hauptsturm-führer Jordan—a murderer and sadist, a typical representative of the ruling body, who during his term of office caused indescribable hardships to the Jews (by the way, on August 7, 1942, he was killed near Dzhev . . . too bad it was a little too late)—concerning the likely very strict repercussions for hiding goods, many did not dig up their gold from the ground. During the house searches, some threw their gold and silver into wells. At the time, one looked upon such Jews as truly lawless people, almost criminals, who, for a little money, had endangered the lives of hundreds of others.

The neighbors in a particular yard or house would watch one another to make sure that everything was given away exactly in accordance with the instructions; if they noticed that someone was avoiding his obligation, this would be immediately reported to the police.

People who, as said, threw their gold into the wells, also came to the police asking for help retrieving these items in order to deliver them.

The police had to fulfill a unique duty: to search the houses of those suspected of hiding their gold, to dig in the yards and stalls, and to force people to bring their valuables to the collection points. The police went from house to house to convey the order once again, to warn and to urge compliance with the obligations that were considered to be so urgent at that time.

Together with the just formed fire brigade, the police went to houses that were reported to have *treyfeh* [nonkosher] wells or toilets, searched the bottom of wells, and frequently removed gold and jewels and delivered them to the collection point. Hundreds of rich people, who did not want to carry large sums of money and gold themselves, would bring their valuables to the police, who would deliver them to the collection point.

The police also had the important assignment of guarding the collection points. Because the delivery deadline was extended twice (until September 10), a couple of millions worth of valuable items had been gathered that our masters had not yet managed to take away. Incidentally, during that time ordinary German military personnel would come and fill suitcases with gold. This may be why it was worth their while to extend the deadline. The police were instructed to keep guard at the collection points day and night, together with Germans sent over from the ghetto guard.

After the gold and silver were removed from the collection points, the mood became somewhat lighter: there was an awakening from the nightmare and relief from the enormous nervous tension that had been suffered from August 9 until September 10.

On September 11 the order came to deliver horses and harnesses, cows and poultry. Again the police were given the task of registering cows and poultry, horses and harnesses, in the possession of ghetto inhabitants.

Development and Expansion of the Police Force

At this point the development and organizing of the work of the police began. The office of the chief—which later became the Headquarters Office ["Central Office"]—managed and directed the work. The Reserve, consisting of most of the policemen, carried out the assigned tasks.

At the beginning, the force was one undifferentiated unit. Only the chief and his few assistants were set apart. The members of the force, all together, carried out the various tasks assigned to them. Gradually the following were set apart: the Reserve, to implement the work of the police force, and the chief's office—Headquarters Office—to manage the force as well as to represent it to the Elder Council and all its branches, to the population, to the ghetto guard, and to other organs of the authorities.

On August 17, the police headquarters was given the assignment to present a draft statute for its activities, including a section on proposed sanctions and arrest procedures for those who refused to obey orders. Soon such a draft was provided, consisting of nine paragraphs. In it were delineated the tasks of the police. The overall objective was to maintain peace and order in the ghetto and to see to it that all decrees ordered by the authorities and the Elder Council were carried out. The police asserted the right to use physical force to maintain peace and order, but only if other methods were not effective, and must make every effort to minimize harm to the subject. Whenever physical force was used, the policeman involved was required to make an immediate report to his direct superior. For not complying with stated decrees, disturbing the public peace, resisting the police, or not carrying out legitimate orders, the chief of the police had the right to impose penalties of up to 500 rubles, incarceration for up to fourteen days, and forced labor, beyond the common work assignments, of up to a month.

Characteristically, this draft was not approved, primarily because of extensive editing of the paragraphs dealing with the application of physical force and the magnitude of the penalties that the chief of police had the right to impose. In addition, the draft was judged to be incomplete; it lacked consideration of the essentials of interrogating the accused, of reporting procedures, and of the sanctioning of the arrest and of the manner in which it is to be carried out.

On August 25 a second statute, of ten paragraphs, was presented to the Elder Council. Here it was stated that the police force was the organ charged with maintaining peace and order in the ghetto and that all inhabitants were to obey its orders and decrees. Further, the statute asserted that the police must be polite to the residents, but that they had the right to apply physical force when all other methods were of no avail. The chief of police had the right to penalize residents for disturbing the public peace and order, or for not obeying or resisting the police, with monetary fines of up to 300 rubles, work penalties of up to fourteen days, and detention of up to ten days. Investigation of the accused was also covered. If the chief of police found it necessary to arrest a suspect in order to deprive him of the opportunity to carry out a crime, the suspect could not be held for longer than forty-eight hours, and the arrest was to be reported to the chairman of the Elder Council.

In its order No. 4 of August 26, the Elder Council approved the statute.

Until a registry office was established, the police force was also charged with the registration of births and deaths. On August 17, the first death—which occurred on August 16—was registered.

The activities of the police prominently mirror the condition of the ghetto in all its forms and nuances. We get a picture of life in the ghetto, its configurations and arrangements. All phases, events, and shocks are reflected in the activities of the police as if in a ribbon of film.

As noted, the police force was where everyone turned, even for matters that were not within the purview of police activity.

From the very beginning, hundreds of people turned to the police with requests to clear up disputes among neighbors sharing the same apartment.

People were jam-packed, and the crowded conditions led to disputes among neighbors, particularly women, over various household matters. They would turn to the police to settle the disputes and at the same time ask to be provided with a different dwelling.

The police constantly intervened in these matters, with policemen resolving the dispute on the spot, and if the neighbors truly could not continue to live together, headquarters would in many instances request the Housing Office to move one or the other to a different apartment.

The housing problem kept everyone busy at that time, with the police function in the Housing Office being important and not easy.

If it was necessary to crowd an additional family into an apartment—to provide for somebody who was roaming somewhere, homeless—this was almost never accomplished by consent and good will, but instead almost always required the help of the police, often including physical force.

Office communications, which had just started to be established, included much correspondence with the Housing Office concerning various matters of moving neighbors—because of unsuitable apartments or incompatibilities or disturbance of the public peace—and also concerning police matters, such as creating room for the planned house of detention, space for the planned precincts, etc.

On August 27, the Elder Council confirmed the decision to divide the ghetto into four precincts. The first was the small ghetto; the second, the old city from Velianos to Braliu; the third, from Braliu to Varniu, including its right side; and the fourth, from Varniu to the end, including Vienozinskio and the Brazilke—that is, the left side of Paneriu.

Police headquarters instructed the assigned chiefs of the precincts to find suitable space and to establish police precinct offices in order to begin normal activity, but, as noted, the house searches taking place throughout the ghetto greatly interfered with the organization of these precincts. Thus the decision remained on paper until after the gold action [September 10].

The work of the police expanded rapidly. Every day new situations presented themselves, demanding immediate attention and requiring greater numbers of policemen.

At that time, groups of dozens of people roamed through the ghetto. Wherever they found a garden, they would fall upon it like locusts and dig everything up.

The digging up of gardens by hungry Jews would not have been such a great calamity, but there were circumstances that forced the police to take up defensive measures. First of all, at the end of August the potatoes were very small, such that when you dug up these little ones, you hardly did yourself a favor and instead led to the loss of hundreds of kilos that could have been had by waiting two or three weeks for them to ripen.

Second, those taking part in the attacks on the gardens were people from the refuges, generally from the lowest class, who did it for a little income, first forming a group that would make five or six garden attacks, then selling the dug-up potatoes. The entire matter had the character not of the actions of hungry people, but of organized acts of wantonness and vandalism, mostly by dark elements.

Third, the authorities—mostly the Lithuanians—made a semiofficial announcement that the gardens were the property of those Lithuanians who had lived there previously, and that the Jews did not have the right to dig them up, threatening that if digging continued, they would shoot into the crowd.

On August 25, the chief of police promulgated an order that it was forbidden, under threat of death, to dig any kind of vegetables, even in one's own garden.[6] But this announcement was of no avail. Morning, noon, and night, hundreds of people continued to attack the gardens like locusts. The police had to assume the role of guards. A large group of policemen from the Reserve were assigned to garden protection duty. During the day, the policemen guarded the gardens from all sides; at night, when the curfew was in effect (at first, even policemen were forbidden to go out after eight o'clock in the evening), the policemen would sit in houses near the gardens and watch through the windows.

This work was very difficult. The police guards had to fight with hundreds of people. There were many instances when policemen were beaten up and the gardens destroyed, and cases of quarrels among the attackers themselves over a few potatoes or a cucumber. The police had a difficult and tiring task; they had to be everywhere, constantly shouting, having altercations, and applying force against those who did not obey.

---

6. Note in the margin refers to the case of a woman shot while digging up potatoes in the small ghetto.

The work of guarding the gardens, later called *garten-shutz* [garden-protection],[7] required many policemen. The number available was not nearly enough to handle all the urgent work.

On August 22, the Elder Council approved a police force of 186 men, and then, in response to a request from headquarters, increased it by 24 men. With these additional new policemen it became easier to organize and handle all assigned tasks.

Police headquarters was also given the assignment of submitting a proposal for the registration of inhabitants according to their addresses.

On August 25[8] headquarters submitted its proposal for the mandatory registration of all ghetto inhabitants, requesting that the proposal be quickly approved, as the matter was urgent and preparation for the job had already been done.

In the draft statute, consisting of eight paragraphs, it was stated, among other things, that every inhabitant, without distinction as to age or gender, must register in the applicable police precinct. Every head of family must come to the precinct office at the specified time with the documents and bread-cards of all family members. Those who moved from one apartment to another were required to cancel their registration in the old precinct and register in the new precinct within twenty-four hours. Those not complying with these regulations were to be penalized in accordance with the sanctions of the Jewish ghetto police.

The mandatory registration of all inhabitants, which the police took upon itself, was important and urgent—first because of internal administrative matters (bread-card misunderstandings and falsifications) and second because of matters external to the ghetto.

As noted, during this early period, when there was no contact with the city, the food problem was very severe.[9] Ninety percent of the population lived only on the rations obtained from the food-supply store. Every household had to show documents and declare the number of family members in order to receive the standard food portions. Since in almost all families someone was, regrettably, missing, many included them in their family

7. A question mark is penciled in the margin, referring to this name for the garden protection function.
8. Margin note appears to question the accuracy of this date.
9. Margin note: "More precise time."

list and received products for them. In most instances, those arrested had left their documents and permits at home; these were presented and rations taken accordingly. Many residents falsely increased the number of family members in their household, thus obtaining more products than they were entitled to. There were hundreds of such falsifications and write-in "angels." People would come to report that they had lost their bread-cards, requesting that they be issued duplicate cards. Some would do so fraudulently, in order to make use of the original (which they had not in fact lost) as well as the duplicate. When informed that a card was lost, the police would conduct an investigation. Six men were appointed to carry out the investigations of lost cards.[10]

These investigations served to establish accurately the size of the families in question and how many were entitled to receive rations. But there were hundreds of other cases of inaccurate registration that could not be uncovered. It was known that improprieties abounded, but it was difficult to expose them.

The problem of inaccurate registration took its toll not only in the area of food distribution but in many other police matters as well. Various penalties and notices from the Elder Council, from the police itself, and from the Labor Office, were addressed to people who could not be found for want of accurate registration. In such instances, the police headquarters office would rely on the files of the Housing Office to obtain the address of the person being sought. But this did little to ease the workload. First of all, the housing files were not very accurate; second, as noted, many people had moved into their lodgings even before receiving a permit and had never registered at the Housing Office, or had received a permit for one place but since moved to another.

The police also had to take care of demands from outside the ghetto. A series of notices streamed in during the first days—from the Kovno apartment management concerning rental fees owed by Jews, electric bills, various orders to appear in civil matters before the district and regional courts of Kovno, notices from the province, advisories from various offices concerning taxes, etc. These were transmitted to the ghetto police via the 7th

10. Margin note: "Why were there falsifications?"

Lithuanian police precinct, and our policemen had to deliver them to the appropriate parties.

Many of these announcements had to be returned to the city because the addressees could not be found. Some of them might not have been in the ghetto at all, not having survived to come here, but, as noted, nothing could be learned without registration—one was groping in the dark.

The first registration was carried out beginning on September 15 [1941].

Either directly or through the Reserve, police headquarters had to take care of various other matters, mostly in connection with the slow settling in of the inhabitants, their moving from one place to another, etc.

During the time of the settling-in and the house searches, many lost items were scattered in the yards and the streets, mostly documents and food ration cards. Policemen or ordinary citizens would bring the found items to police headquarters. The police would post announcements concerning the found items and documents, including the names of their owners, so that they could come to police headquarters to claim them.

When the ownership of found items was not known, announcements would be posted. Those who had lost them could come to police headquarters to claim them based on identifying marks.

During the clearing of Jurburker Street, the keys to the apartments remained with the prior inhabitants; the police made it publicly known that all the keys from the evacuated area must be turned over to the police.

The ghetto was allowed to move medicines and other inventory from the apothecary on Jurburker Street; these were turned over to the ghetto. The police supplied permits for the pharmacists and transport workers needed to move the medicines and inventory to us.

During the first days of the war, telephone connections were completely interrupted, but later the connections were restored. Many telephone sets remained in the ghetto, but, needless to say, they were not connected to the network. An order was received to deliver immediately all telephone sets present in the ghetto. The police went to all the places where the sets were located, took them out, and delivered them to the authorities.

Slowly police headquarters established communications with all the other offices organized by the leadership, especially with the Housing Office concerning various dwelling matters. People who had various problems with that office would bring their complaints to the police. In many instances the police would intervene in writing.

There was also a variety of communications concerning other matters having to do with public peace and order.

There were many homeless, wretched, mentally ill people in the ghetto, wandering the streets hungry and forlorn. They disturbed the public peace, creating tumult and disturbances. It was not possible to place them in a hospital with other sick people. Police headquarters turned to the Housing Office, requesting allocation of a room of 50 or 60 square meters in order to establish an isolated area for holding the mentally ill.[11]

Contact was also established with the Labor Office. As noted, every day the Reserve placed at the disposal of the Labor Office between ten and twenty policemen whose assignment was to supply the number of people required for that day's work in the city.

The task of recruiting people for work in the city was difficult. Early on, after the episode with the 500, people were afraid to go to the city; the police had to appeal, urge, and drag them.

Later, when people had gone to work in the city, had returned safely, and had managed to bring back various products (this was referred to as "making a package"), the crowding at the gate was very great. Now everyone wanted to go to the city in order to bring back packages.

The police—the Jewish gate guard, which had just been formed—had the task of maintaining order at the gate, which at first was simply not possible.

Headquarters maintained constant written contact with officials and managers at the Labor Office concerning the provision of the requisite number of workers, the associated work of the police, etc.

The tale of communication between the police and the [German] ghetto guard, and other official organs of the authorities, is a chapter all in itself. To tell the truth, the contact was always one-sided; that is, police headquarters repeatedly and often wrote to the ghetto guard concerning occurrences in the ghetto, mostly about assaults, robberies, and other acts of violence. The ghetto guard would never respond in writing: throughout all the activity of the police and of other offices, you could count on your fingers the number

11. Margin note: "It was for naught."

of official letters that we received from them, and even these happened only recently. They would answer orally, because it would not be fitting for them to address us in writing; mostly they simply pretended ignorance.

One of the first letters from the police to the ghetto guard was sent on August 28. It is strange that the police would request permission from the ghetto guard to subscribe to the local newspaper then published in Kovno and the Lithuanian *I Laisve* [Freedom], when purchase of and subscription to newspapers was forbidden to Jews. The police did not receive permission for this from the ghetto guard.

Most of the letters to the ghetto guard dealt with the frequent attacks on ghetto inhabitants through the fence by Lithuanian partisans. There is a whole series of letters from the police management to the ghetto guard, where dozens of times requests are made to intervene, to conduct an investigation, and so on.

The attacks happened mostly in houses adjacent to the fence, in Ramigalos and Paneriu Streets, among others. Armed Lithuanians would break in, rob, plunder, and beat, and in many instances bloodshed would result.[12] There were occurrences of attacks and stabbings with knives, and some instances of rape of young girls, described at the time in associated reports by the policemen on duty. The policemen's reports, along with a letter from the headquarters, would go to the ghetto guard, with a request to put an end to the terror and the bloody attacks. Interventions or investigations by the authorities never took place—we are hefker; the letter was the end of it.

Incidentally, there was no penalty whatsoever for robbing or murdering a Jew. We are outside the law. There is no penalty for shooting a Jew, not only early on, when Jews were shot left and right, but even now, when the situation has supposedly improved, there is, in fact, no penalty for shooting a Jew intentionally or unintentionally.

There were dozens of instances at the gate where a guard would shoot a Jew—either for no reason at all or with some kind of excuse. Such deeds were never punished, not even a reprimand. We are shockingly hefker.[13]

12. Margin note: "More specific examples."
13. Margin note: "Examples."

As the ghetto inhabitants slowly settled in, the police headquarters presented a proposal for control of pedestrian traffic.[14] It consisted of eleven points and was sent for approval by the Elder Council on August 30. It warned that those in the street were to stay to the right side, must not assemble in the streets, must not go without a hat, and so on.

Early on, the police began to monitor cleanliness in the yards. It was announced to the public that every house must select a steward from among its tenants, put together an appropriate protocol, and provide a copy to the police, signed by the tenants. Later, public announcements specified that the yards must be clean and that all inhabitants, with the steward taking the lead, must comply with the sanitary regulations.

Reserve policemen were assigned to go from yard to yard to inspect cleanliness.

Inhabitants were ordered to dig garbage pits, to keep the sinks in order, and to properly maintain the toilets. The refuges—where, as noted, large numbers of people did not maintain cleanliness—were particularly dirty. Special regulations for household hygiene and order were prepared for the refuges.

On September 3, a new post was added to the policemen's duties: night-guard in the Elder Council area. Later a higher-ranking functionary was appointed to perform this job—which was called "Area Command," along with a policeman. Initially, however, a single policeman stood guard through the night in the Elder Council area.

As noted, on August 17 it had been decided to divide the ghetto area into four police precincts, in order to permit the start of normal—under the circumstances—police activity.

As will be remembered, until the division into precincts, the Reserve carried out all police assignments (all policemen, with the exception of the chief, his assistant, and his office personnel, belonged to the Reserve). They handled all the assigned tasks, under the supervision of their appointed chief and in accordance with directions from headquarters.

An urgent need was felt for the establishment of police precincts, for the following reasons:

14. Margin note states this was pursuant to an order from the "commandant."

First of all, [before the division into precincts] all work was centralized; everything was concentrated in one place. All activities of the police, all work assignments, the pulse of ghetto life, beat in only one place, in the so-called *naishtot* [new city] on Varniu Street. Those dwelling in other parts of the ghetto had to go there for all matters. For special police matters that needed to be taken care of immediately, a resident had to run from one end of the city to the other.

Second, the policeman needed to know the people with whom he came into daily contact, which was possible only if he belonged to a particular precinct and dealt every day with the same people. He would know almost everyone personally by their appearance, would know where everyone lived, what their work obligations were, and so on.

Initially, the ghetto consisted of about 27,000 souls. Based on normal living space, the ghetto would have covered a very large area, but even under our circumstances the ghetto area was quite large, particularly given that it had to serve such a large community under much more difficult conditions than normal.

Establishment of the precincts was therefore one of the first necessities; the work had to be decentralized, broken down and divided up in such a manner that each resident could easily come to the police unit to which he belonged and which had jurisdiction over him, to be in constant contact, and to have, so to speak, a nearby address to turn to.

Aside from the decision itself, which, clearly, needed to be implemented, the very nature of the ghetto dictated the creation of the precincts as soon as possible; for example, because of its "geographic" situation, the small ghetto was a "country" in itself. In order to come to the small ghetto from the large ghetto, one had to cross the bridge on Paneriu Street, which was quite far, and going up and down the steps of the bridge was difficult, such that the residents of the small ghetto were almost cut off from us.

During the house searches, the small ghetto was entirely closed to us, and conversely, during the house searches on this side it was not possible to go over to the small ghetto. At those feverish times, when every day and every hour was full of unpleasant surprises, the residents of the other side would know nothing, or would learn about what was happening later than everyone else. For this reason, the first police precinct was created there as a top priority. This precinct was created on . . . [no date provided]

The police precinct in the small ghetto became, so to speak, representative of the active and developing life on the other side of the bridge. Before the establishment of the ghetto, very few Jews had lived in the area of the small ghetto, on the other side of Paneriu; the entire dense Jewish population of Slobodka had lived on this side of Paneriu, in the old city. Mostly Christians lived there, in large, spacious, airy houses, many of which had been built in recent years, with modern facilities and gardens and order all around—airy, bright, and clean.

When we had to settle into the ghetto, whether by chance or not, mostly the more wealthy Jews moved into the small ghetto. The largest part of the residents of the small ghetto consisted of the elite of the ghetto. This area contained comfortable dwellings, equipped with amenities, and the crowding was also not as great as in the other districts.[15] Its only deficiency was its remoteness from the center, far from the general Jewish community; if something happened here or there, we were cut off one from the other.

For this reason the population of the small ghetto had an urgent need for its own police precinct so that, in this manner, it would have something of a connection with the rest of the Jews. Whatever happened, they wanted to know it immediately, at the same time as the other Jews. The police precinct of the small ghetto was therefore the first to be established, to serve as the contact point between the two sides of the ghetto.

Somewhat later, on the [no date given], the second police precinct was established, in the so-called *altshtot* [old city].

In terms of area and number of souls, the second precinct was the largest; the largest part of the population was concentrated there. This is the actual Slobodka, whose population had for many years been 100 percent Jewish— the area of yeshivos[16] and houses of study and prayer, crooked streets with dark, small houses, houses built generations ago around dirty yards with trash boxes forever full, chock-full of people, one on top of the other, little houses where poverty emanated from all corners.

In later years, during the time of Lithuanian independence, a few streets were gradually rebuilt; some of the streets in the old city have new,

---

15. There is a question mark in the margin next to this paragraph, referring to the "wealthy" and "elite" moving into the small ghetto.

16. Institutions of talmudic learning.

half-modern, two-story brick houses, and in many places one sees a half-wrecked hut nestling—as if ashamed—against a new two-story house.

In these little houses and modern buildings lived eminent rabbinical scholars along with ordinary yeshiva people, and, at the same time, the famous Slobodka coachmen and scatterbrains, porters and ordinary workmen, the typical Slobodka Khaikes and Yoshkes[17] of our dear *Amkho*,[18] colorful local types, a mixture of deeply rooted, strong, plain people, big-boned Jews, with thick, grimy hands and stomachs undergirded with thick ropes; together with Torah aristocrats, clean, pale yeshiva students with soiled hats, modern short coats with a collar and tie, rabbis with rustling satin gabardines, heads of yeshivos with long, gray beards and high, furrowed foreheads; together with the typical Slobodka proprietor, with his own house and store, half provincial and half city-dweller—all of them the residents of the old city. The new houses and streets were considered, so to speak, the "indigenous" modern old city. But the genuine parts of Slobodka were those crooked, dirty streets and their inhabitants, who did not arrive in Slobodka when the ghetto came into being, but had already been there for years; old residents, living in the small houses inherited from fathers and grandfathers generations before.

When the Jews started to move into the ghetto, and crowded conditions prevailed, the old residents of Slobodka did not want to take in "new" Jews. They argued that, as inhabitants of these provincial streets, they were the proprietors of these little houses and no one could tell them otherwise. For this reason, most of the conflicts and misunderstandings concerning housing were in the first [*sic*, second?] precinct.

Because the second precinct had the largest area and contained the greatest number of residents, a larger number of policemen were assigned to it.

On the [no date given], the third precinct was established on the border of the old city and new Slobodka. As noted, originally, old Slobodka was populated almost entirely by Jews. Fifteen or twenty years ago, the Lithuanian government parceled out open sections of land and distributed them to its first volunteers—to officers as well as to ordinary officials. All the Christians

17. Yiddish first names.
18. Common Jewish people.

who received land around Slobodka built homes for themselves that were very comfortable and surrounded by gardens. The purely Lithuanian quarter started there; a whole row of new houses, modern, with plenty of space, sun, and light. The Jewish types who had long been rooted in Slobodka were not to be found there. The third precinct was purely gentile, aristocratic.

And even now, as the Jews moved from the city to the ghetto, the richer people, who had fatter pocketbooks and, as a result, perhaps, also stronger elbows, settled mostly in this district; here reside some of the so-called yalehs (a ghetto expression, created by the Jews at the airfield; we will dwell on this later.)

At first by the Lithuanian government and later by the Soviet authorities, the neighborhood of the fourth precinct was built up as workers' quarters; many apartment blocks were constructed here.

First of all, the large blocks. These were three-story brick buildings consisting of twenty-four dwellings, equipped with the most modern conveniences.

As in the third precinct, the richer part of the population moved into these blocks, and to this day most of these residents are the ghetto "yalehs."

Here are also streets with apartment blocks, such as Mildas, Gimbuta, and Vienozinskio, where a mixed population once resided.

The Brazilke also belonged to the fourth district, in which a diverse population resided. In the nicer homes lived the more well-to-do, who could afford to pay the gentiles more money for ceding the place; in the smaller, simpler little houses lived the poorer people.

(Incidentally, later, after the gold action, these labels faded, and such distinctions disappeared almost entirely. But later still, when the new way of life settled in, one lived from the sale of one's own clothing, so that whoever had goods and had been able to retain them was rich; those who had not, suffered in silence. Later on also appeared special ghetto *gvirim* [rich men] and, naturally, also newly baked "aristocrats," who had been "clever" at the relevant times. But we will dwell on this topic separately, when we describe the new sources of subsistence that the Jews discovered.)

The borders of the precincts were determined, and for each of them were appointed a chief with an assistant and a secretary, who began to carry out the work.

The work of the policemen became specific, with regular assignments; the precincts had their own established assignments, and headquarters had its separate tasks.

Headquarters had its special work that was not dependent on the borders of this or that precinct, such as service at the Housing Office, and the Labor Office job of bringing people to their workplaces. From this group of policemen, which was at the disposition of the Labor Office every day, a special group later emerged—the gate guard, who maintained order at the gate and in the work columns.

Every now and then the policemen from the Reserve would be commandeered to help carry out large-scale assignments in a precinct. The Reserve—a "non-precinct" group—was under the direct jurisdiction of headquarters, available to meet all contingencies.

Policemen of the Reserve also maintained day and night watch at the Elder Council. When the Reserve was dissolved, a command post remained in the Elder Council building.

Ward policemen had their regular assignments and also took care of general public tasks. These included the effort to prevent trading at the fence. Trading at the fence is a chapter of troubles all its own. As noted, the problem of food was very difficult for us. Everyone sought by all possible means to secure something to eat—first of all by trading through the barbed wire with the local Christians who lived near the fence. The Christians gladly sold everything or, most often, traded for clothing—not because they had compassion for us because we were fenced in by barbed wire—of such feelings one need not "suspect" our "dear" Lithuanian neighbors—but simply because the deal was very advantageous for them: if they sold for money, they charged a much higher price than to the gentiles in the city, and if they traded products for clothing—which was most often the case—they received for a loaf of bread or for a bag of potatoes a variety of good clothing and other valuables, for which they could realize high returns in the city. (All stores selling shoes, clothing, and manufactured products in the city were closed, so that nothing was available.)

For us these transactions were perhaps not advantageous, but we had no choice; one wants to eat.

Trading at the fences blossomed. Jews would come carrying clothing in their hands, as if going to the market with baskets and bags, spreading out the merchandise at the barbed wire fence for the buyers to see. And so the trading would go on, on this side a throng of Jews, on the other side several Christians, usually more Jews than Christians, the Christian haughty with his few potatoes, the Jews competing with one another, showing off their goods as superior to those of the others, only to obtain a loaf of bread, a stick of butter, a little milk for a small child, and so on. The guard outside the fence, the Lithuanian partisan, would be bribed with a few dozen rubles, or some gift, so that he would not see anything. But if it should happen that the partisan had received too little, or that he was simply in a bad mood, then he would begin shooting repeatedly into the air; but there were also dozens of instances when people were shot at and wounded.[19] There were also instances when an inspector would suddenly arrive and the partisan, afraid for his own hide, would shoot into the crowd so they would scatter faster.

In general, trading was rampant at the fence, the tumult and noise great, people shouting and quarreling. The gentiles would frequently cheat: they would sell butter, but, upon cutting it, the buyer would find a stone inside, and various other swindles. Once the Germans found out about this, they threatened to apply strong measures if the Jews and their police did not stop trading at the fence. The precinct police had a difficult time dispersing people from the fences and prohibiting trading, as doing so could lead to tragic consequences for the ghetto. This was one of the most difficult tasks of the police at that time.

At the same time the police also had to maintain order in the lines at the stores, guard the gardens day and night, recruit people for work, supervise sanitation, tend to the public peace and intervene in various misbehaviors, and go from house to house informing the population about various obligations imposed by the decrees of the authorities and of the Elder Council. The precinct was the place where residents would come to become informed of this or that order, or, in troublesome situations, to seek advice and help.

The precincts had their own premises, where the chief and his assistant supervised the work in accordance with directions from headquarters.

They had their own autonomy in local precinct questions. The chief had his own authority over discipline and job issues within the police force. He could penalize his policemen with a variety of punishments for job service

19. Margin note: "Provide examples."

offenses, subject to the consent of headquarters. In more severe cases, he would write a report requesting direct punishment by headquarters.

The precinct chief stays in constant written contact with the headquarters, sending daily reports of his activities and immediately informing the headquarters of special occurrences and happenings in his precinct.

Somewhat later, it was established that each ward—or, as it was later called, precinct—would send a detailed daily report to headquarters, along with a list of assignments, in accordance with a specially designed reporting form, so that each day headquarters had an accurate picture of the work in the precincts.

Headquarters is the eye that watches over the work and issues directives and orders to the precinct chiefs, who carry them out with the policemen at their disposition.

The establishment of the precincts normalized the work of the police. Duties and tasks for each precinct and headquarters were distributed among them.

But then came a series of happenings that interrupted the development of police activities—a whole set of events, one coming rapidly after the other.

The "Jordan Certificates" and the "Rehearsal Action"

The first event was the distribution of the "Jordan certificates."

On September 12, a few days after we had begun to recover from the house searches and their culmination in the gold action, a chain of happenings, events, and shocks began that, during their course, held the entire ghetto in great tension and deathly fear. At first we did not know, or better said, there was as yet no conception of the magnitude of the dreadful tragedy that we were to experience.

On September 12, the infamous Jordan[20] brought to the committee 5,000 certificates for distribution to the Jewish craftsmen living in the ghetto. They were small white cards, blank except for the text in German: "Certificate for Jewish craftsmen, Province Commissar in Kauen (Kovno)—signed

---

20. Margin note: "Kaminski?" Note: Garfunkel states (*Kovna ha-yehudit be-hurbana*, 64) that it was Kaminski who brought the certificates on September 15.

Jordan—Hauptsturmführer [Captain]." The Labor Office was required to distribute to the Jewish craftsmen these white certificates, which were called in the ghetto "Jordan certificates."

A short time earlier it had been announced that all craftsmen and professional workers were to register at the Labor Office. Many people registered, and thus the Labor Office had an assembled list of craftsmen and their professions. The Labor Office began to distribute the certificates in accordance with this list.

At first, the population had no idea why these certificates were being distributed or what kind of certificates they were. For the first few hours the distribution proceeded in an orderly fashion. In the yard of the committee [Elder Council] names were called out by profession, and each craftsman received enough certificates to cover all the members of his family.

But the knowledge spread throughout the ghetto with lightning speed that these were not simply certificates for craftsmen, but that the devil was playing a different game with us—that these were life certificates; it means that all the certificates having been distributed to the Jews, those receiving a certificate would remain living in the ghetto while the others would be taken out of the ghetto, their fate clear to all.

Words cannot convey the fright and panic that prevailed in the vicinity of the committee. Tens of thousands of people flooded the building and the surrounding grounds, each with a little hope in his heart that perhaps he would be favored to receive a certificate. There was colossal rushing and jostling; people were pushing and shoving, storming the doors of the Labor Office and Elder Council, seeking to obtain a life certificate.

The first symptoms of moral deterioration appear in the ghetto during this period, at this point in time: the first step to rottenness, protectionism, and even corruption.

As the great tumult and commotion to get certificates began in the committee, it turned out that those dispensing the certificates had disappeared. One said that a second had the certificates for distribution, the second said it was a third. At one point the mob broke down the door and fell upon the one holding the certificates, wanting to lynch him on the spot. With much effort he succeeded in tearing himself away from the wild crowd and escaped through the window. The noisy, vehement, seething crowd stood waiting, faces twisted with agitation, teeth gritted, and fists clenched.

The population quickly sensed the great injustice being done—that something was not right in the kingdom of Denmark, that there were machinations behind their backs.

It became clear from the first day that the committee had not carried out its assignment honestly.

Those at the helm knew at the outset what kind of certificates these were and what purpose they were to serve. Except for the few craftsmen on the list, the dispensers and minor officials distributed the certificates to themselves and their families, to their own extended families, to relatives, and to close acquaintances—people who had no connection to craftsmen whatsoever. Plain and simple, it turned into a shop: whoever had a good contact on the committee received a certificate; without such an acquaintance, even the best craftsman would not receive one.

Today, perhaps, we view this entire matter somewhat differently. When all is said and done, there were only 5,000 certificates. From the broader Jewish perspective, these 5,000 certificates were to be distributed to Jews, and this particular "allocation" was therefore made use of. From this point of view, all that is important is that Jews should be able to save themselves, whichever Jews they may be—whether shopkeepers or workmen, doctors or shoemakers, it is all the same to us, provided that as many Jews as possible are saved—that's the reality.

But the anger of the public was justified—because which view is to prevail? If only craftsmen were to receive the certificates because the Germans issued them only for workers, then whoever could meet that requirement was lucky; but then must the shopkeepers, merchants, workers, and ordinary Jews accept their fate? If, on the other hand, the certificates were to be given out not only to craftsmen but also to ordinary Jews, then one could justifiably ask the eternal question: How is this possible? Why? Why for Chaim yes and for Yosl no? Is this Jew better than the other? One could create a raffle, a lottery—whoever was lucky would receive a certificate. But why this ugly cattle-trading? How can people's lives be treated so arbitrarily—whoever has protektsia and acquaintances receives a certificate; if not—nothing.

Bitterness and anger against the committee was great. The hatred stemming from the housing days, which had cooled off, flamed anew in the form of great tumult, quarrels, and fighting inside and around the committee. In time, however, the rage of the people spent itself and subsided.

The committee came to the decision that matters could not go on in this manner, that certificates could not be distributed only to craftsmen but must also be distributed to ordinary Jews, so that there would remain, so to speak, a mixed community. It was therefore officially decided that certificates would be distributed to those who were not craftsmen. Part-time workers of the ghetto institutions and of the police and other deserving community leaders would also receive certificates.

Every department of the ghetto institutions hastily put together a list of its workers, including the number of family members (wives and children), in order to obtain certificates for them. But even this was not carried out as it should have been: the higher officials received the full number for themselves and their close family members; the lower ones did not receive enough for all family members; randomly, they were given only a few per family.

The police also received certificates for distribution to 50 men and their families. The police had 120 men. Many more certificates were needed for distribution to the policemen and their families, but altogether 127 certificates were allocated to the 50 men.

One particular police functionary received all the certificates for distribution to the policemen and their families, but even here there were abuses. The above-mentioned police functionary used the task entrusted to him—the right to distribute—to give certificates not only to policemen, for whom they were intended, but also to his personal relatives, who had no connection to the police. It was even thought in some police circles that he gave them to those who could generously pay for them.

When the policemen saw that even the scant number allocated to them were being "suitably" distributed, a group of policemen who were upset by the distribution went to the house of the functionary and made a very great commotion; they wanted to trample him on the spot. But be that as it may, the functionary no longer had any certificates to give out, and those who did not receive them did not sleep and did not rest in their effort to obtain life certificates.

A little later, following intervention by policemen at headquarters and ultimately at the Elder Council, an additional small number of certificates was obtained for distribution.[21] These certificates had to be used sparingly;

---

21. Margin note: "Fritz[?] Fakisan[?] received 150 Jordan certificates."

that is, instead of giving each family member a certificate, only one certificate would be given per family and the names of all family members written on the other side.

There were also some craftsmen within the police force for whom a few certificates were obtained directly from the Labor Office, with the help of the chiefs.

Distribution of the certificates stretched over a period of a few days, until approximately September 15. Those were days of extremely tense moods, as people ran in pursuit of the piece of paper, the so-called Jordan certificate.

Then came a time that showed how important it was to have a Jordan certificate. For anyone who had it, this piece of paper was indeed a life certificate.

On the evening of September 16, nonstop shooting began around the fences, along the length and width of the entire ghetto area; there was firing and shooting from all sides. The sentries—the ghetto guards, Germans and Lithuanians—stood at the fences shooting. People huddled in the corners of their houses, expecting a bullet through the window at any moment. Everyone thought that the houses next door were being shot into, or that people were being taken out of their houses and shot in the streets, because deafening gun explosions were taking place on all sides and in all corners of the ghetto.

The shooting reached a peak in the small ghetto. The fenced-in area was relatively small there, such that wherever one turned there was a fence, and around these fences our murderers stood shooting. But here they were shooting not only in the air, but also into the windows. In one place they fatally shot a nursing baby through the window and gravely wounded the mother. The shooting there was so frightful that the residents were afraid to stay in bed; instead they lay on the floor to avoid a likely bullet through the window.

On the morning of September 17 the small ghetto was sealed. Germans and Lithuanians with rifles and machine guns stood on the bridge over Paneriu Street and did not allow anyone to pass. Then several companies of soldiers arrived, surrounded the entire area, and drove all the people from their houses into the market square. Germans and Lithuanians went through the streets shooting, chasing everyone into the square. The Jews driven from their houses were murderously beaten with rifles for not going fast enough. The old and sick were bitterly beaten for not running fast enough to the square.

The Jews driven from their homes were strictly forbidden to take anything with them. They received murderous blows for holding the smallest package in their hands. Those who had taken from their house a parcel of food or other small necessities had to throw it away on the street.

But not only the small ghetto—the large ghetto was also surrounded. Machine guns and automatic weapons were positioned along the bank of the river Vilia, as well as on the Slobodka bridge.

The entire population assembled in the square, filling it as well as the surrounding streets. The assembled Jews were grouped into columns, and high-ranking German military officers stood before them and began to make the selections. No one knew or could imagine what this meant; it was only observed that people with Jordan certificates were sent to the right and those without them to the left. Occasionally, some who were young and of good appearance, but without certificates, were also sent to the right, but it appeared that there were basically two categories: with and without Jordan certificates. Whoever had a certificate was all right; if he didn't, it was not good.

The work of selection proceeded with full "speed." Trucks arrived to take away some of the people. There were machine guns in some of them. One had no idea where the people who were being taken away were going and what would be done to them, but it was expected to be very bad.

With deadly fear in their eyes, the crowd slowly advanced toward the selector. Those with Jordan certificates were somewhat more confident but still frightened; those without Jordan certificates showed deathly fear in their eyes along with an apathy—"what will be will be; we are in any event already lost."

In the small ghetto there were also a few policemen who happened not to have Jordan certificates. They all had their hats and armbands, however, and they and their families were all sent to the right, that is, to the good side.

The whole crowd, like a large herd of sheep, made its way toward the selectors.

Suddenly an automobile arrived from the city, Jordan jumped out, ran to the selectors, said something to them, and immediately everyone was chased back to the houses, ordered to run more quickly, everyone to his own home.

People ran with joy mixed with fear. What kind of a devil's game were they playing with us? Was the whole thing no more than a game—the staging of a comedy, simply to make us miserable, to laugh at us and mock us, to humiliate us in our and their eyes, or had a miracle truly occurred, had they reconsidered or taken pity—what had happened here?

As we learned from later experiences, this was not just a game, but was based on a preconceived plan for our destruction, which was to have started that day but which was recalled for their own devilish reasons.

The guards were immediately removed from their posts, the machine guns taken away, and one could once again move back and forth from the small ghetto.

Again it became quiet and calm, but how long would we be allowed to remain in our places?

From this show, which we later termed the "Rehearsal Action of the Small Ghetto," we learned above all that not just any piece of paper or certificate would do—clearly, the important thing was to have a Jordan certificate. It was, however, also observed that many without Jordan certificates were sent to the good side. There were also many instances when it helped to say that one worked at the airfield.

It thus became clear to everyone that there was another form of protection besides the amulet of the Jordan certificate, and that was a document from the workplace. A mass rush developed to obtain such documents; along with the development of work at the airfield, this took on the character of a pandemic.

Airfield and City Work Brigades

The start of work at the airfield, the daily increases in demands for workers, the entire "aerodrome" story—that is a special chapter in the history of the ghetto, a chapter full of blood, pain, tears, hardship, and humiliation. All activity and preoccupation in the ghetto was concentrated and tied to producing people for work at the airfield, to which we gave the name "producing the *einsatz*."[22]

22. Work party of a size specified by the Germans.

The beginning of work at the airfield developed in the following manner:

Around September 10 came a demand to provide 500 men for night work at the airfield. Initially, this order was received with alarm, as it bore a resemblance to the first demand for 500 men, who did not come back. In spite of assurances by the Germans that all would return home after work, very few volunteered to go. One way or another, with the help of the police—there were also a few volunteers—several hundred people were "pieced together," and they were sent off to the airfield for night work.

Early the next morning, wives and mothers waited with pounding hearts for their husbands and sons. To everyone's joy, all, without exception, came back. For the next night shift, now that it was clear that this time they were indeed to go to work, more workers could be found. The following work parties also returned in peace, even reporting that the guards, the sentries, soldiers of the Luftwaffe, had treated the Jews relatively decently, that there was no prodding to work, no shouting, and no beating.

The demand, every evening, to provide 500 workers was constant. This number of people had to be provided at the gate every evening.

It was not reasonable to require that those who went out of recognition of their duty, or voluntarily, or even having been mobilized by the police, should go every night, at a time when there were so many men capable of work who did not go at all. Some order had to be brought into this matter.

The Elder Council and the Labor Office began with appeals to the population. Notices were posted on all streets that the authorities required us to provide every day a specified number of people for work, that we must comply with these demands, that we were forced to do so, and that if the required number of people did not come for work, unpleasant consequences could result for all of us. Therefore, all responsible inhabitants must, in their own interest, voluntarily register for work.

A fair number of people did come to register and were told that the names of those who registered but did not show up for work would be remanded to the ghetto commandant for punishment.

But all of this was of little help. The required number of people, the einsatz, was not materializing adequately.

Somewhat later, the number of people demanded was raised to 1,000 men every day. Considerable effort was required to produce this number of people. Policemen and office workers from the ghetto institutions were sent out to go from house to house to register men for work. Many would hide, and of those who were "caught" and registered, only a small number turned up. It became apparent that appeals and haphazard registrations would not produce the required number of people, and that mobilization was necessary. Policemen went from house to house, took people out of the houses and from the streets, and led them to the collection point at the gate. From the very first days, people had to be taken by force. Policemen from the Reserve and from the precincts set out to produce the missing number of people.

Why were the people so reluctant to go to work at the airfield? Why did they respond so weakly to the demands of the Elder Council and the Labor Office to fulfill this urgent obligation?

There were a number of reasons.

Very simply, the first reason was that our Jews—they should live and be well—tend to run and obey only when in fear of a gentile. If one Jew tells another to go to work, he answers: "Why exactly me? Why not the other one, who never goes while I have already gone ten times; and who are you to tell me that I should go? Why aren't you going to work yourself?"

The second reason is the fact that one would leave the house for the gate at four o'clock [in the afternoon] and leave by truck for the airfield around six o'clock after all had been assembled; return to the ghetto was not until seven in the morning. During these fifteen hours the workers received absolutely nothing to eat; whoever could bring something from home was fortunate, but those who could not had to starve, because nothing was given to eat and there was no opportunity to buy anything.

Work at the airfield was not easy. One had to dig dirt, load gravel into wagons and unload them, mix cement, carry boards. At first, the work was not so hard, because the overseers—Wehrmacht soldiers—did not prod the people to work (in contrast to later times when supervision of the Jewish workers was taken over by [German] civilians, the so-called masters, who would strike and beat). But you had to stand on your feet for fifteen hours, and the trucks that had brought the columns to and from work were eventually taken away, so that you had to travel there and back on foot—a distance of 16 kilometers. Clearly, this became very hard, and one also has to take into account the fact that nourishment was quite inadequate.

City brigades began to be formed at the same time. This work was much easier, it was a shorter distance away, and, most important, it was possible to buy food products from Christians in the vicinity.

Initially, the city brigades were formed in response to German demands for a specified number of people for work in various locations in the city. As a first priority, the demand was for skilled workers, locksmiths, carpenters, bricklayers, and so on. Columns were formed consisting of a few skilled workers along with ordinary Jews, and they went to work in the city in discrete columns, each accompanied by an armed German.

Jews working in such brigades got used to their German overseers, would be given food, and, most importantly, had the opportunity to buy products, "to make a package" and bring it home to their families in the ghetto.

Naturally, as the rush to join a brigade became very great, thousands of people would crowd the gate at six in the morning, surging into the square near the gate and the surrounding streets, pushing and shoving in hopes of finding an opportunity to sneak into a brigade.

Work-cards or brigade certificates had not yet been issued. Some brigades issued certificates to their members, but most did not. Some brigades would form spontaneously and by chance. Upon the arrival of a German official with a demand for people, there would be pushing and shoving toward him. Whoever had strong elbows could push and pull his way into the lucky group that would be able to slip into the city to buy something. Whoever was weak or quiet was left behind and returned with an empty stomach.

The Germans coming to take people would most often ask for the same people who had worked there the previous day. They wanted to have "their" Jews. Others who pushed and shoved toward the Germans would be beaten with rubber truncheons and rifle butts.

Those who managed to get into the city were able to arrange to buy food. Those who worked in a brigade every day were the most fortunate. Those working at the airfield worked harder and had nothing.

All those going out at six or seven o'clock in the morning to work in the city brigades would meet the columns returning from the airfield. The returning airfield workers—tired from working, dragging themselves on foot for long distances, standing on their feet for fifteen hours without food or sleep, chilled through, covered in dust and splattered with clay and cement from the airfield, with empty stomachs and pockets—would meet the brigade people on their way to work. These—rested, having eaten and slept, relatively cleanly dressed, with empty sacks under their arms—were marching quietly to work in the city and would bring the sacks back full of products.

The jealousy of the people coming from the airfield toward the brigade members was very great. Everyone thought to himself: "The duty to go to the airfield is the same for all; why then must I suffer at the airfield and have nothing to bring back, while the others have it easy, with food to fill their bellies?"

The following day that person would not go to the airfield, but rather go early in the morning to the gate to try his luck at pushing his way into a brigade. And if he should not succeed, he would rather go back and sit at home than to toil for nothing at the airfield. There were hundreds of those.

With the development of the city brigades, it became increasingly difficult to produce the required number of workers for the airfield.

The police had the assignment of mobilizing the people. They would go from house to house ordering the residents to come to work. But this process was still chaotic and disorganized. There was registration of residents, but control was quite weak, and those who did not want to go could easily hide out for a moment, because it was not known who lived where. There were no lists of those who did or did not report for work.

The Labor Office began to organize columns, so that every ghetto resident would belong to a column with a column leader. The column leader was to register all his people so that the next day it would be known who had shown up and who had not. For a short while this worked, but the required number was almost always not there.

A new work schedule was established for the airfield, with work divided into two shifts: a day shift and a night shift, and for the two shifts we had to provide 2,000 men, that is, 1,000 for each shift.

The police had on their shoulders the heavy burden of producing the two shifts. At that time, this was a very difficult assignment, and, because of the absence of a precise registration, not very fruitful. But the police had to produce the required number of people, and so they would go day in and day out, morning and night, from house to house, and also drag people off the streets.

Columns would assemble near the committee and people would trade places: those who had worked the day shift the previous day had to work the night shift the next, and vice versa.

These early days of airfield work were a test of our internal organization—and a proving ground for the fate of the ghetto—or so it was thought. We were given to understand from German circles that our work at the airfield would provide the justification for our existence.

The large number of Jews trying to shirk their duty to work at the airfield resulted in bloody casualties.

On Friday, September 21, on the eve of Rosh Hashanah of the year 5702 [1941], there was a demand for 1,000 men for the night shift. The time arrived for the columns to march out, and the required number of people was not yet there.

At the gate stood Germans who had come to take away the workers, a few partisans, and the German gatepost. The mood was tense and strained. The Germans, and particularly the post at the gate, were very upset about the shortage of workers.

Jewish policemen were running around from house to house, calling and dragging people out, demanding that people come out to work, because otherwise the situation would be very bad. Everyone was summoned, without distinction as to whether one had worked the night before, because a great storm was gathering at the gate.

The Jew Shtrashunski, who had returned from the city not long before, did not want to comply with the demand of the Germans to go to work. He ran out of his house to the German at the gate and showed him the document from his workplace, indicating that he had returned from work only a short while ago.

The German didn't even look at the document. He pointed his rifle at the Jew and ordered him to run to the house on the corner. When he arrived there, he shot him on the spot.

That was the first casualty.

Germans went from house to house near the gate and dragged people out to work. They pounded on the door at the home of an older Jew who was hard of hearing. Because he did not hear the pounding on the door, he did not open up quickly. The German immediately fired through the door.

When the old Jew, deathly afraid, opened the door, the German dragged him out of the house, chased him to the square near the gate and ordered him to run back to his house. When the Jew reached the threshold of his house, the German shot him in the back on the spot.

The second casualty.

The other casualties were passersby from the side streets. A young man was passing the gate on his way to a house of worship, and a young woman was passing through Synagogue Street. Without any warning, the German shot them both.

Four casualties.

At this time, a work brigade (the Mils brigade) arrived from the city. The post at the gate was irritated and bloodthirsty, and when he saw the incoming brigade with packages of products on their backs, his *treyfeh* blood boiled even more over the fact that people were joining the brigades but not going to the airfield. He started shooting, killing one person on the spot and severely wounding another.

Had it been possible to give medical help to the wounded man, he could have been saved. It is also of interest to note that the German didn't know that the Jew was alive and only wounded—otherwise he would have shot him with another bullet and finished him off. The police pulled him over to the side and pretended to cover him with a little earth so that the German would think he was already dead. Their hope was to take him away a little later and get him medical help. They were, however, not allowed to take away the wounded man, and he bled to death.

Six casualties.

The six casualties had a very depressing effect on the ghetto—this is what we are worth when one Yeke[23] goes wild. However, we learned and understood from this event that, regrettably, we could not change our fate, that we must accept it, carry the yoke, and strive in every way to make the einsatz work better, so as to avoid having to live through such terror and give up innocent victims for no reason.

Everyone was required to work at the airfield, except for police employees and, with some limitations, employees of the ghetto institutions. A special airfield calendar was set up for committee people; they would go from

23. A German (although commonly referring to German Jews).

time to time in accordance with a schedule drawn up by their own offices. At first they went exactly like everyone else; in fact, there was a special airfield column from the ghetto institutions. Later their work requirement was changed to once or twice a week. Meanwhile, the police were still not required to go to the airfield.

It was, however, desired that the police should not be an exception. They should join in the slave labor like all the other Jews—although not as often.

Psychologically, it would make a better impression on the population if all could see that there were no exceptions, that everyone must work, had to work, and that the police, who chased everyone day and night, controlled everybody, dragged, called, and demanded—that they themselves also reported for work.

On September 22, on the first day of Rosh Hashanah, the day following the tragedy of the six casualties at the gate, policemen began to be sent to the airfield—50 men each day. Fifty men were specified sequentially every day from the precincts and from the Reserve. They would march to work in a tight column through the ghetto, wearing their armbands.

It became evident after a short while that this was not useful: the 50 men could not save the situation because removing 100 policemen each day was very harmful (the 50 returning from work had a day off, and those who had to go at night could not participate in the mobilization). People immediately sensed that control was weakened and stopped showing up. As a result of the 50 policemen going, as many as 300 others could be lost. We could not allow ourselves the luxury of showing the people that the police were also going to the airfield, only for the sake of demonstration.

A short time later the order requiring the police to go to the airfield was canceled.

Events and episodes in our ghetto life began to interconnect and interrelate, with the airfield at the center of attention. It was a time when hundreds of people would stream to the gate to report for work at the airfield, without being called or recruited. That was the time of panic, when everyone was seeking to obtain papers and certifications from the workplaces. It was the time when it was thought that working dutifully would save us from all the misery being prepared for us.

A series of events took place that led to the belief that certificates did indeed help, which started a rush to obtain them.

The Actions: In the "Box" (September 26, 1941) and in the "Small Ghetto" (October 4, 1941)

On September 26, partisans and Germans surrounded Ariogolos and Velianos Streets—"The Box"—and chased the residents out of their houses in the direction of Linkuvos Street, all the way to the market square, which is located outside the ghetto. The people were driven from these streets in the customary manner, with the usual methods—with beatings and brutality.

The Jews assembled in the market square were surrounded and the sorting began—left, right, to life, to death.

It turned out that no special attention was given to Jordan certificates; apparently the information had reached the Germans that these certificates had been distributed not only to craftsmen—for whom they were intended—but also to ordinary Jews.

The people were sorted—this one to the right, the other to the left—based on their physical appearance. The old, the sick, women and men with small children to one side, most of the younger adults and others who appeared capable of work to the other side.

The designated "bad Jews" were assembled into columns and led away in the direction of the Ninth Fort, from where they never returned.

Today we can imagine what was done to these unfortunates at the fort. Regrettably, we are sure that each and every one of them was shot. This was the first instance of people being led from the ghetto in the direction of the Ninth Fort—it was impossible to believe, it did not enter our minds, that ordinary Jews, from a ghetto created by the order of the Germans themselves, would be led away to be shot. Why? For what? How can human beings allow themselves to do such things?

It was not possible to believe or imagine this. The Germans themselves—before getting us "accustomed" to the idea that we were worse than dogs—apparently found it unpleasant to say what had happened to these people. The response to inquiries by the Elder Council as to the fate of these people was that they were resettled to a different place to dig potatoes, adding that close family members could submit a request for the return of the resettled.

To some, this information, which spread throughout the ghetto, seemed like a ray of hope. When it became known that it was possible to submit such a request, thousands of people came to the police to submit a plea to the commandant for the return to the ghetto of close family members who had been taken away.

All the requests remained with the commandant, or in someone's waste-paper basket. To this day, no one has succeeded in bringing back the dead.

Those who were sorted to the good side were returned to the ghetto. But they were not allowed to return to the houses in which they had lived—these had been sealed by the Germans.

Among the inhabitants of these streets were a few policemen, all of whom were sorted to the good side; a hat and armband helped once again this time.

The next day, September 27, according to an order of the Germans, Jewish policemen were posted all along Ariogolos Street with instructions not to allow anyone to go through. The Germans went from house to house, took out the better effects from the sealed houses, and carried them off.

The Jews from the "cleansed" streets were later allowed to return to their houses. As a result of this first action—although, as said, it was not possible to imagine and believe that the people being taken to the hill leading to the fort were all, without exception, being killed—it was understood that something fearsome and terrible was being planned for us, and that we must see to it that, as far as possible, we took care of ourselves, and to the extent possible saved ourselves.

It was also learned from this action that, to a greater or lesser extent, papers and certificates from the workplaces did help, because most of the young and those able to work were allowed through.

Rumors circulated in the ghetto that in any future actions the Germans would pay attention to one's ability to work, as indicated by whether he was indeed working somewhere. A rush therefore started in the ghetto for documents and certifications from workplaces. Everyone wanted to present himself as useful and able to work.

The Days of Awe arrived, the first holiday that the Jews celebrated behind barbed wire.

During the entire summer following the occupation of the Baltic countries, the Germans marched ever-forward, occupying more and more Russian cities, swallowing hundreds of kilometers. Then, just before the Days of Awe, they came to a stop for a short while. Great battles took place in the vicinity of Kharkov, Kiev, and other cities.

In addition to our own troubles and pain, we also lived and breathed the situation at the fronts.

We looked for indications of weakness, hoping it might be possible to stop the giant, dreadfully strong German war machine; maybe it would break or weaken. It was thought that if they could be halted or hindered even a little bit, then immediately deliverance would come. There was nourishment and comfort from prognoses, predictions, information from "reliable" sources that they had been pushed back or defeated somewhere, that they had suffered great losses; soon, after a short time, they would receive crushing blows and their end would come.

As the Days of Awe approached, the mystical mood of the people deepened. In normal times, many Jews were mystical and religious and looked for signs and indications to predict a good year. It is no wonder that here in the ghetto, with the constant fear and dread of actions and of annihilation, the mystical mood of the people should grow. Various rumors spread throughout the ghetto—basically foolish and senseless—which many of us nonetheless believed.

Rumors circulated of dreams of rabbis in which they were "informed" from above that on Rosh Hashanah all of us would be released. Deep in our hearts, perhaps none of us believed this empty talk, but we were nevertheless comforted and clung to these dreams and to the rumors of a possible salvation. "Who knows, maybe it will actually come about and we will be freed for the New Year."

Exactly on the eve of Rosh Hashanah there occurred the bloody tragedy of the six casualties at the gate. In the evening of the first night of Rosh Hashanah the Jews went to slave labor at the airfield as usual. The next day, the night of the first day of Rosh Hashanah, the police went for the first time to the airfield. Of all the dreams, talk, hopes, and expectations, nothing, regrettably, materialized.

Many *minyonim*[24] were arranged in the few houses of worship that existed in the ghetto, as well as in private homes. At first, people were afraid to arrange minyonim without appropriate permission from the authorities, who could deem such gatherings to be instances of illegal assembly. The

24. *minyan* (Yiddish, sing.), minyonim (pl.)—prayer quorum of ten male adults, the minimum required for certain religious services.

commandant was approached concerning this, and when he did not object, such minyonim were arranged.

But special precautions were taken: each *minyan* had to register with our police and provide the names of two persons who would be responsible for ensuring order. A minyan was also arranged in police headquarters for the Rosh Hashanah holiday.

The set routine until then was for work at the airfield to be carried out only by a night shift. But on the morning of Yom Kippur, at ten o'clock, an urgent demand was received to provide 1,000 men at once for a new shift— the day shift. We saw in this a power play—they, the Germans, knew very well that this day was a holy day for us, a once-a-year fast day, so they were doing this on purpose—demanding workers in order to make fun of us, to insult our deepest feelings, both physically and morally.

It is possible that they had specifically planned to start the day shift on Yom Kippur, or perhaps it was just a coincidence. But all of us saw in it a new evil decree, a special "gift" in honor of Yom Kippur. Those policemen who were off-duty because of Yom Kippur were immediately mobilized. All policemen were sent out to all the minyonim in houses of prayer and in private homes to announce that all men between the ages of seventeen and fifty-five must immediately leave the minyonim and proceed to the airfield. Hundreds of Jews hastily removed their prayer shawls and ran home to change, while others went directly from the houses of prayer to the gate.

(Incidentally, announcements were posted on all the streets before Rosh Hashanah that the rabbinate permitted work at the airfield during the Days of Awe—indeed, that such work should be considered everyone's duty.)

And so the first holidays passed in the ghetto, all under the whip, all under a cloud of fear, and all under the burden of providing the einsatz for the airfield, which became a very pressing and painful problem—for the Elder Council, the Labor Office, and the police.

Shift notes began to be given out at the airfield; that is, everyone who had worked that day received a slip with a date and stamp. Later, around the beginning of October, the shift notes began to bear an official German stamp, with a swastika and *Bauverwaltung von [sic] der Luftwaffe.*[25] Everyone wanted to have the paper with the German stamp, which led to pushing

25. Construction Administration of the Air Force.

and shoving to be chosen for work at the airfield. Everyone also began to try to obtain family notes. These were prepared, printed notes with the following content: "It is hereby certified that such-and-such ghetto resident works at the airfield and that his family consists of so many persons, signed *Frontbauleitung* 3/1."[26]

The column leaders would take down the family names of those working in their columns, and in addition to a shift note, everyone would receive a family certificate with the stamp of the Front Construction Division. Everyone wanted to obtain such notes, and this is why the people streamed to work, without being asked or recruited.

Everyone wanted to make himself useful, to be suitable for work, to appear younger; many Jews cut off their beards. Older Jews would go to the airfield only in order to get a shift note and a family certificate—it was considered a certain *Karnot Hamizbeakh*,[27] a defense against future troubles.

Women without husbands also wanted to have some kind of paper and crowded into the Labor Office by the hundreds seeking to be sent to the airfield. With the concurrence of the Germans, a few female columns began to be sent to the airfield (it was all the same to the Germans to garner a few hundred more slaves). The women worked under the same conditions as the men—no easier. Certainly, for women, and particularly for Jewish women from the city, it was very difficult to stand in one place for eight or ten hours and to work with a shovel or pick axe. They were not used to it, had never done such work, and it is not within the physical strength of a woman—but the fear of being without a work certificate, without a piece of paper saying that one was suitable for work, was so great that women were not afraid of it. To the contrary, they made every effort to be assigned to a column as early as possible. A queue was set up, each one received a number, and every day a certain number would go.

People armed themselves with pieces of paper and certifications, to have something to show in times of trouble.

The mass psychology motivating people to obtain papers was very great. There was also stirring among the police; in addition to individual

26. Front Construction Management.
27. To seize the "horns of the altar"—to seek sanctuary.

certification, the police office would issue family certificates, listing family members by name. Nonetheless, there was apprehension. Rumors circulated that during a selection only certifications from workplaces would be looked at. Because of these rumors, many policemen were gripped by a fear that maybe it would be better to go to work at the airfield in order to have a paper bearing the stamp of the Front Construction Management. Policemen did not feel secure, as a certificate from the airfield or a brigade was considered to be better and more certain.

At the same time, a series of fictitious marriages began. At first this was in connection with Jordan certificates: people wanted to add a wife to the same certificate. Later these marriages took on almost a mass character— single men and women paired up en masse, leaving the civil registration for quite a while later. Formalities had to be taken care of with the rabbi, and then papers obtained from the registry office. The rabbis and the registry office were flooded with marriage work.

Because of the desire to obtain papers, the einsatz to the airfield went well. However, once people had the stamped papers and family certificates in their possession, the einsatz began to fall off. The police had to be in mobilization mode in order to produce the needed number of people for both shifts. Evening inspections were carried out: since the police were allowed to be in the streets after eight o'clock, inspections were instituted in various streets after this hour, when people were required to show their shift papers, indicating the time that they worked.

What motivated people to go to work was the fear of an action, the "sword of Damocles" constantly hanging over our heads. The fear of likely actions was very great. People were trembling, afraid that early one fine morning they would be chased from their houses and led to the square for selection.

The feared day came in the form of the action of the small ghetto.

On the evening of October 3, people in the ghetto became very apprehensive on account of information that a large pit had been dug near the hospital in the small ghetto; this made people very nervous.

At night, the guards around the fence did a lot of shooting, which was a familiar signal that something was being prepared for us.

Early on the morning of October 4, Germans and Lithuanian partisans surrounded the small ghetto and chased all the Jews from their houses to the market square. At the same time there were strict instructions that it was forbidden to take anything from the houses. And there was no shortage of the familiar beatings, murders, and sadism, especially by the Lithuanians, as the Jews were chased out of their houses.

The Jews assembled in the square. High-ranking German military men—with Jordan at the head—were already there, and the selection began.

With fear and trembling, each one went forward. Slowly the long lines of people wound their way toward the Germans, the sorters, who would seal their fate: who would for the time being remain alive, and who was likely to be going to his death.

Dejected, despondent, morally and physically broken, the Jews dragged themselves before the proud Germans, armed and in uniform, who had come to fulfill the order to carry out the destruction of the remaining help-less, defenseless Jews. Over and above the order that they were fulfilling, the sorters also took great moral satisfaction in observing with sadistic plea-sure how people writhed from fear and pain. They were proud to have been entrusted with such an "important" assignment as to liquidate the Jews. They, the powerful and strong, with their world-dominating iron fist, also opened a "front" against us, a front in which they confidently expected to be victorious.

Here, in the small ghetto action, the Jordan certificates were of little help; the Germans were sorting left and right according to their own notions. Most older men, women, and children were sent to the left, while most of the young were allowed to pass through. There were also many exceptions: a fair number of young people with certificates from their workplaces went to the fort, and, conversely, older men and single women without any certif-icates managed to end up on the good side—it was a matter of luck and fate. There were also many instances when women with small children whose husbands had been arrested in the city and killed there told the German that their husbands had gone to the airfield, and this helped. All in all, there was no uniformity, each German following his own momentary, individual whim, with life and death in the balance.

There were a few policemen in the small ghetto, all of whom were sent to the good side, with the exception of one policemen by the name of Kurtzer; we don't know the details of why he was taken away.

All the people who had been sorted to the good side were immediately ordered to turn around and to run at once, without any belongings, in the direction of the bridge to the large ghetto; they were strictly forbidden to reenter their houses. Everybody pushed in the direction of the bridge. Those remaining in the square, around 1,000 people, were taken away in the direction of the Ninth Fort, and all were killed.

In the small ghetto, a children's home had been established, including orphaned infants of nursing age—all of these innocent children were marked for annihilation and were taken to the fort together with the others. With them was a caretaker, a nurse, who pleaded with the Germans, telling them that her husband worked at the airfield; she was allowed to go over to the large ghetto.

As soon as the Jews went over the bridge, the devil's game began in the small ghetto.

With each action, the Germans would give the Elder Council a sham reason for the "resettlement." (That was the official name for an "action"; after all, they were a "cultured" nation—clearly they wouldn't commit barbaric acts.)

The excuse for carrying out the action in the small ghetto was that in the hospital, which was located in the small ghetto, there were patients who were sick with contagious diseases, who could infect everyone else. That was all, there was no need for anything else, no need for an explanation. (Incidentally, it later became known that a Jewish scoundrel, a certain Levine, a known swindler and thief in Kovno, had reported to the Germans that there were patients in the hospital infected with leprosy. This Levine received his punishment—the Germans themselves shot him later.)

As already noted, when all the Jews were sent over the bridge, the sick people and a few doctors and nurses remained in the Jewish hospital; they were not allowed to leave. Germans entered the building, ordered some of the sick to be removed from the unit, and sent them to the fort. All the sick in the contagious disease ward were shot in their beds. They then set fire to all four sides of the hospital and burned to death all the sick who had not been shot, along with the doctors and nurses.

The flames and tongues of fire rose to the heavens from the burning hospital with its healthy and sick people, the fire and smoke pressing upwards as if to challenge God—if there is such a one in this world—to give an accounting, an answer: why, for what, how much longer will evil rule the world?

All of us who have remained here in the ghetto after all the actions have not as yet "jumped over the grave." The threat of death and annihilation hovers like a specter over our heads to this day. If we should survive and tell all, we will not be believed; all this will be taken as fantasies, or it will be supposed that our misery caused us to lose our minds. If we should not survive, then perhaps the document we are writing here will fall into the hands of Jews, who will read and be astonished by what was done to us in the gloomy ghetto. What we are reporting here are, regrettably, factual events; nothing is exaggerated or fantasized.

On the day of the small ghetto action, a party of about 200 people was brought into the ghetto from Yaneve (a shtetl 35 kilometers from Kovno).

We in the ghetto were then—and remain to this day—isolated and cut off from the whole world. We knew nothing of what was happening a few kilometers outside the ghetto. Rumors had reached us through Christians that in various small towns all the Jews had been shot, down to the last one. But we could not believe this—the notion somehow could not find a place in our minds. What could it mean, that innocent people could be taken away without any reason and all of them shot? How could that be?

From the Yaneve Jews we received a firsthand report about what happened in such a town, which had a population of about 7,000 Jewish souls.

They told us that early one beautiful morning, a grove located 2 kilometers from Yaneve was surrounded. No one was allowed to pass by it, and parties of Jews were assembled to be taken to "work." They were brought to the grove, where they were ordered to remove their clothing and then shot. Throughout the day, dozens of such parties were brought to the grove from the barracks where they had been interned. All—short and tall, young and old—were shot.

In three villages 15 kilometers outside Yaneve lived a rare few Jewish farming landowners. This small group of about 60 or 70 souls had remained alive. In addition, about 130 Jews who had escaped from the town at the outbreak of the war were staying with Jews in the villages or with the few decent [gentile] farmers in the vicinity.

These 200 souls were all who remained of the entire Jewish community of Yaneve. Apparently, after the slaughter, it was "not worth it" to bother with these 200 Jews—they had become accustomed to working on a larger scale. For this reason, they sent this remnant, the few that had escaped, to the ghetto in Slobodka.

We heard from them that all the Jews in the surrounding cities and small towns had been totally annihilated.

Throughout this period, and to this day, individual Jews who by some miracle had been saved from the slaughter in their small towns arrived in the ghetto by various ways and means.

They related horrible stories and details. In many small towns the "play" was organized in accordance with the German love of order.

In the Shavli district, the largest in Lithuania, all the Jews of the countryside were rounded up and brought to the small town of Szhager, where supposedly a ghetto was being established. When all the Jews from the surrounding towns had been assembled, every last one of them was murdered.

In Panevezh, considered one of the finest Jewish communities of Lithuania—with its Hebrew schools, its famous Panevezh Yeshiva, its large chapter of the national youth movement, constituting a new generation, its impressive ranks of Jewish intellectuals, its scholars specializing in Jewish as well as general culture, its dozens of organizations—here, all the Jews of the area were rounded up, taken in groups to a grove outside the city and shot.

Similar news reached us from provinces all over Lithuania. All the Jews from the small towns near the Polish border of the Lozdai district had been rounded up and confined within barracks outside Lozdai, where they were kept for several months. On October 28, the tragic and bloody day when our own Great Action took place, they were all shot.

An eyewitness—by chance a decent Christian from Lozdai—said that SA men came down to the area specifically to carry out the slaughter along with the local Lithuanian executioners. The rabbi of Lozdai, seeing that they were all being led to their death, asked the German leader to allow families to go to their deaths together. The representative of the heroic German military "generously" permitted them to do so. Fathers and mothers embraced their children, babies hugged their mother's necks, brothers and sisters held hands, and so they all met their death together.

In this way they seek to pave the bloodied streets of the new Europe with our bodies, to raise their torch over the world with bloodied fingers, to spread their "high culture."

Aside from the Slobodka ghetto, today there are only two Jewish communities in Lithuania: a ghetto in Vilna with about 17,000 souls and a ghetto in the city of Shavli with about 7,000 souls.

As we later learned, 80 percent of the Vilna Jews have been annihilated. Before the German occupation, the Jewish community numbered about 75,000. Jews who arrived here from Vilna told us about the various actions carried out there. By various means and sophisticated brutality, tens of thousands of Jew were killed.

Vilna, the Jerusalem of Lithuania—a city of wise and learned men, a city pulsating with a rich and vibrant diversity of Jewish life, with its large network of Hebrew and Yiddish schools and gymnasiums, its dozens of Jewish cultural institutions, parties, and organizations—the famous Vilna community with its writers and thinkers, scholarship and learning, world-famous libraries,—the city of the "Gaon."[28] Anything you wanted could be found in Vilna—and this very rich Jewish community was, for the most part, brutally destroyed by the murderers.

The entire realm of Lithuanian Jewry, with their sharp minds, the great scholars and learned men, the dedicated, idealistic Jewish activists, the faithful Zionists, the good-hearted Jews, simple workers with warm Jewish hearts, the bustling shopkeepers who aspired to go out into the wide world but were somehow stuck in a corner in Tshaikishok or Kupishok; the entire beloved Lithuanian Jewish community, the "common people," the shoemaker and the tailor, all the intellectuals, the wheeler-dealers of the small towns, the old and the young, the poor and the wealthy, the short and the tall—all of them were horribly killed.

It seems to us like an evil dream that could not possibly have happened—but, regrettably, it is a fact that all of our close, dear, and beloved people have been killed—as if they were sheep—but still for the sanctification of the nation of Israel.

It is said that here and there a few Jews are in hiding, mostly in the villages inhabited by Poles and Russians, who are somewhat more friendly to

28. Eminent rabbinical scholar.

us, but there are no more than a few of them. The communities themselves have been wiped off the face of the earth.

The Jews of Yaneve who were brought to our ghetto were sent here precisely at the time of the action in the small ghetto, in the "hope" that they, too, would be finished off here. They were saved from the small ghetto action because they were accidentally taken to the large ghetto. But most of them were later taken away in the Great Action of October 28, 1941.

A few days after the small ghetto action, on the first day of Sukkoth,[29] it was announced that Jews [of the small ghetto who had survived that action] would be allowed to cross over the bridge and bring back their belongings to the large ghetto. It became clear that the small ghetto was being liquidated as a dwelling place for Jews; no one would be permitted to resume residence in these houses. An effort was made to allow the Jews who had lived there to cross the bridge in order to retrieve their belongings. It was announced that starting at four o'clock in the evening, and for a period of two hours thereafter, crossing would be allowed, but only for those with Jordan certificates. Again, the value of the Jordan certificates increased. At the specified time, four o'clock, people with certificates assembled on this side of the bridge in hopes of saving some of the belongings they had abandoned.

But others who had not lived there also assembled. Some came to help their relatives, and some went to the small ghetto for no valid reason, simply to take what they could, because the residents of many of the houses were no longer there, having been taken to the fort. An opportunity was therefore sought to take whatever could be taken.

As soon as crossing was allowed, thousands of people ran across. People hurried to go across as quickly as possible in order to make the best use of the miserly two hours.

A picture of complete destruction was seen there: almost all the houses, without distinction, had been plundered, broken, and shattered, all clothing and valuable items hauled out by our "dear" neighbors from the other side of the fence, the Lithuanians. They had taken advantage of the two days when the houses were empty to crawl through the fences and loot and plunder whatever they could.

29. Feast of the Tabernacles.

The Jews who crossed over to retrieve their belongings found very little to bring back.

Following the two-hour time period, the overpass to the small ghetto was again sealed off, the surrounding fence remained in place, and no Christian inhabitants were allowed in. It was apparently already foreseen by the wicked [Germans] that they would want to use the small ghetto as a cover for their carefully planned game of murder against defenseless, innocent Jews. Indeed, as we will presently see, they made use of the small ghetto as a cover and assembly point during the Great Action.

The Great Action

The mood among the Jews following the small ghetto action was depressed and crushed. People were bewildered and dejected: What would happen now? Whose turn was next?

Everyone was convinced that the "cleansing" would be carried out by precincts. First Ariogolos-Velianos, then the small ghetto; the only question now was which streets would be cut off next so that the sorting could be carried out.

One day, Lithuanian partisans came to the Brazilke and ordered all the Jews to leave their houses. It was thought that the hour had arrived for this side [of the ghetto]. People were running from here to there, seeking "protection" on other streets. It turned out later that the fear was groundless.

In any event, there was the conviction that it would soon be the turn of new people and new streets, that one must prepare for it physically as well mentally, that there was nothing we could do—that this was our bitter fate.

Again, we continued to be certain that it was most important for us to work, to fulfill the work obligation, to provide the daily einsatz for the airfield.

Work by individuals and the work of the community as a whole would make us seem useful in their eyes; perhaps the work we were doing for them, the thousands of working hands we provided to them daily without payment, would save us from the threat to our lives.

A more systematic mobilization of all able-bodied men began.

It was established that all men between the ages of seventeen and fifty-five who were capable of work must work either at the airfield or at some other workplace; there were to be no loafers among us. All must work.

Three shifts were established at the airfield: the morning shift beginning at six in the morning, the day shift starting at two, and the night shift starting at ten in the evening.

The police had the job of helping to produce the required number of people for all shifts. This was not an easy task.

In spite of all the warnings from the Elder Council and the Labor Office, in spite of all the remonstrations and admonitions, the einsatz still almost always fell short. The Elder Council and the Labor Office constantly sought ways of producing the workers needed three times a day. Columns were organized; everyone was required to go to his column at the gate and register with the column leader. But people did not do this; those who came attached themselves to any column that was being formed, so that it was difficult to establish who was and who was not reporting for work.

A change came about which improved the einsatz for a time—namely, the white armbands that the German Front Construction Management started to issue to those working at the airfield. (Lithuanians working at the airfield also received such armbands.)

The Labor Office received these armbands for distribution to airfield workers. They were white, numbered, and stamped with the imprint of the German "Front Construction Management" agency.

When the announcement was first made that armbands would be distributed, not many came to receive them. The police were even assigned to block off some streets and not to allow anyone to pass without the ribbon. Somewhat later, people began to sense the usefulness of the new armband: an armband with a German stamp somehow conveyed an association with a real, useful worker. Thousands of people then crowded into the committee, standing in lines in order to obtain such an armband. A few days later, work booklets from the Front Construction Management were also distributed. These were printed cards, numbered in accordance with the number on the armband; the Labor Office would enter into each booklet the name of its owner and his family members.

The rush for an armband and a booklet then became great; everyone wanted to have an armband with a work card. In the course of one week, almost all the armbands and booklets were given out.

Whoever later wanted to obtain a booklet with an armband had to present shift papers verifying that he worked regularly at the airfield.

Following distribution of the armbands, there was a little more order. Each 100 numbers formed a column with a regular, appointed column leader. Daily announcements were posted of the numbers going each day and shift. At the control points, policemen possessing the so-called airfield calendar could quite easily verify whether or not a particular person was working.

In addition, the column leader had a list of the 100 regular members of his column. In the square, he would register those who reported and in this manner could quite easily monitor who was and was not working.

With the armbands and work cards there was, in general, a greater feeling of security. Clearly, the constant uncertainty and fear of what tomorrow would bring did not go away, yet one felt somewhat more encouraged. The pronouncement by representatives of the authorities immediately after the small ghetto action that this would not happen again in the ghetto helped to improve the mood.[30] Although we know quite well the value of a promise by a Nazi, still, the mood calmed somewhat.

The memorandum from the police to the Elder Council requesting, among other things, that policemen should be allowed to go two or three times a week to the airfield, so they would also have the right to receive armbands and work cards like all other workers, is characteristic of the extent to which everyone was convinced that the armband and work card were of great significance.

In the middle of October, various rumors and alarming reports, which could not be confirmed, began to circulate in the ghetto and brought on a disturbing mood.

It is quite interesting that always before some happening in the ghetto, a few days before—or whenever anyone learned something—various rumors would circulate in the ghetto, a phenomenon that we referred to as "the

---

30. A penciled note in the margin reads: "Such a pronouncement was not made. L.B."

women are saying." Curiously, however, many of these rumors would later be confirmed.

The word in the ghetto was that "the women were saying" that something was being prepared for us, that an action was probably on its way. Later it was said that Lithuanians had related that large pits were being dug at the Ninth Fort. A troubled, sad mood descended. People went from one to the other with the silent question: Any news? Have you heard anything? Is someone saying something new? But no one knew anything—until the evening of October 27.

Announcements were posted by the Elder Council that for the purpose of control and oversight of the ghetto workforce, all residents of the ghetto, without distinction as to age or sex, must assemble in the Demokratu Square exactly at six o'clock in the morning on the next day, October 28, 1941. No packages, food items, or belongings were to be carried. Houses, stalls, and yards were to be left open. Anyone found in a house after six o'clock would be shot.

This announcement struck the ghetto like a bomb. In spite of reassurances from officials that the assembly was simply for the purpose of monitoring the workforce, people were despondent, confused, and anxious about what was going to happen.

The tumult and panic following the appearance of the order was very great. Thousands of people were running about; the committee was besieged as if before a funeral. Everywhere, lights were shining brightly in the windows, but in our hearts there was darkness. Those who did not have armbands besieged the Labor Office trying to obtain them. People sought to obtain documents, pieces of paper, certificates, "arming" themselves with all kinds of identity papers. Hundreds of others who already had papers crowded into the committee for no reason other than to hear news. What is being said? What should we do? Which column is it preferable to join?— and more and more such questions for which no one had answers.

What transpired in the ghetto on the eve of the action? What sort of behind-the-scenes play took place between the Elder Council and the authorities?

As we now know, a dramatic act had played out before the action, the outlines of which are known to us in broad brushstrokes.

Representatives of the German authorities had come to the Elder Council with a strictly secret demand to deliver a few thousand Jews, particularly criminals and leftist elements. This the Elder Council had declined to do. The Elder Council held dramatic meetings in strict secrecy. They knew precisely what awaited whoever would have been delivered. It was also said that a representative of the authorities had attended some of these meetings. The situation was extremely tense and painful. The details of these meetings are not known to us, but we can imagine how they proceeded.

After the Elder Council declined to put together a list of Jews to be delivered to their death, the order was received that all Jews, without exception, must assemble at the square on October 28.

The instructions for assembly in the square specified that people were to situate themselves according to their workplaces. Policemen went from house to house repeating the text of the written order and urging the residents to dress cleanly, shave, and see to it that a good impression was made.

The night of the action was a night of *leil shimurim*.[31] Every household was awake, preparing for tomorrow's day of judgment. No one knew where he would be the next day. People prepared a little food to take along in their pockets. Everyone was talking, all asking the same questions: What will happen? Will we survive it in peace?

The Elder Council called in the police leadership for consultation and conveyed to them the plan for maintaining order in the square, where about 27,000 people would gather.

Two higher police officials were assigned to organize the square on the evening of October 27. Placards were prepared with the name of each column according to workplace, and each column was assigned a location of assembly.

Later in the evening of the same day, all policemen were summoned to assemble at the blocks, where the chief informed them of the assignments for the following day and of the placement of the columns.

There would be columns of the city brigades and of the airfield workers, all of whom were to assemble in their assigned locations. In addition to the work columns, there would be several others that would assemble in

31. First night of Passover—night of watchfulness, vigilance.

the following order: the column of the Elder Council, the column of the police, ghetto institutions, firemen, and others. Everyone was informed in the strongest terms that the principal task was to maintain exemplary order in the square, to see to it that each column occupied its assigned place, that the people kept quiet, and, to the extent possible, to avoid tumult and chaos in the square.

Policemen were entitled to bring with them to the police column their wives, children, and parents; it was strictly forbidden to bring in-laws, brothers, or sisters.

The next day, October 28, all policemen were required to come to the square at four o'clock in the morning, to help assemble the columns in the prescribed order and only then to join their own column.

The airfield night shift, scheduled to leave from the ghetto at ten o'clock at night, was not allowed to go out; everyone was sent back from the gate. Those who had gone to the airfield for the day shift at two o'clock on the afternoon of October 27, who were supposed to have been released from work at midnight, were kept for another shift. Not being released from work at twelve o'clock caused great agitation among the workers at the airfield. Some had heard about tomorrow's order before leaving the ghetto and were full of speculation. With fear and trembling, everyone worked with shovels and pick axes at the assigned places, throwing the hard-packed clay into the "lorries," thinking to themselves, "God only knows what is going on in the ghetto, what is awaiting us there." At five o'clock in the morning, the end of the work shift was announced, and the entire shift was taken back home.

Somber, tired, broken, muddy, hungry, and sleep-deprived, the lot of Jews were brought to the gate about six o'clock. Hearing the particulars of the order, they had to run home as quickly as possible so as to be able to collect their families and arrive at the square in time.

From five o'clock in the morning on, thousands and thousands of people lined all the streets and alleys, from the yards and houses to the square. Everyone was present, without exception—the young, healthy people along with the old and feeble, infants in arms or in carriages along with old people with canes or supported on crutches, the sick and invalids carried on stretchers—everyone who was alive in the ghetto streamed by the thousands to the square. It was still dark in the streets; day had not yet broken, and darkness, darkness was also upon our souls. An unforgettable picture was formed by the long, unending processions that extended toward the square, on the way to the prescribed sentence.

By about six o'clock, the entire ghetto had assembled in the square, every column in its place. Shortly after six, there appeared an automobile full of rifle-carrying partisans who surrounded the entire square. Immediately afterwards, the Germans arrived and began their "work"—they began to conduct a selection. First, the column of the Elder Council was allowed to pass through without being sorted: they went as a unit to the right side. They were followed by the column of the police, who were also not sorted—all the policemen and their families passed to the right side without being checked.

After all the family members in the police column had passed to the right, the policemen were ordered to help maintain order in the square. At first, this consisted of their forming a chain around those who were being sorted to prevent people from running from one group to another, and also to maintain order in the line going to the checkpoint.

After the police, they began to sort the column of the ghetto institutions. They were being checked. All the young people were allowed to go to the right; the old and sick were separated and sent to the left. When a group of people were gathered on the left—about forty or fifty—they were taken by armed partisans in the direction of Paneriu Street. It was not known immediately where they were being taken. The hill leading to the famous Ninth Fort is opposite the square where everybody was standing, and although a considerable time elapsed, no one was observed being led in the direction of the fort. We had no idea where they were being taken. A little later it was learned that those sorted to the left were being taken to the small ghetto.

As noted, the small circle of the Elder Council did know what was going on, where the people would be taken, and what would be done with them. But we, the masses, the common people, knew nothing. When it was heard that they were being taken to the small ghetto, many thought that, if this was the case, maybe it was not so terrible. What was the difference whether one lived in the small ghetto or the large ghetto? So long as one was allowed to remain alive, somehow one would pull through.

After the checking of the ghetto institutions column, the sorting of all the other columns began, and this is when all the illusions burst, all the dreams and hopes were washed away. Jordan certificates, ordinary certificates, papers from the airfield, armbands, work cards—whatever one had was of no value. The Germans paid no attention to any papers; they didn't even look at them. The fate of each person, whether to live or to die, was dependent not on a piece of paper but simply on the momentary whim and impulse of the German. It was a simple game of luck, who would pass through and who would be caught—no speculations or hopes survived. Observing how the selection proceeded, people became quite confused. What did they have in mind with this selection? If all those on the left were slated for annihilation, then why among them were such a high percentage of young people? Conversely, why were so many older people going to the right? Why were they being taken to the small ghetto? If a new dwelling place was to be made there for Jews, then why had they liquidated it earlier? Why would they be at all interested in which Jews would live there—were they concerned about how or where we lived? We were only names to them, as worthless as dogs. And, conversely, if they actually intended to annihilate those on the left side, then why were they taking them to the small ghetto—were they ashamed or afraid to take them directly to the fort?

Such were the questions we posed to ourselves, but no answers came to mind.

The sorting was inordinately deceptive. For example, of the column of the firefighters, who were all young, healthy people, three-quarters were sorted to the right, while the rest of the column was cut off, ordered to the left, and taken under partisan guard to the small ghetto. The sorting of the others was equally inconsistent. The German would barely look into the eyes of the approaching people and, as though an expert on this race, one who considers himself knowledgeable about these types of animals, immediately rule on the spot, right—left, right—left, a line of people to the right, a line of people to the left.

At first, it was impossible to comprehend what was going on. One was looking for some kind of indication as to what was considered good and what was bad, what rules they were following, what kind of system they had. It turned out they were following the famous "systemless system": whatever pleased the German at that particular moment, that's how he handled it.

One thing did become clear: that large families were not good. Large families most often were sent to the left, while small families passed through. Policemen were sent to the columns to inform everyone that large families should split up, that they should not go in groups of six or seven, but split into threes and fours. In many cases, this helped many people to go through the checkpoint.

What did the police do in the square, what did they do for the population?

The police had freedom of movement in the square; they could cross without interference from one side to the other because they had already passed the selection and could be identified by their uniform. Their first-priority assignment was to maintain order in the square. All those who had been marched to the right were surrounded by Jewish police guards. From this fact, people gathered that going to the right was good, because to the left they were guarded by partisans, while to the right—by our own Jewish policemen.

Somewhat later, when our eyes had been opened, so to speak, the police—in addition to their official assignment—began to carry out their unofficial mission, and that was to save to the right as many people as possible. The opportunities were few, and the results, as was later found, were also meager.

As it turned out, the Germans had established beforehand how many people they wanted to have on each side. It was almost all the same to them who went where, so long as they had such and such a number of Jews. If a policemen took it upon himself to ask the German to send this or that Jew to the good side, and the German granted the request, it was at the expense of another Jew; he allowed Yosele to go through and sent Chaim away—what was the difference between this or the other Jew? So long as they had their number; it mattered little which Jew went here and which went there. They received frequent reports from the small ghetto as to how many were already there.

But we did not know about these calculations. We thought that when a Jew was led through to the good side, he was thereby saved. The police therefore did all that they could with their scant opportunities.

The police led many people through the checkpoint covertly, that is, when the sorter had turned aside and would not notice, the police would quickly lead some Jews into a column that had already been marched to the right. There were dozens of instances when a policemen would approach the family of some Jewish acquaintance, bring them to the German and tell him that the acquaintance was his brother, uncle, or other relative, and the German would let them go through.

The line leading directly to the control point was designed as a trick by the Germans, in such a way as to deceive and cause confusion: those sorted to the good side were at first ordered to go to the left, and from there the entire sorted group would turn to the right; conversely, those sorted to the bad side would initially go to the right, but a few meters later they would be turned to the left. This confused many people. Thousands were trapped as, too disoriented to know which way to go, they would head to the right on their own. When they recognized their bitter mistake, it was too late: a little further on stood partisans who beat them with their rifle butts and chased them onward toward death and destruction.

The policemen keeping order along the line that led to the control point repeatedly warned the Jews passing before them: head to the left, head to the left, not to the right. This was to little avail: some who headed to the left did go through, but for many, of course, heading to the left was of no use, because the Germans did not let them go through.

In general, the police had little opportunity to seize the initiative. But it must be emphasized that they did all that they could on this tragic day.

It is not easy to convey the various scenes and heartbreaking tragedies that took place in the square to which we were but mute witnesses. There were instances when people lost one another in the square and were unable to reunite. The throng was so large and the congestion and pushing so great that when people became separated it was difficult to find one another again, and so it happened that the wife and the children went to the left and the husband to the right, or vice versa. There were also instances of families being split by the Germans, half to the right and half to the left. In cases where large families had split in two groups [of their own accord], it happened that one part went to the right and the other to the left. There were also instances when people who had been consigned to the column going to the left would run over to the column going to the right. Many times the partisans or the Germans would notice this and drag them out of the column with blows and chase them to the left. But there were also instances when the crossing over was not noticed, and in this way people saved themselves from certain death.

At the very peak of the selection, partisans arrived and informed the Germans, the lords of the square, that Jews had been found in the ghetto who had not reported to the square. What should be done with them?

The order announcing the action had specified that any Jews found in the ghetto on this day were to be shot on the spot.

The partisans went through some of the streets, checking the houses and at the same time doing a little looting. In the refuge, they found several old people from the old age home who had not been carried to the square and were unable to get there on their own. The Germans issued an order to bring them on stretchers and, naturally, sent them all to the left.

By five o'clock in the evening, the checking had become less rigorous. They were no longer meticulous, knowing that the count was to them quite "satisfactory." So during the evening they checked only superficially. The police and the representative of the ghetto institutions, Mr. L., who were present at the sorting (and who, by the way, within their modest opportunities, helped many Jews to pass through the controls), at this point had a free hand and moved almost everybody to the right.

The number of people in the square became smaller and smaller, and at about six o'clock, the selection came to an end. The guards were removed, the Germans and Lithuanians left. All those remaining were told that they would soon be allowed to go home.

When the police announced permission to go home, they first declared that 500 men were required for the night shift and that everyone was asked to report voluntarily; all those who remained here in the ghetto would only be able to continue living here on the basis of work at the airfield. That was why all who were obligated to work should report voluntarily.

It is strange that those who had stood at the brink of the abyss and by chance remained on this side—that they would only a moment later be subjected to propaganda saying that the fulfillment of the work obligation at the airfield was our preservation. Only a few hours earlier we had seen thousands of people with airfield armbands go to the left, yet deep in our hearts we still nurtured the hope that maybe through work we would be able to save ourselves. After a day of standing in the cold without eating and in high nervous tension, many volunteers were found who went on to work at the airfield through the night, driven there by the momentum and gladness of having remained on this side.

The people streamed home; frozen, tired, and hungry, they hurried back—each content that he himself remained, but with a wounded heart for the dear ones who had been torn away.

When all had dispersed, there remained in the square the sick, who continued to lie on the ground, abandoned and forgotten by all, and also a group of policemen and the deputy police chief Mr. B. [Michael Bramson].

This is what happened to the sick: All the sick and the old who could not walk were sent to the left. Since there was no means of transport, the Germans issued an order to place the sick and the old on the ground on the left, all in one line, and later to bring them by wagon to the small ghetto. In the morning, Jordan walked past the line of the old and the sick on the ground and counted them; twenty-eight men were there at that time. Later he issued the order to take them all to the small ghetto. In the evening, when they had assembled their number of people on the other side, they forgot entirely about the sick, whose transfer had been put off. Later, after everyone had returned home, the police who remained to clean up the square found more than forty old and sick people lying on the ground. What should now be done? One thing was clear: twenty-eight—the number that Jordan had counted—must be the number brought to the small ghetto. This could not be helped—but the rest of the forty must be immediately taken back to the ghetto, so there would be no trace left that there had been more sick people who had been allowed to go back home.

Most of those remaining in the square were old people who could not manage themselves because of advanced age; a few were already dead, having frozen from lying all day on the street, expiring from cold and hunger. Others were dying; some were unconscious; the younger sick were simply exhausted and freezing. The very old and the half-dead were to be taken to the small ghetto, the younger and stronger ones back to their homes in the large ghetto. Several wagons were mobilized, as well as a police escort, and they were told that they should rescue as many people as possible from the small ghetto by filling the empty wagons on the return trip. A number of times the wagons took the sick and the half-dead to the small ghetto and, on the way back, rescued some people. Several more trips were to be made, not so much to bring the sick into the small ghetto but primarily to attempt to bring others out. But, not surprisingly, the drivers were afraid to make any more trips. The guards, densely positioned around the small ghetto, were shooting without pause in all directions; the night was very dark; coming into the small ghetto there was the sound of gunshots from all sides—it was dreadful and frightful to take a step.

As for the sick people who were left on the ground in the square, each one needed to be taken to his home. Without enough wagons, many of them had to be carried by hand. Heartrending scenes played out as they begged to be carried or taken by wagon as quickly as possible. There were few wagons, and we did not have the strength or means to carry everyone at once. Family members of several of the sick came and took them away; others, who either had no one or whose families did not know they were lying in the square, were at God's mercy. Some of the sick were therefore brought into houses near the square, so that they could be taken home the next day.

Eight live infants were also found in the square. They were lying among the sick and the old, wrapped in diapers and rags, cold, some unconscious but still alive. The police carried them into nearby houses to be kept overnight so they could be taken care of the next day. Peculiar are the social relations among some of our Jews. The infants had to be left by force in the nearby houses. Under no circumstances did the people want to take them in, to keep overnight these cold, hungry orphans who were lying neglected on the ground. Only by force and with threats that if they did not take in a few infants they would themselves be taken to the small ghetto was the job barely accomplished.

What took place that night in the small ghetto? As related by the few who saved themselves that night or the next morning, many of those taken to the small ghetto were sure that they would remain living there. Many were looking to move into a better dwelling place. Among them were a large number who had previously lived in the small ghetto. They went to their former homes, quickly established themselves there and allowed no one else in. People "arranged" themselves in whatever way they could. Much firewood was found in the stalls; "enough" was carried into the houses to last the entire winter. Friends and acquaintances were located and taken into the apartments. There were many disputes and much bickering over rooms among the unfortunates, each claiming he was there first and that the room therefore belonged to him. Ovens were stoked; potatoes found in the cellars were baked and eaten. Many considered themselves lucky to have landed here; they would live and work here, while the others over there—who knew what would happen to them?

The masters of murder and sadism had disguised things so well, conducting everything with such devilish sophistication, that thousands of people lived a whole day in such bitter, bloody misconception. But there were also many on that side who suspected that something was not right, that it was not good, and who sought all possible means to get away. Several hundred people saved themselves in a variety of ways. Guards were bribed and allowed people to pass through the barbed wire; others—with shooting going on all around them—endangered their lives to sneak through the fence; thus a few hundred people were fortuitously saved from death.

It was said among us in the evening that those whose dear ones had been taken away should submit their names to the Elder Council, because it was promised that some of those able to work would be released to come back. Hundreds of people ran with lists of their family members, but by that time it was understood that something very gruesome was being prepared for those in the small ghetto. Nothing came of all the lists that were submitted.

Early in the morning of the next day, around four o'clock on October 29, hordes of partisans and Germans arrived in the small ghetto and began to drive everyone out of the houses. Everyone was chased from the houses and beaten to move faster. A new trick was devised to bring people more rapidly out of the houses into the street. Those already in the street were ordered to line up in columns and a sham selection was started. Needless to say, this was merely a maneuver, a new mocking trick. Those driven out of the houses were formed into columns that began to be led in the direction of the Ninth Fort. Around 7:30 in the morning, the chairman of the Elder Council and the chief of the police along with several policemen were allowed to enter the small ghetto in order to remove some able-bodied people from the columns that had not as yet been sent to the Ninth Fort.

As soon as they entered the small ghetto and began to rescue these few people from death, a great clamor, wailing, crying, and shouting arose. Everyone pushed and shoved, shouting, "Take me out, take me out." The panic and tumult became so great that the murderers lost patience and started beating everybody, including the ghetto representatives themselves. The chairman of the Elder Council, Dr. E. [Elkes], was wounded in the head with rifle butts and had to be carried away, covered with blood. The other members of the police force were chased out of the square. Nothing came of the attempt to rescue a few hundred more Jews.

They were also shooting at the people on our side, who gathered at the fences by the hundreds in hopes of rescuing some of their dear ones. They shot and killed a young man and badly wounded a woman.

The transport of people to the Ninth Fort began; long columns stretched for hours, without an end and without a break. Ten thousand people extended up the hill in an unending procession of death, driven by the partisans to their death and annihilation. We stood below at the fences and at the windows and watched, our eyes filled with bloodied tears—watched with wounded hearts as our wretched parents, brothers, sisters, beloved relatives and dear ones, innocent, good Jews, ascended to their gruesome, unprecedented mass annihilation.

We are now 100 percent certain that all of these 10,000 Jews were killed, without exception. According to the accounts of the Lithuanians, they were driven in groups to the pits, where they undressed and were shot with machine guns. The children, the innocent infants, were taken away from their mothers, thrown alive into the pits, and torn apart with hand grenades. It is impossible to convey, language is too poor to describe what transpired at the shooting of the 10,000 Jews.

On the evening of October 29, after all the people in the small ghetto had been taken to the fort, an order was received from the commandant demanding that fifty policemen be sent to the small ghetto to search the houses for people in hiding. The policemen searched, and to their delight they did find many people hiding in attics and cellars, people who had had the courage—in spite of the shooting and searching of the partisans—to hide and in this way save themselves from certain death. All those found were immediately led through the fence into the large ghetto; to the great joy of their families, who had already mourned them, they crossed over and returned safely.

That was the end of the Great Action, which will be entered into our painful history in bloody letters.

October 28 will be for us, if we should survive, one of the darkest days in the history of the ghetto.

"Episode" of the German Jews

On the _____[32] the ghetto was again shaken by a tragic event—a continuation of the action that had just taken place behind the barbed wire that fences us in.

A rumor spread that a large transport of German Jews had been brought from Germany to the Kovno railroad station. It was also said that a part of the transport had been led past the ghetto during the night in the direction of the Ninth Fort.

Regrettably, this information was confirmed the next morning. With our own eyes, we saw several thousand Jews—men, women, and children—trudging through Paneriu Street, close by the fence, in the direction of the Ninth Fort. Again we all besieged the fences but were afraid to come near because the SA men and G. [Gestapo] who were leading them threatened to shoot. We stood around the fences with congealed tears, dry eyes—because all our tears had already been shed—with clenched fists and bloodied hearts, and once more we had to experience what had happened to us only a few days earlier.

The episode with the German Jews is the most shocking chapter in the series of persecutions and oppressions of German Jewry. We later learned the precise details of the circumstances under which our unfortunate brothers-in-suffering from Germany and Austria perished. It was impossible to believe that people could sink so low, impossible to imagine such a sophisticated deception. Such cruel, sadistic, contemptuous dealing with people's lives has no precedent in the history of the Jews.

It turned out that the G. had sent letters to various Jewish families in a large number of cities in Germany and Austria, each addressed precisely according to street and dwelling location, family name, and so on. In these letters it was written that they were to be ready by October 28 [1941] for resettlement in the east, specifically, in the Kovno ghetto. It was permissible—the notices continued—to bring along anything they wished; craftsmen could bring their tools, all household items could also be brought, as well as an unlimited quantity of food, because, in addition to passenger cars,

32. Space left blank for entering the date at a future time.

special freight cars would be provided for loading the luggage into the resettlement train. The name and current address of the owner was to be written clearly on each suitcase and bundle.

Many families had received such letters, apparently a few weeks in advance, so they would have time before the specified date to settle their affairs, prepare dried food, pack everything, and be ready to be resettled to Lithuania, into the Kovno ghetto.

The basic fact of the banishment of these families was sad enough in and of itself. But a Jew in Germany was already accustomed to trouble. So be it, they thought, we will live in the Kovno ghetto among Jews—whatever happens to everyone will also happen to us.

It was clear as day to everyone that they were being resettled in another place. Because if not, they would not have allowed time for packing and would not have ordered people to take along tools and so much food. Nor would they have provided special cars. With a sad heart they said goodbye to the few friends and acquaintances who were staying behind, not having received their own resettlement letters as yet, and departed in the train in the direction of Kovno.

They arrived here (we heard that altogether about 15,000 Jews were brought here) and were told to leave their luggage on the train, that it would be sent on to the ghetto later. Everyone was lined up in groups and led past the Slobodka ghetto . . . to the Ninth Fort. A few of the Jews being led along the ghetto, seeing that this was the Slobodka ghetto, asked the Jews standing behind the fence how much farther it was to the ghetto.

About ten or fifteen minutes later, they became aware of their dreadful, bloody mistake. They saw and felt the ugly deception that was perpetrated upon them, the slaughter that was to take place there. But, naturally, it was too late. Apparently, some did have an idea of what was to be done to them, because a few, passing by, shouted to our Jews standing near the fence, "We know already, we are being led to the slaughter."

This is how, by disgusting deception, about 15,000 Jews were brought to the valley of slaughter, all taken to the fort and all murdered.

Later their belongings were brought from the station to the G. For months they were sorted there by Jews working in this brigade. The finest possessions that the eye can see were found in these suitcases: the nicest of foods, all prepared with a generous hand to last a long time, the best clothing, the rarest medicines, and various professional instruments. An endless number of books—scientific, professional, Jewish books, prayer books, prayer shawls—all kinds of equipment, everything a cultured person can imagine could be found among the belongings of the German Jews; all packed with care, prepared with so much hope for their new life in the Kovno ghetto— yet they were so shockingly deceived. Their first step toward their new life was also their last—to the pits of the Ninth Fort.

From the letters, papers, notices, etc., found among their belongings we saw the entire picture, the complete shocking truth of the tragedy, the conclusion of which played itself out before our eyes.

In the first few days after the Great Action, many of us believed that not all who had been taken in the action had been killed. We wanted to believe that a part of them, at least the young and able-bodied, were separated and sent somewhere to work. The episode with the German Jews destroyed even this little hope. If Jews could be brought here from such great distances to be slaughtered, what hope could we have for our own dear loved ones who had been taken along the same route? The Jews in Germany who had accompanied their dear ones to the train and watched as they boarded the cars with their luggage were certain that their close ones were being resettled; to this day they are awaiting letters from them. But we have seen what they meant by resettlement; we have seen the tragic, heartrending end.[33]

Woe, what has become of us, what they have made of us.

The mood that descended upon the ghetto after this was clear. One could not think about anything at all, could not concentrate on anything—every hour of every day one was expecting something. The situation brought to mind the famous curse of the Tokhakhah:[34] "Ba-boker tomar mee yiten lailah u-ba-erev tomar mee yiten boker v-lo-ta-amin bekhayekha"—in the morning you will wish that it were night, and in the evening that it were day,

---

33. Markings in the margin suggested that the following text, to the end of this section, should be moved to a different part of the document.

34. Chapters of the Old Testament listing the punishments awaiting Jews who do not follow God's teachings.

and you will not believe that you will live.[35] People looked upon themselves as the next candidates for the fort; they sat dejected in the houses, waiting for the next action, when the remainder of the Kovno Jewish community would be annihilated.

But life goes on, regardless of our terrible experiences; those who remained, those who survived, had to live and eat. The instinct, the drive, the need to secure a source of livelihood, of a way to exist, drove everyone on, for himself and for his family.

The survivor, in spite of his grief over the loved ones who are gone, still wants to live, clings to life with all his might. With all one's soul, with all one's will, one wants to survive, to be freed from the ghetto and perhaps to experience something good in life.

A few calm days and weeks went by; life was—by ghetto standards—back to normal. All the attention of the Elder Council and almost all the work of the police and of the Labor Office consisted of providing the required number of people for the airfield three times a day.

According to the declarations of the representatives of the authorities, work at the airfield was our preservation, the primary reason for the existence of the entire Jewish community. Great effort was therefore expended to justify our existence in their eyes, and to achieve the einsatz by all available means.

This is what our life looked like in the first few weeks after the Great Action, which we will elaborate on more specifically further on.

In general, the time immediately following the Great Action marked the beginning of a new period in the life of the ghetto. At first, we who remained in the ghetto did not sense or feel it, because, as we said, every day we expected a new evil decree. But to date, a year and a quarter after the Great Action—except for smaller, individual incidents—it was in fact the last action. We can therefore note that the time following the Great Action

---

35. This quotation combines parts of verses 66 and 67 of Deuteronomy 28: "Your life will hang continually in suspense, fear will beset you night and day, and you will find no security all your life long. Every morning you will say, 'Would God it were evening!' and every evening 'Would God it were morning!' for the fear that lives in your heart and the sights that you see." The complete two verses are quoted by Garfunkel (*Kovna ha-yehudit be-hurbana*, 79) at the end of his chapter 4, titled "The 'Actions.'"

was the beginning of a new period, a time when our life changed for the better.

The Great Action was in fact the tragic conclusion of the first period, a time of extraordinary shocks.

These first few weeks, with the intensified work at the airfield and the increased efforts of the ghetto community to provide the required number of people, became the transition to the second period, a time of normalization of ghetto life.

Offices involved with similar tasks would meet on a regular basis. For example, the police and the Labor Office would meet for joint activity and maintained continuous contact to deal with their common assignments.

It will perhaps be of interest to provide an overview of the relationships between the police and the Elder Council and between the police and the Labor Office in order to give a more precise picture of the inner life of the ghetto. We will not restrict these relationships to the time period leading up to the Great Action, but will also take a step forward, somewhat deeper into the second period, in order to provide a picture of both periods and their nuances. We will also examine the moral standards of the offices and of the officials of the institutions and the police, and the relationship of the population to the institutions and to the police, which will complete the picture, and will help to explain many events and happenings that took place inside the ghetto in the second period up to the present day.

Slaughter of Jews brought in by Lithuanians off the street into Lietukis garage yard, June 27, 1941. *Above,* Jews repeatedly beaten by Lithuanians with iron bars. *Yad Vashem Photo Archives. Below,* Local population at the site of the slaughter. *Bundesarchiv.*

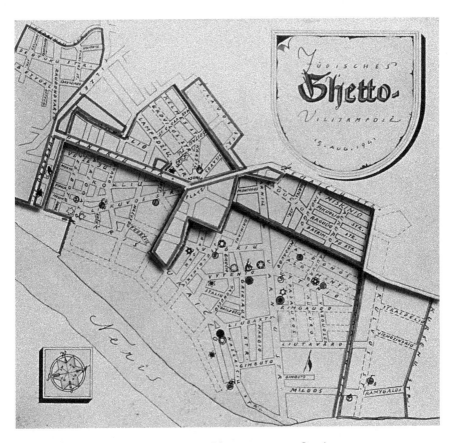

Map of ghetto showing size reductions of August 17, 1941; October 4, 1941;
May 1, 1942; and October 5, 1942. *Yad Vashem Photo Archives.*

Footbridge over Paneriu Street that provided the only connection between the large and small ghettos. Paneriu Street led to the Ninth Fort. *YIVO Institute for Jewish Research.*

Jews move their belongings through a main street of Kovno to the ghetto.
Above, On foot. *United States Holocaust Memorial Museum, photographer George Kadish.*
Below, By horse-drawn wagons. *Yad Vashem Photo Archives.*

Groups of Jews are assembled near the entrance to the Seventh Fort,
where they have been brought for mass execution, June/July 1941.
Bundesarchiv and Yad Vashem Photo Archives.

Field on Demokratu Street in the Kovno ghetto where the selection
of the Great Action on October 28–29, 1941, took place.
Yad Vashem Photo Archives and Beth Hatefutsoth.

Hundreds of Jews are gathered near the entrance to the Seventh Fort, where they have been brought for mass execution. Hebrew caption at the bottom reads "Kovno Jews being taken to be murdered July 27, 1941." *Yad Vashem Photo Archives.*

Jews buying and selling on the corner of Dvaro Street in the Kovno ghetto. *Simon Wiesenthal Center Library and Archives, United States Holocaust Memorial Museum, and Beth Hatefutsoth, photographer George Kadish.*

Ghetto Situation after the Great Action (The survivor must live . . .)

4

After the Action: Moods and Rumors; Camp or Ghetto

On the day after the action, October 29, 1941, all institutions in the entire ghetto were closed. The situation and mood in the ghetto were as if after a great earthquake. One did not know what was happening, where one was in the world, what one should say or think. We were completely paralyzed and dejected. People were running around from one to the other like wounded animals, asking what would be, what kind of affliction had befallen us, and what was going to happen next. It was completely impossible to take stock of the horror we had experienced. Had they really murdered the 10,000 who had been taken away? How could that be, what would happen to us? Were we better than they? Did the Germans value us more, were we privileged, when would they take us away? Was living and doing anything at all worthwhile when, in any event, we would soon be taken to the fort? Holding our throbbing heads in our hands, confused by the sad thoughts that were chasing each other, we asked the same questions for the hundredth time, unable to give an answer.

The entire ghetto was like one grieving family. There was crying and wailing in every house and every yard. There was hardly a house or a family that was not touched; everyone was missing somebody. In addition, for those who were not directly affected by the action, old wounds were awakened. One was missing a husband, a son, a brother arrested early on; another, someone who went away with the 500; a third—someone taken in the two earlier actions. And so the entire ghetto was one grieving community. There was crying and wailing for the loved ones and dear ones who had been so cruelly torn away, crying over our own helplessness and weakness, crying over our shocking situation, our dark prospects. What would be our end, and when? When would there be an end to the troubles, how long would we suffer; if we were not to survive, what was the point in suffering?

Nerves were so weak, people were so exhausted, that they wandered around crying in the streets; women especially ran around in the streets like wounded animals, wailing. People ran to the fences to engage the guards, the partisans, in a conversation: maybe they knew something of the fate of those taken away—because at that time it was not believable that all had been killed, without exception—people would speak to them and inquire, maybe they had seen or heard where the people had been taken to, how many were taken, perhaps there was a possibility to bring someone back. We were still very naïve, thinking that at least some of the younger men had been taken for work.

The partisans, our "good friends," smelled a good source of income, and immediately offered to bring back anyone who was requested; as long as they were well paid, they would bring back anybody asked for, the main thing was "*Yidele* [little Jew], give money." People in despair, seeing a feeble ray of hope, brought money and goods to the fence; they put down a deposit toward bringing someone back. They sought pity from them, stuffed them with all kinds of good things, so that they would do something. They, the partisans, took everything, but needless to say, they brought no one back. They only cheated the Jews of a little more money, a few more valuables.

People did not go to work. Who cares? one thought—what could be worse than what we have lived through? All along we had been implored to go to the airfield because this would help with all our troubles, and here, with the action, hundreds or maybe thousands of able-bodied people had been taken away; they had shown their shift papers at the selection, which had not even been looked at. In fact, people from the airfield had suffered more than everyone else. Since thousands of people with armbands had gone to the Fort, working at the airfield provided no protection—so why should one work? That was the mood of the people, and in the first few days the situation of the labor quota to the airfield was catastrophic; people simply didn't go.

A few days later, the chairman of the Elder Council and the chief of police were received in the city by Jordan. (It was generally noted that he was in a somewhat milder mood toward the Jews than before, having probably observed up at the fort such terrible instances of death and extermination as would move even a stony, murderous Nazi heart such as his.) Among other things, they told him: "The people in the ghetto are confused and dejected; they cannot be sent out to work. As we had instructed them, they had placed their trust and sense of security in the notion that the airfield would save us from all our troubles. But that is not what happened. Airfield workers suffered more than others. Armbands, work papers, and various other papers from workplaces were handed out, none of which were paid attention to. What can we now tell the people? How can we drag them out to work, with what can we win their trust?"

The next day Jordan came to the committee, bringing 100,000 rubles to be distributed as wages to airfield workers, and made the first official declaration that there would not be any more actions, that this was the last one. But he imposed the condition that every day the required number of people was to be provided consistently for all shifts, that the fate of the ghetto, its continuing existence, was dependent entirely upon work at the airfield.

The very fact that a bandit and murderer such as Jordan came not to announce a new edict but instead the opposite, bringing money and promising that there would not be any more actions—this in itself was calming. It was the first time that a somewhat human word had been heard from him. Other representatives of the authorities, who used to come to the Elder Council, declared that what had happened would not be repeated, that there would not be any further actions. The Elder Council posted Jordan's official declaration in placards on the streets and explicitly emphasized in his name that our continuing existence was dependent only on our work at the airfield.

From then on, the entire attention of the Elder Council, the Labor Office, and the police was concentrated on providing three times daily the required number of people for the airfield.

Labor Quota

A few days after the action, the Labor Office carried out a registration of all able-bodied men and women. It was established that women from seventeen to forty-five years of age must also work at the airfield, except for mothers with small children younger than eight years old.

A few days later, it was announced that "all able-bodied men and women of the ghetto must appear on the morning of the 8th of November, 1941, in the square near the committee; everyone must come, without exception, regardless of whether one has worked the previous day. Those found in their homes after six o'clock in the morning will be severely punished." Special large searchlights were set up on posts, which lit up the entire square (it was still dark until seven o'clock). The entire square was surrounded by police, and no one who had come to the square was allowed to leave until the columns had marched off.

From five o'clock onward, hundreds of people, men and women, moved toward the square near the committee. Here, in the square, the people were assembled into columns of 100 with a column leader and sent off to the gate, one after the other, accompanied by Jewish policemen.

It was a picture to remain engraved in memory for a long time. A large, bare square, brightly illuminated by searchlights from all sides, where several thousand men and women are assembled. The square is surrounded by our own Jews, so that no one will be able to avoid going to work, to "slip away." There is confusion and turmoil, talking and shouting, people are hustling, one chasing the other, one Jew driving another to slave labor. The police and the Labor Office are ordering, assembling the men and women into columns, rushing, hurrying to get to the gate early, lest, God forbid, today there should be a shortage, because if Jordan should come to the gate to find out how many have gone to the airfield, and if the number should be short, then one can expect misery from him.

So it was, day in and day out. Everyone had to get used to it, to have it pounded into his head, that one must go to work, that it was our obligation, which we could not, regrettably, avoid or get rid of.

For the first few days, it worked well. People were very much under the influence of recent occurrences and the announcements of the representatives of the authorities. Somewhat later, people cooled off a little and began to dissemble, to fail to come to the square, to shirk their duty. At that time, the police started the most difficult work in all of its existence. The period of providing the large quota, which dragged on for six months, was one of the physically most strenuous and most difficult time periods of police activity.

With everyone required to report to the square near the committee, the police had to go early in the morning to all the houses, to check whether everyone had indeed gone to the square. At two o'clock, the day shift had to depart, and from twelve o'clock on the police were already mobilized to provide people for that shift, being preoccupied with it until around four o'clock, when all columns had been escorted out. And as soon as they had returned from the precinct, wet and muddy, after completing mobilization of the day shift—at around six o'clock—it was already time to go back to the precinct in order to start mobilizing for the night shift.

Somewhat later, the three shifts were discontinued by the airfield management and a single shift was established, which had to leave the ghetto gate around six o'clock, the workers having to start assembling at five o'clock. At first it was difficult to provide the people, and a new arrangement was made that consisted of the police being assigned the task of waking up the workers in the morning to go to work.

For those who did not live through and experience all of this, it might appear comical: it may seem similar to the former practice of pounding [on the door] for *slichos,*[1] or calling the heads of the households to go to the bathhouse on Friday. What is this waking for going to work, and how is it possible to walk around such a large area and pound on the shutters? But it is a fact, this is how it was; that which life compels and teaches, no dreamer can devise.

---

1. Special prayers between Rosh Hashanah and Yom Kippur.

All the policemen would come to the precinct every day at half past four in the morning. At around five o'clock they would go out to the precinct, each having his assigned several streets that he served. Each one would go from house to house on "his streets," pounding on all the shutters and shouting at the top of his voice: "Arise for the airfield." And so it went, day in and day out, the tune known to everyone. Having completed the wake-up calls, they would return to the precinct. At six o'clock they would go out again for the inspections, that is, to check every house and every room to see that people had indeed gone to work.

The inspections extended until around half past seven, the policemen being released for breakfast only when there was a report from the gate that "the airfield has departed." If the required number was not achieved, or if there was some other reason, they were once more sent out to check—more thoroughly, better—in case some had managed to avoid work and were hiding.

The morning wake-up process was conducted with great commotion and noise. The policemen would begin to pound and beat on the shutters, windows, and doors, so that the sleeping people would jump out of bed neither dead nor alive; there would be great turmoil in the house. While pounding, the policemen would wait until there was light in the window, meaning that the inhabitants were indeed getting up. For this reason, many preferred to get up on their own before five o'clock and turn on the lights so that the passing policemen would not pound and wake up the others, who could sleep. To a certain extent, the wake-ups achieved the intended objective. People sensed that an eye was watching, looking out to see that one got up on time and did not oversleep going to work. Conversely, others, who were already used to this, would wait in bed for the pounding on the shutters, for the "signal" to get up.

Checking the houses after six in the morning was the most difficult work. It was necessary to go from house to house, from room to room, from bed to bed, the crowding always being very great. People were jam-packed, one next to the other, beds and couches placed so close together over the entire width of the room that it was difficult to go through. In addition, because of the cramped conditions, the air in the rooms was very stuffy. And so one had to go from bed to bed, to check everyone's documents, to accurately determine when they had worked and for what reason those in question were staying home. Should someone's documents not be in order, he would immediately be taken to the work inspector in the precinct, and if he had stayed home illegally he would be punished. Frequently, if the airfield [columns] had not yet left, he would be taken directly to the gate.

The checking itself, the very fact that the police came to the homes to inspect and monitor whether one was working, led those obligated to work to be careful not to be caught by the police. But there were also quite a few fakers, sworn loafers, who sought to avoid work by any means. They would hide in the attics or under the beds, or get dressed and wander around in the streets, and return home after the inspections, or feign illness, only not to have to go to work. At first, they succeeded in fooling the police. Later, when all these "customers" became known, and all their tricks and ploys became familiar, the police in each precinct knew their regular clients, knew their locations and where they could hide. During the inspections in these houses, the policemen would crawl under the beds, into the attics, into the stalls, in order to remove the band of fakers.

One cannot say that the police treated them mildly. It would frequently happen that once such a person had been caught in his hiding place, after an hour's search, he would get a beating. It is, of course, not good and not nice that one Jew should beat another for not wanting to go to slave labor. On the other hand, however, we understand that those who were hiding were not doing so out of idealistic motives of passive resistance, but were simply the same ones who were always, under all circumstances, the lazy ones. At such a time, when the labor quota for the airfield was an issue of life or death for the entire ghetto of 16,000 Jews, one could not stand on ceremony.

The entire long business of inspections is a very varied one; there were many different ways and forms by which the police checked on the workers. It is not possible to list them all, and so we will provide the most important and noteworthy of them—that is, the extraordinary controls, beyond the daily waking and morning checking.

Night controls. Around ten or eleven in the evening, the entire police force would be assembled to carry out a night control. They were of different types: there were local night controls; that is, each precinct made an inspection in its precinct with its own policemen. Then there were inspections in a particular precinct, but with the help of policemen from other precincts. The largest, most vigorous ones would take place over the entire ghetto area.

While local inspections were frequent, not all the precincts conducted them simultaneously on the same evening. The "nonkosher" or ordinary malingerer would find out which precinct was being checked, and if he lived in the "threatened" precinct, he would simply go to sleep at the home of a friend or acquaintance who resided in a precinct not being checked that day, and in this manner avoid the police inspection. Another time, a night inspection would take place only in one particular precinct, mostly in the first, with all the policemen from the other precincts also mobilized for it. The precinct in which the inspection was to take place was kept secret. Except for the higher police functionaries, no one knew where the inspection was to be carried out, so that no one would escape.

Most of the night inspections would take place over the entire ghetto area. Around eleven o'clock in the evening, the entire police force would be assembled in the central administration building and divided into groups, with each group assigned a group leader and designated streets in the corresponding precinct. The inspection would start in one precinct—each time generally in a different one—and after concluding in that precinct would move on to the next, and so on. Such an inspection would last all night, until five o'clock in the morning. They would go from house to house, pounding to open up and checking work documents. During such inspections, many "rabbits" were caught who did not work regularly. They would be taken to a specified assembly point and from there to the detention house.

The work of the policemen in carrying out such night inspections was difficult and unpleasant. But it was even more difficult for those who were torn from their sleep in the middle of the night, tired, physically and spiritually broken by their work. Sometimes this would take place at two or three o'clock in the middle of the night. Those awakened by the inspection could no longer go back to sleep because in an hour they would have to get up to go to work. The working people were upset over the frequent inspections, over not being allowed to sleep and rest the few hours that they were in the ghetto.

True indeed. But the efforts that had to be applied to meet the labor quotas so that airfield work would function well outweighed all other considerations. The population had to see and know that there was check-ing and that there was accurate observation of where and when everyone worked, so there would not be any loafers. There had to be maximum control over the entire population.

Work at the airfield became even harder than in the early days. It was not so much the work itself, but that the entire environment and conditions changed for the worse.

Supervision of the Jews at the airfield was by soldiers of the Luftwaffe. Except for a few hooligans, they were mostly relatively decent, naïve, sim-ple-minded Germans. Solid people, who did not understand or know of sophistication or politics, they related to the Jews in a friendly manner; they did not urge them on to work, and from many one would even hear a friendly word.

Somewhat later, the guards were changed to civilian "masters." These were simple Yekes, formerly common construction workers in Germany, who supervised the work of the Jews. They were referred to as "masters."

Work at the airfield consisted of digging ditches, doing cement work, and various drainage and construction tasks. Each section [of the airfield] was assigned to a particular German firm, and each firm employed its own supervisors to oversee the work. There were among the masters many hooli-gans, sadists, Nazis, who would beat the Jews for any trifling matter, stand-ing with a stick in hand and violently striking the Jews if they wanted to rest a little or if their work was not fast enough to please them. One had to put up with *gebrente tzores* [dire misfortunes] from them. The steady airfield workers got to know all the firms—which ones were good to work for and which were to be avoided; they became familiar with all the masters and their whims and sadistic habits.

Some firms at the airfield were "famous" in the ghetto—for example, "Fritz Mueller." This firm involved the most arduous work, and its masters were idlers who would beat the Jews who had singlehandedly to push the wagons filled with lime from the notorious lime pit at the airfield.

In the firm "Schultz Dobrick," the work was not very hard. But in this firm was the well-known master who acquired in the ghetto the name of "the white cap," because he would go around summer and winter wearing a white cap. He was a murderer, a dog who would beat and strike; to end up working for him was bitter.

Every firm and every place at the airfield had its own characteristics. Even if, by chance, there was a good supervisor, the work was hard. Often one had to stand for five or six hours in a lime pit, up to one's knees in water. In other places, where the work was easier, bad masters stood over one's head. In other places, both conditions prevailed: hard work as well as bad masters. At work one had to look out so as to rest a little during the few minutes when the bad master turned away. But one had to be careful, or else one could be struck from behind with a shovel; one would pass the word to the other that he was approaching. Since the Germans understood our language, Hebrew words were utilized. Someone would utter the words "Yaleh v-yavo"[2]—meaning that the master, who walked back and forth around the place, was coming, and that one must work. The word *v-yavo* was later left off and it would only be said: "Comrades, get to work, the yaleh is coming."

The airfield expression also became established in the ghetto: gradually, every higher Jewish official in the ghetto was marked with the word "yaleh" and it remained that way—anyone occupying a higher post in the ghetto was referred to as a " yaleh." "The yalehs have the best food to eat at home." Or, "Who can equal him—he is a yaleh." A higher official would be referred to as a "great yaleh," a lower one—a "small yaleh."

Special ghetto folklore.

Before the Great Action, a kitchen was established for the Jews at the airfield. This kitchen was set up by the German management of the airfield; Jewish women cooked there. Neither delicacies nor special platters were prepared there. Twenty field kitchens were set up in a barrack, where every day the same soup of potatoes and cabbage was cooked—every day the same. It had no taste, but it was better than nothing. A little hot soup is very good after standing in the cold for four or five hours; it warms up the frozen bones. The soup at the airfield was given the name *yushnik*, which was also carried over into the ghetto, where mostly *pareve*[3] was eaten, since meat was very difficult to obtain. In the ghetto, to prepare lunch was to cook yushnik; to eat lunch was to "go home to gulp down some yushnik."

---

2. "May it ascend and come"—first two words of prayer recited on holidays and on the first day of the month.

3. Food containing neither meat nor milk.

But all these witticisms, jokes, and gallows humor cannot fill the stomach. Basically, those going to the airfield were limited to the ration distributed in the ghetto. (Later it was arranged for the airfield workers to receive, from the ghetto, a special supplemental ration; that is, the general population received less than what they were proportionally entitled to and the surplus was allocated to the airfield rations.) Unlike the work brigades, there were absolutely no opportunities there to buy a little food, and that was the worst part. The work was arduous, and not only were no wages received, but there were also no opportunities to obtain anything for money.

It is understandable that people would not want to go to the airfield. But this is hardly an excuse—one goes not because one wants to go, but because one must go.

We, who live here in this environment, for us, all the misery, humiliation, and suffering have become normal. We accept it as self-evident, as a commonplace matter. But when one briefly rises above the atmosphere in which we live and which we breathe—released for a few minutes from the nightmare—it becomes strangely terrible and unbelievable: How can this be? How can one live like this, and how can one endure it?

Jews driving other Jews to crushing labor. Dozens of columns marching out of the gate. One following the other, one column after the other, guarded by soldiers with rifles, as though we were the worst criminals; lined up four to a row, one must stay in line, no one must veer off from the row; this is how the Jews drag themselves, with yellow patches on their backs, exhausted, miserable, dejected they go through the wide, bright streets beyond the fence—where there is freedom. We are led in a convoy, as if to irritate, to tease us. You go by the streets where you had previously resided and lived, where you walked and promenaded as free men, where you worked and produced—now you are led through these streets like prisoners, like criminals.

The gentiles, the robbers, who spilled so much of our blood, are walking these streets perfectly free, living in our houses and apartments, wearing the clothing that they robbed from us, enjoying that which we had produced over generations, when they were still running around barefoot, herding pigs. They—standing lined up on the sidewalks—look at us with pleasure and glee as we are led through the street like dogs. Sometimes they see in the lines their former landlords, their employers, before whom they would have respectfully removed their hats, for whom they had at one time swept the street, now trudging along in prisoner garb, humiliated and broken, while he, the shepherd, walks around perfectly free.

They derive pleasure from this entire play and sometimes laugh directly at the face of this or that familiar Jew whom they recognize in the line.

Such scenes really break the heart. Had we been told of this a few years ago and presented with such images, we surely would have said that human endurance was not capable of withstanding such things. But we do endure it and we will endure it, to spite our foes—as long as we are allowed to live, not taken to the fort.

Living for a long period of time under these conditions (it is already twenty months), one becomes used to all these images, so that it becomes normal; one does not pay special attention to it—one becomes brutalized and apathetic, only seeking to obtain something to eat, to bring in as much food as possible for oneself and for one's family. Work at the airfield, and its associated prodding, chasing, and checking, has become ordinary with time. For the one doing the prodding, it has become natural that he should be prodding people to go to work, and for the one being prodded, it has become normal to go.

As noted earlier, the Labor Office and the Elder Council applied all available means to fulfill the labor quota. Toward this end, to bring about as much compliance as possible, it was pounded into people's heads that one must go to the airfield; it was even arranged to stage an action. An announcement was posted one day ordering all ghetto inhabitants to assemble at three o'clock in the afternoon in the square near the committee. The announcement was posted in all the streets. Immediately there was great commotion and alarm. One immediately asked oneself: "What is this, again an 'action'"? People became very fearful.

At three o'clock, a large number of people assembled near the committee although not everyone was there, because many did not come out of fear that maybe "something was up." The Jewish police and the firemen surrounded the entire square and those assembled in it.

A small stage was set up. When the people saw that only Jews were conducting the entire affair, they breathed with relief. The chairman of the Elder Council read an appeal that in the interest of their own existence, and, by extension, also in the interest of the entire ghetto community, all those obligated to work should faithfully fulfill their work duties, because that was the only condition that—in their eyes—justified our existence. We were forced into this and must fulfill our duties without exception and without shirking; we must understand the seriousness of the situation in which we found ourselves. Everyone dispersed after the speech, impressed by the gravity of the obligation facing us.

The city brigades, which also left for work in the morning, had to assemble in the square in the morning—not near the committee where the airfielders assembled, but somewhat farther on, across the road, near the blocks. At first, they were allowed to leave only after the airfield workers had already gone.

The jealous hatred of the airfielders toward the brigade people was very great. They complained, justifiably, that they were going every day, toiling so hard and getting nothing for it. The brigade people took it easy and had everything in abundance. The airfielders had to trudge many kilometers every day and stand outdoors all day in the cold and wet, while the brigade people did not have far to go, mostly did not work hard, and were given food there and could buy something. It would certainly be more just to have people exchange jobs—one who had worked for a few months in a brigade should now go for a while to the airfield, so as to give the airfielder the opportunity to work for some time in a brigade and to revive a little.

Plans were advanced to exchange people, but nothing came of it. Those working in a brigade had their acquaintances in the Labor Office, their "vitamins" [pull, patronage], and quietly continued to go; the unlucky one who was going to the airfield, without protection, remained a dismal airfielder.

Most of the ghetto offices and their staff were far removed from such notions of fairness; in most instances only protection, personal contacts, and other such things applied. So it was from the beginning to this day.

Material Conditions

Parallel with the airfield work—with its development and evolution, and the great effort to fulfill the labor quota—the first offices to develop and expand were those dealing with the labor quota, that is, the Labor Office and its divisions: the airfield division, the mobilization and punishment division, the city brigade division and, somewhat later, the registry division. New people were added to all the divisions, and the work expanded.

The 100,000 rubles brought by Jordan were being utilized to pay day-wages to the airfield workers. It was anticipated that 10 rubles a day would be paid to men and 5 rubles to women. The sum was trivial, but still better than nothing. In addition, it was generally looked upon as a sign of improvement and stabilization of the situation.

In conjunction with the general consolidation, new offices were established and developed in the ghetto. There was somewhat of a recovery and the beginning of a little activity.

The financial situation of the Elder Council and its offices also began to settle. New sources of income were added. From time to time, a little money was received from the Gebietskommissariat.[4] In addition, there were various other sources, such as, for example, profits from the food stores, hospital, outpatient clinic, apothecary, payment for electric lights, taxes, imposed monetary fines, payment for the use of wagons of the transportation division, and so on. Added to these was the income from the warehouse containing the belongings of those taken away in the Great Action.

Along with income, there were also expenditures, which constantly grew. For the first few months after the action, wages of 100 rubles per month were paid to employees of the ghetto institutions and of the police. This sum is ridiculous compared to the price of food products, which were increasing daily. But even so, the Elder Council budget could not sustain these payments as there was not enough money for other public needs, and payment to employees was discontinued.

The expenditures of the Elder Council were large and varied. A large part was taken up with "getting along with Germans." Frequently, valuable gifts needed to and had to be given to Germans who came daily to the ghetto and had a say over us. Many times sad misunderstandings were avoided with nice presents. It was a very important task—it always had to be done; a reserve of money always had to be in the treasury for any such contingencies.

The preoccupation with all of these things—stabilization of all the offices, creation of new ones and getting them started, the slow development of the

4. Gebietskommissariat—office of the regional superintendent.

entire apparatus, the relatively quiet situation in the ghetto—all brought about a general calming and easing of tensions. Slowly one calmed down, ignored one's memories. One was busy dealing with one's own needs, preoccupied with oneself; everyone was worried and very busy finding a source of livelihood, a means of existence.

How did the ghetto Jews support themselves? What was the source of their livelihood, of their daily expenses?

Employees of the ghetto institutions and of the police received no money (needless to say, the 100 rubles paid for only two months played no role). For work at the airfield there is no payment (the 5 rubles a day paid in the early days played no role in the budget; incidentally, payments to airfield workers were discontinued after a few months; city brigade workers were not paid). There were no sources of livelihood, no businesses, no earnings, so how did one survive?

In addition, our money and gold was taken away from us during the gold action; out of terror and fear, everyone—with only a few exceptions—turned everything over, only 100 rubles were kept per family; at the time it was thought that one would stay in the ghetto only a few months and then liberation would come. But four, five, six months went by and Jews still had sources of livelihood, and today, after more than a year and half has passed, Jews still have something to subsist on. In fact, the standard of living has improved greatly, many things are more easily obtained than a year ago; with money one can obtain in the ghetto whatever and as much as one desires. Where did all this come from, by what means was it accomplished?

There was joking earlier that the 100 rubles allowed per family was elastic—"the rubbery hundred rubles"—the 100 rubles stretched out to last a long time. Needless to say, this was only a joke that would not fill the stomach. Jews began to come up with new, unprecedented sources of existence.

Street trading began to develop in the ghetto soon after the action, primarily of items of little utility: cigarettes, saccharine, matches, and other such small things. All these small items were normally not available in the ghetto. In the food stores, Jews would receive only bread, flour, grits, and salt—nothing else. Later on, horse meat began to be given out from time to time, and a few times over the entire time period 50 grams of butter was given per person. The Jews received no other food products. Clearly, these rations were inadequate. Aside from the fact that the ration itself was very small, it was not possible to live and exist on a dry piece of bread and some barley.

Those going to the city would bring back to the ghetto bread, flour, potatoes, and other things that they bought from the gentiles. They would ask Jews to bring clothing to trade for food products. In this manner, at first a little, then more and more, clothing would be taken from the ghetto to the city and exchanged there for food products.

The gentiles learned how to trade from the Jews. They would take the clothing that they had traded from the Jews to the villages, where food was in abundance but not accessible to the Jews. The peasants were not interested in selling food products for money, because they could not buy anything in the city for money. They would trade with the peasants, receiving a lot of products in return for the items for which they had paid a pittance to the Jews, then trade again with the Jews, and so it was repeated over and over.

Exchange-trading developed. In the city, the gentiles were not able to buy anything. With the exception of groceries, all stores were closed, everything was restricted and rationed, the smallest items were not available. They therefore pounced on everything offered from the ghetto. The Lithuanians, whether in the city or in the villages, did not have an abundance of clothing. First of all, the Jews were always the more affluent element, having more clothing than the gentiles. A large number of Lithuanians, who earned more, would drink away in a month what Jews spent in half a year on clothing. Second, many Christians became rich from robbing the Jews and wanted to dress up, to wear nice clothing. They constantly sought to buy clothing; speculation and trading developed among them. They would trade with the Jews and then sell to other Christians in the city itself and in outlying areas, which were not accessible to Jews.

The brigade Jews would trade clothing for food and bring it into the ghetto. They brought in so much that they had enough to also sell some of it in the ghetto. This is in contrast to earlier times, when nothing could be bought in the ghetto for money, because anyone having some food products was afraid to sell it for fear that there would not be any more. Now that everything was being brought in from the city, trading in food products slowly developed. Earlier, Jews in the city had not wanted to accept money for clothing—they only wanted to trade. But, as it became apparent that everything could be had for money within the ghetto itself, trading of clothing for money began. Clothing was sold in the city for money, and with the proceeds everything could be had, either in the city or in the ghetto.

And so, trading slowly started to develop. Almost everyone had some clothing—it was sold and one ate. Product prices were quite high, but the price of clothing was also comparably quite high. And so everything was being sold and traded for food products. This is how one lived and struggled.

But there were also some who did not have any clothing of their own—mostly those removed from the small ghetto with only their clothes on their backs. There were also many who had been driven from their homes by the Germans or Lithuanians without being able to take anything from their houses.

Many of those who were working in brigades found a different source of livelihood. They would take from those having clothing to sell, who were not themselves going to the city but working inside the ghetto itself. They would take the clothing for an agreed-upon price, sell it in the city for a profit, and live on the earnings; or they would trade the clothing for food, bring it into the ghetto, and sell it at the ghetto prices, with the difference between city and ghetto prices being their profit. And so one schemed, plotted, and created the opportunity to endure, a chance to survive, to persevere.

Slowly emerged the sellers, the buyers, the resellers, the middlemen, the agents, who provided the goods to those going into the city, because they themselves had no time to go around the ghetto looking for the items that were asked for by their buyers in the city. An entire category of "merchants" was established: small ones and big ones, those who dealt "wholesale," making large turnovers, and other, smaller ones, making smaller deals, working on a smaller scale. And so trading blossomed. A number of families earned from and lived off every item offered for sale: the agent, the buyer in the ghetto, and then the one who bought it for sale in the city. People earned one from the other and, in this manner, one managed.

An additional category of "merchant" evolved—the trader at the fence. Around the ghetto lived many farmers who had larger amounts to sell: great quantities of food products, primarily potatoes and flour in large amounts, which were normally difficult to bring in through the gate on one's back. There were special traders, who made the necessary contacts with the seller, the Lithuanian, outside the fence; the guard at the fence would be bribed, and at night, the farmer would come with his wagon close to the fence, to the barbed wire, and whatever was needed would be thrown over or passed through.

The Christians on the other side of the fence would most often buy items that were normally difficult or impossible to bring through the gate in the morning, for example, furniture, sewing machines, and other large objects. At night, at the fence, the trade would be completed based on a previously agreed-upon price. As trading at the fence developed further, everything possible passed through it.

And so it came to pass that everything could be had in the ghetto in abundance; anything one desired could be obtained: butter, meat, milk, not to mention bread and potatoes.

Trading in the streets grew mightily. Everything imaginable was offered in the streets. Dark bread was no longer in demand, one became spoiled, forgetting that one was in the ghetto, in a casket.

Brigade people started to bring into the ghetto various higher-quality articles. Whisky, wine, and liqueurs began to come in. Slowly at first, then more and more, people indulged themselves in merrymaking. Needless to say, this does not apply to everyone—the larger majority continued to bear the ghetto yoke. It is however of note that, even in such bitter times, people could be found who indulged in partying and drinking. They were none other than those who should have served as models for everyone—people holding higher positions in the ghetto institutions and the police.

When such things were first heard of, one was shocked by the reckless-ness among us, the thoughtless and disorderly actions that were indulged in. Somewhat later on, one became accustomed to it; it became halfway normal that one should have a drink, enjoy oneself as in former times. In this way, improvement in the food situation in the ghetto—the general improvement in the material conditions—brought with it a great deal of depravity, cor-ruption, cheating, and similar "good" phenomena.

The very fact that the material situation was improved was, of course, uplifting. The recklessness that came with it greatly embittered those who were not as yet completely apathetic and brutalized.

It became almost routine that the best way to get someone's attention was by means of a liter of good whisky; it might be arranged by a go-between, who needed to do something to get something accomplished, or to give thanks for being accepted for a position in some office—a big celebration with a large drink. In many instances, this was, and continues to this day, to be the best way. It all came about as a result of improved living conditions.

That's how this unusual way of life, with its strange sources of livelihood, became established—selling your clothing in order to eat. One adjusted to this way of life, became accustomed to it, and soon forgot how different it was before. One traded, bustled, bought, sold, acted as intermediary, exchanged, made profits from one another, got in one another's way—and made a living.

It seems that what Jews are able to do, no other people in the world can do. We have the physical and material strength, the ability to adjust to the living conditions that we are forced into; a solution is found for each condition and for each circumstance.

The problem of food had, more or less, settled out. One toiled, but, still, most people had their daily bread and potatoes. The problem of clothing and shoes was more difficult in the ghetto, but one managed to find a solution. Some—and they were the majority—still had their clothing from the city, while others utilized the workshops; one managed to cope.

But the most difficult problem was that of firewood; where to obtain firewood became a very urgent issue. The little that people had brought with them from the city had been burned. The winter of 1942 was long and difficult; bringing it in from the city was not allowed, and many residents were therefore freezing. Those working in the city brigades, and even at the airfield, started to bring home from their workplaces, every day, on their backs, a few pieces of firewood. This was illegal, because the firewood actually had to be taken stealthily from the storage places at the work locations, but this did not pose any great difficulties. Also, a piece of firewood was allowed to be taken through the gate, and so it came about that a Jew had to carry on his back a piece of firewood, in addition to his package. Although this was not sufficient to solve the heating problem, still everyone had his piece of firewood to cook a little of his yushnik every day and to warm up.

The shortage in the firewood budget was filled in by tearing down the fences around the houses; almost everyone tore down the fence around his dwelling place. Hosts of people would go out at night for an "expedition" to tear down fences. Tens of meters of firewood were obtained from the fences and used for heating. It went so far that the Lithuanians into whose houses the Jews had moved submitted a complaint to the Germans that the Jews were tearing down the fences and thereby destroying their houses (it mattered little to them that we were completely destroyed; what mattered most was that their huts should not be harmed).

It also happened that little houses, ruins, or ordinary houses standing empty, unoccupied, were torn down plank-by-plank for firewood (after the Great Action, before Vienozinskio Street was taken back, dwelling places were spacious and a certain number of houses were unoccupied).

The tearing down of fences and taking apart of houses took on the character of an epidemic. The Elder Council and the police had to become involved. A special announcement by the chief of police forbade tearing down fences and dismantling houses. The very tearing down of fences and houses led to chaos, fights, and brawls over a piece of wood. There were instances when people were wounded while tearing down houses, and a certain [person by the name of] AZEF was killed on the spot by a log hitting him on the head. A group of collaborating people would converge upon a house in the middle of the night or early in the morning and start to take apart the logs. The guard at the fence, hearing the racket, would start shooting, and the people would disperse in a panic. The Germans—the masters of the house who were by then in the ghetto, the NSKK[5]—also got mixed up in the matter. Once they caught a group of Jews tearing down a house and gave them a good beating and threatened them with their revolvers.

The police now had a new, difficult assignment: to guard day and night all the unoccupied houses in the ghetto so they would not be carried away for firewood. Many times the policemen had to wrangle with everyone, to chase away hordes of people from the empty houses—in their own best interest.

The problem of firewood remained unsolved until the summer of 1942. In the summer of 1942, the ghetto received permission to bring in a few thousand meters of wood. In addition, individuals were allowed to buy a little wood in the city, and so the problem was resolved. Until then it was very difficult and bitter, but it would appear that what Jews are able to do, no other people in the world can do. We have the physical and moral strength, the

---

5. Nationalsozialistisches Kraftfahrkorps—a paramilitary motor organization.

ability to adjust to the conditions in which we are forced to live; a solution is found for each condition and for every circumstance.[6]

Events in the Ghetto after the Great Action

In the preceding chapters we provided a general picture of the development of the ghetto offices as well as of the sources of livelihood we created for ourselves during these times. That was a general picture, in which we looked ahead in order to provide a more complete description of the situation of the developing offices and of material life in the ghetto. Now we will look back a little and describe more or less chronologically the events and shocks that occurred in the ghetto during the last months of 1941 and thereafter.

From the beginning of November, and continuing for a few months, we all had to live through great terror as a result of attacks by Lithuanians on the ghetto through the fence. As if organized, they launched these attacks on the ghetto almost daily. At first, they would assault the houses near the fence. Somewhat later, they became more daring and more arrogant, and there were a few assaults on houses in the middle of the ghetto.

The goal of the attacks by our "dear" neighbors, the Lithuanians, was always robbery. It was not enough for them that they had already been robbing and plundering us continually up to that time, they also had to come in here, where we were closed-in and helpless, and assault us, rob and plunder to their hearts' content.

All these attacks and their sad outcomes are noted in the police archives. The police officer on duty would submit a written report to the Center of all the day's occurrences, specifying the location and time of the attack and the material and physical damages caused by the assault . . . and how it ended. The attackers were never caught, because the authorities were absolutely not interested. It did not matter to them whether the Jews were being robbed or murdered. We mattered to them only to the extent that they could squeeze a workforce out of us for the airfield quota, and nothing more.

---

6. Note nearly identical sentence at end of description of food acquisition activities in the ghetto.

Mostly, the attacks were carried out by armed partisans. In this way, a house near the fence was attacked on November 8, when a women by the name of Baranoff was severely wounded by a number of knife stabbings. There were a number of such attacks in the course of the month in various locations. On a number of occasions the Jewish ghetto police detained Lithuanians at night, and one time even in the middle of the day; they had crawled through the fence with robbery in mind. The detained Lithuanians would be delivered to the ghetto guard, and that was the end of it.

In the month of December, a whole sequence of attacks occurred by armed and organized hooligans. They would knock on a door as if they had some announcement concerning blackouts. But as soon as they entered the house, they would brandish their weapons, rob and plunder. In other places the Jews would not allow the late-night "guests" to come in. Then, they would break down the doors, knock out the windows, force their way into the house, take anything they could find, beat, and threaten to shoot, so that in many instances those being robbed were glad to have gotten off only with material losses and to have remained alive.

A large organized robbery occurred on December 12, when, having done the deed, they set fire to the house in order to destroy any traces of the robbery.

Thus, there occurred assaults throughout the entire month of December—on December 14, 18, 20, 29—when, in addition to material losses, a number of Jews were also wounded by the robbers.

One of the attacks with very sorrowful results occurred on January 8, 1942, when the house of the policeman Vidokle was assaulted by a group of armed hooligans. A party of armed robbers broke in; they shot on the spot the wife of the policemen V. as well as a tenant, a certain Wolf. The policemen V. and his six-year-old daughter were seriously wounded. They robbed everything they could find and ran away. This robbery had a very depressing effect in the ghetto, because the house is located in the center of the ghetto, in close proximity to dozens of other houses around it and quite far from the fence.

As in previous similar instances, this case was also reported to the authorities, but nothing came of it. It matters little to them whether there is one Jew more or one Jew less.

There were a few days when stubborn rumors circulated in the ghetto that a general assault was being prepared with the participation of many armed partisans and hooligans. The talk among ourselves was that we should be prepared. But, unfortunately, how could Jews be prepared—we had no weapons; what could we do against armed hooligans? We had to be content with locking ourselves in the houses, sitting and waiting in fear of what might happen next. Fortunately, the rumors were exaggerated; attacks continued to take place, but, as before, isolated ones. Our life was such that it was enough for someone to spread a rumor, and thousands of people would go around confused, and some would be frightened.

While from the outside, that is, from the point of view of the Germans, life flowed relatively calmly (if one can consider ghetto life as being at all calm—life in the lion's maw), the attacks were like "intermezzos," which embittered the already bitter life.

An event took place in the ghetto on December 27 that shook everyone up. We had to live through a number of very fearful hours before we learned what was happening. On the morning of that day, when people were streaming from their houses to go to work, we were surprised by news from the gate that no Jews were allowed to go to the city—no brigades and not even those going to the airfield were permitted to pass through the gate. Everyone was ordered to return home. There was tumult and panic in the ghetto. No one had any doubt that something bad was about to happen, it was only a question of what that would be, what type of fort action would now take place. That an action would take place no one doubted, because if not, then why was the gate closed and no one allowed to go to the city—this was exactly what had happened before the Great Action; on that morning, too, no one had been allowed to leave.

Hordes of fearful people returned from the gate. Many rushed to go home as fast as possible so as to be together, if something was to happen. Large masses of people gathered near the committee. Perhaps one would hear some news; maybe something was known here.

The chairman of the Elder Council and the chief of police were called to the ghetto guard. Everyone waited impatiently for the news they would bring, what they would come back with.

It is an early winter morning, it is around seven o'clock, it is dark, black, the committee is packed, everyone standing around, tensely waiting for the return of our representatives with new decrees. It turned out that our fears were somewhat exaggerated. This particular time they were not targeting our lives, they just wanted our furs, to carry out a fur action in the ghetto, that is, that all the Jews were to give up their furs for the German army, which was fighting on the Russian front, where, as is known, bitter frosts are pervasive. It appeared that we, too, were to be called upon to help the Germans achieve victory.

In the fall of 1941 the German advance came to a halt. Not only did they not go forward, but in many places the Russian pushed them back—luck abandoned them, Mars turned his head away from them. In addition, the winter was a very difficult one, and they were not adequately prepared for the extensive Russian frosts. This wasn't just hearsay, but a fact, because they started a large-scale action everywhere—in all the countries under their domination—to secure furs and fur products for the army.

A fur action was also announced to the gentiles in Kovno, nor did they forget us in the ghetto; we should also help conquer the Jewish-Bolshevik, plutocratic alliance . . .

To carry out our fur action, they ordered the closing of the ghetto in the morning and issued an order that all furs in the Jews' possession must be delivered in the course of this day. House searches were to be carried out after this deadline, and anyone found having furs would be severely punished.

In the "famous" Demokratu Square, where the Great Action had taken place, a number of large, long tables were set up, to serve as the collection point, where people would bring their furs. Having lived through the earlier couple of hours of fear, people were pleased to have gotten off only with this, that it was limited only to the furs; such were the "good fortunes" of the ghetto.

Fearing that house searches might indeed take place, many Jews who had furs and fur products in their homes carried them to the collection point. But there were also those who, having learned from earlier practices during the gold action, hid their furs and did not give them away. Many removed the inside fur linings and either delivered them or destroyed them, keeping the outer garments for themselves.

The Jewish police, the announcers of all rules and punishments, again went from house to house and read the text of the order saying that all fur products must be delivered, that the given order must be complied with. Be that as it may, many furs were collected at the square.

In the evening of the same day, Lithuanian police went through the houses making searches. In some houses they searched only superficially, but there were also many places where they made thorough house searches. Others would, at the same time, engage in some robbery—if they liked something, they would just take it without asking any questions.

It turned out that many Jews, out of fear, gave more than was required. They brought to the collection point furs that were torn, tattered, worn out, greasy, dried out, dirty, which the Germans would not touch. After a few days, they sent back to the ghetto a few wagons full of these plain furs.

Incidentally, when turning in the furs, we were told that everyone should sew on a note with the first name, family name, and address of the owner. When the returned plain furs came back, many of those that had such notes were returned to their owners. The rest, without notes, were turned over to the Labor Office, which distributed them through the social commission to the poor, primarily to airfield workers.

That was the end of the fur action, which today appears like a small episode, although at the time it held everyone in fear and tension.

The year 1941 is going away, a new year 1942 is coming. There is among us Jews a new proverb, said on the eve of Rosh Hashanah: "Tichleh shanah v-klalose-ah, techel shanah v-brachose-ah," may the old year end with its curses, may the new year begin with its blessings. The old year had brought terrible curses, unbelievable afflictions and pain, one of the most horrible in the life of the Jewish community of Lithuania. A year in which more than 80 percent of the entire Lithuanian Jewry was annihilated, in which we experienced such cruelty as to make the hair stand on end. The pogroms of the other world war, of the Petliurites and all the other gangs that raged in Russia at the time of the civil war, all the other oppressions and afflictions which the Jews suffered over the last hundred years, they are all like child's play compared to what we lived through. Let the old year go and take with it all of our afflictions.

The new year is coming. What does it bring for us, can we hope for something good, will our situation improve somewhat, or will a new flood of afflictions and oppressions be poured upon us? Whether or not we want to, we are continuing on the dark road, into the gray, cold unknown.

From the situation at the front we could not expect a quick salvation. The fight of the giants was in its full force and growing more and more intense. From here [from Lithuania] the Russians beat a hasty retreat. In the course of three months, the Germans continued to advance, almost reaching Moscow. In some places they were stopped for a few weeks, and colossal battles developed. But they broke through and continued to advance. In the winter months, with their great Russian frosts, they were stopped. The Russians went on the attack and recaptured a few places. Optimists in the ghetto started to hope that maybe they would collapse, but, regrettably, nothing good could be anticipated; quite the opposite, it was evident that the game was in favor of the devil. A war to last for years: in the winter the Russians advance, in the summer the Germans—a story without an end.

In the month of January, a new, powerful factor was added to the struggle of the giants: the United States of America entered the war. The Jews began to make new conjectures and combinations. On the eve of America's entry into the war, the opinion in the ghetto was that this would impact badly on the situation of the Jews. They, the Germans, see in America the fortress of the "international Jewry" of the world. They would surely propagandize that it was the Jews who had incited the Americans to join the war against them.

Indeed, following the entry of America into the war, there was a lot of incitement and propaganda in the press and radio against the Jews: it was our fault that America had entered the war, we were the cause of it all. Well, what could we do—we could not respond, nor could we argue against this. We put up with the flood of invectives and the hail of accusations and continued to carry the ghetto yoke on our backs.

Many said that the entry of America into the war indicated that the war was coming to an end. The basis for this was that in the earlier war America joined the fighting six or seven months before the end—perhaps it would also be that way this time. One always consoled oneself and kept up hope, because what else was left to us besides hope for an end to the war and, as a result, an end to our unbelievable afflictions?

That was the mood in the ghetto in the area of "foreign policy." One inquired, debated, interpreted, analyzed, and came to the strangest conclusions. The pessimists—saddened, and the optimists—cheerful.

In the month of January, various events followed one another, which today appear as passing episodes, but made a strong impression on everyone at the time.

On the January 11, around twelve noon, a sudden order came from Jordan that the Jews living in the Vienozinskio district and the adjacent streets of Strazdelio and Kulvos must clear the district by four o'clock that night. The district consisted of wooden block-houses, eight rooms to the block, as well as other houses in the remaining streets not built in block form; all together, 1,300 souls resided there.

It was a very cold day. A large area had to be cleared, including many families with infants and old and sick people. Where should they all be placed? It was already tight everywhere and, in addition, such bitter cold. But, true to himself, Jordan's order sounded cold and murderous, requiring that the entire district be cleared in the course of a bare four hours.

There was commotion and tumult in the streets. As quickly as possible, people grabbed their few possessions and took them wherever they could. Fortunately, the day fell on a Sunday, when all the men were at home. Quickly, ladders and planks were used to make sleds, to haul their belongings swiftly, in order to take out more of their effects, as well as firewood. All policemen were immediately mobilized to help those being evacuated, to carry their belongings, to pack, to haul, to guard against theft, and so on. Employees of ghetto institutions and all means of transportation—horses, sleds, and wagons—were put at the disposition of the people being chaotically evacuated. Once more with the bundle on the back, again dragging oneself from one place to another. One had already settled in and suddenly had to be uprooted, to run around looking for a new place again, a different roof over one's head.

The reason for the order to evacuate that part of the ghetto soon became known. The Elder Council was officially informed that German Jews, scheduled to arrive by train that same evening, would be settled in the area being evacuated. Immediately afterwards, the order received from the authorities was made known by means of an announcement from the Elder Council.

The announcement contained fourteen clauses. It was dated January 11, 1942, and stated the following:

1) Today, January 11, 1942, the entire district to the right of Demokratu Street must be cleared by four o'clock;
2) All belongings and moveable possessions may be taken along;
3) All means of transportation including support personnel are to be immediately mobilized and placed at the disposition of those being evacuated;
4) German Jews will be settled in the above-mentioned district;
5) The German Jews are not allowed to leave the district; the Jewish ghetto police will guard it day and night, with two policemen at each of three locations along the entire Demokratu Street;
6) The German Jews will arrive through Paneriu Street and will be met at the corner of Demokratu and Paneriu;
7) Upon arrival in the ghetto, the *Kenn-Zeichen* [ID/registration number] of the German Jews (author's note: instead of a passport for German Jews) will be taken away. As a replacement, a card index will be arranged for them later;
8) The German Jews will not be included in the labor quota;
9) They will not be given any food because they had been provided with food for three weeks;
10) A ten-man commission will be formed in our ghetto whose task will be to collect from the German Jews whatever furs they may have. The number of collected furs must be reported to the authorities by tomorrow;
11) The sick among the arriving German Jews must be quartered in separate rooms;
12) Order will be kept by the Jewish ghetto police;
13) Only the chairman of the Elder Council and the chief of police have the right to enter the area in which the German Jews will reside;
14) Anyone disobeying the clauses of this order will be severely punished.

As we could see, a detailed plan had been worked out for the arrival and absorption of the German Jews. Various conjectures were voiced among us in the ghetto. Some said these were Jews from Czechoslovakia. Be that as it may, one was consoled by the fact that if Jews were being brought here, it was a sign that we were still allowed to remain alive; in fact, our number was even being increased. To be sure, these other Jews would live separately from us, we would be unable to come to them and they to us, but, still, we would live side by side.

A few days passed, a week, and there was no trace of the German Jews. No one knows where they were or where they had disappeared to. A few weeks passed and they did not come, and so it remains to this day.

What kind of a devil's game was this, was another comedy being played out on us? Such detailed plans had been worked out for their arrival, with all the particulars concerning their settlement and stay—was it all nothing more than a game of deception, as with the other German Jews? All kinds of rumors circulated—that they had been brought here, but instead of being led to the ghetto had been taken to the fort. It was also possible that they had been murdered somewhere along the way. Everything could be believed, precise information was impossible to obtain, the entire episode remains a dark secret for us to this day.

A few days after this episode of the evacuation of the Vienozinskio district, a new event occurred in the life of the ghetto, which greatly affected the shape of the inner life of the ghetto—its fundamental material existence: the arrival in the ghetto of a new ghetto-guard, the NSKK.

The Elder Council, the Ghetto Institutions, the Police, and the Ghetto Population

Mutual Interrelationships

5

As noted, the police and the Labor Office were set up and organized during the very first days. According to the established order for such institutions, the largest organizations—in size and influence—were subordinated to the Elder Council. These were the organizations that, within the limits of their capability, had a say over the entire inner life of the ghetto.

The Elder Council is the highest organization of the ghetto; everything and everybody were subordinated to it. It has veto rights over all decisions of the various offices. But, customarily, the Elder Council does not involve itself directly with the daily issues of the police or the Labor Office, such that the police, as the implementing organization—the "eye" of the ghetto—and the Labor Office, as the organization dealing with the distribution of the Jewish work force, are largely autonomous in their fields of endeavor. These two organizations, although subject to the oversight of the Elder Council, are in fact the decision makers within the boundaries of their fields of activity, which encompasses the entire administrative life of the ghetto.

The Elder Council is our official representative to the outside world, maintaining contact with the authorities, conveying in their name various instructions to the ghetto population, issuing direct orders to the ghetto inhabitants and to the offices of the ghetto institutions concerning all internal matters, and setting and approving the fees of all the offices. The Elder Council is the *balebos* [master of the house] over everything and everybody.

The chief of police Mr. K. [Kopelman] was also a member of the Elder Council, meaning that the chief of police, as top man in the police, was at the same time also a member of the ghetto management. The Elder Council and the police force, although the latter is subordinate to the former in all matters, are essentially one entity, one complementing the other. The Elder Council makes decisions with the concurrence of the chief of police as its member, and the police, as its implementing arm, carries them out. That's how it looks officially, and that's how it also was in fact during the first days of the ghetto.

But it is also true that in normal life not everything put on paper looks the same in practice. "What one eats is not as hot as when it was cooked." As actual work began, as we entered the pace of ghetto life, mutual relationships took on different forms. In the course of their work, the relationship between the police and the Elder Council encountered various difficulties. Little disagreements grew into larger misunderstandings, which later developed into subtle struggles between them. Clearly, it could not be considered a struggle between equals, because, in the end, the police were subordinate to the Elder Council. But a critical attitude developed in police circles toward the Elder Council and a grudge or anger developed among the latter toward the police.

The first misunderstandings were due to differences of opinion between the leaders of the police and the Elder Council as well as due to various interventions by the police that were not given any consideration by the Elder Council.

It is well known that it is easy to be critical of someone else, much easier than to have your own work exposed to the criticisms of others. But there were many matters in which the police intervened, believing themselves to be in the right, but without success.

As previously noted, many of those who first joined the police believed that they were doing so without ulterior motives—only for the well-being of the ghetto. There is no such thing in the world as an idealistic "ghetto huckster." But there does exist the ideal of working for the benefit of all, regardless of where and in what condition the community may find itself. The first group of people to join the police did so to work for the well-being of the ghetto Jews.

Later, things became quite different. During the following times of persistent struggle not only for bread, but also for bacon, butter, and whisky, not only did all traces of idealism disappear from the police force, but many of our functionaries became like animals and lost their normal human countenance. But in the early days, when serving in the police still had some of the taste of public activism, the first young men to join it and to lead it were quite naïve and simplistic, thinking that the police force was created as a control and oversight institution and, to some degree, also as the defender of justice and decency in the ghetto.

Many of the employees of the ghetto institutions, less naïve than our first police functionaries, behaved, from the very first days, in a manner somewhat different from that prescribed by the *Shulchan Aruch*.[1] From the very first weeks, the distinction between theirs and mine was forgotten; they did anything they chose to do, as long as it was done quietly so that no one would hear about it.

When supervisory men of the police would bring to the attention of the Elder Council various injustices committed by this one or that one, the first answer was: "It is not your concern. The assignment of the police is only to carry out orders, to maintain peace and order in the ghetto—all other matters which take place here are not within your authority."

Factually, they were right. Indeed, the police must only carry out orders, submit to the decisions of the Elder Council, and implement them in

---

1. "Prepared Table"—book published in 1565, containing all Jewish religious laws.

practice. But from the perspective of the overall interests of the ghetto, such an attitude and answer were insulting, creating a critical attitude toward the Elder Council.

There were instances when the police would bring to the attention of the Elder Council various abnormal and unlawful occurrences committed by other persons or offices, as, for example, the distribution of vegetables from the gardens. The population was starved for a few potatoes and other vegetables, while the yalehs or institution functionaries who strutted around the food distribution office obtained as many potatoes from the public gardens as they wanted. The general population, the "ordinary mortals," received nothing. It was plain robbery at the expense of the starving population.

When people were being mobilized and recruited for the airfield, there were, in the same house, in the same yard, people who would go to slave all day at the airfield and receive nothing for it, as well as others who had not gone to the airfield their entire life, because they were provided and were "armed" with papers from the Labor Office such that, for the police, they were "taboo" and untouchable. They would obtain these papers where they could do so on the basis of acquaintanceship and protektsia. Why should it be so? Why should one be dragged to unrewarding hard labor while the other sits around the house in his morning-coat reading a book, playing the dandy, as if on vacation in the countryside?

To the daily relevant occurrences that the police brought to the attention of the Elder Council, the response very often was: "Maybe we are also aware that certain injustices are taking place, but we must tolerate them and that's how it must be." Sometimes the answer would be quite stereotypical, that this was not within the domain of the police.

If the attitude of the police toward the Elder Council was critical, then, as a consequence, the attitude of the Elder Council toward the police was also not overly friendly.

If the police needed to arrange material provisions for the policemen, this was not easily accomplished. For example, verbal and written negotiations were carried out over an extended period of time concerning the provision of vegetables to policemen. It took a long time and was accomplished only with great difficulty, and when the vegetables were finally received, they had to be immediately returned. There exists a copy of a letter to the food supply office—which, by the way, would sabotage the police at every opportunity—where it is stated that: "The cucumbers which had been designated for the police must, regrettably, be returned, because they are only fit to be eaten by pigs, not by people." The police saw this as a representative case of our being treated as stepchildren, because, at the same time, other employees of the ghetto institutions were effortlessly receiving good vegetables.

It was thus only with difficulty that the Elder Council was persuaded to allow the opening of a police store. Lengthy negotiations took place before its opening was permitted at the beginning of September. The following motivations drove the effort for a separate food distribution center for the police:

First, there were long lines in the food distribution stores. Since policemen received everything without having to wait in line, there was great resentment on the part of those waiting their turn.

Second, a separate line would build up of those "receiving without having to wait in line," consisting—besides policemen—of other privileged people, employees of ghetto institutions, friends and acquaintances of the store employees, such that the policeman, even though entitled to receive without having to be in line, also had to wait a long time, which was, at that time, when the police were constantly on their feet, a difficult matter.

Third, various irregularities were practiced in the central distribution place: the population would receive less than what was allotted to it. The population in general, and the police as a part of it, suffered from this, because one was entirely dependent on the ration.

For all of the reasons listed above, a separate store was desired, where one would receive directly from the central distribution point the full amount of products to which one was entitled, to be dispensed to the policemen and their families.

Opportunities began to develop for the acquisition of food products beyond the distributed rations, as, for example, bringing them in directly from the city. It was therefore thought that food products obtained from other sources could be given over to our own store, where they would be sold and distributed to everyone. Only after protracted efforts did the Elder Council allow the opening of the store. They had their own reasons: that the police were no more privileged than anyone else, that tomorrow the Labor Office will also want to open its own store, and the day after the

Housing Office, and the ghetto would be flooded with distribution centers. It may well be that their concerns were justified, but, on the other hand, the Elder Council knew very well that none of the employees of the ghetto institutions had the burden of doing such difficult and thankless work as the police. They all sat comfortably in their offices doing their work, while the police were the ones who were day and night on their feet, quarreling with everybody, everyone against them. They therefore sought to have some compensation, even if it was only in this form. The difficulties made by the Elder Council left a certain aftertaste.

Notwithstanding the fact that the relationships were strained, this did not have any serious consequences. For example, one cannot point to any occurrence of the police not obeying and not carrying out a given order. Criticism is one thing—order and discipline are something else.

How did the relationships between the police and the Labor Office evolve?

Whatever the relationships between the police and the Elder Council may have been, the police force was, in any event, subordinate to the Elder Council, having to carry out all of its orders. But, in a certain sense, the Labor Office was a parallel institution to the police. They came together in a common field of activity, having to collaborate in one of the principal tasks for both of them—the provision of the daily labor quota to the airfield.

Initially, it was determined that the Labor Office, as the institution in charge of the ghetto work force, must also be the one to provide the required number of people for the airfield; the police must maintain order during the recruitment and bring the assembled people to the gate.

Somewhat later, when the provision of the required number of people encountered great difficulties, the police also started to recruit workers, such that, slowly, it came about that the entire burden of producing the labor quota, all the dirty work, fell upon the police. People had to be grabbed from the streets, dragged from their homes to work. As a result, the resentment and anger slowly grew in our hearts, that all the dirty work was put upon the police, one had no day or night of rest, while the employees of the Labor Office arrived like lords after everything was done and issued orders.

That was the start of unfriendly relationships between the police and the Labor Office. Although, to tell the truth, it was the fault of the policemen during the initial period, who were the first to start dragging people to work, as though this was a sport. Had they not started, then perhaps the entire burden of providing the labor quota would not have fallen on them later. Be that as it may, there were strained relationships right from the start. Later on, relationships sharpened further because of subjective as well as objective reasons.

First, psychologically, there is an internally directed loyalty in every branch; everyone wants to boast about his own branch, that it works in a more timely manner, better and faster. As a result, a situation was created where the employee of each branch wanted to be superior to the other. Each branch—and, as a matter of course, the employee himself—wanted to make itself more conspicuous, to be in front. A sort of competition developed between the two branches.

Second, somewhat later, when the registry had already been set up, and it was already known roughly where one lived, where he worked and so on, the police would conduct inspections in the houses according to lists of people provided by the registry division of the Labor Office. But this did not work well, as there was no correspondence between the provided lists of workers and the facts. One would look to take people for work at false addresses, or several pieces of information were simply mixed up, so that you could not make head or tail out of it, at times looking for people who were not even in the ghetto. On the basis of the lists put together in the Labor Office, which had been sent over to the work-inspectors in the precincts, the policemen had to drag themselves out to do inspections early in the morning or in the middle of the night, in rain, mud, snow, or cold, and then drag them-selves back to the precinct. Frequently, things would turn out topsy-turvy, where the concerned person would actually be working regularly but had been given leave, or where the lists of addresses were inaccurate, or where family names and addresses did not match. A man who had returned in the evening tired from work would be ordered in the middle of the night to get dressed and come to the precinct, where it turned out that it was all nonsense—it had been quite unnecessary to drag the man out of bed in the middle of the night.

Those affected by such orders, or, better said, "disorders," would be very upset and would pour out their bitter heart on the heads of the policemen, as if they were responsible for them not being allowed to rest, not letting them sleep. Not only did they have to suffer from the Germans, they also had to suffer at the hands of their own Jews.

But from their perspective, the policemen knew that they, and even the chiefs of the precincts who sent them, were not at fault—they were only the sticks. They received already completed lists from the Labor Office, which they must take care of—they were only the enforcers of the orders. Thus, the Labor Office was the real cause of the disorder and tumult. The irritation over the unnecessary work, the drudgery and sleepless nights, dragging oneself with wet feet, in the dark, through all the attics and cellars—for all of these only the Labor Office was considered responsible; it alone was the cause of our distress. That's how the anger and irritation with them swelled in our heart.

In the course of time, as work proceeded, our anger, and to some degree hatred, became deeper and wider; a struggle developed between the two independent branches. There became, so to speak, two sides—us and them—who hated and had ill-will toward each other.

Substantively, for someone looking at it from the outside, the whole matter may well seem comical; it could look like children playing. What do you mean "a struggle," who is fighting whom and for what, who are we, where are we, what are we worth?

Without any doubt, it would be sufficient for a German sergeant to yell only once and all of our "higher ups," *natchalnikes* [chiefs], with their rank insignia and cockades, all these seekers of glory, plotters, plate-lickers, all these highly placed personalities with their assistants and subassistants—all of them, together, would scatter in fear to "where the black pepper grows." And what can be the meaning in the ghetto of a struggle among ourselves— why and for what? Do we know how long we will remain here, do we know what will happen to us one hour from now? We are weary and don't know our fate; so what is the purpose of this struggle?

But it would appear that in practical life, sentiments and feelings are one thing, while greed and the quest for power are something else. One who is alive and breathing, regardless of the conditions in which he may find himself, keeps on elbowing his way forward, without any consideration of sentiments or logic.

Along the way, a competition developed between the two branches for influence in the Elder Council and, as a consequence, also in the ghetto. Each branch wanted to be at the head, to be important; each one fought for dominance, for the public trough. It is an old and perpetual struggle for power and influence in public life.

Initially, the police force was almost the sole authority in the ghetto, the central place that everyone turned to. Later on, the general influence of the police diminished—it was wrested away by the Labor Office. To this day, the police remains only the implementing instrument of the decisions of the Elder Council and of the Labor Office, without any significant say in the making of these decisions.

The reason the Labor Office was able "to beat a path for itself," to achieve influence, to become the spokesman, was, first of all, because the police force, for reasons previously enumerated, was not viewed with favor by the Elder Council. Second, there were a number of energetic and, most important, solid people, who made personal contacts and achieved influence in the Elder Council; they were listened to and they were depended upon. They pushed their way through and achieved a dominant influence not only in matters of labor quotas, but also in many matters having nothing directly to do with the labor quota. By contrast, the police lacked such people, who could create status for themselves through personal relationships and conduct—some because they were too young, others being too phlegmatic and not sympathetic. That's how it was, and, with time, it [the Labor Office] increasingly occupied the top position in the ghetto.

What is the moral level of the offices and employees of the ghetto institutions? Had we matured morally to lead the Jewish community in these dark days? Did the population feel tied to the functionaries as to brothers in suffering, or was a wanton mood pervasive, as among the gentiles in wartime? We will dwell on these questions a little in order to, as much as possible, sharpen the image of the inner life of the ghetto.

From the very beginning, after August 15, 1941, when the offices of the ghetto institutions were being formed, when we had barely "gotten our feet wet" in the ghetto, abnormal phenomena started to show up; various small illegalities began. They first appeared during the gold action, when many of those who found themselves at the public trough—at the collection points—made much profit from the entire show. Later, during the distribution of the Jordan certificates, there were, as previously pointed out, many illegalities. Afterwards, many offices and people followed the already "paved" road. In particular, endless schemes were concocted in the food distribution centers—a whole series of illegalities with the distribution of food products, at the expense of the population. Smaller amounts of products were given out than the required size of the ration; all kinds of games were played with the distribution of vegetables. The bottom line is that the schemers had no limit, whoever had the opportunity and the "cleverness" took all at the expense of the starving population.

In the Labor Office, where various sections started to develop, a well-known *protektzionism* [system of privileges] grew rapidly. Someone with "vitamin" was assigned to an easy brigade, never went to the airfield, transferring from one brigade to another. It was only necessary periodically, about once a month, to "have a chat" with the appropriate persons, to send a *shalach mones* [presents exchanged during the Purim holiday], and to continue going undisturbed to the brigade and to do some business. Others, who had already gone to the airfield a hundred times and were already exhausted from it, were seeking a little "piece of brigade" in order to get something to eat, but were only seldom rewarded. Such people were not given any consideration—the supplicant standing at the door, begging like a poor man, was ignored. No attention was paid to the material condition of others, the size of their family, and so on. Whoever had protektsia was well off, if not—it was difficult and bitter. For hours on end one could be standing before the doors of the yalehs of the Labor Office, tired, exhausted from the day of work at the airfield, and if God made a miracle and rewarded one with luck, then one was told to come back the next day—they would look into it, investigate whether one was entitled. Such was the lack of consideration for the honest ones, for the ones without protektsia, for the hard-working people.

Without any doubt, the Elder Council knew of the injustices being perpetrated in the offices. There is also no doubt that the two principal leaders of the Elder Council were personally very clean and kosher. However, the trouble is that they did not adequately react—they did not undertake really energetic mass measures against all these dark elements. They never were, and to this day are not, sufficiently energetic, lacking the personal initiative to tear out the evil by its roots. In addition, there were those who interfered, because for them, for some of the assistants, it was more worthwhile to allow matters to go on as they were, since they personally derived benefits from this.

However, for the sake of objectivity, we must emphasize that in every instance it is necessary to differentiate among the people in the offices. We do not wish to imply that the office, as such, was in its entirety operating on the basis of protection or illegality. Many solid, honest people in the various offices did not want to and could not tolerate all these machinations, the horse trading going on in their offices, but there was nothing they could do about it—it became our common evil, a general affliction of our "autonomous republic"! An organization came into being and started to handle everything, building and organizing. To the extent that our sad circumstances permitted it, development and organization went on unabated. But the foundations, the bases of all these developments, were rotten from the first moment and remain so to this day.

Was everything in order with us, in the police? No, here also things were not as they should have been. Many things happened to put us "on a par" with the accepted "general pattern" of the ghetto institutions. There were abuses and illegalities by individual policemen who took advantage of their position and did things that should not have been done.

The abuses started at the time of the gold action. The policemen standing guard at the collection points noticed that some of those sitting at the counters were not quite on the level, so they joined in. There were policemen who attended to the searches in the private homes "with life and soul," searching and finding buried gold and diamonds. They would search very diligently in order to bring the found items to the police headquarters or to the collection points. But while they were carrying things to the collection points, some of the treasure would "leak out" on the way.

Firm regulations had been established for the policemen, but inside thieves are difficult to contain. There were therefore those who took.

Not withstanding the great fear that they instilled and the terror that they applied, it was very difficult to resist the temptation; the innate craving for money and gold was very strong, and when a "golden" opportunity presented itself, one took.

From that time on, a certain demoralization began among a great many policemen. There were many instances when individual policemen would take advantage of their close personal acquaintanceship with Germans for their own purposes. For example, almost every day various Germans would come into the ghetto demanding to be given a variety of things—suits, coats, shoes, women's clothing. Immediately, a number of policemen had to be sent out to the houses to collect for the German the demanded items. The people, rather than receive a visit from the German in their own house, would, of course, give; better to give something and to be done with it. The policemen—the collectors—at first indeed delivered the collected items to the German. But later they concluded that they themselves could also benefit; they would take for themselves a share of the items collected for the German. Later, there were a few cases when some policemen, on their own initiative, would go through houses in the name of a German, simply making demands, threatening that if people refused to give to the representative of the authorities—in whose name they were supposedly making the collection—the alternative would be worse and it would cost them dearly. The people were afraid and they gave. In this fashion, with threats and with plain deception, a number of policemen appropriated belongings from Jews. A few policemen "excelled" in these neat activities. Some of these policemen were removed during the cleansings of the police that took place in the course of time; some are still members of the police to this day. It may be that specific proof of their guilt is lacking, or that they posses a good vitamin.

The leadership of the police knew of these doings, at least in part, and, at times, they tried to react to them, but it did not produce any significant results. First of all, because the chief, Mr. K. [Kopelman], although without any doubt personally clean and crystal-clear, was nevertheless of weak character, not strong-willed, not energetic, and subject to being influenced by those surrounding him. And those surrounding him, knowing his weakness, exerted their influence so as to let matters remain as they were.

Second, there were always people in the background, not visible publicly, who in roundabout ways, through the back streets, exerted their influence, interfered, made impossible the removal of people if this was not to their liking. In many instances, Caspi mixed in—a Jew who lived in the city and went around without yellow patches. Officially, he was in their service and did not allow us to do what we wanted, only what he told us to do.

The period before the Great Action was a time of living in constant terror. There was not a minute of peace; every hour, every day brought new decrees and plight, so that there was never any time, no opportunity to do anything on our own initiative.

There was also the police incident, when one of the then-masters of the ghetto, Tornbaum, was persuaded to allow a couple of policemen to travel to the city accompanied by a guard to purchase food products for the police. A few policemen went and bought flour, potatoes, and other things. But everything that they had purchased they kept for themselves; policemen received nothing. They fooled their own comrades in a loathsome manner, taking advantage of the name of the police for their own purposes.

All of this implies that, from the very beginning, and more so with the passage of time, and to this day, immoral and demoralized behavior settled in among us. One became coarse and dulled, all human feelings became atrophied, one ceased to be embarrassed for one's own actions or for those of others.

By the Germans we are treated like animals. They look upon us as if we were scabby beings with whom one should have no contact, not offer a handshake, not utter a friendly word. We, who are not supposed to know or understand anything, must bend our backs with their yellow patches and silently and patiently bear the yoke of slavery, work like horses and receive beatings as our wages, be cheap and worthless in their eyes—like dogs, to be content upon return from work that "thank God, we have good Germans—they are not beating us," looking, with flattery and submission from below, at the pig-like stuffed German murderers above us; what is the master going to order now, maybe he will, in his generosity, grant us a smile. They, the dull, idiotic bandits, murderers and sadists, scoundrels and drunks, who kick us with their feet, rule over us and suck our blood. All of this—their dreadful treatment and attitude, our worthlessness in their eyes and arbitrariness toward us, made us deaf and turned us into animals, cheapened everything that had been dear to us before, produced a reckless attitude toward everything that, over generations, had been instilled in us that one should not do. Everything that was soaked into our blood, rooted in our hearts, was torn out, shattered, destroyed, emptied. Everything that we had achieved in life disappeared, as though it was never there, everything that we had experienced, learned, studied—all a worthless effort. At first one was shocked, but then you let yourself go, give up trying, let matters take their course. When one recovered somewhat, one became like everyone else. The struggle for bread, for survival, drove one to work, to be bold, to be enterprising. The animal in each one of us took the upper hand and the animal instincts, which came to the foreground after the apathy, remained dominant.

Without being aware of it, one became so atrophied that even the great pain of the missing loved ones, who had so gruesomely been killed, was no longer so sharp. From time to time, one would remember, moan, and carry on. One was so bewildered and worried over the daily problems of getting a piece of bread that one became dulled and insensitive to past and recent happenings.

Events, starting with the first day after the ghetto was sealed, when the series of actions began, the anxious intervals between them, the uncertainties of each day, of every hour—to this day—the likelihood that something could happen any moment, brought on the mood of *ekhol v-shte, ki machar tamut*—eat and drink, because tomorrow we die anyway. Who cares whether you should or shouldn't, it is all nothing anyway, as long as one is allowed to live, one should at least have a little enjoyment. In this way the limits are being erased, one jumps over all the fences that, in normal times, one rigorously stayed within.

For many of us, this mood resided in our subconscious. Later, after the Great Action, when life, within the framework of ghetto conditions, more or less normalized, this mood became more entrenched. Whoever had the opportunity, let himself go. At this later point, it became easier to obtain food products, new sources of livelihood opened up, and people started to live well. A certain segment of the population, among them mostly the yalehs of the ghetto institutions, the police, and members of the privileged brigades, partied and drank. There were many men and women whose spouses were taken away during the first days of the war or had gone with the 500. In the course of time, recklessness could be observed—some of these women without husbands allowed themselves to follow an undesirable path.

Clearly, only a small number lived this way—the so-called *slivke* [cream] of the ghetto. The others, the majority, continued to bear the yoke as before.

But it is a fact that among those who had the material means, the mood of recklessness dominated.

This may, perhaps, explain the weak response of some of the people and of the leadership of the offices to the various abuses that were done in the offices, because nearly everyone was at heart—whether factually or morally—not kosher. Each one possibly had on his conscience something that he would not have allowed himself to do in normal times and therefore had to tolerate the sins of others to some extent.

That was the general situation in the offices, the nature of their work during the early times, the moral level of the functionaries in these offices and their mutual relationships.

How did the population relate to the institutions—the deep layers of the working masses, who dragged themselves day in and day out to work—what was their relationship to their own Jewish *natshalstvo* [authorities].

As already said, the population as a whole had an unfriendly attitude toward their own authorities. There were various reasons for this, mostly justified.

It started during the time of searching for housing. At that time, the committee did not display an appropriate stature. The commotion, chaos, and disorder were great; there were many to whom an injustice was done, who were wronged, and they harbored an unfriendly feeling in their hearts toward the committee.

Later on, in the ghetto, during the money and gold action, when in the mood of terror everything was delivered, retaining only 100 rubles per family, persistent rumors circulated in the ghetto that those who received the verbal orders from Jordan did not properly understand him, they simply did not communicate: one was allowed to retain 100 rubles not per family but per person. Under the then-existing conditions, that made a colossal difference.

A few weeks after the money and gold were delivered, the house searches by the Germans, which had been so threateningly announced, did not take place. Soon, the Jews forgot all the fears that they had experienced. It was quickly forgotten that only a few weeks earlier one would have been content to be rid of all one's valuables if only the house searches and shootings would stop. Everything was forgotten. One was only "biting one's fingernails," meaning: How could one have done such a foolish thing as to have listened to the committee and to have given everything away? How could one have been so blind and afraid as to have been taken in by the threats of the committee and of the police, to dig up the buried treasures, which no one would have found, even if they wanted to look for them?

The entire anger and fury was taken out on the committee, the Elder Council, and the police. It was argued that had the Elder Council not created such a commotion, such panic, such fright, had they not sent out the police to make house searches, then a great deal would have been hidden and would have been kept by the Jews. It was considered to be the fault of the committee for being more cautious than was necessary.

Later on, the episode of the Jordan certificates, food distribution, various abuses in the offices, the wrongs that were perpetrated without there being anyone to complain to, the outrageous protectionism, the so widely practiced "vitamin system," the abuses of the Labor Office in the assignments to the brigades—all of these direct and masked injustices created a hateful attitude by those wronged and affected, and scorn toward those associated with the Elder Council and its offices.

From the very beginning, there did not exist the relationship that should have been there between Jews in such bitter times—when everyone bears the same yoke and shares the same fate. The contact, the warm feeling from one to the other, did not develop. Hearty, Jewish relationships were not established. That which would unite everyone, which would make one feel like brothers in need, like a community, did not develop.

Those sitting in the warm, bright offices looked down upon those who dragged themselves day in and day out to the airfield, muddied, filthy, and ragged. They didn't want to understand that they sat in the offices on the account of and at the expense of those who labor every day, and that it could have been the other way around, that it was only by accident that he was there, only temporarily privileged. This gave rise to pronounced snobbishness among many of the functionaries. The privileged, the functionaries of the ghetto institutions and the police, stood apart from the "ordinary mortals"—from the rest of the people. Each one started to make gestures as though he was some kind of commander. A typical bureaucratic machine came into being, without a shred of heart or soul. Dry pen-scratchers, bureaucrats were at work. A coldness developed and was displayed in the attitude of the functionaries and the police—arrogance and, frequently, cruelty learned from the Germans, as well as rudeness and empty pride.

Of course, this should not be said about everyone, without exception. There surely are sincere, understanding people and Jews in the offices of the ghetto institutions and in the police, but they are nullified in the commotion; their voice is not heard among the majority of indifferent, angry, dry, and self-centered voices.

This attitude arose, perhaps, because of the makeup of the Elder Council. Almost all of them were decent people, cultured and polite, but had never mingled with the Jewish masses. In the good days, they had no daily contact with the average Jew; they did not see or had little interest in their daily needs, their deprivations and sorrows. They were mostly from the free professions, doctors and lawyers, who dealt largely with their professional matters. There were a few who had been involved with public work, but they were soft. The insufficient energy, to some extent idleness, and the inability to firmly take leadership in hand—all this led to others, on the sidelines, also placing their hands on the steering wheel and putting their stamp on the leadership.

The makeup of the Elder Council was also not entirely successful, even though there is no doubt that they had, and to this day have, the nicest, best, and most honest intentions. But good intentions are, by themselves, not enough; one must also know how to implement them in practice.

According to what we hear from the other, nearby ghetto in Shavli, the interrelationships there are much better—warmer and more friendly. Maybe that's because Jewish merchants are also members of their Elder Council, people who are mixed in with everyone, who have a Jewish, businesslike, practical approach to everything, who harbor no illusions or have pretenses of being above others, of being leaders—they are from the masses and a part of them. With us it is different: the Elder Council and the committee are not mixed in with the population but the opposite—they are separate from it, a *nachalstvo* [authority] with all its appurtenances. Indeed, we obeyed them, but love them we did not.

The relationship of the population to the police was also not friendly—it was the same as the relationship of the people to the ghetto institutions and, in many instances, even worse. The reasons for this are manifold, including the fact that one had an unfriendly attitude toward one's own officials in general, and also because of the specific unfriendliness toward the police, in particular.

First of all, some of the policemen treated the population not simply as keepers of order, not as comrades-in-suffering—sharing the same conditions and troubles—but as the privileged: it is the same attitude as of one who thinks he is at a higher station to the one below him. This is not a general rule—not all the policemen were like that; there were many understanding, sincere people in the police. But the overall impression was that the police were a special class of the privileged, the chosen.

There is also a psychological reason for the unfriendliness of our Jews toward the police.

The civilian population in normal times, under normal conditions, and in orderly societies, always hated the police. A policeman's coming into the home of a citizen smells already of a citation, of punitive action, arrest, or other such unpleasantness. Jews, in particular, certainly always hated the police—they had a deeply rooted hatred toward anyone in uniform. In addition to suffering a great deal from the police as citizens during the two decades of Lithuanian independence [between World Wars], they also had to put up with the police uniquely as Jews. The Lithuanian policeman would treat a Jew more harshly than a gentile; a Jew would be given a citation faster. In a commotion, or in the case of a public disturbance of the peace, if a Jew was involved—whether guilty or not—he would suffer more than the gentiles.

Here in the ghetto, when the Jewish ghetto police force was first created, the average Jew assumed a psychologically mixed attitude. On the one hand, the ingrained disapproval of the police as such; on the other, the lack of regard by a Jew for a Jewish uniform. We are already used to the fact that a Jew will fear and obey a gentile in uniform. But that our very own Yosel or Shmerl should become some kind of decision maker, whom one should listen to, defer to, whose orders one should carry out—for that one was not psychologically prepared. There were therefore cases, as previously noted, when residents not only would not listen, but actually would apply physical force against the police. The masses, the ordinary people, would frequently resist the police when the latter came to enforce some kind of a regulation. They did not obey, and the policeman was powerless against the crowd.

In such cases, when they were unable to deal with the swarming mass of people in a vegetable garden, in a queue, in the refuge, at the gate, and the like, many more policemen had to be brought to the place of the encounter and to restore order by force so as to carry out the task that they had been assigned. Needless to say, this immediately caused bad blood. When they were fighting trading at the fence, the police would confiscate the products of the traders and bring them to the precinct. Some of them would be sent to the Center for distribution to the hospital and to the poor, and some were given to the policemen. The traders at the fence would be in a rage. A rumor spread that the police were robbing food products at the fence and were dividing them among themselves.

When the police were rounding up people for work, there were many incidents with a variety of malingerers. It would frequently happen that the police would apply force—whether justifiable or not—against the malingerers, when someone would refuse to leave home to go to work. The special group of policemen at the gate—the gate watch, whose activities we will dwell on separately—had a particularly difficult time dealing with the swarming thousands of people, all coming early in the morning to the gate, so as to go to the city. They would press, pull, and push. The Germans would strike with their rifle butts and truncheons—left and right. The Jewish policemen, wishing to somewhat contain the crowd, to maintain some kind of order with their own strength, tried at first to hold back the crowd with their own hands, to bring about at least a minimal order. When this failed, they also took up truncheons, striking the shoulders and heads of Jewish sons and daughters.

We wish to note here that it should not be said that the police were always justified in everything that they did. But it must also be emphasized that some order, more or less, needed to be maintained so that our "dear" masters should not have to come into the ghetto themselves, to establish their kind of order, which could result in the sacrifice of people. There must be a firm hand, there must exist an organ so that the people would maintain discipline out of fear of it—for the sake of everyone's well-being. The individual pressing at the gate to go to the city, he doesn't want to know anything—he wants to eat and must join his brigade. But there are thousands of those who want to eat, and if all of them recklessly push and shove, then no one will get to go. Surely, there must be a definite queue, some kind of system and order. To appeal to thousands of people is of no value, as they will in any event not obey, they will continue to push and shove. The policeman, who is also only human, loses his patience; he forgets all the relevant considerations at the time when this goes on—where he is in the world, who his adversary is—and beats Jews, at first partly ashamed of himself, with pity, the second time somewhat more boldly, and later, when he has become accustomed to it, he beats with brutality and strikes as well as the Germans. There are many good teachers at the gate, from whom one can learn.

Be that as it may, the word in the ghetto is that the police are hitting and beating, one must obey or they give you a beating or throw you in jail, that they are all "robbers, even worse than the partisans." While physical force was used only by a few isolated ones, it was attributed to everybody.

The police carried out all the dirty work. Wherever there was a commotion, a brawl—the police. They had to mix into everything, working day and night, always ready to be mobilized, always available wherever and whenever it was needed, receiving no remuneration for it. It could be that in other places, under different conditions, such young men would be considered public servants. But that is far from being the case with us: the innate unfriendliness toward the police in general, the many instances of lack of tact and understanding by some of the policemen, the brutal approach, the self-importance and conceit, pride, and arrogance, the mechanical implementation of orders and the associated attitude—all of this led to the population fearing the police and obeying it. But in their hearts they were hated—this was not to be uprooted or changed.

This is how the interrelationships between the police and all the offices of the ghetto institutions and the population were formed and that's how they were viewed during the first gruesome months of the ghetto. They later remained that way, with only small changes.

The first gruesome months put their stamp on the entire life of the ghetto—months that cannot be erased from memory, whose anxiety still hovers over our heads to this day.

Life after the Great Action slowly began to normalize. But the impression of what had happened was indelible. The nature of these events, their form and results, the struggle to stay alive that followed—the jostling of the strong while paying no attention to the weak who are left behind, that is the background of the evolving ghetto. Those are its foundations to this day, the basis of the formation of the interrelationships between offices and between people themselves.

With this chapter we close the first period of ghetto life and move on to the second time span, when living conditions in the ghetto began more or less to normalize. The formation of the normalized life, and the transition to it, were not without birth pains. We will dwell on this in more detail in the next chapter.

Development of the Administrative Apparatus and of the Police after the Action

6

AS NOTED, WE SLOWLY entered a new period after the action, a time when everything began slowly to stabilize and calm down. At that time, it was not possible to observe the transition, the evolution period, but now, as we look back upon those days, we readily see that it was the beginning of a new time period.

New offices were being created, and existing ones were reorganized and stabilized.

The first office to be established immediately after the Great Action was the commission for the liquidation of the property of those taken away. By order of the Elder Council, all the houses of residents who had been taken away were sealed and transferred to the jurisdiction of the commission. By means of public announcements, the Elder Council made it known that it was forbidden to take any belongings of those taken away without permission from the commission, even belongings of parents, brothers, or sisters. The commission returned some of the property in the sealed houses to very close relatives, and the rest was transferred to specially arranged rooms in the clothing warehouses. The purpose of the Elder Council in arranging these warehouses was to distribute the belongings to those in need.

Many quarrels took place in connection with this—altercations among the relatives themselves concerning inheritance items as well as various other incidents involving the commission and other parties interested in the properties. Later on, when the ghetto court was established, it was overwhelmed by quarrels over belongings. Many who shared quarters with someone who had been taken away grabbed or hid their belongings. With neither the relatives nor the commission able to find very much, the result was hundreds of quarrels and court cases.

The commission was also not entirely pure. It was said in the ghetto that the employees of the office—the lower-rung and even the higher-up officials—were also not beyond being on the take. The more alert, the swifter, and the bigger the thief, the more he could steal, as there was no accurate accounting, the warehouse was not inventoried, and there were no controls—at least not at first.

In spite of the fact that before reaching the warehouse the belongings were handled by many hands—they would go through various "transmigrations"—many items valued at hundreds, even thousands, of rubles were assembled in the three warehouses. A welfare division was created by the commission, whose assignment was to distribute the belongings to those in need, first of all to those working at the airfield.

Many items were distributed to the poor, particularly shoes and clothing. To some extent, this reduced somewhat the need for and the shortage of clothing. There were also a great deal of utensils, furniture, and other items of secondary utility, which were sold for money and the amounts received transferred to the Elder Council treasury.

The Labor Office was reorganized at the same time. The former manager, Mr. F.,[1] an unsympathetic person without social manners, was removed from his position and Mr. G. was appointed in his place. The mobilization,

---

1. Dov Levin provides the full names of the eleven people referred to in this chapter by initials only—see "How the Jewish Police in the Kovno Ghetto Saw Itself," *YIVO Bleter*, new series, 3 (1997): 284–290 (Yiddish).

penal, and city-brigade sections were established; work assignments were reorganized and rearranged and new people brought in.

The seed of the future ghetto court was established in the form of the rapid-response court specifically to resolve work-related problems. If someone was caught not going to work, he would be turned over to the rapid-response court by the mobilization section. The matter would be handled publicly the same day and the accused given his punishment. The most common offense at that time was that of shirking work at the airfield. In addition to punishment, the task of the rapid-response court was also educational—a means of instilling fear in those wishing to malinger. The public sessions of the court, attended in the evenings by many people, led to the shaming of the accused: he would be reproached in the presence of everyone as being lazy and a malingerer. Many people—those having a sense of shame—were impressed by this. On the other hand, there were many who were not at all impressed. The rapid-response court had the authority to impose effective sanctions as, for example, to take away a bread ration-card for a specified period of time, or to evict a person from a dwelling. The most severe punishment was to be turned over to the ghetto commandant, who would whip the person. This last punishment was seldom practiced—altogether only once, with an intractable malingerer. The other punishments were frequently utilized and carried out. We would quite often read on the walls public announcements that a bread ration-card had been taken away from such-and-such a person for a specified period of time, or announcements of other punishments imposed for failure to fulfill the work obligation.

The rapid-response court did not exist for very long. In accordance with a special decision of the Elder Council of December 8, 1941, it became the ghetto court.

While the need for a court was very much felt in the ghetto, its creation passed through a number of stages. A so-called Conflict Commission was created by the Housing Office in the early days, whose task was to resolve quarrels concerning housing. Later, after the Great Action, when the housing problem was no longer urgent, the Conflict Commission dealt with ordinary quarrels. But its work had no relevance because it had no authority or defined jurisdiction, nor did it have any means of enforcement against those choosing not to obey its decisions. Later, after the rapid-response court was created and before the establishment of the ghetto court, there was no institution for dealing with civil matters. Aside from the general population, it was the police who mostly felt the need for such a court: citizens would come to the police with complaints of, predominantly, civil disputes. But the police force was in no position to resolve these issues because it was not a judicial institution—only an implementation organ of Elder Council decisions, and, along with the Labor Office, provider of the labor quota. It was unable to resolve private (civil) quarrels, and, because of the absence of a court institution, it encountered great difficulties day in and day out.

The newly created court was given wider authority and jurisdiction. Professional people were assigned to it—well-known Kovno lawyers, who managed its work with a practiced hand. In addition to the civil matters that the court had to handle—mostly quarrels among relatives over the belongings of those taken away—it also handled criminal matters that were brought to it for processing by the police headquarters and, later, by the criminal division.

At the same time the Housekeeping Office established a professional body whose task was to organize the ghetto artisans into a workshop. Tailors, shoemakers, furriers, and other craftsmen were assembled into a collective under the auspices of the ghetto administration, working for the benefit of the population. Shoes and clothing gradually deteriorate from walking 10, 15 kilometers [6, 10 miles] per day, and garments become ragged from carrying loads. Since new ones could not be bought, there remained only one solution—to repair them. In the newly established small workshops, later referred to as the "artisan houses," clothing and shoes would be accepted for repair for a relatively very small price. For airfield workers, or for those without means, clothing and shoes would be repaired at no cost. Old shoes and garments that were not suitable for use would be selected in the warehouses for use as raw material for repair work. A few times the airfield column leaders were organized on Sundays to carry out a collection in the ghetto of old clothing and shoes and to turn them over to the artisan house to be reworked.

Toward the end of December 1941, the [German] regional commissar established the ghetto workshops, or as they were referred to by us—"the large workshops." These were set up by Jordan and were required to do work exclusively for the army. Gradually, various departments were established—clothing, shoemaking, laundry, carpentry, and others—all of which worked for the army under the direction of a Jewish works-manager, with the supervision of a German from the regional commissariat. The workshops developed at a rapid pace. Today (July 1943), 2,800 men and women work there.

A new, important factor was added to ghetto life. Many not otherwise obligated to go to work were employed in the workshops because they were recruited as specialty craftsmen. Many who had worked at the airfield, who had torn garments and shoes and were exhausted from walking 16 kilometers day in and day out to work in the cold and wet, were transferred to work here, in the workshops. After all, here it was better and easier. Later on a kitchen was arranged in the workshops, where all workers got lunch. Aside from that, there was a conviction in the ghetto that the workshops gave us security. Their various commissions come, first of all, to the workshops. The Germans from the regional commissariat, who lead the commission members on tours of the facility, praise our work to high heaven. They, our local managers, have their own calculations: they are not doing this because they love us, but simply because they want to show their superiors that they have done well with the Jews. But for us this is, indirectly, a big favor, because the impression is left with them that we are accomplishing a great deal for their army. Who knows, maybe each of their visits results in our life being prolonged so they will be able to squeeze more work out of us. And when the day comes when they no longer need us, then, as repayment, they will perhaps do away with all of us. Who knows?

During these times of organization and arrangement of all the offices, administrative and technical changes were also made in the Labor Office. These reforms were intended to regulate and to bring more or less better order in the allocation of the work forces and their orderly utilization. Order was established in the brigades. Cards were introduced; that is, anyone working in a particular brigade received a brigade-card with a number. Each brigade had its own number and, so that people would not run from one brigade to another, the card of each brigade was of a particular color. Everyone passing through the gate had to hold his card in his hand. In this way it could be verified that each person would go to work in the brigade to which he was assigned.

Men had to work every day. If someone became ill, he had to present a leave authorization from a special commission created by the Labor Office. (Until the spring of 1943) women worked every other day. For them it was also arranged that they must work on the days prescribed for them by the Labor Office and could not select the three days in the week of their own choosing. Every day the column leaders had to provide a report to the Labor Office listing those who went to work. From this report, the registry division could easily determine the names of those who had failed to go to work. The registry division would assemble a list of those who had not gone to work, for transmittal to the mobilization and penal divisions, who, in turn, passed it on to the work-inspectors in the precincts. Policemen would bring the people to the work-inspector, and if this was a malicious case, the person in question would be placed overnight in the jail and early next morning sent off to work, but if the person had leave or some other valid reason, this would be noted in the list, which would then be sent back to the mobilization and penal divisions.

The Health Office was organized to oversee the sanitary life in the ghetto, to arrange—based on directions from the Elder Council—the hospital, and to establish clinics in a few locations.

Everything began to be built, to be created, to be organized, to be reorganized at a faster pace; things began to assume a shape and to have a face.

Before the Great Action, the children in the ghetto went around idle. After the action, the Education Office was created, which, in turn, established two public schools and a trade school. It was publicly announced to everyone that the children could resume their studies. An entire teaching staff was established, and the little children studied enthusiastically. The teachers worked unselfishly, devoting themselves with heart and soul to the education of our children—with the last small hope that perhaps they would survive to get out of here, to tell and describe the seas of trouble and pain that we have experienced.

It was a joy to see the Moishelekh and Shloimelekh playing during breaks in the meadow near the school, at Demokratu [Square]—just like in the good old days. In this way everything began to be arranged—one forgot how it once was, one became so merged with the troubles that one no longer remembered that things had once been different.

All of these reforms and reorganizations took place in the ghetto administration and its offices, and the police, too, were swept up with the times— for us matters also became different. A whole array of reforms were made, which changed our method of working and gave it a different, more orderly appearance.

Before describing the reforms, we will provide a brief overview of the development of internal police operations from the beginning, and then gradually come to the various changes and transformations that took place in the police force from the time of its founding until March 1942.

The organizers of the police force did not have a clear picture at the time of its founding what its future assignments would be; there was no conception of what it would look like, what form it would take, or how it would be organized, much as we had no idea at all what life in the ghetto would be like. But one thing was clear to the organizing group—that the police force needed to be and must be an organization built on military discipline. The policemen must be subject to a strict discipline, they must obey and carry out orders like soldiers; an organization such as the police could not exist in any other way. Organization of the police began on this basis, but there were many practical obstacles that interfered with normal organizational work during this early period.

The orgy of house searches, which we have previously described in detail, was started by them immediately following the closing of the ghetto. During those few weeks it was impossible to do anything. One sat hiding in the houses, and there could not be any talk among the police of any kind of organizational work, although there was an abundance of plans.

Before the Great Action proper police conditions had not been established; the situation and mood in the ghetto were too tense, the uncertainty and fear too great, for normal police work to be instituted. Every day, every minute, some kind of new affliction, new lamentation, here an action at Ariogolos, there in the small ghetto, then all kinds of rumors, which in the interim times had wide circulation in the ghetto. Psychologically, one was prepared to stand every day with a bundle in hand, ready for some kind of trouble. The entire situation was chaotic and the general mood weighed down like lead on the soul, affecting everything and everybody.

As noted earlier, an administrative office was established during the first days, its work having been more or less provisionally defined. From the beginning a registry unit was set apart in the administrative office, where all birth and death cases were noted. Slowly, contacts with the population began to be established; gradually a police presence started to be felt, one which guarded, protected, and watched over everything and everybody.

In general, a police force is everywhere an authority factor—one obeys it because one fears it. Every police force has at its disposal means to punish those who rebel against it. That was not the case with us. In the early days, the police force was not feared (later on our policemen learned to give beatings) because it had no sanctions. As yet there was no jail and, after the gold action, it was not possible to apply monetary penalties. And so, since the police force had to function with moral persuasion alone, it could not get far in the accomplishment of its police duties. A policeman would have to eat his heart out arguing with every Jewish woman. It therefore frequently happened that, because of lack of respect for and fear of the police, hordes of people—especially in the gardens and when tearing down fences—would attack the policeman who forbade them to do something, and would beat him up.

In the early days all the work bore an organizational-social character, rather than that of a police nature. This situation persisted until the Great Action. After the action, when all the ghetto offices began to rearrange themselves, the situation became somewhat more regular and more normal; the ice budged and the first reforms began.

The first, smaller reforms started immediately after the Great Action, when sifting of the police rolls began, to remove the undesirable elements, particularly those who surfaced in the police during the panicky times of the gold action. Among these were also some of the first ten to twelve men who were found to be physically unsuitable for police duties. For all practical purposes they had already been dismissed shortly before the Great Action, but because of the restless mood in the ghetto on the eve of the action, they remained on the police force for a short while and were released immediately after the Great Action.

The proper, larger reforms of the police, following which the internal work was finalized and instituted, began in the month of December. A change in management took place on December 1: the deputy chief [Michael Bramson] was removed from his post and the chief of the third ward, Mr. Z., appointed in his place. The chief of the second ward, K. G., was appointed to the post of police inspector. In the administrative office, the former chief Mr. Sh. Z. was removed from his post and the secretary of the second ward, Mr. A. Sh., appointed in his place.

A new work attitude began with the arrival of the new management. Whether the work of the new management was always good and at the proper level, that is a question in and of itself. But it must be noted as a fact that the new management achieved important, useful, and timely reforms in the work of the police; it must be recognized as having brought more youthfulness, more liveliness into the work of the police.

The former deputy chief, himself a solid, deliberate man, had a patrician approach to everything, even though he was a former army officer. It was accepted that the police force was an organ seeking to appeal to the citizen's sense of justice, not a hand to be feared and obeyed. In addition, the administrative office was not properly organized: it was the administrative office not of an organization based on military discipline, but rather of a normally functioning Jewish establishment.

The new deputy chief, Mr. H. Z., himself quite a young man with very little life experience, but possessing much youthful courage and energy, only recently having completed officers' school, widely and energetically applied to the police force the knowledge that he had acquired there—although often overdoing it—and one must admit not without success. He certainly had his shortcomings, being somewhat too young, too hotheaded and hasty in decision making; he did not have the influence that he could have had, had he been more solid and deliberate. On the other hand, he ruled with a firm hand, which the police needed, and gave to the internal work a different spirit and direction, narrowed and militarized it, and brought about more discipline and order.

Slowly everything began to be reformed and to achieve a different appearance. For the sake of objectivity, it must be emphasized that working conditions were now much better than they had been before the Great Action. It was possible to get things done. It is quite possible that the prior management, had it had the same working conditions, would also have been able to institute the needed reforms and to implement them in practice. Be that as it may, the new management can take credit for reforming and reorganizing the entire police apparatus.

The chief's office—which was now called the "police-central" or "central" [headquarters] for short—was the first to be reformed. A genuinely government-style administrative office was set up and moved to new quarters. The new chief of the administrative office, Mr. A. Sh., who had extensive experience as a government functionary—a typical bureaucrat—set up the work of the administrative office in an orderly manner. In the new quarters, which consisted of three rooms, one room was arranged for the management, one for the administrative office, and one for investigation personnel.

In the month of December, the new management carried out a staff reduction. Basically, it was not so much a reduction as an exchange of people. The older, physically weaker were let go, and later, in January, an entirely new group of younger and more energetic men were brought in. It was, so to speak, a rejuvenation of the apparatus.

The overall numerical picture of the size of the police force changed many times; it shifted up and down, parallel to the general situation in the ghetto. In addition, the food supply problem also played a role in the numerical stability. Many, mostly those with large families, relinquished their police service in favor of finding a brigade in the city, in order to be able to secure a source of existence. A few left during the first few months following the creation of the police because they thought that working in the city was more secure than being on the police force.

It would be interesting to provide some statistics of the numerical size of the police force, its ups and downs, because these reflect the entire life of the ghetto, its conditions and moods in the corresponding time periods.

As previously noted, the Jewish ghetto police was created on August 15 [1941]. On August 18 there were 120 police officers. This was too small a number of policemen for a population of about 30,000 people. The police also had to carry out urgent, special ghetto activities, as, for example, the moving in and moving out of people by a permanent group of policemen in the Housing Office. In addition, the Labor Office required 15 to 20 men every day to help provide people in response to various demands from the authorities. The 120 number, which had been approved by the Elder Council, proved to be too small. On August 25, the police requested the Elder Council to approve an additional 24 men.

On August 27, the Food Supply Office requested the police to place 14 police guards near the vegetable gardens. The management therefore asked the Elder Council to approve an increase of an additional 28 men (two shifts

217

of 14 men). The Elder Council approved this. And so, by September 1, altogether there were 172 men on the police force.

In the beginning of September, in connection with the gold action and the house searches, there were not enough men to carry out the work. At that time policemen were taken in without regard to the budget, so that the number jumped to 270 men, not counting the 17 men in the address bureau created by the police.

Quite a few left the police during the month of September. There were a number of reasons for this; first, the episode of the Jordan certificates. There was disillusionment with the security provided by the police force to its members. In addition, the material situation played a large role—working in a brigade provided the opportunity to acquire something to eat. There was a flight from the police. There were instances when the precinct chief did not himself know who was still in his service and who had left. On September 20, headquarters circulated an inquiry in the precincts as to how many officers were in fact still in their service. Two hundred thirty-five men factually remained in the police by the end of September (excluding the address bureau, which we always consider separately, because later, after the reforms, they were "picked off" the police and established as a special office of the administration, called "Residents' Certification Office"). About 15 men either were released or left on their own during the month of October. Thus, around 220 men remained (excluding the 17 of the address bureau). This number included:

> Chiefs—15 men (1 police chief, 1 assistant, 3 instructors, 1 reserve,
>   1 assistant, 4 precinct chiefs, 4 assistants).
> Guard commanders—13 men.
> Administrative employees—12 men (administrative office,
>   medical personnel, investigators).

Until November 30, the numerical picture of the police was as follows:

Policemen in active service, including management	182
Administration: investigators	4
Administrative office (1 woman)	12
Medical personnel	3
Address bureau (6 women)	17
Total	218 men

At that time, couriers were also taken in by the police, the so-called *Eilboten* [German: messengers], as well as some others outside the budget.

Couriers	3
Cleaning women	3
Craftsmen (barbers)	2
Total	226 men

The picture on November 30 was somewhat different. During the month of November, 8 men were released from active service (some were taken back somewhat later), as well as 5 bread-card investigators. Thus, only one investigator remained on the police force.

In the month of December, in connection with the reforms and reduction, 29 men were released from the police, consisting of the following:

Investigator	1
Employees of the administration (employees of the Housing Office having police privileges)	2
Address bureau	4
Active service policemen	22
Total	29 men

During the month of the reforms, the criminal division was also created. On the one hand, the size of the police was reduced, but on the other hand, it increased in numbers with the creation of a new office. To some degree there was an attempt to partially cover the budget of the criminal division with those previously let go. For example, four who were removed because of budget reductions in the address bureau were taken into active police service. Of those four, three were assigned to the criminal division and one to the police store.

External reforms were made at the same time. Ranks were introduced and the position of duty-officer was established, previously known as *Budintis Viršininkas* [Lithuanian title]; that is, every day a different precinct chief, or his assistant, was designated to be on duty in the police; he had to be available for a full day and night, to oversee all police organs, to be the "eyes" of the police for twenty-four hours.

(The ranking and duty-officer position had already been established earlier, but not in a very businesslike fashion. These were later introduced in an orderly and systematic manner, providing a better and more efficient appearance.)

The newly established criminal division consisted of 17 men according to the following table:

Chief and assistant	2 men
Secretary and assistant	2 men
Manager of the investigation division	1 man
Investigators	3 men
Information personnel	2 men
Supervisor of the arrested	1 man
Guard commanders	2 men
Policemen	4 men
Total	17 men

As noted, Mr. B. [Bramson], the former deputy chief of police, was appointed chief of the criminal division; as his deputy, the chief of the disbanded reserve, Mr. P.—two men from the previous management. The former secretary of the fourth precinct, an attorney, was appointed manager of the investigations division. One investigator came from the address bureau, two were new people. The information personnel and commanders of the guard came from the active police service.

The numerical tabulation for December 1941, that is, as of January 1, 1942, was as follows:

In active police service, including management	58 men
Investigators, information personnel, and prosecutors	10 men
Administration	12 men
Medical personnel (doctor, dentist, and nurse)	3 men
Address bureau	9 men
Total	192 men
Couriers	6 men
Cleaning women (4 in the precincts, 1 in headquarters, 2 in the criminal division)	6 men [*sic*]
Craftsmen	4 men
	208 men

The table shows that the numerical size changed in various ways—on the one hand there were reductions, on the other hand, a criminal division was added; thus, relatively, the overall size was not significantly reduced. However, the number of assignments to be carried out increased; the workload became more diversified.

The December reduction, initially seen as a reduction due to the reduced size of the population after the Great Action—a smaller police force therefore now being needed—later became not a reduction but an exchange. Those somewhat less suitable were removed, but after only a short while, with the growth of the number of assignments, the available number of people was consistently inadequate for the work. And so, as previously noted, new people were added in January. Eight new policemen were taken into active service in the course of the month of December, an additional 13 men in January. The new recruits had to pass a special examination. A special commission was established in the month of January, consisting of two representatives of the police management and one of the Elder Council. Each applicant would appear before the commission so that, in addition to his personal data and recommendations, it could observe the personal impression made by the candidate.

On January 31, 1942, following the reductions of December and the additions of January, the numerical picture of the police was as follows:

In active police service, including management	170
Investigators, information personnel, prosecutors	9
Administrative office	14
Medical personnel (doctor, dentist, medic, and nurse)	4
Address bureau	9
Total	206
Couriers, cleaning women, and craftsmen	18
	224

This number is almost identical to that in the table of November 30, 1941. However, as noted, the total number is, in effect, reduced, when taking into consideration the addition of a new office in the police—the criminal division.

A small change took place in the administrative section, specifically, with the investigators. With the last two bread-card investigators having been let go, only two permanent investigators remained, located in headquarters. Their domain encompassed investigations of administrative infractions by the population and of service-related discipline violations by policemen.

Not only the internal, but also the external work procedures were established at that time. Things began to work almost as in a normally functioning state apparatus. Everything—the entire service establishment, the relationship to the population, all the rights and duties, all were made pursuant to the same underlying basis. The basis of all police work was the statute, the law of internal order. This statute was made public on December __, 1941. It encompasses the entire internal operation of the police, setting forth the rights and tasks of all functionaries in the course of fulfilling their duties.

The statute consisted of sixty-three paragraphs, arranged as follows:

1. General rules
2. The police employees
3. The police organs

Item 3 includes subsections: A. headquarters office, B. police chief and his assistant, C. duty-officer of the police, D. police inspector and special case officer, E. police prosecutor and investigator, and F. precincts.

4. Punishment rules
5. The police and the population

The first category, "General rules," consists of four paragraphs, which set forth the following:

> The police is organized on the principle of discipline, the highest disciplinary and punishment authority being that of the chief of police.
> Members of the police, as disciplined residents of the ghetto aware of their status, see to it that the population complies with all the decrees, themselves being a model for everyone else.
> Members of the police faithfully carry out the orders of their direct superiors.
> If a policemen commits an offense, he is to be punished by his immediate or higher superior in accordance with the penal regulations of the Jewish ghetto police, provided the general laws do not require more severe punishment.

Category 2, "The police employees," contains five paragraphs setting forth employee ranking in accordance with the following order, from the bottom up:

1. Policemen
2. Commander of the guard
3. Assistant precinct chief
4. Precinct chief
5. Special case officer
6. Police inspector
7. Deputy chief of police
8. Chief of police

The rank of administrative police employees can be equated to those in active service in the following manner:

1. Administrative office chief—to a precinct chief
2. Police prosecutor—to a precinct chief
3. Investigator—to an assistant precinct chief
4. Chief of the jail—to an assistant precinct chief
5. Administrative officer (secretary)—to an assistant precinct chief
6. Precinct secretary—to a guard commander

Category 3

A. Headquarters Office
Headquarters manages and oversees the activities of all the police organs. It is directed by the chief of police and his assistant, who have complete authority over the ghetto police. They are responsible to the Elder Council and to the state organs for the activities of the police and are obligated to report to the chairman of the Elder Council the work done by the police in the entire ghetto area.

Headquarters consists of the following organs:

1. The headquarters administrative office
2. Three police precincts
3. Criminal division
4. Resident information office
5. Ghetto jail

The central administrative office corresponds with the Elder Council and its divisions, with the police divisions and with the authorities. The central administrative office is directed by its chief.

The organs of categories 3, 4, and 5 carry out their work in accordance with special internal instructions.

B. The police chief and his assistant
The police chief and his assistant, in order to carry out the tasks entrusted to them, must:

Monitor and control the work of all divisions;

decide on matters brought to them by the chiefs of the precincts or on requests and complaints from the population;

seek approval from the Elder Council of newly engaged policemen or of the discharge of police employees;

promote or demote police employees (except for the deputy chief of police);

issue daily orders concerning duty assignments and the maintenance of order within the borders of the ghetto;

punish police employees for disciplinary violations;

cooperate and maintain contact with the special commission (ghetto control and investigative commission of the Elder Council).

C. Duty-officer of the police

For the purpose of overall oversight over the entire ghetto, a duty-officer of the police and his assistant are appointed each day.

The duty-officer is appointed from among the higher police officials, starting with the assistant of the precinct chief.

The duty-officer reports directly to the chief of police.

All police organs must obey and assist the duty-officer.

The tasks of the duty-officer are:

To tend to order in the entire ghetto area; to follow up on all events in the ghetto, and to check on those on duty in all the precincts, on the assigned posts, and on the guards in the jail.

In case of an emergency, he has the right to alert the entire police force, but must immediately inform the chief of police of his action.

He must report to the chief of police upon taking on and when completing his tour of duty.

D. The police inspector and special case officer

The tasks of the police inspector are to inspect and check on the activities of the police organs, and to monitor policemen discipline, behavior, and appearance. The special case officer carries out various assignments of the chief of police.

The position of police inspector was created later—when the new management came into being. The inspector belonged to the management, all three making up the triumvirate—chief of police, assistant, inspector.

The special case officer had to deal with special housekeeping matters and to carry out various assignments concerning internal police matters of discipline and order. Mr. L. was the first special case officer, who had to carry out the above assignments.

Later, after the reforms, two additional special case officers were added. They were: the former inspector K. G. and P., the former assistant chief of the criminal division. The first had the assignment of paving the streets, the second was given the task by the Elder Council of organizing the guarding of the vegetable gardens by the police and, in the fall, of guarding the ghetto firewood stores.

E. Police prosecutor and investigator

The police prosecutor is assigned the duties of prosecution in the ghetto court. The chief of police is the direct superior of the prosecutor.

The prosecutor reviews all cases brought to his attention from the precincts and the criminal division, prepares the charges, and delivers them to the court.

He has the right to control all investigative organs.

F. Precincts

Policemen are assigned to carry out their duties in two shifts. Attention must be paid to the proportional allocation of the heavy work (assignments) among the policemen.

All policemen must, in accordance with Form No. 1, be familiarized with the duty-assignment sheets a day in advance.

A duty-roster is to be established in the precincts, in which the names of all employees of the precinct are to be entered every day. The policemen must register in the duty-roster upon arrival for service and sign out when leaving. The duty-roster is to be administered in accordance with Form No. 2.

The list of all permanent guard locations and posts, in accordance with Form No. 3, is to be posted on the bulletin board. Daily reports are to be sent from the precincts to headquarters every day. The daily report is to be composed in accordance with Form No. 4.

The remaining clauses define the duties of the precinct chief, his assistant, of the commander of the guard, of the duty-officer, and their authority.

4. Penal Regulations

For the work of the police to be carried out promptly, police activity must be built on the principle of discipline. Anyone violating established discipline rules must be punished.

Those of senior rank, who penalize the policemen, must rely not on any kind of sentiments, but on objectivity; they must thoroughly research the matter and only then penalize the offender.

Penalties consist of:

Warning
Reprimand
Extra service
Service reprimand
Arrest
Demotion

All of these penalties are applied by the chiefs of the precincts and their assistants, by the police inspector and the chief of police. Only rarely should the full penalty be imposed. In addition, a procedure is provided for the policemen to appeal to the chief of police regarding the penalty imposed by his direct superior.

5. The Police and the Population:

Members of the police must treat residents courteously, strictly, and justly. Only in rare cases do the police have the right to use physical force against undisciplined and disobeying citizens.

For every event or crime, an appropriate report must be prepared by the policemen on the spot, according to established forms. The report is submitted to the immediate superior, that is, to the precinct chief, who reviews the matter and imposes a penalty within the bounds of his authority, or transmits it, with his remarks, to the chief of police. The police chief considers the entire case and makes the appropriate penalty decision. A copy of the penalty decision is given to the one to be punished, together with instructions as to where and to whom he can appeal the decision of the chief of police (if such an option exists at all in the case).

Residents are penalized for disturbing the public peace, for creating commotion and not obeying rightful demands of the police. The precinct chief has the right to impose monetary penalties of up to 50 rubles and arrest of up to three days. The police inspector—up to 100 rubles and arrest of up to five days. The chief of police—up to seven days. The decision of the chief of police can be appealed to the chairman of the Elder Council via the chief of police, in accordance with paragraph 18 of the police statute.

This, in broad strokes, is the police statute on the basis of which all the work of the police was established and carried out.

To the extent that life itself and its normalized conditions dictated, a consolidation also began in all the other offices. But elsewhere the form and manner of the work were not fixed or set; it was done "Jewishly"—without statutes and paragraphs. In the police force, things were quite different. The internal work was set up in accordance with a specified order, by statute, precisely defining everyone's rights and duties; everyone had to know his assignment and the limits of his authority.

Characteristically, the work of the police was conducted in Lithuanian. The orders, reports, accounts, protocols—all paper work, official communications among officials, everything was in Lithuanian (until February 1, 1943, when everything was changed to Yiddish). This was not because policemen loved the Lithuanian language so much; the opposite: the hatred of the Lithuanians, who carried out such unprecedented, horrible massacres of the Jews, was very great. They, as well as their language, were hated to death. But there was a different, deeper psychological meaning here.

From military service, from the schools and universities, the entire youth population was familiar with the Lithuanian language. One was psychologically used to a command—an order to be carried out—being heard in Lithuanian. It appeared that an order given in Yiddish was somehow out of place; it would not be obeyed and would not sound military.

From the beginning, the work of the administrative offices, that is, in the offices of headquarters and of the precincts, was set up in Lithuanian. The chief of the administrative office as well as the secretaries and people in the precincts who had previously been officials or attorneys and conducted all their work in Lithuanian, knew its routines, were experienced in its use, familiar with its terminology, knew in their heads all the texts of a variety of forms, and were able to deal with the language concisely and practically. All in all, it came about, in any event, that all work was conducted in Lithuanian. But, psychologically, this led to a gentile approach to everything, that is, not to debate, not to ask questions, not to argue, but to do what one was told. The ordinary policeman had respect and obeyed the commander of the guard, the precinct chief, and all together they maintained an appropriate distance from the management—which was feared and obeyed. A certain military discipline prevailed everywhere—an order that was given, must be punctually carried out.

The order of October 28, 1941, established the ranking of police officials. The same order-of-the-day listed all the ranks and depicts their insignia.

A guard commander had on his hat a blue leather circle with one horizontal silver stripe; an assistant precinct chief—two silver stripes; a precinct chief—three silver stripes; police inspector—a blue leather [circle] with one horizontal gold stripe; deputy chief of police—two horizontal stripes; the chief of police—three.

These insignia were instituted by the order of October 28 only up to the rank of precinct chief. Later, with the entry of the new management, the insignia of the police inspector was designated as a blue leather circle with an empty silver diamond; the deputy chief of police—a full silver diamond; the chief of police—a gold diamond.

Ordinary policemen had only a number on their hats—a leather form in the shape of the Star of David with the number written in it. At first the numbers of the policemen were assigned in the order in which each one was taken into the police force. Later, the numbers were assigned in the precincts. Policemen of the first precinct were given beginning numbers, those of the second, the following numbers, and so on. Commanders of the guard in active service, of whom there were about twenty in number, had the numbers from 1 to 20, with their rank below the number. Those not in active service, such as chief of administrative office, investigator, precinct secretary, doctor, housekeeping manager, and so on, who had the rights of the rank of commander of the guard, of assistant to and of precinct chiefs, had on their hat a leather star of David with the [Yiddish] inscription *Y.G.P* [abbreviation of *Ydische Ghetto Polizei*—Jewish Ghetto Police]. Precinct chiefs and their assistants in active service, as well as management, had the same leather form on their hats with the *Y.G.P* inscription and their rank marked below the Star of David.

The level of discipline was heightened during the time of the new management; there were objective as well as subjective reasons for this.

The preceding few months were terribly anxious; day and night, one was subject to the effect of actions and terror. In addition, during the last month, the deputy chief Mr. B. [Bramson], sensing that his position was shaky, eased off. All of this affected the discipline of the staff. The new management viewed things quite differently. From the first day, it paid attention to outward appearance and to discipline. It was particularly strict in seeing to it that policemen made a good external impression, that they carried out their duties without questioning, that they were—to some degree—soldiers.

The new management was, perhaps, not loved, because it made too much of external effects, smelled somewhat of snobbery, which, in the ghetto circumstances was entirely inappropriate. While this may indeed have been true, it must be emphasized that the new management introduced more order—one was afraid of being penalized, and obeyed.

Outwardly everything also began to be better organized. As noted, headquarters moved to a new facility that had been renovated. The management office could be entered only with prior announcement. The precincts were also renovated—there was some prettifying, cleaning up, so that headquarters and the precincts began to look like state institutions.

In a certain sense, the administrative office of headquarters served as a model for all ghetto institutions. Every item, every piece of paper had its place, its location—nothing was lost, everything was registered and kept in order. Every resident who submitted a request or a complaint received an answer—a positive or simple one—but nothing was misplaced. Everything was attended and responded to. If a resident was to be penalized, he was informed of the reason for it and the relevant statute paragraph and, at the same time, where and in what manner he could appeal the penalty. Four men carried out the technical work in the headquarters administrative office: one chief of the office, two secretaries, and one typist; these were the technical workers who performed the strictly office functions. In practice, a whole array of additional employees not in active service also belonged to this number; they did not belong to any of the precincts but were at the direct disposal of the chief of police, that is, in headquarters.

Including personnel of the administrative office, headquarters maintained a small unit of its own:

Office personnel	4 men
Housekeeping manager	1 man
Prosecutor	1 man
Investigators	2 men
Medical personnel	3 men
Police store	5 men
Office couriers	2 men
Telephone operators	3 men
Total	21 men

On January 26, 1942, based on the permission granted by the regional commissariat, telephone service was installed in the ghetto for internal use. It was a great achievement, to have been allowed to do something that actually made life easier. All previous decrees only aimed to make life more difficult. Earlier, there were special messengers who would run from the gate to the precincts, as needed. Now, if the number of people required for the labor quota was inadequate, it was no longer necessary to send off people, as telephone contact could be made and everything taken care of.

Actually, permission to install telephones was given not for our benefit but in their own interests. The [German] ghetto guard was inside the ghetto and they had to have a telephone. Be that as it may, we benefited because of them, as telephones were installed in all the police units and all the important offices of the ghetto institutions. Later, telephone utilization grew so much that installations were made in almost all offices as well as in the private homes of the leading personalities of the ghetto.

All the technical work of telephone installation was carried out by three police telephone technicians who had had work experience in this field during the good years. The telephone center was set up in the police headquarters, in a special room. The three telephone operators served it at all times. These three men were a part of headquarters, not of any other unit.

A separate room was arranged for the investigators. Their task consisted of investigating residents concerning various complaints of one against the other, as well as investigating charges against policemen in service-related matters.

If a report (or complaint) was received from any unit against a policemen concerning a disciplinary infraction, the investigator called the affected policeman to come to headquarters, interrogated him, and provided the material, with his comments, to the chief of police for penalty determination or for annulment of the matter.

Complaints and claims of one resident against another in civil or criminal cases would be forwarded to headquarters from the precinct in which they originated. (With the creation of the criminal division, this became superfluous; that is, headquarters was relieved of court matters, which from then on were processed through the criminal office. All complaints of residents concerning criminal matters would go directly to the criminal division, which would, after an appropriate investigation, send all the indictment documentation to the court.)

Headquarters also had a treasury. The police had all kinds of expenses, and money was needed to cover them. This was also set up in an official manner. The "cabinet of ministers," in this case the Elder Council, gave the police money in the form of advances against an accounting system; that is, headquarters had to provide from time to time a detailed accounting as to how much and where the received amounts were dispensed. The police force contributed to the income of the Elder Council by virtue of its various fines and penalties, which were delivered to the treasury, and, naturally, also benefited from these funds for its own needs. A veritable government style: contribution to income combined with expenses according to an accounting system; a regular state, almost like in the Land of Israel . . . what can one say . . .

As noted, on December 5, 1941, a new office was created in the Jewish ghetto police, at the same time as the new management—the criminal division. The criminal division was created, first of all, because along with the development and normalization of ghetto life, the number of instances of thefts and break-ins kept increasing. Jews learned to do this work as well as the gentiles. "Vee es kristlt zikh, azoy yidlt zikh" [As the Christians do, so do the Jews]. Aside from this, the creators of the criminal division had several other incentives for bringing about its establishment. First of all, as already noted, there were many nonkosher people in the various offices. There were instances of abuses and thefts without the ability to expose the guilty ones, cases of corruption and similar offenses committed by these "trustee-thieves." An office was therefore needed to deal with this entire gang, to quietly check on their activities, to investigate their source of income and find out from what and from whom they made their living.

The creators of the criminal division set for themselves an additional task—a unique one, specially appropriate for the conditions in which we live. The ghetto leadership was aware that there were among us in the ghetto Jews who served the G. [Gestapo]; regrettably an ugly and sad phenomenon, but a fact. These Jews informed the G. about everything that took place in the ghetto, maintained contact with them, went there quite often, and caused us a great deal of trouble.

The names of the Jews serving the G. were known, as well as where they worked and where they lived. The creators of the criminal division made it their task to keep an eye on them, to observe and follow where they went, with whom they were meeting, what they were saying—to accurately know everything about them, every step that they were taking, what they were doing, in order to be able to intervene in due course and, as much as possible, to constrain their activities.

The criminal division did not fulfill its assignment of keeping an eye on the activities of officials of the ghetto institutions. Only a few instances can be noted of their uncovering unscrupulous officials—more plainly said, ordinary thieves, as, for example, a few employees of the warehouse for the belongings of those taken away, who were caught stealing. The criminal division discovered this and they received their punishment. In other instances, when the criminal division wanted to pursue an investigation of a particular official, a button would be pressed from high up that such an investigation should be stopped, because it was not appropriate and was not needed. The criminal division had to abandon the matter for "technical reasons."

However, for the sake of objectivity, it must be emphasized that, judging from their conduct, few officials of the criminal division were qualified to carry out such investigations. Be that as it may, they did not accomplish anything in this area.

Very little was accomplished in the area of watching over the people serving in the G. [Gestapo]. The names of the informers were known, as were their workplaces, and that was the end of it. Because of fear, this activity was not expanded. And so, in practice, the criminal division was limited to being an organization for fighting criminals, and, as such, it remains to this day. In this field the criminal division accomplished a great deal. Hundreds of thefts were uncovered, the stolen properties returned to their owners, and the criminals punished. Here the internal work was also set up with a system and order. Every investigation involving a resident had its file and number; each individual case was investigated in detail, with witnesses and confrontations. Officials of the criminal division would search the exact place where the theft or break-in occurred, make detailed inquiries, question all the neighbors—much as it is done in proper societies.

Over time, the criminal division had its steady "clients," whose identities and hiding places—*malines*—were well known. In case of a large theft, some of the gang, who in many instances had a part in this or that "piece of work," would be taken into custody. The gangs of thieves feared the criminal division because they knew that they would be treated there unceremoniously—pressed against the wall, given a good beating, so that, willingly or not, they had to confess.

The criminal division is a separate unit that, like the precincts, is subordinated to headquarters, but with the difference that while the precinct operates in a limited territory, the criminal division carries out its work over the entire ghetto area, though in a restricted field of activity. The chief of the criminal division is a rank higher than the precinct chief and has the rights of a police inspector.

The administrative office of the criminal division was set up much the same as in the precincts. Every day a report is sent to headquarters detailing its work and listing the thefts or other crimes that occurred the previous day. Later, the reporting system expanded, with the criminal division submitting detailed statistics on a monthly basis, itemizing the number of crimes, how many were uncovered, how many investigations were concluded, how many were in progress, and what were the results. All events and occurrences were noted in detail, classified, and assigned their appropriate place in the police archives.

The jail was also established in the ghetto at the same time. Something new in the ghetto: Jews—prisoners—one arresting the other; a jail within a jail.

Establishment of the jail was a necessity. With the existence of the threat of the jail, many troubles were avoided—whether associated with crimes, administrative matters, or the labor quotas.

The question of punishment for avoiding work was pertinent from the very beginning. The work rapid-response court, and later the mobilization division, would penalize the malingerers with internment or monetary fines. Some people would pay the fines; those unable to pay had to fulfill their punishment by internment. Absence of a jail interfered with the work and undermined the general discipline. Without the availability of an effective sanction, appeals and warnings were not effective. The authority of the Elder Council, of the police, and of the Labor Office suffered from the absence of sanctions against those who did not obey. The authority of the official institutions grew with the creation of the jail. The fear of landing in jail, or, as we referred to it by its Lithuanian name *daboklė*, led to a more prompt fulfillment of work responsibilities by many people. In general, a means became available with which to penalize people in cases of malingering, for crimes and other infractions.

The jail was set up in the courtyard of the refuge, in a block that became vacant after the Great Action. The administration of the jail consisted of six men: a chief, one secretary, one commander of the guard, and three guards.

Internal operations of the jail were conducted in accordance with statutes and instructions approved by the chief of police. It will be of interest to briefly note the main points of the internal procedures of the jail, established according to Instruction No. 1, as well as of the "Rules of the Internal Procedures of the Ghetto Jail," issued on January 23, 1942 (both based on police statutes), and approved by the chief of police on December 18, 1942.

Instruction No. 1 consists of thirteen paragraphs which set forth that:

All those arrested and put into the jail must be registered in a special ledger.

All belongings, except for clothing, are to be taken from the prisoner and remain in the custody of the jail administration until the release of the prisoner. This must be noted in the registration ledger.

Prisoners must be examined by a physician to determine whether they are ill with any kind of infectious disease.

Men and women are to be held separately. Administrative offenders are to be held separately from criminal offenders.

The prisoners must work eight hours a day. They are to get up at five o'clock in the morning and go to sleep at eight o'clock in the evening.

Prisoners are fed by the jail kitchen. Food products are obtained from the food distribution center, based on their own food ration cards.

Prisoners who work receive an extra 100 grams of bread a day; three times a day prisoners are given hot beverages.

Those who do not go to work because of illness or for other justifiable reasons are permitted to walk thirty minutes every day.

Those whose trial has already been concluded are allowed to meet with their kin once a week for fifteen minutes in the presence of a jail official.

Those still under investigation are allowed to meet with relatives only with the concurrence of the official or office having custody over them (chief of police, prosecutor, or the criminal division).

All prisoners must maintain cleanliness in the jail.

Those transgressing one of the clauses of the instruction, or interfering with the general discipline and order in the jail, are penalized by:
a) denial of walk privilege
b) reduction of food allowance
c) cancellation of visitation right
d) lock up

Prisoners have the right to submit to the chief of the jail complaints concerning unjust treatment by jail officials.

Rules of internal procedures, consisting of fifteen paragraphs, set forth the work day of the prisoner: when he must get up, wash, eat breakfast, go to work, eat lunch, return to work, eat dinner; when floors were to be washed, bedding aired, baths taken, and so on. Those were all rules and instructions to serve as the basis for maintaining internal order in the jail. At first, order was very weak, the entire jail was no more than a joke—it was somehow inconceivable that Jews would create a jail in the ghetto. Order was at first maintained as if "while standing on one foot." Somewhat later it was taken more seriously. The chief of the third precinct, Mr. G., was appointed temporary chief of the jail to systematically bring about order; slowly, it indeed came about that it became a real jail—a place where people were found who must fulfill a punishment; not a joke but a penal instrument, to be feared and avoided through appropriate behavior and by prompt fulfillment of work responsibilities.

Administratively, the jail was at first not considered a separate entity; rather, that it belonged to the second precinct because the building was located within its area. At first, the second precinct would provide two guards and a supervising commander to guard the prisoners, that is, as if the jail was a part of the second precinct. But there was also another factor in play here—the workshops set up by the Stadt Commissariat, which placed the jail at the center of police duties.

As previously noted, workshops were established in the ghetto that functioned exclusively for the Germans. According to their order of the day, policemen had to guard the workshops day and night. The jail was located in the same courtyard as the workshops, and both places had to be under guard day and night. For this reason, everything was combined, and the chief of the jail simultaneously also became commander of the policemen on duty in the workshops. A larger number of policemen was needed to provide for continuous, twenty-four-hour guard service, organized in shifts, with defined times of guard duty and rest. The second precinct, with its limited number of men, was unable to provide people every day to guard the jail as well as the workshops. As of November 21, five men from a precinct—from a different one every day—would have guard duty at the jail and the workshops. Every day the police order of the day would specify which precinct was to provide guards for the workshops on that day. A different commander was appointed for these guards each day.

On December 5, Mr. B., commander of the guards in the second precinct, was appointed temporary chief of the jail. He was also assigned an assistant, who also served as secretary, and two policemen as foremen. (December 5 is the official date of the creation of the jail because this is when it was formally announced in the order of the day and its chief appointed. Actually, the jail had already existed for two weeks, operating as previously described.)

The temporary chief, Mr. B., began to set up the internal procedures of the jail. But it became apparent after a short while that he was not suitable for this position, not knowing how to establish and maintain order. Guards were not at their posts; in the jail—neglect and filth; everyone did as he pleased and B. was unable to control it. As noted, headquarters assigned the chief of the third precinct, Mr. G. [Joshua Greenberg], to bring order to the work.

On January 24 it was arranged for each precinct to send two men every day, the group of six making up the guard unit. Later on, when the workshops were enlarged and expanded and more policemen were needed, each precinct sent five men each day; that is, a unit of fifteen men was assembled every day from all three precincts. These fifteen men were divided into shifts, standing guard for two hours and resting four hours throughout the twenty-four-hour period, until the relief shift arrived from the precincts. The chief of the jail had a permanent staff of six men; [an additional] fifteen men were at his disposal every day.

On January 28, B. was released and the commander of the guards of the second precinct, Mr. M., was appointed chief of the jail.

(The task of the temporary chief Mr. G. [Joshua Greenberg] was only to establish order. He developed the jail statute, introduced discipline, arranged duty assignments, worked out the documentation of the prisoners and of the functionaries—he properly carried out the task entrusted to him. Afterwards, he returned to his specific duties as chief of the third precinct.)

It was announced in the order of the day of December 30 that the jail was being detached as a separate unit and, like the other three precincts, would report directly to headquarters.

As a separate unit, the jail—just like the precincts—functioned in accordance with established procedures, reported its daily activities to headquarters, the number of prisoners that day, how many were brought in during the twenty-four-hour period and for what reason, how many were released and on what basis—everything was set up according to procedures especially worked out for it. It functioned on the basis of an established program and order.

A variety of offenses could land one in jail. Many of these, as, for example, criminal offenses, theft, fraud and administrative infractions, disturbing the public peace, fighting, and so on, are daily occurrences in normal states and are everywhere subject to punishment. But in the ghetto conditions many things were different. Ghetto inhabitants were charged with specific offenses that, under normal circumstances, would not be considered offenses, or would not have happened at all. In the ghetto it was different. There were unique laws in our unprecedented way of life, and punishments were meted out for violating these particular laws.

Administrative offenses were committed by citizens out of dire need, desperation, and indifference. In many instances the police would take into consideration the circumstances and the person committing the offense and look the other way. But in most cases it was necessary to intervene, to punish as required by law, in order that behavior that caused chaos and disturbed the internal order should not happen again.

There were many causes for the punishment of citizens. Every month, every week, and, sometimes, even every day, a variety of decrees were issued by the authorities, the Elder Council, and the police during the panic times.

It would not be uninteresting to provide a short tabulation of the number penalized for administrative offenses from the beginning of the ghetto, that is from August 15, 1941, up to the beginning of the second time period, that is up to and including February 1942.

Penalized in August 1941:

For insulting police and administration officials	2 persons
For avoiding work duties	3 persons
For digging up potatoes	1 person
Total	6 persons

Many more were, of course, charged, but during this half of the month everything was still in the process of formation so that it was not possible to follow up all those charged—the police force was not as yet in full swing.

Penalized in September 1941:

For resisting the police	5 persons
For creating commotion and for fighting	3 persons
For destructive activity	2 persons
For beating policeman	1 person
For theft	1 person
Total	12 persons

This is already a different picture. The police intervened in brawls and fights, mostly because of the vegetable gardens. Like locusts, crowds of people would attack various gardens and dig them up. Everywhere the police had to intervene, often resulting in big fights and brawls, with the citizens often being punished.

Penalized in October 1941:

For resisting and insulting policemen	17 men
For making commotion and disturbing the peace	2 men
For breaking up a fence	1 man
For using police insignia	1 man
Total	21 men

There are many offenses in this month for resisting the police in conjunction with the prohibitions against tearing down fences and entering other people's vegetable gardens.

Penalized in November [1941]:

For insulting and resisting the police	16 persons
For avoiding work duties	2 persons
For making commotion and disturbing the peace	5 persons
For forging a document so as not to work	2 persons
For obtaining food products by fraud	5 persons
For willfully breaking into a dwelling	1 person
For not keeping sanitary regulations	80 persons
Total	111 persons

The picture in November is entirely different from the first three months; the start of normal activity is already noticeable in different areas.

As a top priority, the police began systematic roundups for work. As noted, one would go from house to house, dragging, appealing, and demanding that people fulfill the work obligation because the existence of the ghetto depended on it. Many managed to evade the obligation. Those who were not caught "were in luck"; those found in the house were punished. The will to evade work was so great that some went so far as to falsify documents concerning their age in order not to have to go to work.

The table for November shows that the police force applied itself quietly to its work. The major effort consisted of fulfilling the labor quota. But other areas also received attention—checking cleanliness in the courtyards also began. After an appropriate warning, residents of the yards were penalized for lack of cleanliness with monetary fines and, later, also with time in jail.

Penalized in December 1941:

For insulting and resisting the police	14 persons
For sanitary offenses	76 persons
For escape from jail	2 persons
Total	92 persons

In this month there was already a jail, where people were completing their punishments for a variety of offenses. Penalties generally became much more effective. For administrative infractions, such as cleanliness in the yard, if the citizen was unwilling or unable to pay the fine, he would be put in jail. There was more fear and, because of it, there was more obedience. In this month there was also the offense of escape from jail, a transgression for which one was specially punished.

The police force started to intervene everywhere, to have its say, to penalize, getting the citizenry used to the fact that a Jewish official—not just a gentile—must also be obeyed and his orders carried out; that maintaining public peace and order was in our own best interests.

Penalized in January 1942:

For insulting and resisting the police	18 persons
For making commotion and disturbing the peace	7 persons
For sanitary offenses	34 persons
For escape from jail	1 person
For blackout infractions	9 persons
For disobeying orders of the authorities by the German commandant	15 persons
For trading in the forbidden area	2 persons
Total	110 persons [sic]

Here can be seen the major role played by the new situation of the ghetto guard, the NSKK,[2] being inside the ghetto proper, rather than outside it, as before. Arrival of the ghetto guard inside the ghetto—which we will cover in more detail later—made its mark on the entire inner life of the ghetto. They, the Germans, were in every nook and cranny; every place was full of them. They would check to see whether Jews had properly sewn on the patches and instruct the police to check this and to punish for it. (Earlier the instruction was to wear yellow Stars of David made of cloth, but somewhat later they ordered them to be crocheted into the clothing out of yellow wool. A few months later they changed their mind and ordered us to wear the Stars of David made only out of yellow cloth.)

2. National Sozialistische Kraftfahrer Kompanie—National Socialist Motorized Company.

A number of times they caught Jews on the ghetto streets whose patches were either not properly sewn on or not well crocheted and beat them for it. In such instances the Jewish police had to intercept their route in order to check the streets and to punish those whose patches were not in order.

The Germans would also check on the blackouts of windows. If a blackout was inadequate, they would frequently shoot through the window. Luckily they mostly missed people, and one would get away with fear and damage.

The Jewish ghetto police started to pay strict attention to blackout requirements. Special announcements and warnings by the chief of police would alert the population to the dangers and warn of the likely consequences of inadequate blackouts. The police would go around in the evening to check the blackouts and punish with monetary fines and jail those citizens who did not follow the instructions and thereby endangered their own lives as well as those of people sharing their quarters.

The ones punished for "disobeying the orders of the authorities" were mostly those caught by the Germans trading or walking near the fence. It also included those found to have a "nonkosher" package during the inspection at the gate upon return from the city. The commandant would turn these people over to the Jewish police with associated instructions as to how many days or weeks the person was to be kept in jail.

Trading among people was another "sin." Street trading had developed even though trading was basically forbidden. When trading was done in side streets, the police looked the other way. The police and Elder Council let it be known that only in the vicinity of the Elder Council and other main streets, where Germans and Lithuanians were frequently around, was trading strictly forbidden. But Jews did not obey, trading exactly where it was forbidden to do so, and the police, following Elder Council orders, penalized the offenders.

And so a variety of "sins" accumulated, unique to ghetto conditions. The police and the jail already had their regular "clients."

Penalized in February 1942:

For insulting and resisting the police	37 persons
For applying physical force against the police	1 person
For using police insignia	5 persons
For sanitary offenses	5 persons
For escaping from jail	4 persons
For going without patches	3 persons
For trading in the forbidden area	1 person
For disobeying orders of the authorities by the German commandant	34 persons
For disobeying compulsory registration requirements	114 persons
For tearing down a building	1 person
For disturbing the public peace	2 persons

207 persons

The month of February was marked by the roundup of 500 men from our ghetto for work in Riga. We called it the Riga action; we will dwell on it later in greater detail.

As always, the entire dirty job of rounding up the people and leading them to the jail fell on the shoulders of the police. It was obvious that no one would want to go voluntarily to an unknown place. The roundup therefore had to be done by force. There were many instances of resistance, beating, and disobedience, for which people were also punished.

In order not to end up among those being sent to Riga, many people copied police armbands and hats and wore them to the infamous Demokratu Square, where Jordan ordered everyone to assemble, and where the people were sorted. The police discovered this and the offenders were punished.

The largest number of penalties of this month was for failing to reregister. An order had been issued that all former residents of Vienozinskio must reregister, namely, that they must register their new address in the police precinct. The people who had been transferred from that area had scattered to various parts of the ghetto so that their location was not known. Reregistration was also needed for control of the bread rations, because many people would continue to obtain food products from distribution centers for people who were no longer in the ghetto. Everyone had to reregister by February 15. After this deadline, the police checked and penalized those who had not reregistered.

The police force was everywhere. It mixed into everything—reacting in every place and to every circumstance, intervening, bringing order, punishing, trying to impress upon the population that the police force must be obeyed and that it must be feared; that the police force was an authority factor to be reckoned with by the population because it had at its disposal effective punishments for those who disobeyed orders. On the other hand, even though the police force took forceful measures and applied strict punishments, it thereby avoided greater troubles that would result if Germans or Lithuanians were to intervene under the same circumstances.

The police developed into a large organization with a variety of divisions. The precincts, the criminal division, the jail—each with its duties—contributed to the wholeness of the entire police apparatus.

It was also no coincidence that the creation of the "triad"—the court, the criminal division, and the jail—occurred almost at the same time. With them the administrative apparatus was completed—a "state" behind bars.

People become used to every situation, particularly officials of the ghetto institutions and of the police who sit in the ghetto all day. One no longer sees the barbed wire and the armed soldier—the guard, in front of one's eyes. We actually think that we are like ordinary people. But only 10 meters from the fence we can readily see that we are just prisoners confined to jail, and for an unspecified duration at that. We do not know when the day of our liberation will come, for which we all yearn so much.

The feet of two men on a street in the Kovno ghetto. The man on the right stands beside baskets of bread. He is wearing sandals held together by strings. *United States Holocaust Memorial Museum, photographer George Kadish.*

View, after liberation, of the Ninth Fort, where an estimated 40,000 Jews were shot to death between the fall of 1941 and the spring of 1944.
United States Holocaust Memorial Museum, photographer George Kadish.

Ghetto hospital burned by the Nazis with doctors, nurses, patients, and resident orphans locked inside. "What Was Left of the Hospital," etching by Esther Lurie. *Beit Lohamei Haghetaot and Féderation Nationale des Déportés et Internés.*

A Jewish policeman helps a family carry its luggage to the assembly point for deportation from the Kovno ghetto. *United States Holocaust Memorial Museum, photographer George Kadish.*

A group of Jewish women return to the Kovno ghetto after a day of forced labor on the outside. They line up to be searched. *United States Holocaust Memorial Museum, photographer George Kadish.*

Deputy Police Chief Yehuda Zupovitz at his desk in the Kovno ghetto.
United States Holocaust Memorial Museum, photographer George Kadish.

Left to right, Chief of Police Moshe Levin and his two deputies Yehuda Zupovitz and Tankhum Arnshtam. *Beth Hatefutsoth, photographer George Kadish.*

Police orchestra. *Above,* Violinists. *United States Holocaust Memorial Museum. Below,* Michael Leo Hofmeekler conducting. *United States Holocaust Memorial Museum, both photos by George Kadish.*

Jewish police assembled in a courtyard before being taken to the Ninth Fort, where the leadership was tortured and killed March 27, 1944. *Beth Hatefutsoth, photographer George Kadish.*

The Ghetto Guard and the Jewish Police

7

The New Ghetto Guard (NSKK) Located inside the Ghetto

As previously mentioned, until now there had existed a ghetto guard near the ghetto fence but outside its borders. The sentries guarded the fence but did not enter the ghetto itself; it was an external patrol carried out by the German police unit—the 3rd Company of the 11th Police Reserve Battalion.

The new ghetto guard, the NSKK, which was to be stationed inside the ghetto, arrived on January 15. They made their first entry into the ghetto with violence and commotion, casting fear and terror over everyone with their behavior, rudeness, and brutality.

From the name of the unit, which smelled of National Socialism, one could not expect anything good. Their first move in the ghetto was to select for themselves a location in the center of the ghetto—an entire block-house at Stulginskio 20.

Levrentz, a soldier of the NSKK who was later to become known as a famous hooligan in the ghetto, showed up with a big truncheon and immediately ordered all the neighbors out of their premises, entered each dwelling one by one, "honored" a few Jews with his whip, and chased them like dogs out of their dwellings. Within one hour all the neighbors were out, each grabbing and running with his meager belongings. But not everything was allowed to be taken. As the guards went through the dwellings, if they found a good sofa, cupboard, or buffet, they ordered it to remain in place and took it for themselves.

After removing the neighbors, they immediately had to be provided with Jewish craftsmen to make repairs and women to clean and scrub. Within a few days, they moved in.

The arrival of the ghetto guard brought up various observations and caused many troubles. We basically did not know how our community was viewed by the Germans: Did they consider this a ghetto or a camp? As a ghetto we had the privilege of living together as families, that is, men and women together leading their own inner lives, with their own administrative organization, and so on. In a camp, by contrast, men and women are separate, children and old people are not there at all, and life is subject to a strict regimen. The latter we did not have, thank God. On the other hand, the Germans never informed us officially of our situation. We were never officially addressed in writing; they did not recognize us as any kind of concrete entity. The question therefore remained: Are we a camp, not a camp, a ghetto, not a ghetto?

Various rumors began to spread at that time. It was said that we were considered a camp and, as a result, families would probably be separated, husbands from wives. These rumors brought on a great deal of unease; one asked oneself what would happen to the small children, to the old, and to those simply not able to work. The arrival of the NSKK in the ghetto intensified the uneasy mood. Many concluded that it implied our being considered a camp, with the NSKK our camp guards. Others said the opposite, that in a camp the guards are never inside, only outside. Therefore, quite the opposite, the arrival of the guards inside the ghetto was a sign that we were considered a ghetto and the guards were the same as a posted police precinct.

Be that as it may, their very entry into the ghetto depressed everyone's spirits. Here, among ourselves inside the ghetto, we had seldom encountered their vicious faces. We did not see nor did we want to see any of them, content to live out our forced separate existence. Now we would see them all the time as they went to and from their posts.

Immediately the old order was renewed, requiring that all Jews meeting their people on the street must greet them by removing their hats. And so, as the hooligans with their rifles walk around the ghetto, Jews who pass by them must remove their hats for them.

Together with the NSKK, Lithuanians also came into the ghetto, the so-called Hilf-Polizei [auxiliary police] (the former Lithuanian police). Together with the Germans, they kept watch at the fences. For the Lithuanians, the swineherds, it was also required that hats be removed, which was even more painful.

At the beginning of the ghetto, guarding of the fences was done entirely by Lithuanians, the so-called partisans, almost all of whom had joined the Lithuanian partisan groups that were forming during the first days of the war, whose objective was to fight behind the lines of the Russians, who were retreating in panic. That was their official task. But their actual assignments were to slaughter Jews. They were the ones who dragged thousands of Jews from their homes and took them to the Seventh Fort, never to return from there.

Each one of the partisans had on his conscience—if he possessed such a thing—the lives of hundreds of Jews.

All along, the partisans who stood guard around the fences were from the 3rd Company (the former ghetto guard). The large majority of them were thorough hooligans, many with a criminal past—thieves, murderers, ordinary outcasts, and operators capable of doing anything in the world. That was the face of the partisans who guarded the ghetto.

The Germans sensed whom they were dealing with. They recognized the physiognomy of their helpers and, looking at the matter from their own point of view, did not trust them. They understood that the sentries at the fence were a type who were prepared to sell out their entire service for a whiskey, with whom anything could be arranged for money, who was himself capable of robbery and murder; to the Germans this was a completely untrustworthy type.

With the arrival of the NSKK, the watch around the fences was kept entirely by Germans. Lithuanians also came with them, but they were no longer partisans, only policemen, that is, policemen of the former Lithuanian police who were taken in selectively and were called auxiliary police. They were no less antisemites and hooligans than the partisans, yet conveyed the character of a regular police force that had been recruited in a somewhat orderly manner, and not a band of partisans hurriedly assembled during the time of confusion.

During the first days of their arrival in the ghetto, the Germans and Lithuanians showed their "good deeds." By January 13 there were already two victims. One, a Jew by the name of Gempl, was shot by the German sentry Schimkat [or Shimkat] at the gate, as he came from the city. The reason for this was that the Jew Gempl came with a wagon from the workshops in the city, the German asked him whether he had any food products and he replied that he didn't. The German searched and found some. He then ordered the Jew to run and shot him in the back.

The same day a woman, Dvora Everowitch, was shot by a Lithuanian policeman because she walked close to the fence.

Many Jews were beaten for not greeting [the guards]. It was not an infrequent occurrence for them to badger people at the slightest opportunity, to go into a Jewish house and beat people up for inadequate blackout. There was one case, on January 22, of a German sentry shooting through the window at Linkuvos 88 because it was insufficiently blacked out, severely wounding the Jew Zelik Altman, who died the next day from his wounds.

A pair of Lithuanians were walking through the ghetto on January 30. Coming from the opposite direction was the ghetto resident Dr. Gerber. He did not greet them properly. They stopped him and ordered him to go down on his knees and to remove his hat. He refused to so demean himself before these swineherds. One of the hooligans ordered him to run and shot at him. He immediately fell to the ground in a river of blood. While he was thus lying on the ground, one of the Lithuanians came over to him and asked: "Have you had enough, or would you like another bullet?" Dr. Gerber was taken to the hospital, where he died the following day.

These are all recorded cases. But who can recount the dozens, perhaps hundreds, of abuses to which we were subjected by them during the first days?

During the early time, one was afraid to go by the house where they were quartered, and not without good reason. There was the case of a Jew passing by their guardhouse and being called inside, ordered to dance and sing Jewish songs and "The Internationale," beaten with a truncheon so that he would dance better and sing louder. The battered Jew stood in the middle of the house, surrounded by a band of hooligans, having to dance while they roared with laughter, mocked and jeered him. To the extent possible, they were therefore avoided; it was better to go around another street so as not to pass by them, because failing to greet them to their liking meant fiery slaps in the face in the middle of the street, being kicked with their feet, and similar deeds, which were such frequent occurrences that they were no longer recorded.

The principal new item introduced by the NSKK, the great new game that they started in the ghetto, was the new procedure at the gate. Until then, brigades going into the city had been allowed to bring back as many food products as they wanted. The principal difficulty was in the basic procurement of the products; it was difficult to "make a package," but once the package was acquired, bringing it into the ghetto was not a problem. Sentries of the 3rd Company occasionally searched what was being brought in from the city, but, in general, one could bring in anything one desired. The NSKK introduced a new procedure: they started to check the Jews returning from the city and took away whatever they wanted. They established this procedure and it remains this way to this day, even as we write these lines (end of August 1943)—only the forms and variations changed, the control principle remaining the same.

Control at the gate is a chapter all by itself, soaked in sweat, tears, and also blood, a new series of murders and afflictions that were visited upon our heads in order to humiliate us physically and morally, to daunt and starve us.

To describe the scene of evening controls at the gate is not an easy matter; one must have personally experienced it to have a more accurate picture of what took place there every day. It is sometimes impossible to believe that human beings can be so corrupt and rotten, so brutal and so beastly—and on the other hand, that physical and moral human strength is capable of withstanding such things.

Three or four Germans are standing in a line with truncheons in hand, the sentry with his rifle, awaiting the arrival of the Jews from the city. When a brigade arrives, all are ordered to line up, individually, in one row, one behind the other, each having to advance in his turn toward the German who thoroughly scrutinizes the package. Beatings and curses are common during the inspection.

Initially, the Jews at the gate informed the outgoing brigades in the morning that, as of that day, nothing was to be brought in from the city because everything would be taken away at the gate. Not everyone knew this and, besides, our Jews cannot resist offers in the city to buy food products. Some brigades indeed returned empty-handed, but many came back loaded with packages.

Arriving at the gate, those carrying packages saw that things were not good, that everything was being taken away and that beatings were being given. That day everything was taken from everybody. The Jew works, takes risks, is covered with sweat acquiring the package and carrying it a distance of 4–5 kilometers [2.4–3 miles], brings it to the gate, and here it is taken away accompanied by a beating.

Some adjusted to the situation immediately. They threw the package that they had brought over the fence, which extended 100 meters before the gate. There, on the other side of the fence, many people had assembled—family members of those coming with the brigades, awaiting their return. Those returning on the other side of the fence threw the packages through the wire, the others picked them up and brought them home through side streets.

But throwing a package over the fence is hardly sensible; should someone notice it, it can easily result in death—shooting a Jew for such a thing is a small matter for them. The following day nothing was carried in—everyone returned empty-handed. Things remained that way for a few days. But one cannot live that way; without the ability to bring something in one is sentenced to death by starvation. With the rations, which became smaller and smaller (100 grams of bread were issued per person per day), one could not possibly survive. So the Jews came up with new strategies: since carrying packages was forbidden, they began to bring in things in their pockets—a half a kilo bread, a few hundred grams of fat, a little flour in a small bag inside the pocket.

As these "experiments" slowly succeeded, more and more was brought in. The Germans realized that the Jews were "smuggling" in food products, and they started to body-search each person, to see whether something was being hidden. They would indeed find hidden food products, take them away, and administer beatings.

So began the long history of control at the gate.

At first, it appeared to be a terrible, evil decree. How was one to survive? What will happen? But according to the popular saying, one only has to sleep with an affliction one night to become used to it. Fortunately, we are a nation that, through thousands of years of troubles and persecution, developed a remarkable ability to adapt; we can orient ourselves, endure and survive that which other nations could not bear. One became used to the situation, racked one's brains and sought out ways to bring the package into the ghetto.

The NSKK had a system of placing every day a different senior German of their unit as the supervisor at the gate. Checking was done by some Germans and a few Lithuanians, and every day they had a different supervisor over them. Within a week, the Jews sensed that a different one was assigned every day. Some of them took everything away, but there were among them a few who allowed packages to go through. While passing through the gate in the morning, one would inquire and establish who would be controlling the gate that evening, in order to be oriented as to what to do. If the dog Bara was to be there, nothing should be carried because he would take everything away; if it was the hooligans Levrentz or Hempler, things were also miserable, even though they sometimes allowed something to pass through, because they were dangerous sadists and hooligans—for the smallest matter they gave murderous beatings. There were a few better ones, as, for example, Yung, Dikart, and others who would allow small and sometimes larger packages to pass through.

A brigade is coming to the gate, hearts pounding with fear of the impending danger, each one wondering whether he will pass through in peace, wishing to be on the other side as quickly as possible. Everyone is ordered by the Germans to stand four or two in a row so that the searches could begin. Wanting to get over to the other side as quickly as possible, people start to push and shove. Immediately, a German or a Lithuanian, and, shortly thereafter one of our own policemen of the gate guard, steps up and starts beating with truncheons on heads and legs to make people line up properly.

The inspection begins—the Germans or Lithuanians searching the Jews in the line. While the three or four searchers are busy inspecting, the other Jews waiting their turn are looking for opportunities to sneak through. Frequently, one or the other succeeds in scraping by past the searchers, who are busy at the time with someone else, and in slinking past the barrier. But it also often happens that one of them notices it, the Jew is returned and, if he has any kind of a package, woe is to him—he gets a really large portion of a beating, in addition to having his package taken away from him, which he had endangered his life to acquire.

Slowly it developed that small amounts—a few kilos of potatoes, a kilo of bread, and such, were allowed to pass through. Somewhat larger quantities of potatoes or fat would be taken away.

Jews started to arrange hiding places, to conceal things on their own persons. These hiding places were given the name *malines;* to hide something was referred to as *farmalineven.* One tries hard to sneak in a little food for oneself and for the family, *farmalinevet* it on yourself—inside your coat lining, in the sleeves, in the trousers, or, for women, under the corsets; one sews a wide bag, buys flour and pours a little into it, wraps it around the stomach like a bandage; money and a newspaper go in the shoes. In some workplaces the Jews get soup for lunch and everyone brings with him a tin can, pouring the soup into it to bring it back with them, which was allowed, and concealing in it eggs and other things. One obtains a little sour cabbage, places butter or bacon at the bottom and covers it with a little cabbage and one is kosher. Jews thought up hundreds of schemes and ploys only to sneak in a little food. Eventually, the Germans, even with their dull minds, managed to figure out that the Jews were outsmarting them. They made the personal searches even more rigorous, inspecting from head to toe. It happened often that they would order a Jew to undress almost to the point of nakedness, or to remove the shoes, to take off the shirt. A bitter pity for the Jew if, upon making such a body search, they found something treif on him. Your heart could burst seeing the cruelty with which they threw themselves upon the Jew with their truncheons and rifle butts.

They searched women with roughness and brutality. If they suspected a woman of concealing something, she would be rudely and without shame searched by the hooligans. They intruded everywhere with their paws, ordering the woman to unbutton, prying and searching. And the Jewish daughters stood at the gate bearing these morally disgusting humiliations.

It happened frequently, when it was seen that the situation at the gate was not good, that carrying things or "swimming" was impossible that day (to swim through meant to sneak through the gate unnoticed by the controllers), that the forbidden packages would be given to the escort of the column—a German or Lithuanian soldier, who was well known and was often bribed, for him to take back to the workplace in the city, to be picked up the next day, so as to pass through the gate kosher, empty-handed.

Frequently, a higher-up [German] yaleh would come from the city and stand at the gate for a few hours to check to see how the control was proceeding, whether the students had learned their lessons well. It is bitter at the gate then—literally everything is taken away, whatever it may be. Those who are treif, who have forbidden packages, their fate is bitter, because, in addition to having everything taken away, they are beaten, slapped, and sometimes even taken to the G. [Gestapo]—for buying forbidden things and for illicit trading.

At such times one looks for any and all means to pass through the gate, most of which involve risking one's life. First, you throw the packages over the fence, then crawl through yourself. This "operation" carries the threat of death if someone should notice it. But one takes the risks, seeking all kinds of means: one sneaks away from one's place in the brigade, sneaking into the nearby courtyard of a Christian, waiting "for the fury to pass," maybe the higher-ups will have gone away and one will be able to pass through; others throw their packages into a nearby courtyard at the mercy of God and pass through with only their clothes on their backs. It also happens that people consume at the gate many of the food products that they have brought, distributing some to the others, who have nothing with them, for them to eat. It is better to stuff yourself as much as possible, than to let them have it.

Gambling with death from all directions, from every turn, with every move—every side step and combination smacks of death. To shoot a Jew for no reason is of no consequence for them—one is not punished for it in any case.

A new evil decree arrived one early morning—the NSKK started to search everyone before leaving for the city. They had, apparently, come to the conclusion that the Jews still had ways of buying food products, by taking along items to sell for money and buying food with the money, or by trading the items for food. They therefore started to inspect before departure; just about everyone was being searched. The first day, before this became known, they took away various items from many Jews. The next day, much less was being carried and, those who did carry things concealed them on their persons. Jews would put on two pairs of pants, one on top of the other, women—a number of dresses and three or four sets of underwear. But the Germans were not bashful and would make body searches early in the morning, including unashamedly searching women in the middle of the square or, in the best case, taking them to the guardhouse of the Labor Office or of the police, ordering them to undress completely and touching and searching them with sadistic pleasure.

So we were tormented and continue to be tormented to this day at the sorrowful gate, where such gruesome, heaven-rending deeds are done as to make it unbelievable that one could have the strength to bear it.

The cruelty that they displayed, the humiliations and insults that one had to tolerate every day at the gate, are indescribable. Jews standing with their hats in hand, the German or Lithuanian searching them; if the way the Jew is standing does not please them, or if he has "God forbid" forgotten to remove his hat, he receives a blow on his head with the truncheon. From time to time they hit over the head those standing in the back so they will not push and shove. And so it went, day in and day out, month in and month out—for more than two years, and one became used to it. Sometimes one thinks that this is the way it must be—it has become "natural."

In spite of all of this, there was no shortage of food products in the ghetto. Quite the opposite, as time went on, more and more products could be found in the ghetto. Despite all the difficulties, something was still brought through the gate, trading at the fence blossomed, dozens of kilograms of flour, potatoes, fat, and meat were brought into the ghetto every day. As long as one is allowed to be alive, it is apparently difficult to block the path for Jews; if one cannot go through the door, one crawls through the window.

The Jewish police at the gate are a separate chapter. They began to carry out specific assignments that greatly increased their value.

The Gate and the Gate Guard

In addition to the Germans and Lithuanians, Jewish policemen also stood outside the gate. Their assignment was to maintain order in the incoming columns, to see to it that people stood in line and did not push or shove. Being at the gate every day, they met up with and saw the same Germans and Lithuanians, gradually got to know them and, as a result, achieved a certain role in the control process. While less so at first, in time they had increasing opportunities to bring Jews through the control. They had become acquainted with the Germans and the Lithuanians, and if they asked permission to pass someone through, most of the time it helped.

The Jewish police helped hundreds of people to pass through the control, helping to bring food into the ghetto, doing Jews a favor. Slowly, doing Jews a favor by passing them through the control turned into a business. The gate became a store, a source of wealth for those ambling around it, deriving a living from it—one became fat at the expense of another. The control at the gate was trouble for the overwhelming majority of the population. For those roaming around the gate the control was a business, a means of getting rich.

At the very beginning, a Jew who was passed through by a policemen would, out of gratitude, oblige the policemen with something. At first, the policemen might possibly not even want to take it, but later they became used to it and a whole system came into being: the policeman would pass one through who would then give him something. Higher-up policemen and members of the Labor Office serving at the gate (in addition to the policemen of the gate guard, there was also a group of people from the Labor Office whose function it was to release the brigades and to check the work papers; they were present at the gate when the brigades were returning) acquired their own people to carry food products for them, and they would pass them through. They also passed through other, unrelated people from whom they received a certain fee in the form of money or food products. And so it came about that gate guard and gate service became an important factor of the gate inspections.

Those serving at the gate explained to the Germans and Lithuanians that it would be advantageous for them to be paid off for allowing a Jew to pass through without being searched. So it came about that lower-level

Lithuanians or Germans would receive a fee for each person whom they unofficially allowed to go through without being searched. Needless to say, the policemen and Labor Office employees who collected the fees from the brigade Jews so as to turn them over later to the Lithuanian, also did not lose out from the deal. The Lithuanian, who only received the money later, could not remember how many people had passed through, so that there were always "mistakes in the calculation." A unique situation came into being, where they, the gentiles, would rob us, and we Jews would take one from the other—everyone behaving like animals.

In many instances the Jewish policemen would save Jewish goods and, perhaps, even souls from their clutches without any compensation. The Jewish police helped many people pass through the gate without receiving any reward for it. They have a difficult and responsible job, to know how to, on the one hand, balance their duty to the Germans who allow them to be there to maintain order, and, on the other hand, to help Jews to pass through and bring in as much food as possible into the ghetto. We have no other sources of existence here, the gate being the provider of food for everyone because it is not possible to live on the ration given to us—hundreds of people would have long ago died from starvation.

On the other hand, the brutality of our policemen at the gate is unbelievable; it is not possible to imagine that a Jew could be so brutal toward another, to have such a murderous heart as to beat another Jew in the ghetto. One shudders sometimes seeing a Jewish policeman beating Jews with a stick or with a truncheon over the head or body, or wherever he can, no less than a German would. It is a shame, a disgrace of the nation of Israel before the eyes of the gentiles who stand around and see how one Jew is beating another Jew. One is sometimes amazed at what the ghetto turned us into. There are those who, by nature, are indeed sadists, Jews with hearts of gentiles, as, for example, the policeman T. A.—a mean creature, deriving pleasure from beating, hated by everyone for his rudeness and also feared. For him it is a small matter to hit a Jew over the head with a board. There are also a few more who, by nature, are capable of rudeness and beating—this is not surprising. It is surprising, however, that people who were quiet in the city, calm people, intelligent people with a higher education, who had never harmed a fly on the wall, that they would turn into animals, would become so crude, brutal, murderously beating Jews, foaming at the mouth. Such a metamorphosis of people is difficult to understand or to believe.

Granted, it is difficult to get along with Jews amicably, particularly during the return from the city, when everyone is pushing toward the gate so as to sneak through as quickly as possible. A certain order must prevail; it is not possible for everyone to press forward at the same time—there must be a line. It would not do for the Germans or the Lithuanians to be the only ones to maintain order, it would inevitably lead to human sacrifices. The Jewish police force, by maintaining order by itself, is preventing the eventual occurrence of woeful incidents. Politely requesting Jews to stay in line doesn't work. There is no compliance, people continue to press ever forward, bringing chaos and disorder into the lines. It is perhaps not surprising that a policemen would give somebody a push or shove him to keep him in his place. In this fashion, getting used to a push and a shove led to ordinary beating. It became "natural" for the Jewish police to beat everyone while the Germans and the Lithuanians stand on the side content to be spared from having to do this work . . .

All of this came about and developed because the NSKK established controls at the gate during departure and, particularly, upon return to the ghetto. We had to change, to reorient ourselves to our new masters, to adjust to the new conditions, and, most importantly, to learn how to reach them in order to establish some contact with them.

The gate was one of the most important places in the ghetto. It was the key to everyone's stomach, the nerve of the ghetto and its most important factor, the place through which several thousand people pass every day, going out and coming back, the mirror of our unbelievable troubles and humiliations. The gate was also the place where the Jewish functionaries of the police or the Labor Office were able to begin to establish a certain contact with them. At the gate the policemen and Labor Office functionaries would see the same Germans every day, get used to them. The Germans also got used to these same Jews—they became "my Jews."

We have previously described the role played by the gate guard, the role that the policemen played there, and have shown the more-or-less negative side of some of the policemen at the gate. We will now show a little of the other side of the coin, not to offset their beating of Jews at the gate—their being rude and brutal, but simply to provide from an objective perspective the complete picture of the gate chapter, which is soaked with our sweat and blood.

Even before the era of the 3rd Company, at the start of the large labor quota for the airfield, the police had an important mission to fulfill at the gate, namely, to let through the airfield workers and the city brigades.

Morning at the gate!

Dark, wet, and cold; the large square is lit up by a few electrical lamps, casting a yellow, dead light on everything and everybody. Jews flocking toward the gate from all the streets and alleys, sleepy, downcast, trekking in the mud or in the snow. They had returned only last evening from work, soiled, cold, and hungry, without as yet having had the time to dry out their clothing and to properly rest up, and being awakened again at four in the morning, having to rise and go to the unrewarding slave labor.

At the gate people start to assemble, to form the columns for marching out.

(Almost everyone going to the airfield knew and was familiar with all the workplaces at the airfield, knew all the firms, what type of work each of them required, where the work was easier and where it was harder, the kind of overseer in each workplace. Each of these Jews had had the taste of the overseer's truncheon on his back. Many of our airfielders were used to working at one and the same firm, always scheming at the gate, before departure, to land in the column that worked at "their firm." Each one was almost adjusted to it, knew all the overseers, the masters, and their caprices and whims. The inverse of this was that the overseer got used to the Jew working there every day and treated him better than a newcomer.)

More and more people gather at the gate, streaming to the gate from all directions, dozens of columns having formed in the entire area ready to march out. There is pushing and shoving, everyone who has been with a column wants to go again with the same one, but a column cannot have more than 100 men. The people are counted before going through the gate, and if the count is greater than 100, the last rows are cut off. For this reason everyone is pressing to be in the earlier rows; there is jostling and pushing.

The police line up the columns, seeing to it that everyone is arranged to stand four in a row so that twenty-five rows can be counted off. Jostling leads to commotion, the rows come apart, the policeman with the stick is pushing and must hit people to keep them in place, but many pay no attention, run forward, and press themselves in front of those standing ahead of them. A knot of people is formed, others fall down in the mud or snow, those behind them step unseeingly on those who have fallen, there is screaming and yelling, crying, groaning and shouting, tears, sweat—steaming breaths in the cold, dark morning at the ghetto gate.

The Germans in the square with their truncheons are only waiting for such opportunities so they can hit the Jews on the head with all their might, to bloody and to batter them.

These were daily occurrences. One cannot let up or avoid it. The Jewish police at the square were convinced that the required labor quota must be provided, that commotion and chaos must not be allowed at the square. Whether we like it or not, the required number of people must go out to work. The Jewish police had to form the columns, to see to it that the people went out in an orderly fashion—that was our duty; in their eyes, the only justification for our existence.

The task at the gate was not an easy one; most of the time the required number of people was not there. There were also days when the number of people exceeded the requirement, but that was rare; mostly there was a deficiency. The noncommissioned officer coming to the gate with his guards to take Jews to the airfield, if he was not in a bad mood on that day, or if he was generally a person to whom one could talk, might be persuaded to take somewhat fewer people. But this could only be done a few times—on a permanent basis it could not be arranged.

The police at the gate got the idea to "fudge the numbers." In all situations, Jews find a solution, a way out—they don't get lost in times of trouble. This is how the numbers in the columns were fudged:

The noncommissioned officer is arriving with his crew to take away the Jews. A few thousand Jews are assembled in the square near the gate, ready to march to the airfield. Based on a special list, provided from the airfield to the ghetto, a Jewish policeman determines which column is to be sent to work at the assigned firm. With people standing four in a row, the Jewish policemen had to count twenty-five rows to form a column. The policeman would count the rows and "miscount": one, two, three, six, eight, eleven, and so on. Thus, while the officer and the policeman noted 100 men to have gone out, in fact, there were 80 or 72. Ten or fifteen such fudged columns could result in a reduction of 300, which could be used to patch on to other columns.

To do this one had to be lucky, swift, and, above all, nimble, because if the noncommissioned officer or some other German should catch on, one could get a good beating, and, sometimes, they might also honor one with a bullet. The Germans don't fool around.

In the late winter or in the fall, the noncommissioned officer coming to take the people, already being known, would be asked to come into the Labor Office room at the gate, to warm up, to drink a cup of hot coffee, which had already been prepared for him, and in the meantime the Jewish police in the square would work at full speed sending out the workers, patching and fudging the columns and passing them through the gate.

Except for the early days, there were no controls after leaving the gate or at the airfield. They, the Germans, had no way of knowing how many people arrived at the airfield, because the work area was very large, Jews were working there in the most diverse locations and it was difficult to check the count.

That was one of the most important activities carried out by the police on behalf of the entire ghetto at that time. The policemen of the precincts would run around to the houses and, at best, with great exertion, drag out forty or fifty people. Here, at the gate, hundreds were fudged. One only had to be nimble and lucky for everything to go smoothly.

In addition, interaction with the noncommissioned officer, who came to the ghetto with his soldiers to take the Jews, was good—that is, he was bribed. Whether he needed a suit, a coat, a pair of shoes—he was supplied with all of it, through the Elder Council. One always had to live in peace with him, to keep him happy, because a great deal depended on him.

There were days when the Jewish police were unable to do anything. That was during the early days of the NSKK, when they, the Germans of the gate guard, started to count the people going out through the gate themselves. Nothing could be done—they did not allow the Jewish police to come near. It was then necessary to arrange with the noncommissioned officer for him to accept a smaller number of people, but to tell the NSKK at the gate that the number was adequate.

The police and gate-service members of the Labor Office established connections with individual Germans and, with bribery, tried to soften them so they would be responsive to their requests.

The bribing of the Germans began to develop primarily during the times of the NSKK. At first it consisted of providing a liter of whiskey or a bottle of beer, which made them more accessible and made it possible to arrange a variety of matters with them. Later on, and more and more so in time, they were given whatever they asked: one wanted gloves, the second a pair of shoes, the third a pair of pants—everything was provided to them. This led to the police and Labor Office members being able to help people pass through the controls. A policeman leads a Jew to his German, winks, and he is allowed to go through without inspection; or the policeman "covers" him, that is, he screens with his back the controller standing in front of him, and the Jew slinks by behind him—this is referred to as swimming through. In this manner the police passed through thousands of people, thereby saving Jewish money and also preventing likely beatings.

The policeman at the gate is the one who maintains order and is the bad guy, but he can also be the rescuer and protector. The role of the policemen was an unpleasant one—in the ghetto, in general, and at the gate in particular, because people most often viewed him as the plunderer, overlooking his role as mediator, as go-between, as spokesman and as defender—to the extent that circumstances allowed. The day-to-day, personal contacts established at the gate contributed a great deal to raising the material level of the ghetto and to easing the struggle for survival, the battle for the daily bread.

The Ghetto Guard and the Police Intermediary (Relations with Germans and Lithuanians)

The second police precinct was the second place where contacts began to be established with the ghetto guard, the NSKK—a lively and important contact set up by the police in the person of the chief of the second precinct, Mr. D. T.

The contact was established on a strictly personal basis—officially we were nothing to them. The Elder Council had official contacts with them but only for the purpose of receiving orders, mostly verbal, to be announced to the population. The principal contact was unofficial, maintained by the Elder Council through the chief of the second precinct, Mr. T., and through the supervisor of the gate service of the Labor Office, Mr. K. M.

On the first day one feared even to approach them because, as noted above, they, the NSKK, entered the ghetto by storm and with much commotion. In one hour they displaced the Jews from the block of houses that they had selected to live in, going through all the dwellings to inspect the furniture in these apartments, taking for themselves whatever pleased them. On the very first day T. had to come in contact with them because of a need for an intercession. A family that had lived there and, like all their other neighbors, had had to leave in a hurry, possessed a sewing machine. A German ordered them to leave the sewing machine in place because they were going to take it for use by the ghetto guard. The owner of the sewing machine, a seamstress who relied on it for her livelihood, rushed to Mr. T. asking him to intercede with the Germans to return the sewing machine to her. He asked them and was successful—they gave the machine back to the woman.

That's how, slowly, it began. At first T. would come to the ghetto guard only occasionally and by chance, later on more and more frequently. While settling in, the ghetto guard needed various items: furniture, desks, and chairs for the apartments, writing desks, writing utensils, pictures and implements for their offices—they had brought very little with them and needed to obtain everything here, in this place. T. made an effort to get everything for them, to always be ready to serve them, for the benefit of all of us. But, at the same time, he did not give them the impression of a subservient Jew, of one who tries to flatter and ingratiate himself, rather approaching them in a practical and purposeful manner, always trying to keep his word—what he promised, he fulfilled, and, if unable to accomplish something, he would say so. Regrettably, we must be obedient, stand with hat in hand and say "at your command." But even in such circumstances one can maintain a certain dignity, although to a very limited degree. T. possessed such a measure of dignity, coolness, and practicality, not a Jew seeking attention but a police official, a former officer who is, at the same time, a Jew having to be subservient to them, but as a necessary adaptation, not as an innate subservience.

All of this resulted in their having a certain confidence in T., of their trusting him. He became a frequent visitor with easy access to all the Germans, seeing them often, talking to them—he became somewhat of a member of the household. A little later, he was not the only one going there—his assistant L. B. and the master of the guard, Z., also went there. He became the official representative of the Jewish police to the ghetto guard, raising, to some degree, the prestige of the police in their eyes, and, to the extent that this was possible, he also made the effort—through his personal influence—to dull their intense hatred toward us.

As noted, almost everybody considered the coming of the ghetto guard into the ghetto itself as trouble. But trouble invariably also brings with it something positive. It is true that their being in the ghetto was indeed a burden to us, but our contacts and communications with them were entirely changed.

We had had almost no contact with the earlier ghetto guard, the one located outside the ghetto—"the 3rd Company of the 11th Police Battalion"; it was as though we were blind. To go to the ghetto guard was an event—the chairman of the Elder Council, Mr. E. [Elkes], and the chief of police, Mr. K. [Kopelman], would go there. It would happen often that the sentry at the ghetto exit-portal to the guardhouse would not let them through (the ghetto guardhouse was exactly opposite the fence at Velionos Street). He would only inform the commandant that some Jews were waiting below, at the fence. The commandant would open the window on the second floor and shout to them across the street: "What do you want?" They, our representatives, would stand on the street, with hat in hand, and would have to shout back across the street what it was that they had come for and wait, with bared heads, to be granted entry. Needless to say, one was not eager to make such "visits" frequently—one would only go there when it was absolutely necessary.

Here it became quite different. The ghetto guard is inside the ghetto itself, the people in contact with them can go there almost at will, there is an opportunity to talk to them frequently, to learn all kinds of things, and, most important, to save Jews who have fallen into their hands for various "sins."

We in the ghetto knew and understood that they, the ghetto guard, with the commandant at the head, were what one would call "little people." The commandant, with the help of his crew (troops), has the task of guarding the ghetto, to see to it that there is peace and order there, that the Jews are working, are loyal, and so on—all police and administrative functions and tasks. But they have no say and influence on the fate of the ghetto as such. He, the commandant, could send people to the G. [Gestapo], punish them with jail sentences, beat them, take away their property and personal belongings, but fateful decisions he could not make—that belonged to the center, to the SD,[1] to the Generalkommisariat, and to other angels of destruction. But the day-to-day inner life of the ghetto, its food supplies, the treatment of the Jews by the sentries, the calm in the ghetto itself, reports about the ghetto to higher authorities, control at the gate, and so on—all depended on the commandant and the ghetto guard. It was also very important to know the private opinions of the commandant and his attitude toward the Jews. Very often, his personal opinion was a decisive factor in many ghetto matters.

We had an entire gallery of different types of commandants in the ghetto; they differed in character and in the manner in which they related to us; there were good ones and bad ones, those with whom one could come to an understanding, those who disliked us because they were ordered to do so, as well as those who were indeed committed antisemites. To each one, individually, one had to adjust, learn how to approach him, how to communicate with him, find favor in his eyes; to each one of them one had to have a different approach, learn how to adapt.

The first commandant of the NSKK in the ghetto, with whom contacts began to be established and an acquaintanceship engaged in, was a certain Lot. He was a genuine, not overly sharp-witted German type, strict but honest and straightforward, a small-town bourgeois with a small head, small ideas; what he was once taught and what was hammered into his head remained there unchanged; simplistic good-naturedness mixed with German love of order, blandness, and cruelty. His relationship to Jews was not particularly antisemitic, but rather the typical attitude of an official, a German who dislikes Jews according to the laws and the rules. He considered himself complete master of the ghetto, full of confidence in himself and his abilities, believing that he knew everything and understood everything.

---

1. SD—Sicherheitsdienst, security service of the SS, under the authority of the Reich Security Main Office.

The first ruling to be introduced by him into the ghetto guard was that flogging was to be the penalty for infractions committed by Jews. He lectured Mr. T. (he was a big talker and chatterer) that flogging had two virtues: first, the one receiving the lashes received his punishment for the transgression that he had committed, and second, flogging was a good educational tool.

To beat a Jew who, because of some transgression, fell into their hands was an entertainment and source of pleasure for the entire German crew. If they got ahold of someone, he would be beaten murderously. After the flogging the commandant would send the Jew to the ghetto jail, specifying the number of days he should be kept under arrest; in addition, the Jew frequently also had to go to work every day (incidentally, that was the first time that a German sent a Jew to the ghetto jail to serve his sentence, a sign of a certain amount of trust in us).

"Ghetto-Guard" was a word feared by everyone. To fall into their hands meant to, first, simply receive an "advance" beating from the sentries, and then an additional, official flogging based on the order of the commandant.

Flogging was administered in the following manner: the victim would be placed on a chair, his clothing well taken down, and two Germans, standing on either side with thick rubber truncheons in their hands, would whip him over his seat with all their might. Forty lashes was the "normal portion." The pain experienced by the unfortunate one is obvious; for long weeks afterward that person was unable to sit—his skin was literally cut up; others were not even able to lie—the smallest movement would cause great agony.

After such a serving of lashes the commandant would frequently send the punished one to the ghetto jail via the second police precinct and, as noted, also order that he go to work every day. T. brought the fact to his attention that a person cannot go to work after such a punishment and that in order not to lose his availability for the labor quota, the commandant should order such beatings to be discontinued. The appeal was to no avail—he only instructed that, in the future, rags should be placed on the seat of the accused as this would draw out the pain . . .

The greatest impression was made on him if the one being flogged did not scream during the punishment. Most of those being beaten would cry and scream because of the great pain. There was the case of a certain Antzel, a young man of about seventeen, who was caught with a forbidden package. He was fearfully beaten. The young man absorbed a great many lashes

273

without a peep, as though it was not he who was being beaten. This made a very deep impression on the commandant, and he would mention the strength of character of the young man at every opportunity.

Nor did the Germans spare the women—they received beatings just like the men. They had no regard or pity for women, flogging and breaking the skin as much as possible.

There was the case of a young girl, a certain Vilentshik, who fell into the hands of the ghetto guard. They started to flog her with the thick rubber truncheons—the girl did not make a sound. The commandant, standing nearby, was surprised by her strength and ordered execution of the punishment to be stopped in the middle. By his then-current standards, he considered it a courageous act on his part, one giving "recognition" to that person.

There were hundreds of instances of outrage; we provide here only a few noteworthy ones in order to show what we had to put up with, who we had to deal with, the role played by the police in this or that case.

Trading at the fence went on all the time and continues now. During the first few weeks of the NSKK it was more quiet; then it continued as before. The majority of the fence-traders were butchers, who would bring in cows and horses, slaughter them in the ghetto, and sell the meat.

In the winter, when the river was frozen over and Jews would bring ice from the river for the hospital, a few of the guys thought up a scheme for bringing horses into the ghetto to be slaughtered for meat. A gentile from the other side would bring over a horse, and it would be hitched to the sled with the ice so it could "help" move the sled up the hill. Along the way, the purchased horse was unhitched and the deal was done.

A certain Teinovitch carried out such an operation. A certain Gritzmacher, a Jewish informer working as a laborer at the ghetto guard, informed the Germans, and they found in the home of Teinovitch the meat of a slaughtered horse as well as a live one.

Teinovitch, having learned that he had been denounced, went into hiding. The Germans arrested his mother, an elderly woman, well into her sixties, demanding she tell them the location of her son, the meat trader. She responded that she didn't know. A hail of blows fell upon her. She stood in the middle of the room while a German beat her with a truncheon over all of her body—angrily, with force and ferocity, and asking her with each blow: "Tell us where your son is, or we will kill you." She coolly and calmly wrapped a bandage around a finger that had previously been cut, back and forth, and responded with the same answer: "I don't know." They did not succeed, no matter how much they beat her. T. appealed to them that they should stop beating her since, as they could see, she really didn't know; otherwise she would not have been able to withstand such terrible torment. It was to no avail. They continued to beat her, they grew tired from beating her, but she was not weakened by her suffering—she stood in one place and continued to repeat the same tune: "I don't know anything."

Later, they captured the son and, needless to say, gave him a terrible beating, and put him in jail for forty days.[2]

There were various and similar instances of their nabbing Jewish traders at the fence, in every case, always, severely beating them, causing fearful torment. T. would often intervene, asking that the victims should not be subjected to such terrible torment. Many times it helped, many times it didn't. There was the case of five butchers caught trading at the fence whom they transferred to the SD, where they were later shot.

There was one noteworthy instance when a Jew was saved from death by the intervention of the police. The Jew Visgordiski was caught going through the fence, and a gold ring was found on him. Jordan arrived at the ghetto guard precisely at that moment, and having learned about this episode, he ordered the Jew to be hanged and the execution carried out by the Jewish police. Later he would issue further orders as to where and when this should be done.

Visgordiski was immediately taken to the ghetto jail without knowing just what sentence he had been given. T. learned about this episode from the commandant Lot. He reported it to the Elder Council, and they deliberated together as to what could be undertaken to save a Jew from death. First of all, T. succeeded in getting the commandant to ask Jordan to officially convey the order to hang Visgordiski. Knowing the commandant Lot well, T. also arranged with him that when Jordan came again to the ghetto guard, the commandant would not remind him of this matter, unless he spoke of it himself. Afterwards, Jordan came once to the ghetto guard and was not

---

2. The paragraph that follows is repeatedly typed over to make it illegible. It possibly describes the fate of the informer, a story that would not be included if it involved activity by the underground.

reminded of this matter—the commandant kept his word and did not speak to him about it. In the meantime it came about that Jordan went away and did not live to return. And if the prince dies, his decrees are annulled. In this manner Visgordiski was saved from certain death by the chance of a simple maneuver by T., and the ghetto avoided an ugly execution that was to have been carried out by the Jewish police.

It is of interest to note that, to this day, in the entire ghetto only two or three people from the Elder Council and a few persons of the police know about this episode. The fact that no one knew about it, that the general population did not chatter about it, helped to let the matter pass quietly and for it to be suppressed.

The commandant, the troop leader, had under his jurisdiction a team of Germans and Lithuanians. Only Germans guarded the fences the first few weeks—Lithuanians were few in number, like a fifth wheel of the wagon. Germans guarded the gates and the important points of the fence; Lithuanians were at the remaining locations. Among them were better ones and worse ones, committed antisemites and simply average Germans, who hated the Jews but did not cause special problems. In general, the ordinary sentries, the Germans, had no say in the ghetto. But over the Jews everyone is a master, and we feared every German, regardless of his rank. During the time of Lot there was a large German contingent (later they decreased in number and Lithuanians took their place). A few occurrences are associated with one of them, a certain Shimkat. As noted, on the first day that he came, he shot and killed the Jew Gempl at the gate, who was returning with a wagon from the city workshops.

Later on, after he got to know the Jews better, particularly members of the second police precinct, he said once that he was not sorry for having shot the innocent Jew, that he had his reasons for it: first of all, he said, it is wartime now . . . Second, "before coming here we were taught that when shooting a Jew one should make the effort to hit the target because otherwise it will be a wasted bullet."

Later he told T. in confidence that a few weeks before coming here to the ghetto they were systematically lectured about the Jews, being told that the Jews were the source of all evil, thieves, deceivers, and loafers. In their already poisoned minds was planted the idea that they should treat the Jews as badly and as brutally as possible.

Lot was the commandant in the ghetto for about five months. He left in the month of May, and Katein was assigned to replace him. He was an entirely different type of a man—one of the rare Germans to be encountered in these current, dark times of blind, deathly hatred of the Jews.

He was in his late forties. As an established Hamburg merchant, wise, intelligent, very sensitive, with a fine upbringing and good character, he was very far removed from National Socialism. He was accepted into this Nazi NSKK by means of good connections. He wanted—according to his own words—to serve in the NSKK only because it was more comfortable here and chances were better of remaining in the rear and not having to face frontline fighting.

The first thing he did upon his arrival was to discontinue the floggings—he prohibited beatings.

On the very first day of his arrival to the ghetto guard, T. presented himself to him as chief of the second precinct. The commandant immediately entered into a conversation with him. He said that he had much compassion for our bitter fate, that his assignment to the ghetto was very painful to him, that he could in no way treat the Jew badly, to further oppress the already oppressed and suffering.

"Should you sometimes see," he continued, "that I am shouting at a Jew, punishing him or even beating him, you must know that I am only doing this because I must, as mild treatment of Jews, or interceding on their behalf, can cost me my head." Those were his first words to a Jew in the ghetto.

He would frequently walk around in the ghetto, particularly in the old city, observing how people lived, deploring the crowding and the difficult existence. It particularly irked him that people were afraid of him. He once passed a large, vacant lot in the old city where a large group of children were assembled and were playing. When they saw a German coming from a distance, they started to shout one to the other: "Kids, the commandant is coming." The children scattered fearfully. Katein observed the entire scene, how the children were scared off by him, and his eyes filled with tears. "Look," he said to Mr. T., "what the Nazis have accomplished here—little children are afraid of me, as of a wild beast."

Katein didn't last long—for them he was too kind and too soft. He left, and in his place came Tiele. He was a young man, a cunning businessman, a journeyman by trade, a seasoned city-dweller and a clever, spirited young man. He wanted no part of parties or programs—he only sought one thing: to have money and live well.

He was not a great antisemite, hating the Jews only to the extent that orders required it. In general, he had little interest in the Jewish question and did not dwell on its issues. Being a practical man, he knew only one thing: he was not going to lose out by allowing the Jews to do some trading, to bring in products. Mostly he only wanted more money—let the Jews do some business, as long as he benefited from it. A lot of products were brought into the ghetto during his time. One time, with his permission, 2,500 kilograms of flour and other products were brought into the ghetto in one day by wagon and by truck.

At the end of August, Tiele left and Barro arrived. He was the terror of the ghetto, especially at the gate. A great antisemite and hooligan, a bad person with a rotten character, he never uttered a friendly word to a Jew. Not even to T., who would come to the ghetto guard a few times a day, whom he knew well and saw every day, would he respond with a good morning, never looking him straight in the eyes. He hated Jews organically, deep from his heart. He was like a wild animal at the gate, seldom allowing anyone to go through with a package. There were various attempts to "break him," to give him a present so as to make him somewhat milder, but it was difficult to "take him."

One time, Barro needed a shaving device. Characteristically of the Barro type, when T. obtained it for him and he came to the second precinct to get it (a splendid shaving apparatus in a leather case), he didn't even raise his eyes, did not thank [T.] for the present, did not smile, just stood there with his back to T., inspected the present that he had just received, and left without saying a single word.

At the end of September 1942 the NSKK left, and in their place came new people: the Viennese Protective Police [Schutz Polizei]. From one perspective this might have been expected to be better for the ghetto, because the NSKK is a political organization, a branch of the Nazi party, while the new ghetto guard is a police unit, which has nothing to do with politics. But experience has demonstrated that, in some respects, it was worse.

During the times of the NSKK, when an accused Jew was brought to the ghetto guard, he would be punished on the spot—with flogging or jail, or both. They were not afraid to decide for themselves. After implementation of the punishment, the matter was closed. It was also possible in many cases for the police to come to the commandant of the NSKK, to clarify, to say a good word for the Jew and so on.

The new ghetto guard, a police unit, was afraid to make decisions on its own: in every significant matter they would send the Jew away to the SD. During their time dozens of people were turned over to the SD for a variety of transgressions; many of them never returned, and those who did come back had experienced great fear and were beaten there.

Compared to the time of the NSKK, the number of Lithuanians increased greatly with the arrival of the Viennese Protective Police. Things changed to the point where the guards around the fence and at the gates were exclusively Lithuanians; there were only four or five Germans in the ghetto: the commandant and his immediate assistants.

The police, in the person of T., and the Labor Office, in the person of N., began to also establish some contacts with the Lithuanians. During the time of the NSKK, particularly the first few months, the Lithuanians were hardly to be seen—they didn't dare raise their heads. The Germans, according to their own words, hated the Lithuanians maybe even more than the Jews; they always liked to remark that "the Jews we are ordered to hate— the Lithuanians we hate from the heart." Although, regrettably, this is not so—they also hate us from the bottom of their hearts—it is a fact that they would come to pour their hearts out to the Jews, say the worst about the Lithuanians; in any event, they did not consider them equal to themselves, but rather looked down on them, just as they looked down on the Jews.

The Lithuanians repaid them in the same coin—with hatred. The relationship between the two partners was strained. The Lithuanians would also come to the Jews to pour out their hearts about the Germans, who wronged them, didn't let them raise their heads, didn't let them have any say, didn't value them, and most important—what made their blood boil—was that the Germans took everything at the gate for themselves, eating all the best and the nicest things themselves without giving them anything.

The basic fact that they are quarreling among themselves would be of little concern to us—let them quarrel to their heart's content, but the trouble is that we are in the middle, we must jockey it so as to not allow their mutual hatred to land on our heads. They must have the impression that we are completely neutral, having no sympathy with the one or the other.

The Lithuanians suspected that we sympathized more with the Germans, because Jews could converse with them so fluently, and the Germans were almost friendly with the Jews. Conversely, the Germans suspected that members of the second police precinct incited the Lithuanians against the Germans.

Once such a suspicion took on a serious form. The commandant Tiele accused the assistant chief of the second precinct, L. B., of inciting the Lithuanians against the Germans. On our behalf, T. explained to him that the accusation was without basis, because the Lithuanians were our worst enemies, having murdered on their own initiative dozens, thousands, of Jews and that, except for work-related matters, we had nothing to do with them. Quite the opposite, T. went on to emphasize, with the arrival of the Germans inside the ghetto, there was more order, day and night shooting around the fences stopped, life became somewhat more secure. The arguments didn't help and the assistant chief; L. B. was transferred out of the second precinct.

The majority of the Lithuanians were coarse young men, simple Lithuanian peasants, many of them dull-witted, crude, and intense antisemites. A large majority of them knew little about the Jewish question; they knew nothing, except for the two things that they knew and understood: to hate the Jews and to be fond of _____ [illegible word]. One could arrange anything one desired with them; all of them, from the first to the last, only wanted bribes; allowing one to bring in through the fence or through the gate whatever and as much as one desired, as long as they were well paid.

All of the above refers to the ordinary policeman. They also had their supervisors—the chief of the gate guard and three or four controllers. Among them were also different types: some with whom one could get along, some even half friendly, and others great hooligans, antisemites.

The most noteworthy of them was Petkunas. He was an intelligent Lithuanian, a former officer in the Lithuanian army, not an antisemite. He was a man with a firm hand, straightforward; his crew, the Lithuanians, feared him and greatly respected him as their chief of the gate guard. The Germans also had a good opinion of his behavior and, as a result, he was able to secure more rights for the Lithuanians. When he arrived in the ghetto, there was an effort to get close to him; he was given presents, more and more he allowed himself to be bribed, helping the fence traders to bring in and out larger objects; at the gate he was also all right, and, in general, he was seen as a clever man with a personal sympathy for the Jews.

There was the case of the police chief, Hauptmann Birger, coming from the city to the ghetto and making a speech to the assembled guards, where, in addition to service-related instructions, he mostly poured venom on the Jews, using the well-known oratorical phrases, that the Jews were responsible for the war, they were our enemies, one should not have anything to do with Jews, and so on. Later, the speech was translated into Lithuanian for the Lithuanians.

The next day Petkunas had to communicate the speech to the members of his crew who had not heard it because they were on duty. He conveyed that part of Birger's speech that concerned service-related matters, saying not a word about all the poison against the Jews.

He spoke many times with T., expressing friendliness toward the Jews, emphasizing that the Lithuanians must now make contact with the Jews and help them in the current sorrowful times. The Germans would disappear from here and Jews and Lithuanians would again have to live together.

A meeting was arranged, mediated by T., between Petkunas and the vice-chairman of the Elder Council L. G. [Leib Garfunkel], the general secretary A. G. [Avraham Golub], and member of the Elder Council H. L. [Hirsch Levin]. They had a lengthy conversation with him concerning "the Days of the Messiah," which left a good impression on both sides. The general help that we could expect from the Lithuanians at critical moments, particularly during the transition period, was talked about, and many other issues of the present and future were touched upon. On his part, he promised collaboration and help. But we know quite well that the majority of the Lithuanians—particularly the ordinary element—is set against us. Aside from that, we also know that the Lithuanians have little say with the Germans; they themselves are being terrorized by them. Nevertheless, such a conversation was of great moral significance in the sense that this was the first time that representatives of the Jews came together with a Lithuanian official around the same table and considered matters of justice and human relations in a friendly manner.

Besides him, a variety of different types of people passed through the ghetto. We will describe in a few lines the most important of them. They were Kalasauskas, Marzinenas, Lafshis, and Ratnik.

Kalasauskas is a heavy-set peasant, by nature honest and not bad, would not take any bribes from any Jew, but his material condition is difficult, which forces him to be on the take. He is bitter, and it galls him to have to accept bribes not because he wants to, but because he needs to. Who always has money to give him?—the Jews. Who has all kinds of food to eat?—the Jews. The Jews have everything, but he doesn't. All of this led to his being bitter and to his letting out his anger on us. While in the ghetto he became an ardent antisemite, hating the Jews even more than when he first arrived here. Needless to say, he caused us great suffering.

Marzinenas, a type of intellectual antisemite, a former schoolteacher, who read all of the Nazi—and *Sturmer*—"literature," derived his entire knowledge of Jewish issues from newspaper articles, and hated the Jews with all his heart.

Lafshis, a former army sergeant, was an honest, good-natured peasant. While honest and good-natured in his relationship with the Jews, he hated the Jews, although in a good-natured and cordial manner, without the gentile venom. He was quite honest at the gate and sometimes did many favors for the Jews without any compensation.

Ratnik was the most "popular" in the ghetto. He was the genuine policeman type, much like the ones in crime novels—in his eyes, all people are criminals, especially the Jews. By nature a bad person of crude character, a virulent antisemite, he considered himself quite an expert on Jewish questions, saturated himself with material from cheap filth-pamphlets against the Jews, and, while in the ghetto, insisted that he be provided with a translation of the *Zohar*[3] because he wanted to study Kabbala. . . . He was the only one not to yield to being bribed or broken-in, a dry formalist, honest—by his standards, to the point of madness. In addition, he was somewhat depraved, always angry, irate, and glum, on guard day and night, never at rest, morning, day, and night—always running around the gates like a tracking dog, going to all the fences, looking in all the corners, poking, rummaging, and searching everywhere. And if this were not enough, he would go to the city on his bicycle, wait for the returning brigades and check them while on their way back. In the ghetto streets he would stop ordinary Jews who were

---

3. Principal source of the Kabbala—the complex and esoteric body of Jewish mystical tradition, literature, and thought, based on a mystical interpretation of the Scriptures.

passing by, search them, confiscate their money and other items, and take them to the ghetto guard. It seemed as though he always appeared out of nowhere, no matter where one turned. He would stand at the gate keenly looking over the people lined up for inspection as though they were a horde of criminals, remove from the line those who appeared suspicious to him, and search them from head to toe. In short, his was the dreaded name in the ghetto.

He was in the ghetto about five months and caused quite a lot of trouble, having sent not a few Jews to the SD, never to return. On June 1, 1943, he was transferred out of here.

The police, that is the second precinct, maintained daily contact with the Lithuanians just as they did with the Germans, providing them with everything possible and, on that basis, prevailing upon them as much as they could. All this effort, establishing contacts with the ghetto guard, is, in fact, intercession activity, petitioning, which, before the ghetto, we had left behind a long time ago. It all had the taste of Tsarist Russia of old—we are going backward, just as everything else of our generation is going backward. We had to return to intercession, and of the puniest and most insulting type. We come not to demand, but to plead, not as citizens, but as creatures without any rights, who are given something not because it is their due, but mostly because of personal considerations. In spite of this, we are pleased to have succeeded in establishing some kind of contact with these little people.

That's how life became established in the ghetto, that's how one worked, struggled, and obeyed, ears always sharply tuned, listening for good news that is, regrettably, far off; apparently, we must still trudge through a large swamp before we reach freedom, and who knows whether we will last until salvation comes; we must wait for miracles, which are so rare these days in the world.

The Ghetto during the Time of the NSKK, Wiedmann, and Hermann (Spring and Summer 1942)

8

Jordan's Last Actions (the Riga Action and the Book Action)

Half the winter had passed and, in general, it was quiet and calm in the ghetto, everyone doing his work, settled in, adjusted, and getting on. At the end of January 1942, the ghetto experienced a shock associated with an action.

It became known that 500 men and women from the Kovno ghetto were needed for work in Riga. There was a great commotion in the ghetto. Repeated, explicit assurances that the people would be taken to work in Riga were not believed. Most were convinced that the people to be taken out of the ghetto and led away would meet with the same fate as those who had previously been taken away. The Labor Office displayed announcements seeking volunteers for Riga, to report by January 30. Except for three men, volunteers were not to be found; they had to be recruited by force.

On the evening of January 31, Germans of the Third Company came into the ghetto, with the assignment of carrying out the roundup, together with Jewish policemen. The Labor Office assembled lists of the people to be taken, some of them work-truants, some simply shady characters; included in the lists were also single young men and women. The lists were sent out to the police precincts corresponding to the places of residence, and there the Jewish policemen went, together with the Germans, to take them out of their homes.

The police had to carry out an ugly and dirty task, compelled to deliver our own Jews to the Germans by force, to be sent away to a strange land, far away, to work, and who knew whether they would reach that destination, or perhaps be done away with en route.

The recruitment action was not successful. The majority were not to be found at home, as the upcoming roundup became known in the ghetto and many people, particularly unattached ones, went into hiding as much as possible, not sleeping in their own homes, so that instead of 500, 150 were rounded up. The following day they were taken through the gate to the railroad station. The authorities, having learned of the small number of people who had been rounded up, ordered that they be returned to the ghetto and demanded that the full number be provided.

Jordan came to the ghetto, threatening in his typical hooligan tone that there would be an explosion in the ghetto if the required number of people were not produced. Everything had to be started all over again, the 150 men and women who were brought back could no longer be found, as all of them had gone into hiding. Many went to work in the city and remained there overnight. The situation was very strained and tense. The Elder Council prevailed upon Jordan to allow three or four days to provide the people. New lists were put together, and the rounding up started again.

On the evening of February 5, the second roundup was in progress all over the ghetto, and the following morning it became known that the required number was still not there. There was the feeling that something was about to happen.

The next morning there was an order from Jordan that all men and women in the ghetto must assemble at Demokratu Square. Following the specified hour for assembly, the Germans would check the houses, and anyone found at home would be shot. Children up to the age of fourteen, nursing mothers, and old people were not required to come to the square.

A great panic came over the ghetto; frightened, everyone wondered what was going to happen. Immediately, the Jewish police were sent out to all the houses to communicate the text of the order.

Friday, February 6, around one o'clock in the afternoon, the Jews of the ghetto assembled at the bloody Demokratu Square. But this time the square looked quite different from October 28 of the previous year, because only a small number of people had assembled. All those working in the city or at the airfield went to work normally, as on any other day. Only those remaining or those working in the ghetto went to the square, so that in the square were assembled the police, workers of ghetto institutions, and a few members of the general population.

Everyone was ordered to line up according to their work columns; Jordan arrived with his staff and the sorting began. There was a lot of noise and great disorder in the square. The people knew from previous experience that the police column passed without being checked, and so everyone was pushing into it. It went so far that a third of all those assembled stood in the police column. Many people copied the armbands and hats, put them on and stood together with the police. This caused great commotion in the square, people pushing to and fro; it took a few hours before the entire spectacle was concluded. The Germans selected some of the people for Riga and ordered the rest to return home. But the number of people was still short. At around three or four o'clock in the afternoon, an order was issued to seal off a few streets in the old city, and Germans along with Jewish policemen went from house to house and took out whomever they found at home, because they either couldn't or didn't have enough time to go into hiding. But even after all this, the required number was not achieved, and they went to complete it with people returning from work in the city. Germans, and a few Jews from the Elder Council, placed themselves at the gates, removed people from the columns of workers returning from the city, and took them, heavily guarded by Germans and Lithuanian police, to the assembly point at the former New Synagogue. Later that evening, these people were taken in groups to the railroad station; from there, they were all transported to Riga.

Here the police also did some rescue work. On the one hand, they were forced to discharge their duties—to accompany the Germans, to grab and recruit; and on the other hand, they snatched people away from them whenever they could and smuggled them out of the house of prayer, where they were locked up. Among those at the railroad station were also the police official M. L. and the Labor Office official P. M. Taking advantage of the darkness, they took people out of one of the open railroad cars, until a German noticed it and beat both of them with the butt of his rifle. The police official M. L. was bedridden for three months as a result.

The train with the Jews left for Riga. A few escaped from the railroad cars on the way; the rest arrived there unharmed. Letters were received from them shortly afterwards saying that they were all alive, healthy, and working. This time, the predictions of the pessimists did not come to pass. This was the first time in the life of the ghetto that people taken out of the ghetto were not killed but were in fact transferred to a different place to work.

After the Riga action, life continued to flow normally, until the coming of a small shock, this time not a physical one but a deeply moral one, shocking everyone to the depth of our soul.

It was announced on February 26 that all ghetto residents were required to deliver all books in their possession. The locations where the books were to be delivered were specified, and, as usual, it was announced that the Germans would conduct house searches after the deadline and that anyone found to possess books would be severely punished.

As always in case of a problem or a decree, the police went from house to house informing everyone that all books in one's possession, including religious books, must be delivered. A large part of the population obeyed the order out of fear and delivered the books.

The best that we had was removed from the Jewish homes, the greatest spiritual treasures, pearls of world and Jewish literature, religious books revered by fathers and grandfathers with great love and devotion, books sometimes acquired by being thrifty so as to obtain this or that masterpiece, pages telling of the quiet sighs of fathers and grandfathers as they sat bent over them, deriving from them their vital strength, their spiritual nourishment and strength to cope with the coming gray day, books telling of the suffering and joys of entire families, of entire eras in their various transformations and manifestations—all of this we had to deliver to the Germans; they wanted to deprive the nation of the book of the last weapon that it still had—the book.

This test we also withstood, delivering the largest number of our books to the collection points. But a large part of the population had learned from previous experiences; they hid their books and did not give them away.

Departure of Jordan and Kaminski

Shortly after the Riga action and the delivery of the books (it is difficult to pin down the date), Jordan departed from Kovno.

Jordan, that was the dreaded word and specter of the ghetto; one trembled with deathly fear of him. A cold shudder would pass through one's spine when hearing that he was coming to the ghetto.

That was a person—an animal, an unparalleled sadist and murderer, an incomparable antisemite. His face would change into a dark grimace when coming to the ghetto; he hated Jews pathologically, with passion.

The following characteristic incident is known about him.

During the early days of the ghetto, a certain workplace wanted to bring in a few hundred Jewish workers to clean up the burnt-out barracks in Schantz. From this workplace came a request to Jordan for permission to take the Jews. They also asked him how many hours the Jews should work, whether they should be given food, whether in the evening they should be transported the long distance back to their homes by truck or whether they should go by foot, and so on. To this Jordan gave a short answer: "The Jews working during the day should be shot in the evening and new ones gotten early next morning; there are enough of them, the dogs . . ."

Lithuanians also related that when one talked to him about any random topic, he was very friendly, polite, and spoke to the subject matter. But if the conversation chanced to turn to the subject of Jews, his countenance changed immediately, his face went red—he became a totally different person.

This was the type of master that we had ruling over us. No wonder therefore that people would shake with fright when he came to the ghetto. He was ready and able when walking or driving through the ghetto to pull out his gun and shoot the first, most convenient passing Jew.

He was once traveling in his car in the direction of the ghetto when an airfield column returning from work stopped at the market, with the permission of the noncommissioned officer, to make some purchases. Jordan drove to the market, and when the Jews saw his car, they scattered in panic and fear. A few remained in the market, as they had not as yet managed to run away. He came to a twenty-year-old young man, Rabinowitch, took him into the toilet in the market and, without saying a word or asking a question, shot him on the spot.

He would frequently come to the Elder Council to announce new decrees, to give new orders. To ask, to appeal, to attempt to intercede, that was not allowed under any circumstances; only to hear him out and to say: "Jawohl" ["Yes, Sir"].

As previously noted, he became somewhat milder after the Great Action, probably because what he did and observed at the Ninth Fort was so cruel and shocking that even such a scoundrel as Jordan was somewhat affected. He allowed himself to be spoken to a little; one could ask a question or say something.

Thus, for example, during the Riga action, after the failed first roundup, the Elder Council succeeded in getting him to allow the recruitment to be extended by a few more days so that the Jewish police would have more time to accomplish the task. To have prevailed with Jordan on any such matter was, at the time, quite an accomplishment.

He came to the Elder Council after the Great Action and, as noted above, made the famous declaration that there would not be any more actions, promising then to establish workshops, to provide work for the Jews in the ghetto, and to increase the rations.

The workshops were later created by him in January 1942.

One fine day it became known that Jordan was leaving, and, although this may sound absurd, it is nevertheless a fact that many regretted it. First, because one had become used to him and adjusted to his type of wickedness. He, on his part, always dealt with the same few Jews, and, notwithstanding his horrible hatred of the Jews, he became, willingly or not, used to the Jews with whom he always dealt; they became "my Jews." Perhaps even against his own will, he treated the few Jewish officials differently from the other Jews. Second, having had a preview of this type, one was sure that he was not the worst, that there were, possibly, more wicked ones than he. Who knew who would replace him, how many victims, horrors, terror, and troubles we would have to live through before we got used to a new master.

New Masters, New Winds
(Wiedmann, Hermann—German Labor Office)

In his place came a new master, an entirely different person—Wiedmann. He was a completely different type of man, also an AS [SA?] man, outwardly very strict, but by nature a person of good character, except that he had the habit of shouting at the top of his voice, but did not mistreat either the ghetto as a whole or individual people. Relationships became much milder, the exchange was a very good one; with him it was possible to talk, to appeal, to intervene.

Various smaller events occurred during that time, which intertwined one into the other, but each separately and all of them together kept the population in constant uneasiness and fear.

On February 25, the registration of all men, with or without a specialty, and of women only with a vocation, was announced. Persistent rumors started to circulate in the ghetto at the same time—the end of February— that 1,500 Jews would be taken out of the ghetto to work on peat in Praven- ishok. This led to a very anxious mood, because being in one of their work camps involved hard labor, starvation, beatings, and so on.

Some said that the registration was ordered so as to send to Pravenishok those without a specialty. Others said the opposite, that the registration was a separate matter and that people needed for Pravenishok would be taken from the airfield columns and from brigades. All these rumors led, on the one hand, to a fear of registering; and on the other hand, fulfillment of the airfield quota suffered greatly—it took on a simply catastrophic scope. It went so far that the Elder Council made an official announcement in the name of Stadts Kommissar Kramer, dated March 15, wherein it was said, among other things, that rumors of a forthcoming removal of Jews from the ghetto for work elsewhere were baseless, that the question was not active and had not been decided in principle.

The announcement further said that the worker turnout to fulfill the labor quota had diminished greatly in recent days—it was short seven or eight hundred workers every day. The Elder Council therefore gave notice in the name of the Stadts Kommissar that the question of taking Jews to work away from the ghetto would be completely taken off the agenda only when the labor quota was properly fulfilled. Every attempt to shirk work would have consequences for the associated individuals as well as for the Jewish community of the ghetto as a whole. The Elder Council therefore urged all Jews, in the interest of the entire community, to go normally and punctually to work so as to avoid calamity and troubles, because the ghetto lived and existed only for work.

The announcement calmed the public somewhat, although the rumors about moving people out of the ghetto did not cease.

Registration of men and women with specialties was for an entirely different reason—it was in preparation for establishing in the ghetto a German labor office. There existed in the city, in addition to the Lithuanian professional associations and labor office, also a special German labor office that had at its disposal the entire Lithuanian labor force. It was decided to also create in the ghetto a section of their labor office so as to have control over the Jewish labor force and its utilization. A registration of the workforce was therefore carried out, and shortly afterward, a division of the German labor office was established in the ghetto.

Everyone saw a change for the better in the coming of the German labor office into the ghetto, implying that our labor force and its administration were worth something and needed to be taken into account.

We don't mean to imply that they became friendlier toward the Jews, or that they somehow changed their program—that is out of the question. But they have apparently reoriented themselves to further exploit the Jews for work, to extract from them even more work effort. Looking at it from this point of view, one cannot simply shoot a Jew. Those who are shot cannot perform work for them . . . There was a certain transformation in the relationship, which we can now observe in past events. Creation of the German labor office was the beginning of this somewhat new attitude. The manager of the German labor office, a German, an SA man, Hauptsturmführer [Captain] Hermann, himself a Nazi, was nevertheless a human being who could be approached.

He is an elderly man, in his fifties, of an earlier generation, who perhaps dealt with or traded with Jews in past years. Solid, not so full of hatred of the Jews—disliking them as a German and a Nazi, as required by the laws. He is readily approachable, one can talk to him, deal with him, prevail on him, convince him—he is not crass. He hears us out and often does what this or that Jewish representative asks of him. The following characteristic case is of interest: He once expressed himself as follows: "We are now short of workers, of skilled men. It was very foolish to have annihilated so many able-bodied men and women who could be very useful to us now." This opinion was characteristic of him and of the office that he managed.

He does not regret the fact that so many innocent Jews were slaughtered, that tens of thousands of Jewish souls were annihilated without mercy—to regret it would be contrary to his nature as a German Nazi. But he does regret being deprived of so many workers, of whom there is now a shortage, who might have been at his disposal. From this perspective he was often, whether directly or indirectly, an advocate on behalf of the ghetto.

There were cases when a large number of people were to be taken out of the ghetto to be sent to work someplace far away from here, which he did not allow. He intervened frequently, not out of compassion for the people who would be separated from their families and lost in some camp, but because he needed the people for his local workplaces, which are in his jurisdiction and which he must supply with Jewish labor.

One can draw a certain parallel between the two new people, Wiedmann and Hermann. The first, not at all a bad person, does not especially look to do harm to the Jews; the second, because of his position, intercedes on our behalf.

In general, the above-mentioned change that the Jew is a source of labor, a property of the government that must not be damaged, comes increasingly to the foreground. In the attitude that crystallized, the Jew is a slave, belonging "to the state," and if he is to be able to work, he must be allowed to live and given something to eat.

On the other hand, they, the G. [Gestapo], considered it an unconditional rule that the Jews must be strictly isolated from the Lithuanians, not only in the sense that they must be in the ghetto, but also, when in the city, they must have no contact with the Lithuanians, not have any dealings with them.

But the Jews in the brigades had to acquire food products. In many brigades the Jews worked in an enclosed site, where people from the outside could not come in. If he wanted to buy something, the Jew had to sneak out of the workplace and go to the nearby gentile houses. In many places one had to go quite a ways to find something to buy, before reaching providers of food products. It was life-threatening for a Jew to walk down a street without a guard—any passing Lithuanian could stop him and turn him over to the G. [Gestapo], which entailed beating, jail, and sometimes even death. Jews therefore resorted to a different method: one would leave the work site, remove the patches, go up onto the sidewalk, and walk to one's destination. Very many Jews, particularly those who did not look particularly Jewish, succeeded in accomplishing what they set out to do and returned to their workplace, or waited for the brigade to return to the ghetto and joined it.

Many Jews made this dangerous trip—it became a daily occurrence; dozens of Jews in various brigades did this every day. This was known in the ghetto, and there were many warnings that this was a dangerous undertaking that would eventually lead to disaster, that they were risking their lives every moment.

One day, the G. [Gestapo] conducted an extensive hunt of Jews going without patches, caught twenty-four Jews in various city locations, and shot every one of them. On March 10, they officially informed the Elder Council that they had shot twenty-four Jews for being in the city without patches and required that the Elder Council inform the population and warn it that similar crimes would result in the offender being shot. Jews should take this into consideration and know that no one should dare to move around freely in the city and, especially, to go without patches.

Going without patches meant to them mixing with the Lithuanians, to which they reacted very strongly. Jews must be in strict isolation and not come into any contact with the Lithuanians. By comparison, if they caught a Jew on the street but with patches, he would be punished by beating or jail— for such an offense there would not be any shooting. (Only a few exceptions can be noted, among them the shooting of thirty-four Jews on February 4, 1943, a case that does not fall into this category because it was an act of revenge for Stalingrad! . . . It is our fault that they experienced such a great defeat there.)

Evacuation of "Brazilke"

On March 25, an order was given to evacuate by May 1 the entire left side of Paneriu Street, the so-called Brazilke.

Because of the housing problem, which was already acute, the evacuation of Brazilke created, to some extent, new difficulties. But, in general, this evacuation was carried out without the usual hooliganism, and we were given a deadline of over one month. This served to highlight the difference between Jordan and Wiedmann. The former gave us a period of four hours to evacuate Vienozinskio, while here we had a full month. One could quite calmly pack up and take along whatever one wished.

The Lithuanians also contributed to the order to evacuate Brazilke—they begrudged us the spaciousness in which we lived. The owners of the homes of this district began to petition the German authorities to remove the entire district from the ghetto. The priest of Slobodka also joined them, on the basis that the Christians from the surrounding streets going to church had to walk a long distance around the barbed wire to reach the church, which was located adjacent to the ghetto. Negotiations stretched over a long period of time; there was a struggle between the Lithuanians and the Germans; commissions came on a number of occasions to inspect the district, until they prevailed and, at the end of March, the order came to evacuate.

The police were given a large task in the evacuation. The ghetto commandant decreed that all houses in the district abandoned by Jews must be left in complete order; nothing was to be broken or disturbed, the doors, windows, ovens, electric lights—everything must be left in good order; trash and dirt that had accumulated in the houses during the winter must be removed. The commandant made the police responsible for the exact implementation of the order. The police therefore decreed that all inhabitants must straighten out the houses before leaving and, upon their departure, lock up and deliver the keys to the third police precinct.

The policemen inspected all the houses every day until late in the evening, checking to see whether everything was in order. When a resident brought the key of his former residence to the precinct, a policemen, before accepting the key, would first check the corresponding dwelling to see whether everything was in order as required. A tag with the address was attached to each key, to be turned over later to the ghetto commandant. He would frequently come to the precinct and check the houses himself to see whether his order was being carried out.

By May 1 the entire district was evacuated. The ghetto firefighters built a new fence around the reduced ghetto area. Until the fence was completed, the police patrolled the vacant district day and night.

Workers for Palemon

End of May there was again a small shock to the ghetto. A demand was received to provide 100 men for work in Palemon, about 7 or 8 kilometers from Kovno, for peat-work in a work camp.

The police had to recruit the people, again doing the dirty work, force-fully grabbing people at night from their beds for hard labor in a camp, dis-lodging them from their homes, to endure beatings and a life of starvation.

During the nights of June 1, 2, and 3, people were brought in according to lists put together by the Labor Office—a large number of people, all taken to the jail, where they were kept for the few days until the required number was reached. Germans and Lithuanians arrived on the morning of June 4 and took all the people to Palemon under heavy guard.

A few weeks later, they—the ones sent away—had become accustomed to their workplace, adjusted to their supervisors. Some even received per-mission from their supervisors to travel on Sabbath eve to the ghetto and to stay there until early Monday morning so as to be with their family members and to rest.

Within a short period of time, a tragic occurrence liquidated the entire workplace.

Saturday, June 30, in the evening, the guards of the Palemon camp, the Lithuanians, got drunk and thought up the amusement of shooting Jews. They pointed their guns at the Jews and fired. They immediately killed two Jews, and a few others were wounded. The next day, Sunday, July 1, a group of Jews came down and brought with them the two who were killed—Chaim Ackerman and Strassburg. At 11 o'clock in the evening of the same day an additional group of workers came and brought with them the deceased Sha-lom Levine, who had been wounded and who died from his wounds. The manager of the German labor office, Hermann, traveled to the site of the event to clarify what had happened there. In the end, the workers who had come here did not return there, and after a short while, the Jews who had remained there were also brought back, which closed the tragic first phase of the Palemon chapter; the next spring and summer of 1943 Jews were again sent to work in Palemon.

The Labor Quota

Throughout the entire spring and summer of 1942, the police had the cease-less task of providing the day and night labor quotas. All that time, start-ing in the month of March and continuing through the summer, persistent rumors circulated in different variations that the Germans were preparing to relocate some Jews to the Pravenishok province and that the people needed would be taken from the columns going into the city.

All these rumors had a negative effect on the labor quota, as people would hide, and even those who didn't want to malinger were afraid to go to the city because the rumors concerning trimming at the gate and relocation were very intense. Every morning there were great problems, brawls and shouting at the gate. The noncommissioned officer who would come to take the people to the airfield would be outraged, more than once slapping the policemen because the required number was not fulfilled. Bringing the people out to work every morning was a problem—hundreds were short every day.

This also reached the Gebietskommissariat [regional superintendent] and the SD. Representatives of the authorities came to the ghetto and quite sternly and explicitly warned that the entire ghetto would suffer greatly if the situation continued; they warned that they would publicly hang twenty men in the ghetto who would be snatched from the streets or from the houses and that they would also apply draconian measures against the Jews.

The Elder Council, the police, and the Labor Office were very worried; the situation was very serious, the mood depressed. Numerous meetings and consultations took place on how to extricate the ghetto from this painful situation and what measures to take.

It was a vicious circle: The restless mood and the rumors of relocation had a negative effect on achieving the labor quota and, at the same time, the shortage of people for the labor quota led to a restless mood and a variety of rumors.

On May 22, the Elder Council published a notice (similar to the one of March 13), which emphasized the difficult, disastrous condition that we were in. The shortage of people for work, the notice continued, would lead to serious and sorrowful consequences for us. Each and every one should consider that by not going to work he endangered not only his own life, but also those of his wife and children, as well as the entire existence of the ghetto. We existed and survived thanks only to our labor and our work output. To avoid one's work obligation was a frivolity that could cost the life of the entire community. All the rumors being spread that Jews would be sent out of the ghetto were groundless; if we worked regularly and consistently, there would not be any reductions of the ghetto population.

This notice was posted in the entire ghetto. The entire Jewish police was mobilized that evening to go from house to house with the text of this notice; all residents of the house were led into the courtyard and the text of the notice read to them.

In addition, the police systematically carried out strict controls. Entire streets and entire districts would be sealed off, streets surrounded in the morning and in the evening, and work documents checked. On Sundays, when everyone was at home, the police would encircle entire streets and check whether people had worked consistently the previous week. For improperly skipping a day, that is, without permission from a doctor or from the mobilization section, the penalty was arrest. That person would be in jail that day and throughout the night and be sent off directly to work the following morning. The police worked very hard in this domain, day and night; controls could not be allowed to be neglected to any degree, not even for one day—malingerers and sluggards would watch where the policeman was going; controls had to be constantly maintained; one had to always be on guard, to keep one's eyes open, to keep sending people off to work.

Economic Conditions; Gardens

Ghetto life during the entire spring and summer was varied. On the one hand, there were various shocks and experiences—evacuation, Palemon, rumors concerning Pravenishok, and so on; on the other hand, economic conditions in the ghetto improved significantly. Not only for those who, materially, lived very well in the ghetto—the so-called yalehs, and others who worked in good brigades and were, materially, no worse off in the ghetto than they had been in the city, but also for a large majority of the population, material conditions were significantly improved. Almost everyone had sufficient bread, and vegetables and fat were also available in significant quantities.

However absurd this may seem, it is a fact that the average ghetto Jew lived better than the average German in Germany. We, the segregated, expelled from society, smeared and persecuted by them, whom they confined within barbed wire, who every day anticipated annihilation, live better than the privileged Aryan, who lives in his own land and rules over almost all of Europe.

The improvement of economic conditions in the ghetto was due to many factors. The most important of them was, as we already noted above, the bringing into the ghetto of food products by trading at the fence and carrying them in through the gate, as well as by various other means. It was a daily occurrence for almost every office to arrange to collect money and to send a few of their people with an escort of an armed German guard (who had been well paid off) to buy food products for an entire group of people. Wiedmann, as noted, did not inquire into these matters, and the ghetto commandant Tiele would do anything for money, so that all the best could be had in the ghetto.

A provision commission was created during that time by the ghetto institutions, whose task it was to supply ghetto employees with food products. A cooperative was set up; any employee who wished to be a member of the cooperative had to acquire a share. The cooperative would bring in food products and sell to its members at cost.

The abundance from the planted gardens also contributed greatly to the improvement of economic conditions. It became a positive source of livelihood, providing substantial quantities of vegetables and potatoes. Initially, ghetto Jews looked with disdain upon planting in the gardens—people had "no faith" in it—but later it became quite an important element of the food supply process.

There was a plot for a garden next to nearly every house, over the entire ghetto area, particularly in the second and third districts. In addition, there were the large, public vacant lots that could also be planted.

The first push toward intensive planting came from the ghetto guard in the person of commandant Lot, who was, by nature, a domestic sort. He ordered that all vacant plots of land must be planted. It was also announced by the city that all vacant lots must be planted. The Elder Council ordered all vacant lots to be plowed and planted by a specified date. In accordance with the order of the commandant, Germans went around the ghetto to check whether the order had been carried out, so that, willingly or not, the Jews planted, and later each had his own place that supplied a part of his food needs.

Later, in July, a special organization by the name of ESCHEL—Irgun Shmira L-ganim [Hebrew—Organization for the Guarding of Gardens] was established for the protection of the gardens. The members of this organization were girls and boys aged ten to fifteen years old, with leadership and supervision by adults, whose assignment it was to patrol and guard the gardens of the ghetto institutions day and night so they would not be trampled and vegetables would not be stolen. The police also detailed a special group, called Garden Security, because the boys and girls could not carry out such an assignment by themselves. The policemen of the Garden Security group maintained day-and-night watch over all the gardens in the entire ghetto area.

As a result of the [improved] economic condition, the sources of income of the Elder Council also grew—it became a rich Elder Council, rich institutions, and all kinds of new offices were created in the ghetto.

The Social Office would distribute free bread and lunches to those without means. The Health Office established two institutions in the ghetto for the maintenance of health and hygiene: the bathhouse and the delousing facility, with a special room for disinfecting the clothing. The commandant was prevailed upon to allow the Jews to bathe in the river, and a beach was fashioned at the edge of the Vilia, just as in the days of freedom. The Education Office was expanded and filled out, the Garden Security organization ESCHEL, in addition to its official task of guarding the gardens, also carried out educational activities with its members. In a word, there was building, organizing, reorganizing, and the entire summer may be considered as a blossoming-time in the material sense and a reenergizing in the organizational-administrative sense.

In general, one felt a little more calm, somewhat more secure; there were no special evil decrees in these three or four months.

The Vilna Letter Episode

A small "intermezzo" occurred during that time that could have ended badly, with the most dire consequences especially to the Elder Council, but, fortunately, all ended well: it was the Vilna letter episode.

Here in the Kovno ghetto we knew that a large Jewish community existed in a ghetto in Vilna, but, except for one occasion, we had no contact with them.

A Lithuanian was encountered who made work-related trips every week from Kovno to Vilna. He met a few Jews in Kovno who were working in a brigade near the railroad station and he brought them a bundle of letters from the Jews in Vilna. While turning the letters over to them he told them that he would be returning [to Vilna] in a few days and if the Kovno Jews wished to write from Kovno, they should give him a bundle of letters that he would take there. The correspondence was set up in this manner: the Christian would come to take the letters from the Jews at their workplace and also bring them the replies. It happened once that the Christian did not show up for a long period of time, and the letters remained hidden at the workplace until a German accidentally found them and turned them over to the SD. This led to a big investigation; for Jews to correspond was strictly forbidden, especially illegal, uncensored correspondence in a foreign language from one city to another. The investigation showed that a legitimate office of the ghetto institutions was involved—the address bureau (that would collect the letters destined for Vilna), and that the general secretary of the Elder Council, J. B., had received a few letters. There was great danger that the G. [Gestapo] would accuse the Elder Council of organizing an illegal, subversive connection from one place to the other. What this implies in time of war in general, and for Jews in particular, is quite clear.

On May 7, the general secretary of the Elder Council, Mr. B., the assistant manager of the address bureau, Ch., the Jew who carried the letters back and forth to and from the city, Z., and the courier of the Elder Council, J., were arrested and taken to the central prison in the city.

Fortunately, the matter was successfully obliterated, with Caspi being of considerable help. The four arrested Jews remained in prison for three weeks and were released on May 28.

The result of this entire matter was that the general secretary of the Elder Council was removed from his position at the request of higher-ups, and his former assistant A. G. [Avraham Golub] was appointed in his place—a young, very energetic person, who occupies this position to this day, and is the right man in the right place.

Ghetto Commissions

Throughout the month of August, the ghetto was inundated with visits and commissions—a new German official or commission continually came to the ghetto. Among others, we were honored with a visit by the leader of the

SS and by the chief of the police of Lithuania, General Visoki, in addition to various high officials and commissions.

What do the commissions want, what is their objective, what is the purpose of their coming here, are they preparing new evil decrees for us—all these questions were on everyone's lips, but no one was able to figure it out; there were thousands of conjectures, but no specifics were known.

Before the arrival of such a commission in the ghetto, our regular Germans would inform the Elder Council or the workshops that important people were coming here and that an effort should be made to have everything in order. The Jewish police would seal off all the streets, prohibit all movement, and, except for the policemen on patrol, no one was to be found in the streets, because it was in our interest to show the commission that there were no people in the ghetto who did not work—everyone was occupied.

Our own Germans from the Stadts Kommissariat and from the SD also made an effort to have the ghetto make a good impression on the visitors, not because they loved us, but because each wanted to protect his own post. Should the commission or some higher-up official find that something was not in order in the ghetto, the person in question could be sent off to the front, and this none of them wanted.

Upon arrival in the ghetto, the first visit was usually to the workshops. They would be accompanied by the city commissar, who provided the explanations. The lies and exaggerations that he told them are unimaginable. He provided astronomical figures of the numbers of boots, military coats, and uniforms produced by the Jews in the workshops. He informed them that there were no non-able-bodied Jews in the ghetto, only healthy men and women. Such lies as to take one's breath away.

The German giving these explanations is only looking out for his own well-being. He raises his own prestige in the eyes of his superior officials, but for us this is, indirectly, beneficial.

The results of these visits had their effect somewhat later, by bringing about a new way of life in the ghetto. The new order consisted of a strict prohibition against bringing food products from the city into the ghetto and of a change in the entire financial structure of the ghetto—in accordance with the famous orders (decrees): orders No. 1, 2, and 4 of the Stadts Kommissar, dated August 25, 1942, which remain in effect to this day and which we will describe in detail in later segments.

The Police in the Spring and Summer of 1942 (the Caspi Period)

9

The Appearance of Caspi

The recent change in life inside the ghetto was characterized by the fact that, following the departure of Jordan, we had commissars and commandants over us who—some more and some less—were approachable and could be talked to. Higher-up functionaries of the ghetto institutions, the general-secretary of the Elder Council, A. Golub, and others, would frequently come to the relevant city commissariats in order to be informed, to be given orders, sometimes to plead or to intercede—specific contacts were established. They, the official [German] institutions, treated our Elder Council like an official Jewish entity, turned to it, and, on some occasions, gave consideration to its opinions concerning various ghetto matters.

The entire stabilization, whether on an internal basis—in the sense that material conditions had significantly improved—or on an external basis—in the sense that our general condition had settled into that of a legitimate community—led to reorganization, rearrangement, and reform of the entire official life of the ghetto.

Many changes also occurred in the police force in the course of that year. The system was reformed and rearranged a number of times, the management of the police was regrouped and partly changed, and lower functionaries were reassigned. But the reforms did not introduce any great innovations. In the end, it was no more than "a storm in a glass of water"—there is commotion, people run here and there like ants in an anthill. However, at the time, the reforms and internal shocks in the police force, particularly during the time of Caspi's rule, elicited much discussion and bad blood in the ghetto. There was commotion in the upper police circles, there were debates, altercations, something decided one day only to be regretted the next day, starting all over again the following day, everything swirling as though in a vicious circle.

One of the principal factors of this entire period was the person of Caspi, who exerted his influence on ghetto life in general and on the police in particular.

The Caspi chapter is a chapter unto itself—with a secretive beginning, a dramatic course, and a tragic ending. Were it not for the latter, that is, the tragic ending, it would not have been possible to write about it, because the people around him would not be talking, and authentic information would not have been available. Now that the person who created such a furor, who for a time was the center of attention in the ghetto, has disappeared from the horizon, one can sum up his work, his activities, the tumult and commotion that he caused, how he came to us as a dictator, what power he had at his disposal, and by whose authority he ruled.

It is indeed a difficult undertaking to provide a comprehensive picture, to describe this complex person, this raging volcano, this crazy rebel.

As soon as we came into the ghetto, Josef Caspi-Serebrovitz, who was well known in Kovno, started to show up. (His proper family name was Serebrovitch but, from the Russian word *serebro*—silver—he Hebraicized it to Caspi [*Kesef* = silver in Hebrew]).[1]

He did not move into the ghetto like all other Jews, but continued to live in the city, walked around without patches, was completely detached from the community, as if he was not a Jew at all. Word immediately got around

---

1. Roman C and Hebrew "K" are equivalent as are Roman p and Hebrew "f."

that Caspi worked for the Gestapo, that he was one of their agents, and that they had allowed him to remain in the city.

In Kovno he was known by all as a rebel, a hothead, a wild man. A couple of dozen years before, he had been a teacher in a Hebrew school in Rokiskis, where he had been dismissed because of his difficult personality. Local Jews also reported that he had been expelled from the school because of diploma abuses, which led later on to criminal proceedings against him.

Then he moved to Kovno. He inveigled his way into the Yiddishist newspaper *Folksblat;* later he moved over to the Revisionist *Moment* and became a passionate Zionist-Revisionist.[2] There he quarreled and argued with his comrades until they expelled him from the party. He was an average journalist, but had a light and smooth pen. Because of his ability to sneak and push his way in everywhere, he had many acquaintances in Lithuanian circles and was able to get in everywhere and secure interviews with higher-up personalities; everyone knew him because he was everywhere, whether or not he should have been there, and mingled in some Lithuanian circles that did not do us honor.

Later he became a shareholder and advertising manager of a large soap factory in Memel, earned very good money, and lived with his wife and two daughters a rich and prosperous life. It was also said in Kovno that he was working for the Lithuanian Okhranke[3] as a secret agent.

A few weeks after the Red Army marched into Lithuania, he was arrested and spent a full year in the Kovno jail.

When the Germans came in and the prisoners of the jail were freed, he was released along with everyone else and began to mingle in various Lithuanian circles where he had previously felt at home.

When the order came out on July 12 that Jews must wear patches, Caspi was observed bustling about in the streets as before, without patches; it was understood that he was working for the Gestapo. At that time, even before the Jews moved to the ghetto, he tried to persuade some of the Jews who were in the Soviet prison with him to remain with him in the city, saying that he would obtain the required permission for them to do so. All of them

2. Militant branch of the Zionist movement.
3. Secret police of Tsarist Russia.

refused categorically, so that, in fact, he remained the only Jew living legally in the city.

Jews in the ghetto talked about it a little, shrugged their shoulders at how it could be that at a time like this a Jew could be found who would agree to serve our bloody enemies for a pot of lentils. This might have been the end of it—there would have been some talk and then it would have stopped. But he began to frequently show up in the ghetto. Having the appropriate permission from the Gestapo to come into the ghetto, he would use it often to come here, at first quietly, as if he was ashamed of being set apart from everyone else, but coming more and more often as time went on.

His assignment in the police (to the extent that it was possible to confirm this later) consisted of being an informer concerning Lithuanian matters— Jews were not in his sphere of activity; he had nothing to do with them as such. In addition he had the task of providing goods to the higher-ups of the Gestapo, obtaining for them various items that could not normally be purchased. He was given permission to come to the ghetto to get these goods for them, for where is there a better place to buy various luxury items than from Jews in the ghetto, who are glad to be able to sell something or to trade it for food products?

Because of these assignments he would come to the ghetto, so to speak, on business. He would frequently come to the home of a Jew who had been with him in prison and make extensive inquiries about all ghetto affairs. The exact nature of his assignments was not known, but knowing that he was an agent of the Gestapo who must be feared, willingly or not, people would give him information about everything, and, with his nauseating noise and commotion, he began to mix into internal ghetto matters, more and more as time went on.

Later on he became a frequent visitor to a second Jew in the ghetto, became increasingly more involved, had an opinion and something to say about everything; one feared him and obeyed him. He spoke in the name of the Gestapo, loudly proclaiming that he was a trusted man of theirs, that he had important tasks to carry out, and that he was very much accepted by them. Since no one could prove that this was not so, out of fear he was allowed to go everywhere, to stick his nose into everything, and to be connected and master of it. As noted, except for his assignment to supply the Gestapo people with goods, he had, in fact, no business in the ghetto. It is known that one of his direct superiors, Rauca, warned him not to overdo his coming to the ghetto as he had nothing to search for there, but he always found excuses for coming here.

At first he would tell his superior that he must come to the ghetto to visit his friends with whom he was together in prison in order to obtain from them specific information about Lithuanians that he needed to investigate. He would also say that concerning some matters involving Lithuanians he must also question some Jews and that he therefore had to frequently be in the ghetto.

From a psychological perspective, this is easy enough to explain. Being a native Jew who, from his childhood, was brought up as a Jew, who lived all his life with and among Jews, he would find it difficult to live alone, separated from everyone, among gentile enemies. With his very stormy nature, he had to be with Jews, to be among his equals, where he could converse in a genuine Jewish manner, to argue and to shout. He was therefore drawn to a Jewish environment, he was drawn to the ghetto.

To be truthful, it must be emphasized that he did not, personally, cause any harm to Jews. The opposite, he tried at every opportunity to save Jews in trouble. A number of instances attest to the fact that he covered up many early investigations against Jews that would have led to sad consequences for those involved.

To do in Lithuanians—that he pursued wholeheartedly. He sought out opportunities to cause trouble to Lithuanians, investigating them, attributing crimes to them; he derived moral satisfaction from causing harm to a Lithuanian. He would not miss an opportunity to pick on them and to discredit them in the eyes of the Germans.

In spite of the warnings from his superior, he came to the ghetto more frequently and for longer periods of time, becoming involved and entangled in ghetto matters. Slowly he got them used to the idea that he was needed in the ghetto as contact man for the Jews, and, later, he acted as such.

After the two individual Jews whom he had visited often had had enough of him because of his carrying on and shouting, he settled into the police force; that is, upon coming into the ghetto he made police headquarters his quarters. He argued that the police force was his organ and relished being called chief of police. Officially and unofficially he had absolutely nothing to do with the Jewish ghetto police, but since he wanted to express his opinions about a wide range of ghetto matters, he needed a place where he could rule, and he therefore slowly inveigled himself into police headquarters, because here there were properly repaired and comfortably furnished, nice rooms; he settled in there and played the lord. He argued that the police were loyal to him (what this loyalty consisted of no one knew, apparently including also himself). The police force belonged to him, he was its chief, it was at his disposition.

The police belonged to him as much as anything else in the ghetto belonged to him, but there were motives, associated with internal "house politics," that thrust the police management into Caspi's arms, allowing him to become entrenched, causing them to tolerate him, to honor him, and to be ruled by him. The motives leading to this had to do with relationships with the Elder Council, which, as previously noted, were not particularly friendly for a variety of reasons.

Numerically, the police force was the largest organized entity in the ghetto—a large organization but without a head, without leadership. The leaders, or, more precisely, the chief of police, had no influence there; he was not able to have his opinions accepted, which he, by the way, never had been. He allowed everyone to influence him, and whatever the Elder Council wished to do, they did, even in his name.

The influence of the "competing" organization—the Labor Office—became increasingly greater in the Elder Council. The police had to fight them during their parallel assignments for the production of the labor quota, because they always wanted to be over the police. But the police were unable to fight them for influence in the Elder Council, because the police had no leadership, and those in management positions didn't know what they wanted, and their influence was nonexistent. In the labor office there were always people able to advance their points of view and be reckoned with. These were solid, deliberate people. By contrast, the police did not have such people and, even if there were such people, with the energy and courage to strive to gain influence, they were either too young or were not personally liked.

The police wanted to and needed to have a backup, a representative in the Elder Council. When Caspi appeared on the horizon and, as noted, began to come to the police more and more often, they started to make use of him and made him their "spokesman" in the Elder Council. Whenever something needed to be accomplished there, Caspi would be prompted to do it. He, who, as noted, constantly sought to be with and among Jews, looked upon such missions as trust in him and gladly carried them out. He allowed himself to be prompted by the police and would run there to win the case. The police saw him as a good trump card and used him increasingly more and more.

The Elder Council, seeing that Caspi was the patron of the police, was annoyed by the fact that the police utilized an outsider as their spokesman; rather than coming themselves to present their complaints and demands, they sent Caspi instead. They resented it very much, and rightly so. The disagreements, the unfriendliness between the Elder Council and the police, became sharper.

The police probably also understood that it would have been better, nicer, and more comfortable for them to come themselves to seek influence for themselves. But, because of the previously listed objective reasons, this could not be accomplished, so that, willingly or not, they held on to Caspi, leaning on his broad shoulders. In this way, in the course of a short period of time, he became the de facto master of the police. He would sit all day long in police headquarters, from there exercising his rule.

Somewhat later, when the tumult and unease caused by him could no longer be tolerated, and also by his own special request, he was provided with a separate room in block B, across from headquarters, the famous room 19, where he would sit all day and conduct his affairs.

Very pleased with his power and the respect bestowed upon him in the ghetto, ten times a day he would proclaim himself chief of the police. The latter obeyed him and honored him first out of fear and second because they needed him.

It will be of interest to provide a picture, to characterize the Caspi type, because as a type he was, in some sense, one of a kind.

The Caspi Personality

He was a man who never knew what he wanted, who was never content, never quiet, unable to sit for ten minutes in one place, who, it would seem, jumped asleep out of bed, always sweating and puffing, hustling and bustling, constantly pacing back and forth in the room, constantly looking for something to pick on to give him the opportunity to bang on the table, to shout, to make noise, to make a racket, to intimidate, to scream his head off with mayhem and pandemonium, to vent his anger and dismay over trivial and silly matters, and at the same time to take the opportunity to settle accounts with someone who might have made him angry, and to accuse him of silly personal offenses which that person supposedly committed against him years ago. At the same time, he would talk about himself, about his greatness and his importance in the eyes of this or that personality. He would describe, with great aplomb, how this or that one did not think much of him and how he got even with him and how he told him off. In the middle of his shouting and anger he would start to tell stories, tales, parables, pouring out witticisms and anecdotes, episodes, experiences, and happenings that, in themselves were interesting and sometimes even informative, but they stuck to the subject, which initially had made him so angry, like peas to a wall.

He was very astute, quick-witted, intelligent, possessing a large supply of general as well as Jewish knowledge, but, just like his entire being, his acquired learning was so chaotic, such a mixture of this and that, that he himself got tangled up in it all, kicking like a young horse reined in for the first time.

He never carried out a task to its conclusion, becoming so entangled, so twisted up in it that he was unable to disentangle himself from it. The large-scope activity that he had just undertaken with so much noise and commotion, he would abandon the next day. He would start something different with his customary tumult the day after that, again abandon it, and so on, constantly. He was capable of working all day and night and would not let those around him sleep or rest.

He had good qualities, afflictions, and obsessions. He had the affliction of preaching—randomly holding forth with lectures. In the midst of dealing with the most important issues, he would begin to lecture, talk, describe, pour out words, become entangled, no longer knowing what he started with and how he was going to end it, simply talking for the sake of talking, to unburden himself. Each story and tale a pearl by itself, but a hodgepodge when taken together—a preposterous concoction, mixing the lowliest dirty words with quotations from the Gemara[4] and spicing things up with a parable that had nothing to do with the matter. In the midst of talking he would suddenly remark that this or that higher-up functionary was somehow not present and, forgetting all about his topic with its lectures and fables, shout at the top of his voice, "Where is he? Doesn't he know that I am here? Where did he go? He must be brought here immediately." After a while, he would forget about him and continue to lecture. Or he would order everyone to immediately leave the room—he had important matters to take care of— remain sitting by himself in the room for a few minutes, then start again to run around from one place to another, bringing up or seeking out matters that had already been taken care of or that he had himself abandoned a long time ago, unfold new matters, and drag everyone out of bed, quite frequently at twelve or one o'clock in the middle of the night.

Seeking respect was also a kind of affliction of his. He very much relished being respected, being admired and praised, being considered defender and savior of the ghetto community, being called its leader, having everyone stand in awe before him, not out of fear, but as if internally driven to give him—the great one, the powerful one, the perfect one—the respect that was his due.

If, God forbid, someone raised doubts about his honor, it was as though the sky had opened up; he could not take it—how was it possible that someone should so offend him? He would become very agitated, recount his distinguished background going back ten generations, recount for the hundredth time his biography with all its great accomplishments for the Jewish community, and conclude—in a flood of words that jumped from one thing to another—with: "This or that one had the audacity to speak ill of me. I, Caspi-Serebrovitz, say that I will show him who I am, I will teach him good manners and he will know who Caspi-Serebrovitz is."

Physically he was ill. He had a heart ailment, was a diabetic, was not supposed to eat excessively, was to be on a diet, not to drink any alcohol, not to become excited. He paid no attention to any of this, doing the opposite of what was needed to preserve his health, eating anything that he fancied,

---

4. Second part of the Talmud (writings on Jewish civil and religious law), providing commentary on the first part, the Mishna (oral interpretations of scriptural ordinances).

frequently enjoying having a good drink, partying with young, pretty women—a regular playboy.

His external appearance made a very good impression. Somewhat taller than average with a full, round face, with quite nice facial features, large restless eyes, very pronounced wrinkles at the sides of the nose and mouth, a head with constantly disheveled dark hair, whose constant disarray gave him a certain charm, pale lackluster complexion, always smoothly shaven, clean, always dressed according to the latest fashion, he emanated a pleasant scent and presented a spotless appearance. Heavy, with a substantial round belly, strong broad shoulders that imparted a certain importance, the fingers on his hand adorned with a number of rings, always with an elegant cane and gloves, depending on the weather—his external appearance gave the impression of quite a healthy, energetic man.

In addition to his sick heart he also had a sick soul. In addition to the chaotic confusion of his spirit, he was also prone to contradict himself.

He was an amiable Jew, a fervent nationalist, constantly proclaiming to be a Zionist-Revisionist.

On the other hand, it did not bother him, as a Jew and as a Zionist, to sell out to the Gestapo; it did not at all shock him to be an outsider with respect to the community, not to be with or share the troubles of all the Jews in the ghetto, but to live in the city, one Jew among the gentiles; to be the one at whom fingers were quietly pointed, "here goes the Jew who serves the Gestapo." For him it was one and the same—Jewishness, a warm Jewish heart, nationalism, and, at the same time, selling his body and soul for money to the worst murderers in the history of the Jews—one did not interfere with the other; apparently, his conflicted soul could digest it all.

It can readily be imagined from this brief description of the Caspi type how difficult it was for the police management, and for the official Jewish offices of the ghetto in general, to work under his direction. Each time, over every small matter, our officials had to maneuver, to scheme, to conceal from him so as not to provoke his anger, to avoid feuding with him, which, given his difficult character, was unavoidable. It was particularly difficult for the police management, where, as noted, he continuously located himself, entangling himself everywhere and into everything, and proclaiming every day with great pathos to be the chief of the police.

Police Reforms and Reorganizations; New Management[5]

In the spring of 1942 and throughout the entire summer various reorganizations and reforms of the police took place in which, needless to say, Caspi played a major role.

In accordance with a decree of the authorities, a reduction in the staff of all ghetto offices took place at the beginning of April. Their explanation was that it was necessary to release more people from the administrative apparatus to meet the labor quota. Fifty percent of all employees of the ghetto institutions had to be let go and fifty men from the police. After long meetings, arguments, and commotion, where Caspi shouted and made noise louder than everyone else, the police reduction came about. It was announced in the order of the day of April 6 that forty-six men had been removed from active duty, that the address bureau was being separated from the police, and that the eleven men who worked there were considered to have been removed from the police budget. Also let go were two investigators, four medical personnel, and a few craftsmen and workers who had been part of the budget—a total of seventy-seven men.

A small reorganization was carried out among the middle functionaries whose positions could not be justified. The reduction of the middle police officials consisted of having the deputy chief of the second precinct, Tabakin, and the chief of the gate guards, Birger, who held the rank of deputy chief, downgraded to the rank of master of the guard. Two masters of the guard were downgraded to ordinary policemen. Actually, a few higher officials, in addition to the four, should have been downgraded or let go, because some among them didn't do anything, or, more accurately, they did do something, but not that which was needed; their behavior was such that their wearing the police hat and armband did not do us honor. But that is the case in all ghetto offices as well as in the police; when it comes to a reduction, the ones to be removed are not the ones who should be let go, but the ones who could be removed, the ones who allow it to be done to them.

As noted, the large reduction of April 6 did not come about without "birth pains." Meetings went on day and night, where the list of those to

5. This heading is provided in the table of contents of the manuscript, not in the text itself.

be discharged was constantly being revised. Use of vitamin and of protektsia began; whoever had connections rushed to seek intervention, and there were such policemen who were able to reverse their expected discharge. The commotion associated with the force reduction went on in this manner for a long time.

Simultaneously with the reforms and reduction there were also reassignments of the managing functionaries.

The police inspector Gudinski, although an intelligent man and no fool, had nevertheless caused the police much bad blood with his behavior. Along with a few more high police functionaries, he went on drinking bouts. Rumors spread in the ghetto that the police were carousing, and so it is, always and everywhere, that when two or three people who occupy a higher position in a particular office do not conduct themselves properly, the entire unit gets a bad name.

This reached a culmination point with a big drinking bout that took place on April 13 at Vienozinskio 3. A number of high police officials assembled there as well as a few women, and drinking went on until late into the night.

The entire matter was publicized by the chief of the third precinct, who submitted a report concerning it to the Elder Council. It became a scandal. The Elder Council appointed a special commission to investigate the matter and to punish the guilty ones. The commission called in all the participants of the drinking spree, questioning and investigating them. The Elder Council, which even before then had not had a particularly friendly attitude toward the police, especially toward some of the high functionaries, took advantage of this affair to insist that some of the higher officials be discharged. It was necessary to persuade Caspi, who stood up for the officials. Caspi, being a drinker himself, was in fact the "spiritual father" of all the prearranged drinking sprees; he was almost the first one to have made this into a custom, and there was no lack of followers.

No matter what happened, this affair could not be easily covered up; a reorganization of the higher and middle functionaries had to take place. Inspector Gudinski, aside from his misbehavior, generally abandoned interest in his official duties, did absolutely nothing, only serving as an example of malingering to all policemen—he was dismissed from his position and appointed official of special matters. The Elder Council wanted to get rid of him entirely. The police management would have gladly agreed, but, once more, Caspi, who had something to say about everything, gave his opinion, and one had to follow his instructions.

From the precincts there was also a demand for the rearrangement of the chiefs and their deputies. The prevailing tense atmosphere associated with the reductions and the commotion in management had an effect on the work of the precincts. In the precincts as well as in service locations, groups of policemen constantly congregated and talked, discussing politics, listening to each other's stories and gossip, which were passed on from mouth to mouth, embellished with a wealth of fantasies.

The first precinct, the largest one in the ghetto measured by the number of people in it and the one most burdened with work, ceased to function properly. Its chief, Robinson, an honest and quiet man, but without energy or initiative, was unable to supervise the work, not having the enterprising spirit needed for it and also being lazy. In the criminal department, the deputy chief Padison, one of the creators of the police, otherwise quite an energetic and capable person, now became one of those who engaged in drinking and who contributed to the creation of a bad name for the police.

After lengthy arguments and negotiations it was decided to make some reassignments; on May 6 they were carried out in the following manner.

Grinberg, chief of the third precinct, although quite young—almost a boy—displayed unusual honesty, a firm hand, directness, and sincerity. He was appointed chief of the first precinct.

The former deputy chief of the third precinct, Panemunski, was promoted to chief of the same precinct. The former chief of the first precinct was appointed deputy chief of the criminal division. The former deputy chief of the criminal division, Padison, was appointed deputy chief of the third precinct; a few weeks later he was removed from the third precinct and appointed functionary for special matters. Later, he supervised the garden protection unit, the firewood guards, and so on.

Caspi played a large role in all of these reassignments; he would come every day with a new project, with new plans. He was the main commotion-maker or, as he was called in the ghetto, the "principal storm-maker." Unable to sit still, he would constantly look for new plans, new ideas.

For example, at the end of April he had the idea of creating a special unit in the police, and in the middle of May such a unit came into being. As chief of this unit he appointed the functionary for special matters, Gudinski. He needed this unit because he apparently wanted to justify in the eyes of his Gestapo supervisors his frequent coming to the ghetto; so he spun all kinds of plans and built castles in the air.

In addition, because he had a mania that people were not faithful to him, he wanted to establish a group of people in the police with whom he could work. From among the policemen he selected a group of individuals who would regularly be at his disposition and whom he could trust. Why he needed this none of us knew, nor did he himself . . . because, other than to run around for him as couriers on all kinds of errands, they had no special assignments; why he needed them was not clear, but, like all his other crazy and wild ideas, they had to be tolerated.

The personal selection of the people for this special unit was, like all his doings, made haphazardly and with commotion.

First of all, he selected a few [Zionist] Revisionists from among the policemen—they became the nucleus of the special unit who were to be faithful to him and to his "ideas." To them he added: a few relatives, a few good brothers, with whom he had had some good drinks in Kovno, a few of those whose stores he used to patronize in the old days, and some who had placed advertisements in his newspapers in the past . . . He assembled all of them and from this concoction he created this special unit, a "faithful group of policemen."

Everyone laughed about this entire matter—which was a joke, the fantasy of a hothead—but feared to say anything against it; there was no desire to bring on his rage and gain his displeasure.

But he had his reasons for all of this—he could brag to his chief that he was "accomplishing things in the ghetto"; that he had created a police unit consisting of particularly reliable and trustworthy people.

From an objective perspective the management can therefore in many instances not be blamed for the commotion in the police during those times, because everyone was overshadowed by the Caspi figure.

On the other hand, the absence of a proper chief of police—a man with a firm hand and of strong character—made many things possible that could have otherwise been avoided.

Kopelman, the chief of police, while a very intelligent and decent man, displayed absolutely no energy or any kind of initiative. Caspi would cause him great troubles, insult him in front of everyone, shout at him that he did not understand anything, was not good for anything, that he was a chief on paper only. In a certain sense he was right, because his only good quality was that he didn't bother anybody, but on his own he did nothing—with his decency, intelligence, and good manners he was no more than a label. As a result of this, the idea of reorganizing the police management ripened.

From the very beginning Caspi intended, and proclaimed to every one, that, first of all, chief Kopelman must be removed because he was not appropriate for this position. But he was unable to bring this about. Kopelman was the chief of police from the very first day, who, because of his modesty, had many supporters in the Elder Council and, in a certain sense, was also a contact with the authorities. Because of this it was decided to bring a new person into the management. Until then the management consisted of three persons: the chief, Kopelman, the deputy chief, Zupovitz, and the inspector, Gudinski. After the inspector was removed from his position, only two remained. Since Chief Kopelman showed little interest, Zupovitz was in effect the chief of police.

A new addition to the management was now needed, a person with social stature and a good name, who would raise a little the prestige of the police. The vice-chairman of the ghetto court, Abramovitz, was selected and appointed deputy chief of the police.

For the moment this was a way out of the situation. The chief, K. [Kopelman], remained in his position and, in order to have new blood in the police, A. [Abramovitz] was brought in. The former deputy chief Z. [Zupovitz], was released from his position and appointed police inspector and member of the management.

There was another reason why A. [Abramovitz] was appointed deputy chief of police, namely, because the function of the ghetto court was incorporated into the police.

In the month of July, by order of the authorities, there was a reduction in the staff of the ghetto institutions, which included the elimination of the ghetto court; it was only allowed to create a penal division within the Jewish ghetto police.

An activity statute was worked out for the penal division, within the scope of an addition to the general police statute, which was confirmed by the chairman of the Elder Council on July 20. The penal division (which we will consider separately later) and all other matters dealing with administrative and judicial issues were handled by the new man, A. [Abramovitz], who was a known Kovno jurist.

Abramovitz is a good jurist and a specialist in his profession, but not a chief for a police organization. About matters of duties, discipline, and internal order he understood absolutely nothing; he has no initiative, no energy, and does not bring forth from the policemen good manners or fear toward himself, which must be there toward a chief. In the internal life of the police, besides his management of the penal division and of administrative charges, he did not introduce any great changes and is, to this day, quite an unimportant person.

In the same order-of-the-day of July 2, 1942, establishing the new reorganization of the management, there was also an announcement of the furloughing of the chief of the criminal division, Bramson, who was later—on July 20—removed entirely.

Bramson, the de facto organizer of the police and its first deputy chief of police, had lately become completely negligent. On the one hand, he fell into the disfavor of Caspi, who was constantly looking for ways to have him dismissed, and, in addition, the Elder Council lost its trust in him. He was also involved in the Vienozinskio affair—a participant in the festivity. As noted, after the investigation undertaken by the commission that had been established by the Elder Council, reforms had to be made. Bramson became the scapegoat for the whole affair; the dislike of him as well as the loss of trust in him led to his being dismissed from the police. In his place as chief of the criminal division was appointed the former manager of the address bureau and later police headquarters functionary for special matters, M. Levin.

Levin is an unusual person. He is one of the few people in the police to display unusual energy, to exhibit skill and devotion to the task at hand. It is a fact that while others cause aggravation because they have little energy, his deficiency is that he has too much of it, that is, that no matter what position he occupies or what task he is given to carry out, he works with such energy and intensity that he overshadows those above him in rank with his unusual agility. This caused many quarrels between him and management. There was also an unstated reason for transferring him to be chief of the criminal division: so he would not meddle too much in headquarters, just manage his own office.

He distinguished himself in his position as chief of the criminal division, applying his great energy and devotion day and night, and accomplishing a great deal in combating criminal offenders. Many crimes were uncovered as a result of his initiative. He did not rest, did not sleep, going around with his policemen for entire nights in rain and cold (despite his ailing heart), looking, searching until he accomplished what he set out to do.

Following the management reorganization and all the other previously listed changes, an additional staff reduction of twenty men occurred in the police on July 7. Incidentally, following the reductions of April 6, sixteen of those released were taken back on May 10. Caspi bragged at that time that this was his accomplishment, that he had arranged with the authorities to allow an increase in the staff.

And so it went during the spring and summer—constant commotion in the police, increases, reductions, reorganizations, and so on.

Caspi's Departure

A rumor spread in the ghetto at the end of summer (the end of August) that Caspi was being transferred to Vilna. He himself came to say: "I am being transferred to Vilna, but I feel that these are my last days; I think that I will never return from Vilna." Rumors also circulated that he would be sent there to the ghetto, like all other Jews. Apparently, he and his work were no longer needed; he was not useful to them any more, and they decided to liquidate him.

One nice day he, his wife, and both of his children were taken to Vilna. To this day we have heard nothing further from him, and, to tell the truth, no one was interested. But, as we learned from reliable sources, he and his family were brought to Vilna, and all were shot the same day.

This is the end of the Caspi episode, the end of the life of an uprooted Jew, who sought to come out of his own skin, to be someone that he wasn't, to escape from the ranks of the weak and attach himself to the strong.

He attached himself to the grinding wheels of bloody Nazism and perished. A pity, one more Jew perished, albeit a bad Jew—he did not do us honor, but, still, a Jew, one more gone. How many of us are still left.

The Ghetto in the Times of Koeppen, Miller, and the Vienna Protection Police (Schutz Polizei)

10

An Economy without Money

The financial regulation of the various offices of the ghetto institutions was arranged according to a municipal system designed to suit the ghetto conditions. All moneys received by the Elder Council treasury through the various offices—for example, the Food Distribution Office, Housekeeping Office, Housing Office, and so on—were dispensed through the Elder Council for payment to the various offices and institutions and to cover various obligations. The payments were always very large, and balancing the budget always entailed certain difficulties. Basically, however, an established financial system was in place and existing arrangements worked well.

The famous new decree of August 25 [1942] completely transformed the internal economic life of the ghetto and marked a new period of ghetto life—an economy without money.

Decree No. 1 stated: As of today, food products (rations) in the ghetto will be disbursed to the population at no cost. Bringing in supplies from the city, or in any other way obtaining food products beyond the rations, is strictly forbidden.

Decree No. 2 stated: All ghetto inhabitants will be provided with foot-wear, clothing, and heating supplies, in addition to food, as needed. Any kind of money exchange in the ghetto is strictly forbidden. (As a consequence of this, all treasuries in the offices are dissolved, taxes and salaries are forbidden; the ghetto must fulfill its labor quotas to the city-commissariat at no cost.) All ghetto facilities belong to the city-commissariat. The immediate closing of all schools is ordered, and future private tutoring and religious services are forbidden.

At first all these regulations had a very depressing effect on the ghetto. Later, one became accustomed to them and they became tolerable. Initially, this was something very new to us—housekeeping without money: one receives everything without the exchange of money, there is no income and no payments; a starvation-ration is thrown at us and we are expected to survive on it.

Two or three weeks before the new decree of August 25, it was known in the ghetto that bringing products into the ghetto would be allowed until August 27; after that it would be prohibited. During the same time period, in the course of the entire month, there were constant visits and commissions; it felt as though something new was afoot.

About a week before August 26, the city-commissariat inquired of the Elder Council how much money was held in its treasury. They ordered the council to retain only a few thousand rubles and to turn the rest over to the commissariat. Koeppen came to the ghetto a few days later and took away the remaining money in the Elder Council treasury. Koeppen was the representative of the city-commissariat to the ghetto (Wiedmann's replacement). He was a young German, a Nazi, and a zealous foe of the Jewish people.

Removal of the money from the ghetto created a great stir. It was remembered that on October 27, 1941, the day before the Great Action, all the money in the ghetto was seized by Jordan. Perhaps there was no basis for thinking that an action was to take place in a few days, but nevertheless there was much fear.

During the ten days preceding August 26, the ghetto population hurried to acquire food products, to bring as much as possible into the ghetto. The week before the 26th, controls at the gate became weak; the NSKK people looked the other way. The Labor Office distributed a great many one-time passes for those not working in brigades; thousands of people pressed to go to the city in the morning, each seeking to bring back as much as possible.

On August 26, the bringing in of products was shut off. In any event, almost nothing was brought in the first week. The authorities also announced that, in addition to the German and Lithuanian gate controls, the Jewish police was also responsible for assuring that nothing was brought into the ghetto; the Jewish police would be responsible for each attempt to do so. The chief of the Jewish police also publicly informed the population of this.

Experience showed a short time later that the entire commotion over August 26 was somewhat exaggerated. Initially it was indeed not possible to bring in products, but this hardly affected the ghetto food supply. Slowly people started to carry products through the gate, at first in their pockets, and then more—the sentry at the gate was bribed and products were brought in. The fence-traders also actively applied themselves to their work, with hundreds of kilograms of various products coming through the fence at night, such that there was no sense of food shortage in the ghetto. The one difference was that money, as such, became nonkosher in the ghetto. It was important to be very careful not to have any money on you, particularly at the gate. Because if money was found on someone, it would be taken away, and, in addition, he would be punished for having it.

Days of Awe, Again Palemon

The summer passed and we advanced to the Jewish New Year, Rosh Hashanah *T.Sh. "G.* [5703].

Optimists made the calculation that the preceding year was *T.Sh. "B.*, that is, *tavo shanat b-hala* ("a year of panic will come"), while the new year was *T.Sh. "G.*, which means *tavo shanat ge-ula* ("a year of redemption will come"). The interpretation fits, and the interpreters are well-meaning, but whether this will indeed be so, whether the new year will be a year of salvation, for this there are at present no indications.

On Rosh Hashanah eve, September 11, we received a "surprise" in honor of the New Year: from the columns returning from the city, people were separated out at the gate for Palemon.

A new Palemon chapter, precisely on Rosh Hashanah eve. A demand for people for Palemon was received; parts of brigades were separated and taken to the jail; from there they were supposed to be transported to work. By evening the required number of people had not been assembled, and so people had to be taken again the next day. As this stretched to another day, the protektsia with the vitamins came into play.

Relatives of those taken by the police ran to intercede for their release. Many who had acquaintances and connections succeeded. But those released had to be replaced with others, and so, rather than one or two days, the recruitment dragged out for a whole four days. This resulted in a tragic-comic situation.

The police are given a list of people to be taken. The list is quite long, and the police run around and assemble the people according to the list and are relieved to have taken care of the problem. But that is not the end of it. Through influence some of the assembled people are released, so that the required number is not achieved; the police are given a supplemental list, they continue to assemble these new people, and, again, relatives run to intercede for the newly assembled; some of them are released, again the required number is not there, the police receive a new list—a story without end or limit, a sack full of holes. The policemen are made to run around like dogs, four days without food or sleep, and the people who were assembled the first evening and have no one to intercede on their behalf are sitting for four days shut in prison for no good reason, all because there is no order.

Had the first list been accurately and properly prepared, without those whom it was decided should be taken having recourse to appeals and influence, then everything would have been accomplished in an orderly manner. But the opposite impression was given, that the police were the evil ones—they were the ones who drag people from their beds in the middle of the night, having no pity for their brothers, even though the police themselves owe their souls to God. But, in fact, the guilty ones were those who were unable to carry out a task in an orderly and systematic manner—that is, the Labor Office.

The Palemon action was concluded only by September 15.

The New Year arrived—for the second time, Days of Awe in the ghetto. In accordance with decree No. 2, praying was strictly forbidden; Koeppen had already taken care of that. But this did not stop Jews: whether secular or orthodox, they made minyonim for Rosh Hashanah and Yom Kippur, arranged secretly and in hiding; in private homes, in side streets, in a room in the hospital, on the third floor of the blocks, minyonim were arranged wherever it was possible and wherever it could be done. Many who in normal times would not go to the synagogue went to pray in the ghetto to spite the bloody enemies and their prohibitions, like the Marranos[1] in Spain, all together appealing to God to have pity and bring to an end our terrible troubles, *ki sa-avor memsheles zadon min ha-aretz.*[2]

Two episodes from the Days of Awe are of interest. One occurred on Rosh Hashanah and the other on Yom Kippur; they could have ended badly, but, fortunately, we got off with only fright.

The second day of Rosh Hashanah fell on a Sunday. A group of policemen and employees of ghetto institutions, who had not had the opportunity or the time to go to pray on the first day of Rosh Hashanah, collaborated to make a minyan on Sunday, the second day.

It was decided to make the minyan no more and no less than in the German labor office, in the room of SA Hauptsturmführer Hermann. Not a minor audacity. Since it was Sunday—a day when the German labor office was closed and Hermann never came to the ghetto—what better place for an illegal minyan under Hitler's regime than in the room and office where a Hitlerite conducts his affairs? They prayed, the morning prayer was completed, the Torah reading was done, the shofar [ram's horn] was blown—all was well and good.

In the midst of the afternoon prayer, as the deputy chief of police A., who was leading the afternoon prayer, was in the middle of the *unesahne toikef*,[3] spinning the *mi le-khaym u-mi lamohves* ["Who shall live and who shall die"], one of the congregants gave a shout: "A German is riding toward us!" Everyone looked through the window and saw in the distance that a uniformed German was riding straight in their direction, toward the German labor office. There was a great commotion and panic, prayer shawls were hastily removed, some jumped through the window to the courtyard, and the rest crowded together into a second room so that, if he should come in,

---

1. Secret practitioners of Judaism.
2. "That the rule of malice should pass from the world."
3. Prayer of the day of judgment, recited on Rosh Hashanah and Yom Kippur.

it would be possible to slink out from this adjacent room, because it was no longer possible to leave directly by the entrance door.

It turned out that the German riding toward us was the commandant of the ghetto[-guard]. Quite calmly he rode by, without stopping, and everyone breathed with relief. But they were bewildered, depressed, and disheartened, imagining how they would have looked if the commandant had entered the German labor office and found Jews at prayer, most of them members of the police and of ghetto institutions. They got off with a scare.

The second episode occurred on Yom Kippur. Around twelve noon, one o'clock, Koeppen arrived in the ghetto. He came to the Elder Council by car, together with another German, a doctor, whom he brought to show how the ghetto hospital was organized. A minyan had been arranged in a room in the hospital, including a cantor and all the paraphernalia. One can imagine the sad consequences if Koeppen had come and found in an official branch of the ghetto administration, in the hospital, a large crowd engaged in religious service contrary to his just-decreed strict prohibition.

The policeman on duty at the Elder Council, having learned where Koeppen was preparing to go, sent a policeman to the hospital to tell the assembled people to immediately disperse. The policeman went as fast as he could and arrived a few minutes before the car. The assembled worshippers managed to get away. Koeppen came into the hospital with his guest, looked around for a while, and immediately went back. Fortunately, he did not go into all the rooms.

Marranos of the twentieth century.

Our ghetto offices were concerned about the labor quota for the day of Yom Kippur. There were hundreds, perhaps thousands of people who did not want to have to work on this one day of the entire year. But exactly on Yom Kippur they could demand more people for work than any other day, and great unpleasantness could result to the ghetto if many people were missing from the labor quota exactly on that day. Because of this, the Kovno rabbi made a public announcement that because of the present conditions of our existence, not going to work threatened the life of thousands of Jews. The matter involved *pikuakh nefesh* [the saving of lives], and all Jews were therefore required to go to work, so as not to endanger the Jewish community. Several hundred copies of this announcement were printed; the entire

Jewish police force was mobilized on Yom Kippur, and they went from house to house to distribute and to proclaim the printed announcement.

Vienozinskio Area Cleared Again

On September 25, which fell on a Friday, the eve of Sukkoth, an order was received to vacate the area of Vienozhinskio for the second time. (After the first evacuation on January 11, German Jews were supposed to have been settled there, but, as previously mentioned, they did not come, and after a few months, when the Brazilke area was evacuated, Jews were allowed to return and settle there.) In fact, rumors had been circulating for a while in the ghetto that this area would be evacuated, and people were already moving out a few days before the official order. The official announcement was made on September 25 to evacuate the area by October 5—an interval of ten days.

From then on, and to this day, the problem of housing became very acute. Two areas were taken away from us—Brazilke and Vienozhinskio, where, all told, there lived about two and a half thousand souls.

All those evacuated were resettled throughout the entire ghetto region, thereby further crowding all the other residents.

Riga a Second Time

Once more rumors began to circulate in the ghetto that people were again needed for Riga. The mood became dark; people were nervous, which had a negative impact on the fulfillment of the daily labor quotas. Even though there were letters and greetings from the first party of Jews, who had gone to Riga in February 1942, that they were alive and working, that they were, relatively speaking, not doing badly, no one wanted to go there; everyone wished to remain in the place that he was accustomed to and settled into, to remain with his loved ones and acquaintances.

As a result of the earlier recruitment, when people were taken directly from the work brigades to the square, quite a few families had been torn apart—many men were taken at the gate whose wives and children remained in the ghetto, as well as women whose husbands remained in the ghetto.

When the recruitment for Riga became a fact, the Labor Office immediately let it be known that those who had family members there should report voluntarily. Ten or fifteen women and men showed up to report voluntarily.

The required number was 300. Since volunteers alone would not be enough, the second forced recruitment for Riga started on October 16. Recruitment lasted a whole week, from October 16 to 23.

This time the recruitment dragged on for a long time, in part because of our own lack of promptness. The police had already assembled around 500 [*sic*] people, but the number was still insufficient, all for the same reason—the police arrested and the committee released, constantly in and out. Finally, the required number was achieved on October 23, and they were sent away to their workplaces. It is possible that their being sent out from here, although forced, will be to their benefit. Who knows whose fate is better?

Although the entire recruitment activity was not orderly, the office work of the police was carried out very well. After the first transport in the month of February, the belongings of those sent away were taken by strangers, and it was not accurately known who was sent away, who were the members of each family, their profession, where they worked, and so on. There were practical reasons for this at that time, since some were taken from the square and from the gate with only their clothes on their backs. This time, however, the police headquarters had an accurate list—according to the wards—of those taken away, by name, family, address; if they left belongings, these were given to relatives in accordance with the wishes of the deported. Everything was accurately written down and all relevant documents were attached.

October 28, 1942.

A year has passed since the Great Action—the 28th according to the conventional calendar, the eighth of *Cheshvan T.Sh. "B.* [5702] by the Jewish calendar.

Yizkor![4]

May God remember the fathers, mothers, and children who were killed by the murderous sadists.

---

4. "May [God] remember!"—first word of the prayer for the deceased, part of the Yom Kippur service.

The spilled innocent blood of the gray-haired old people, the simple honest people, good, devoted Jews, who raised generations and lived productively.

The spilled blood of the babies, whom they threw alive into the pits and tore apart with hand grenades, innocent, amiable Jewish children, nursing infants with their mothers' milk on their lips, older children who understood a little of what was being done to them and with indescribable pain in their naïve faces and eyes asking: "why?," "why?"

Yizkor! The heaven-rending crying and wailing of the ten thousand whose screams should have split the skies.

If there is such a one as you, God, your throne is immersed in blood; how can You allow such terrible things on this earth—albeit filthy—but still Your world.

If truth and justice are indeed to come to the world, it will, no doubt, be too late. As Bialik said: "Im akharey mosee ha-tzedek yofiya, yimoogar na khiso la-ahd"—If only after my death justice will appear, then let the throne of justice be broken forever. A new world will come after the war, we will be mourned with false tears; a large number of nations friendly to us will rejoice in their hearts that they were able to rid themselves in such an easy manner of a difficult problem—the headache of having to deal with the Jews and their just aspirations.

But in the meantime the pain remains with us. The large wound is somewhat closed, but will never heal. Should we survive, the great grief will forever hang over us like a dark cloud.

We all remembered this anniversary, some more, some less, reliving the terrible days of the past year, wounds that bleed and are not healing.

A year has passed. Had anyone told us at this time a year ago that we would survive another year, we would not have believed it, because it appeared that the extermination of the entire ghetto was imminent. But we did survive another year, and while our situation has not improved, still, we are a year closer to the conclusion.

The Meck Episode

Sunday, November 15 [1942], the entire ghetto trembled from a unique event, unprecedented in the life of the ghetto.

A certain Noah Meck fired several shots from a revolver at the German commandant [of the ghetto guard] near the gate.

The matter developed as follows: Sunday evening, about six o'clock, a Jew without [yellow] patches crawled through the fence near the ghetto gate intending to go into the city. The German commandant, who was standing nearby, noticed this and ran to grab the Jew. The Jew Meck pulled out a revolver and gave a shout: "Herr Commandant, let me go or I will shoot," and fired several times. Luckily for the entire Jewish community of the ghetto, he did not hit him. Immediately, Meck was grabbed by the other Germans and Lithuanians in the vicinity, disarmed, and taken to the ghetto guard house.

The news spread throughout the ghetto with lightening speed, causing panic and turmoil in the ghetto. We remembered very well that thousands of Jews were taken to the fort and murdered only because they had the "audacity" to be born Jews. We remembered very well that Jews were shot for not greeting a German, for not properly removing the hat. We could therefore imagine what we could expect when a Jew wanted to shoot a German. They have an old, favorite rule—Jews are responsible for each other.

Everyone awaited with anxious expectation what would happen next, how we would curtail the calamity that had stricken us, that a Jew should have taken it upon himself in these times to shoot at a German and thereby bring about the destruction of an entire Jewish community.

Soon Germans arrived from the city—from the G. [Gestapo] and from the police. They immediately arrested the entire Elder Council, sent them to the city, and imprisoned them in separate cells. One member of the Elder Council happened to be sick. He was taken, ill, to the ghetto guard house and from there sent to the city.

The German chief of police Binger ran around the ghetto guard house as if poisoned, with a revolver in his hand. He didn't know himself what punishment he should think up for the Jews.

The ghetto streets became deathly quiet. All the residents were hiding in their houses, afraid to stick their noses into the street. The entire police force was mobilized, on the alert in the second police precinct located near the ghetto guard house, including the police leadership and other high officials, waiting from there for the order. A short while afterwards came the anticipated order, instructing the Jewish police within a half hour to provide twenty Jews to be shot, and to hold them locked up overnight in prison, until further instructions were given.

The Jewish police faced an unprecedented, terrible assignment: to arrest twenty Jews and to deliver them to the Germans, fully aware that they would be killed. Who should be delivered, who among us were the good and the bad, how could we ourselves be the angels of death to our own Jews?

But the choice that was given, that the Jews themselves should provide the twenty people, represented—paradoxical as this may sound—a certain relief, because if the Germans were to take the twenty men themselves, they would take the first and the best to fall into their hands; there would be among them young fathers and mothers, family breadwinners, who needed to live for themselves and for their children. In this case, since they did not specify which Jews should be delivered—that was not important to them, as long as they were Jews—the task was accomplished by Jews themselves in the following manner: a list was put together and people were assembled from the hospital, where a number of old men were lying, near death—one of them was already at death's door; from the insane asylum (such a place was also arranged in the ghetto) where there were incurable, abandoned old people; from various other places where [there were] old people, deep in their nineties, who, because of old age and weakness, were lying in bed awaiting death any day; also a few physical and mental cripples—all of them were assembled, and, because almost none of those taken were able to walk on their own, they were carried on stretchers or taken in carts to the jail, for delivery to the Germans.

Dreadful was the task of the Jewish policeman, to go into a home, to take an innocent, sick, elderly person and to deliver him to death. Most of those taken did not understand anything, nor did they ask questions. A few old people, who were still of sound mind, asked: "Where and why are we being led away? We have not done any harm to anyone."

They ordered the police to include among the twenty people the mother and sister of Meck and the sister of Meck's partner, a certain Gelson, who had escaped from the ghetto.

In the evening, the commandant came to the prison to determine whether the required number of people were there. On our part, there was no longer any fear that he would perhaps reject the victims and demand young and healthy ones. But he said nothing and departed.

The night passed. In the morning the imprisoned members of the Elder Council were released. We saw in this a certain change for the better and waited for what would happen next.

A day went by. Quiet. The next day it became known that the Gestapo had decided to bring Meck back to the ghetto in order to have him publicly hanged, the execution to be carried out by the Jewish police. In addition, they ordered that a public announcement be made that all Jews who had arms were to deliver them to the specified locations by November 18 in order not to be punished. After this deadline there would be house searches, and anyone found with a weapon would be shot.

On November 17 the Jewish police, as ordered, conducted house searches in various homes looking for weapons. Needless to say, no weapons were found anywhere.

The day of the execution of Meck arrived—Wednesday, November 18.

A gallows was built opposite the building of the Elder Council, in the center of the ghetto. Exactly at twelve o'clock noon he was to be hanged. The previous evening, when it became known that the Jewish police were to carry out this assignment, the police administration faced the question as to who should be the hangman. Clearly, no one wanted to undertake such an assignment, and, even more so, the police officials did not want to have the responsibility of designating the person. It was decided that the appointment should be made by lottery, to be administered by fifteen men.

A lottery was organized, witnessed by the leadership, the chiefs and assistants of all the units, and a drawing was made separately for each unit. But it turned out later that the police were relieved of this assignment. A pair of thieves, well known in the ghetto, were confined in the prison, sentenced to long terms of imprisonment for thefts and break-ins. This pair would not shy away from any dirty work. They were offered release from prison in exchange for carrying out the execution. They immediately agreed.

Exactly at twelve o'clock the entire Gestapo gang arrived in the ghetto. Almost the entire police were assembled near the committee, near the gallows. Meck was brought in a car, a beaten, battered man, his hands tied behind his back. One of the Germans called the chief of police and the chief of the criminal division and ordered them to bring Meck from the car to the gallows.

Meck was a young man of twenty-seven or twenty-eight, a watchmaker, a gold dealer, who speculated and traded in watches, gold, and diamonds. On the unlucky day, he had wanted to go to the city on account of his business. Of short height, thin, he gave the impression of a pitiful, terrified young man. Going to the hanging he was quiet and cool, not saying a word, except that when walking from the car to the gallows he quietly asked the chief of the criminal division: "What is heard of my mother and sister?" When he received the answer that they are in the ghetto, he said: "If so, then thank God." He did not say another word, didn't even blink an eye, as if the entire matter did not concern him.

The two hangmen placed a rope around his neck, kicked away the table, and in a few seconds his body was quivering in the air.

While Meck was still shaking in his death convulsions, one of the Germans shouted to the assembled people: "This is what will happen to every swine who dares to raise his hand against a German."

Immediately everyone was told to disperse, and instructions were given to leave Meck hanging until twelve noon the next day, with a guard of Jewish policemen standing near the hanged man for the twenty-four hours.

Meck's was an ill-considered and foolish deed, which could have killed hundreds of Jews. But he died like a hero, not a word, not a tear, no weakness, just like a martyr going of his own free will to *Kidush Hashem* [Sanctification of the Name of God]. Even the Germans marveled that such a creature should have within himself so much spiritual strength and manly courage.

Immediately afterwards Schtitz of the Gestapo drove to the ghetto prison, took out from there the mother and sister of Meck, drove them in his car to the Ninth Fort, and shot them there. The remaining seventeen hostages they released.

Following this event, with its drama and suspense, calm returned—forgotten as if nothing happened. The monotonous, sad ghetto life continued to flow.

Assaults

The year 1942 is coming to an end. During the last months of the year, much the same as in the previous year, we face disturbing experiences due to the frequent assaults by the Lithuanians through the fence. The bandits take advantage of the long nights and darkness to embark on robbing the Jews.

This is not a difficult task for them; they know very well that no one will stand up for the Jews, that we have no weapons. In addition, they have often worked hand in hand with our guards, the policemen at the fence, with whom they have shared the spoils.

There have been instances when tracks in the mud or snow clearly showed that the robbers came in through the fence or directly through the gate. The Lithuanian guard never saw anyone or heard anything. Jews who lived in the neighborhood would hear suspicious footsteps, running, talking. The guard would not "hear" anything.

The assaults started in October, primarily in the houses near the fence.

On October 2, 4, 11, 14, and 15, assaults took place in different parts of the ghetto. The attackers were always armed and, brandishing the guns in their hands, they took everything they could. On October 24, two uniformed Lithuanian policemen broke into a house near the fence and carried out the robbery, brandishing their revolvers.

On the night of November 2 a number of Lithuanians with intent to rob came through the fence into the ghetto. Jews noticed them and reported it to the first precinct. Greenberg, the chief of the precinct, and the policeman Avtshinski went to the reported place and encountered four Lithuanians. Two of them immediately ran away, and the policemen ran after the remaining two to capture them. A fight started, resulting in one of the bandits cracking the head of the policeman Avtshinski with a brick. Both robbers escaped. The policeman remained sick for two months from the serious injury.

There were also organized assaults in various parts of the ghetto on December 2, 5, 8, 10, and 12.

It was almost never possible to capture the robbers or to find their tracks. Every time our criminal office would report the assaults and the police headquarters would prepare and send a number of disclosures to the commandant of the ghetto guard, to the chief of the Lithuanian guards, and to the S.D. That was the end of it; they never took any steps to investigate the robberies.

Chanukah and the New Year—Beginning of the
Ghetto Bright Period (the Time of Miller)

We are already into December 1942; it is Chanukah for the Jews. Even though we are still behind barbed wire and the threat of death still hovers over our heads, there is a big difference between Chanukah of a year ago and this year.

A year ago it did not enter anybody's mind to remember and to celebrate Chanukah in any fashion. It was shortly after the Great Action, we were still under the effect of the events that we had just experienced, the problem of food was still with us in its full intensity, trading of our belongings had not as yet developed. This year it was different. Food products in the ghetto were in abundance, general conditions in the ghetto had more or less settled down, and, besides this, the overall political-military situation had changed to the detriment of our enemies.

The Elder Council arranged a Chanukah gathering for specially invited guests; the police headquarters also arranged its own Chanukah gathering, and so did other offices for their coworkers and for community activists. All these were the so-called official gatherings, but there were also unofficial ones, arranged by organizations that had started to develop under illegal circumstances—Zionist, spirited Chanukah gatherings, where comrades who had worked together in the good days for the common ideas could meet for a few hours, with party differences erased. Many of the Zionist comrades are no longer with us; they are no longer among the living. In all of the gatherings in which one assembled with his circle of intimates, the missing ones—old and young—were remembered, people were encouraging each other, rising for a few hours above the grayness of the daily lives in which we are all immersed.

While all these were spiritual events, drinking parties spread throughout the ghetto like an epidemic, with an entirely different character. Various groups would come together in order to get drunk. Frequently one would hear the sounds and shouting of the guzzling gang or see intoxicated passersby in the night. Often high-ranking functionaries of the ghetto institutions or the police would take part in these bands, which gave rise to all kinds of talk and commentary.

The year 1942 is passing. We are again facing the unknown. What will the new year bring us? More slavery and humiliation? Or will deliverance perhaps shine upon us?

We enter the year 1943 with a somewhat lighter heart than the year 1942. During this period we had been reassured several times that nothing would happen in the ghetto for the present. In addition, little by little their foundation has been shaken, their glitter has receded, they are starting to retreat; every day given to us is a day closer to the end, one day less to wait for the hour of our liberation, which, we hope, will surely also arrive for us.

The Police in the Last Quarter of 1942[1]

11

New Units (Gate and Detention-House Guards; Jail and Workshop Guards)

After Caspi left us, the police revived somewhat, breathed a little more freely. Before, whatever one wanted to do, it was first necessary to ask what Caspi would say about it. If everyone said day, he said night—it was difficult to deal with him. Now, after his departure, one became somewhat revitalized, one could get something done independently, without regard to his craziness and capriciousness.

Throughout the fall and the beginning of winter 1942, various changes took place in the internal operations. In addition, new units were added, and the activities of existing units were rearranged. To some extent this was perhaps related to the ability of police management to pay more attention to direct, internal organizational matters, rather than being constantly preoccupied with Caspi politics. Basically, however, all the changes that took

1. The manuscript Table of Contents refers to this chapter as the last "third" of 1942.

place were the result of daily activity and practice, requiring the introduction of modifications in order to make police activity more purposeful and practical.

On August 15, a second detention house was established in the ghetto. The reason for creating an additional jail was basically a purely geographic one. As previously mentioned, the existing ghetto jail was located near the workshops, at the other end of the ghetto.

Regulation of the entire work force, all the maneuvering to meet the labor quota—all this took place at the gate. There were dozens of cases every day when people had to be separated from their brigades only to be sent half an hour later to a different place, because of an urgent demand for manpower, or because people simply had to be forcibly mobilized for a particular work site. There was no available place to hold the people assembled by the police until the required number was achieved. It was not possible simply to hold them in place because they would disperse; to take them to the other jail for a while was too far—everything at the gate had to be done quickly. It was therefore decided to establish a detention house at the gate, especially for labor-quota purposes. Initially, the detention house was called "detention house for work duty evaders." Here, in this detention house, were held all those whose offenses related to work-duty compliance. There, in the other jail, were kept criminal and administrative offenders as well as those punished by the commandant and the SD; they, particularly criminals and those punished by the SD, were not sent to work outside the ghetto. All those arrested for work-duty offenses and jailed for a specified time period would be sent to work in the morning and returned at the gate in the evening to the detention house.

The guards in the new detention house were policemen from the first precinct. The new detention house, located near the gate at Krishchiu-kaichio 23, was set up in the former prayer house of Abba Chatzkel. Jews themselves made a jail of a prayer house. This will certainly not be believable to future readers of this material, but it is a fact. The prayer house had already been partly destroyed before, because during the early days of the ghetto, when each square meter of living space was in demand, many homeless people moved into houses of prayer and study, causing their devastation. Later, when the housing problem became somewhat more regulated, particularly after the Great Action, surviving families moved out of the houses of prayer, which then stood empty and semi-destroyed. Adjacent neighbors dragged out the benches and all other available firewood. The detention house was set up in one of these. In the same house where previously prayers to God had sounded, where generations had passed through the house of prayer and study with their sufferings and joys, within these very same walls could now be heard the groans and cries of Jews who were arrested by other Jews for not properly fulfilling the orders imposed by our rulers.

The detention house served the needs of fulfilling the labor quota and, consequently, also those of the labor office, but being under the jurisdiction of the police, was conducted according to the statute that had been approved by the chief of the police and by the Elder Council on September 23, 1942, called "Regulations of the Detention house for Evaders of Work Obligations in the Ghetto." The regulations contained thirteen paragraphs, which included the following:

In the detention house are to be confined:

> those penalized by the decision of the Labor Office for avoiding their work obligations;
> those to be held until further notice based on a decree of the Labor Office;
> when there is a need for it, those assigned to work in a specified place until their departure for work;
> those detained in the course of inspections for avoiding work obligations;
> those being sent out with police escort certificates (the latter being under police jurisdiction).

People subject to instructions from the Labor Office, to be carried out by the police, were taken into the detention house.

Men and women were kept separately.

Those held in the detention house (sentenced for a prescribed period of time) would be sent every morning to work and returned to the detention house in the evening. One person would remain in the detention house every day to maintain cleanliness in the rooms.

Those held in the detention house would be penalized for offenses against discipline and for failure to fulfill their work obligations.

The Labor Office controlled and regulated matters dealing with work issues pertaining to those held in the detention house. Policemen of the gate guard—in effect from the first precinct, because at that time the detention house as well as the entire gate guard belonged to the first precinct—managed the administration of the detention house. While the official chief of the detention house was the chief of the first precinct, the actual one was the chief of the gate guard, who was the second deputy chief of the second precinct. There was a great deal of confusion and chaos concerning issues of the official and actual fulfillment of duties.

The detention house expanded, with hundreds of people passing through it every morning on the way to work. The police of the gate guard had a lot to do, maintaining order at the square and at the detention house—it was more than they could handle on their own. Every day policemen from the first precinct were therefore sent to help them. But the policemen from the precinct had their own daily task—the morning inspection of the houses. Sending a part of the precinct force to help maintain order at the gate produced more harm than good—the early morning inspections were not carried out properly, and the help given to their associates at the gate guard did not amount to much because work at the gate required familiarity and experience; a newcomer could not accomplish much, and in the end nobody was pleased.

In addition, the chief of the first precinct carried the responsibility for the entire gate guard, in whose activity he, in fact, did not get involved because theirs was a world of their own. All of this combined to ripen the idea of separating the gate guard from the first precinct, to make it a unit by itself, with its own permanent staff, having under its control the detention center as well as the gate—a unit having its special assignments and duties. As a separate unit it was much like a precinct, subordinated directly to headquarters.

This reform was announced in the order of the day of September 27.

The same order of the day also included the transfer of all policemen from the first precinct to the second and third and transfer of the latter to the first precinct. This was the result of a tragic event involving four policemen, one of whom paid for it with his life.

It came about as follows: As previously noted, very many products were being brought into the ghetto in the summer of 1942, during the time of commandant Tiele. Employees of various offices would collect money and send one of their people to purchase food products. This was also arranged by policemen of the first precinct. They collected money and sent a policemen to buy flour for all the policemen of the precinct. The sentry at the gate stopped the vehicle and, precisely at that moment, a senior Lithuanian official came to the gate. The machine containing the flour, along with the people, were sent to the ghetto guard and from there to the SD. An investigation was initiated that included four policemen: Reibstein and Feinberg, who had organized the trip, and Grossman and Lifschitz, who had collected the money in the precinct. Two ghetto residents were arrested along with them—Gutman and Krieger, who were the intermediaries.

All were taken to the central jail, and from there they were sent to the Ninth Fort. The fear in the entire police force was very great—here, in the ghetto, everyone thought that they had already been shot. A while later it was learned that they were all alive and that they would be returned to the jail and, indeed, three weeks later they were taken to the Kovno jail.

The policemen Feinberg, Grossman, and Lifschitz were freed; the policemen Reibstein and the ghetto residents Krieger and Gutman, along with their wives and children, whom the Gestapo ordered arrested and delivered to them, were shot and killed.

Following this event, the SD ordered all the policemen of the first precinct to be dispersed into the other two precincts. So ended the sad episode.

Continuing with the reforms, a reform also came about in the workshop guard, in order to improve internal services and the guarding of this important location. Smaller reforms had been instituted earlier, but did not produce the desired results.

As noted earlier, guarding of the workshops and of the jail was done by policemen sent from the precincts.

With time, the number of assignments increased, the workshops expanded; storage places contained goods worth millions, which the authorities strictly directed the police to guard diligently. Many instances of theft from the storage places by workshop workers were noticed. Policemen posted at the gates were instructed to search workers on their way out. But police posts were not always at the same location, they would not stay exactly at the assigned place, thus allowing people to pass without being checked—they did not watch adequately. On a number of occasions, the chief of the workshops and of the jail was reproached by the German administrator of the workshops and by the Jewish management of the workshops; a long series of correspondence ensued between the workshops and police management. As a means of improving the situation, the workshop management requested police headquarters to assign three permanent policemen to control the police posts. These assignments were made on September 5.

The three permanent appointees did not accomplish much—it was the same with them and without them. A reform had to be made that would fundamentally improve the guarding of the workshops. Police management therefore decided to designate a permanent unit for guarding the workshops. This was announced in the order of the day of November 1, specifying the policemen who were being transferred to this unit.

In addition to seeking to improve the guarding of the workshops, these changes had a further objective, namely, to facilitate the normal day-to-day work in the precincts.

Until then every policemen in the precinct had one day of normal precinct duties, night duty in the precinct the following day, normal precinct duty the next day, and then a shift at the workshops for twenty-four hours. After completing workshop duties, the policemen would be free until the morning of the day after, so that, in effect, the policeman would serve his normal precinct duties three days a week, the rest of the time being outside the precinct. Work in the precinct suffered from this, because the policeman was like a guest in the precinct.

Expansion of the Administrative Work of the Police (Penal Department, Criminal Department, "Passportization," Administrative Penalties)

As we will elaborate further later on, it was arranged that summer to divide the entire ward into districts and sections, each policeman having his own section, consisting of several streets that the policeman was required to visit a few times a day, to monitor cleanliness and to carry out various assignments from his precinct. According to existing work schedules, the policeman was able to visit the precinct only three days a week, and normal work suffered from it. Consequently, this new reform had a twofold effect.

Along with the growth of the units and their being reformed, the tasks of headquarters, as the highest command and oversight organ, also expanded.

Headquarters had under its jurisdiction six police units: three precincts, the criminal division, gate and detention house guards, jail and workshop guards, and, in addition, the court—the penal department.

Every day, from all units, headquarters receives reports and various written communications to take care of; all court matters are also processed through headquarters.

Headquarters expanded because of the quantitative increase in the number of units as well as because of the increase in number of tasks. This field of headquarters activity included matters of an administrative nature, which, under normal circumstances, would belong not to the police but to municipal organs or to other administrative offices.

With time, the police force, as a whole, became not only the implementing organ of the decisions of the relevant offices, but also a court and penal institution, handling all criminal matters and civil disputes among residents (penal department). In the case of an offense or a crime in which a resident is punished with arrest, again, the police by itself, having resolved the matter, decides the punishment and implements its decision.

Normally, three offices would be involved in such matters: the police, the court, and the jail—separate offices, independent of one another. In our case, everything was concentrated in the hands of the police.

The penal department, the new office, was incorporated into the police; it was created August 16 and carried out its activities according to a special statute confirmed by the chairman of the Elder Council on August 20 as an addendum to the general police statute.

The rights and authority of the penal department were established as follows:

The Jewish ghetto police is temporarily commissioned to deal with all criminal offenses and civil matters of residents of the ghetto.

The penal department consisted of a panel of three persons, appointed by the chief of police explicitly to carry out these duties. In addition to their duties as members of the panel, these officials also fulfilled their daily police duties. (This was changed later so that those who functioned as judges in the penal department carried out only this assignment.)

The panel dealt with and rendered rulings on all matters submitted to it by the criminal division, by the precincts, and by others, including requests and accusations by private parties.

Work of the panel was based on the judicial statutes of the former Lithuanian Republic, to the extent that they applied to ghetto conditions and were not in conflict with decrees issued by the Elder Council.

Rulings of the panel went into effect, and became final, only after having been confirmed by the chief of police.

In exceptional cases, or when requested by an interested party, and also on his own initiative, the chairman of the Elder Council could void the decision and order reconsideration of the matter by a panel made up of different members, designated by the chief of police.

All matters of the former ghetto court that were left unresolved were transferred to the headquarters of the Jewish ghetto police.

In time, after the three panel members became permanent, the penal department became functional. They took over all matters of the former ghetto court as well as new cases flowing from the criminal division and from other sources. They arranged for themselves a special meeting room, a secretary with extensive court experience was assigned to them, and work proceeded in a normal fashion, much like in the earlier ghetto court.

All matters requiring a decision by the chief of police in order to be transferred to the penal department, and all matters handled by the criminal division that needed either to be transferred to the court or to be voided, were processed through headquarters. In addition to this there were complaints and claims of inhabitants against one another, administrative penalties for various offenses submitted via the precincts—all of these matters were processed through headquarters and represented an important part of the administrative activity.

It will be of interest—and it will highlight the work of the police in this area—to provide a few statistical tables of the work of the criminal division and of the penal department, as well as statistics of those penalized for various administrative offenses.

From April 1 through December 31, 1942, the criminal division had to deal with various matters of theft, fraud, forgery, and so on. There were many complicated and tangled matters that the criminal division was able to clarify, punishing the guilty and returning to the victims their losses. Crimes that had been committed mostly by local thieves were mostly solved. In time, employees of the criminal division became experienced in their work and developed a special approach and a certain routine.

The following table shows the matters processed through the criminal division during the period of its existence from April 1 until December 31:

	April	May	June	July	Aug.	Sept.	Oct.	Nov.	Dec.
Theft, fraud, forgery	90	133	62	104	42	52	68	62	97
Cases solved	15	88	12	117	114	51	19	5	3
Cases in process	519	626	709	769	569	374	105	81	38
Cases forwarded to the court	13	29	5	20	24	32	35	26	38
Interrupted cases	18	59	7	97	90	62	24	24	22
People tried	24	51	12	20	27	36	29	20	39
People detained	4	5	—	24	34	5	19	17	8

As may be seen from the table, during the three-quarters of the year of normal criminal division activity, a total of 700 criminal offenses were committed in the ghetto. Of these, 424 were solved, 222 were transferred to the court—a total of 646, that is, around 90 percent.

These numbers are not quite accurate as we are missing the statistics for the period prior to April 1, 1942 (beginning with April 1, headquarters received precise biweekly and later monthly reports, detailing the activities of all police units during the month). In addition, cases flowed into the criminal division from the discontinued ghetto court, and there were also many cases that had been handled before April 1 but were resolved only a few months later. All in all it can be concluded that of the crimes committed by Jews here within the ghetto, 80 percent were resolved.

The penal department, which began normal operation as of September 1, handled the following cases for the period ending October [*sic*—December?] 31:

September	Handled 24 criminal cases	Penalized 18	Freed 6
	" 11 civil "		
October	" 21 criminal "	" 17	" 4
	" 43 civil "		
November	" 16 criminal "	" 14	" 2
	" 21 civil "		

| December | " | 18 criminal | " | " | 15 | " | 3 |
| | " | 38 civil | " | | | | |

Total handled: 192 civil and criminal cases

Resolution of all of these hundreds and dozens of cases, the number of which greatly increased in the months of July and August, when the court was shut down and all of its incomplete cases transferred to police headquarters, represented a significant part of the administrative activity of police headquarters.

Another non-police assignment that the police were drawn into, or, better said, that was incorporated into the administrative activities of the police, was the issuing of ID cards ["passportization"].

The question of every ghetto resident having a personal document became very pertinent. Typically, it was difficult to establish personal information pertaining to a resident, particularly when there was an interest in concealing something.

From the beginning of the war in June 1941 until after the Great Action, we lived through endless trouble. All were uprooted from their homes and abandoned to the vagaries of fate. The condition of the Jews of Kovno was greatly changed during the period from the beginning of the war until entry into the ghetto. Thousands of people, particularly men, were among the first to be arrested and taken to the forts. Of the women who were at the forts, some perished and some were freed. During the first days of the war, many Kovno Jews fled the city, going to the provinces. Some of them perished on the roads and in the villages themselves, and a small number returned to Kovno after much difficulty. A whole series of evacuations and actions followed the sealing of the ghetto. During the first three evacuations, one had to grab a bundle and run from the area—the commotion was great. No wonder then that thousands of people lost their personal documents in the forts, on the road, during the evacuations, and during the actions. There were many, particularly among the German and Polish refugees, who deliberately destroyed their personal documents. Also, many who had the new Russian documents destroyed them because, during the house searches, people were afraid to have documents issued by the Russians. Thus, many thousands of people had no personal documents.

In order to establish personal data, everybody's information had to be believed. During the issuing of the first bread-cards in the ghetto, as many family members were included as were claimed verbally. Many used this for falsification purposes. Such falsifications were present in all the offices. In the Housing Office, for example, the number of people was exaggerated in order to secure a room of a larger area. In the Labor Office, when the issue of work responsibility was already somewhat regulated, there was great difficulty with the question of a resident's age: a younger age would be given, not yet subject to work assignment, or older—no longer required to work. There was also the question of children. The Labor Office also imposed work duty on women, except for women with small children under the age of eight. This provided a wide field for various schemes—women listing their children as younger than they actually were. There were even instances of women who had no children stating that they had a small child. The situation provided a "wide field" for deception in various areas for dishonest residents.

Within the police, when detaining someone, or when preparing a report, anyone could in the early days just give a false name, then "go look for him." Later on, when work-obligation cards were instituted, if the person detained was not subject to work duty, then that person would not have such a work-card. Even if he had such a card, because of moves or simply because of inaccuracies, addresses would be incorrect. Such schemes were used by various people at work inspections, in the Welfare Office, and so on.

The aggregate of all of this gave rise to the idea of introducing a uniform, general document for all ghetto residents, without exception, the so-called ghetto *pass* (*oisveiz*) [*Ausweis*—German, identity card].

The idea originated in the Elder Council and was initially dealt with by the secretary, Golub. The decision was made to introduce a mandatory identity card in the ghetto, and implementation of the entire matter, theoretically as well as practically, was turned over to the Jewish ghetto police.

On June 7 the chief of police announced that between that day and July 1 every ghetto resident must acquire a ghetto identification card. The order specified that:

> The cards will be provided to residents in their houses by the
> appropriate police precinct and the house manager, who will later

carry out a general inspection to verify that all residents of their
district have a card.

Every ghetto resident must have a card, regardless of gender or age.

Cards for minors under the age of fifteen will be issued to their parents
(father or mother). If the minor has no parents, the card will be
issued to the person with whom he resides.

Every ghetto resident above the age of fifteen is obligated to have the
card on him at all times and without exception, upon request, to
show it to members of the Jewish police and to persons instructed by
the police or by the Labor Office to carry out an inspection of able-
bodied workers.

Every ghetto resident is obligated to keep the card clean and in good
condition; the holder must not make any notations on the card.

Every ghetto resident who changes his place of residence must register
in the police precinct of his new residence within twenty-four hours.
His registration is to be noted on the card by the police precinct.

Minors will be registered by those persons to whom the card is issued.

House managers are required to carry out within twenty-four hours the
registration in the police precinct of persons moving into or out of
the house.

Residents and house managers who do not comply with these
instructions will be penalized by the chief of the J.G.P. [Jewish
ghetto police] with a monetary fine of up to twenty marks, detention
of up to seven days, or both.

No one may obtain from the J.G.P. more than one card. Circumventing
this restriction will be punished with detention of up to three
months.

The order for issuing the cards specified that all the information in the
card is to be entered by the resident certification office (the address bureau),
who then forwards it to police headquarters. The chief of police signs the
cards, and then they are sent out to the appropriate police precincts. Policemen bring them to the house managers, who distribute them to the residents
of their houses.

The shape of the card was somewhat smaller than the format of a post-
card—one page of light-gray, hard paper, on which the following was written:

At the very top, in German and Yiddish, "Jewish Ghetto Community, Viliampole" and then, in German, "Identification Card No. . . ." Below this was the following information: family name, [first] name, father's name, age. At the bottom, an imprint—"Chief of the Jewish Ghetto Police" and signature. On the left side, a stamp—"Jewish Ghetto Police Viliampole." Below it, on the right: "Viliampole" and date of issuance of the card. On the left side of the card, a stamp in German: "Resident Certification Office, registered on the . . . date, resides on . . . street, No. . . . , signed: Registration Office official."

The information in the identity card was quite minimal. It may be that this was purposely done to limit the information on the card only to the most essential facts needed to identify the person. For example, the following question is absent in the card: "where do you come from." This is omitted out of consideration to the refugees who ran from Hitler, from Germany, Czechoslovakia, Austria, Memel, and so on. There is no question on the card as to whether or not one is married, because the issue of weddings in the ghetto was a painful one. There are here hundreds of men and women whose first husband or wife is not here, having run away, been lost in the actions, missing in the provinces, and so on. Many of them registered with someone else. The missing ones are considered by us to be dead, but it is possible that some of the lost ones will reappear sometime in the future. This painful question was therefore left open.

The identity card contained adequate information to serve the needs of ghetto offices for work-duty checking, for police work, the food supply office, and so on.

In order to anchor the identity card into ghetto life, the Elder Council issued on August 1 a compulsory decree to all its offices that as of August 5 (by then all ghetto residents had already received their cards) the ghetto card was the sole identification document for ghetto residents.

To avoid misunderstandings and mistakes, all offices of the ghetto institutions were required to demand a card of every ghetto resident for the purpose of establishing his identity. Employees were required to note the card number. In particular, office employees were to demand that the card be shown under the following circumstances:

When submitting a request, when issuing certifications, when paying out money, when issuing food supplies or clothing, when compiling reports, issuing notices, confiscating, when issuing orders for housing.

In addition to these general circumstances, offices needing to establish the identity of a person must use the card in the following manner.

Food supply office. In the food supply stores, the customer lists must also include the number of the identity card, in addition to the first and family name, the same as on the wood allocation cards.

Labor office. The files of the labor office must include the number of the identity card next to the first name, family name, place of residence, and work-card. This also applies to the files of the welfare office.

In the hospital. The number of the card must be noted next to all the information about the patient.

Police. In all official reports, statements, and various other matters in which the police deal with an individual resident, the card must always be demanded and in each case its number noted. When admitting into jail, the jail administrator must, in order to receive bread for those arrested, provide the number of the identity card, in addition to the first name, family name, and place of residence of the detainee.

In the address bureau, the number of the card must be provided next to all the other information.

Housing office. When issuing an order for housing, the number of the card must be written next to the names of all the residents of the corresponding space.

By means of this decree, the basic principle was established that the identity card is everything and that without it a resident cannot come to any office. Of importance here was not only the entry of the number of the identity card, but that the appropriate official must request the card. If the resident does not have it with him, then his matter cannot be taken care of, and, most important, the information needs to be taken directly from the identity card.

The documents, and all the preparations leading to the issuance of the identity cards, had been carefully taken care of some time earlier.

The undertaking of issuing a standard card did not come about as a sudden project. The idea matured over time because of the hundreds of difficulties encountered in office activities, which led to the ripening of the idea. A few months before the official announcement, the Elder Council, at whose initiative the entire matter was set into motion, provided on April 17 general directions for the issuance of the cards.

Registration of all ghetto residents began on April 1. This was the third registration (the first was on September 18, 1941, the second on November 15). A new resident file was created from this registration in the residents certification office. Later, all house managers were required to provide their police precinct with a detailed list of the residents in their house, by families, including the accurate age of each person, family association, and number of the work-card. All the lists were sent by the police to the address bureau, where their own lists were checked against the house lists.

The address bureau prepared the identity cards from these lists, sent them to the appropriate precinct; the precinct then distributed them to the house managers, who then distributed them to the residents of their houses, each resident having to sign, verifying that he had received the card.

Hundreds of entwined matters, generally unavoidable in a registration, were clarified, mostly attributable to simple mistakes, wrong addresses, and so on.

We also introduced the requirement for small children to also have a card, which was done primarily to avoid misunderstandings, so that whoever claimed to have a small child had to present its card.

Following the issuance of identity cards to all ghetto residents, misunderstandings and fraud became nearly impossible in all the activities of the ghetto offices.

The police force devoted itself principally to the "passportization" and the work deriving from it. All the work was done with the principal participation and direction of the police and occupied a significant part of the administrative activities of the police.

The ghetto identity cards had one basic deficiency—they did not include a photographic picture. This allowed for the possibility of a resident's taking someone else's card and claiming it to be his own.

By virtue of the creation in the police precincts of districts and sections, whereby every policemen had his section where he would go every day, visit almost every house, in the course of time getting to know all residents personally, misunderstandings of one person's using another's card occurred very seldom.

The entire administration of the districts, which was in the hands of the police, was, in fact, not a police function but, rather, a purely municipal one.

In addition, the police also carried out the function of an administrative penalty organ, being the ones to decide the punishment as well as the ones to implement the sentence. This had been the case from the first days of coming into the ghetto.

The essential aspects of population punishment progressed through a number of stages.

At the very beginning, police punished with fines or detention. As noted in the first chapters, these punishments were not effective, because immediately after the gold action, monetary penalties were waived, and detention sentences were not implemented because there was no jail. Later, the jail was created and, because trading produced an abundance of money, penalties became effective. The offender had to serve his jail sentence or pay the corresponding amount of money.

Later, in August 1942, when the moneyless economy was introduced, financial punishments were discontinued (officially, any kind of money transaction was forbidden, and it remains so to this day—November 1943), the only remaining means of punishment being detention. The number of offenses was extensive—it was necessary to intervene and to surmount this challenge.

Types of offenses were diverse. They included those of common character, such as making a disturbance, fighting, resisting, violation of decrees, sanitary offenses, and so on. But there were also ghetto-specific offenses, such as, for example, going without [yellow] patches, not carrying the ghetto identity card, not reregistering [when moving]. Not having with you the identity card is, actually, carelessness rather than an offense, but in order to implant the card into ghetto life and to elevate it to the status of an absolute necessity, it was necessary to also intervene in such cases and punish with detention. The length of the jail sentence for these offenses was hours of detention. To detain someone for twenty-four hours for such an offense was excessive; lesser administrative offenses were therefore punished with four, six, or eight hours of detention.

There was a very large number of offenses for violation of sanitary decrees—for dirty yards or streets. These were also punished with hours of detention, a "recidivist" being punished with an entire twenty-four-hour period.

A whole series of people, punished administratively for a variety of offenses, were processed through police headquarters, recorded, and listed in accordance with the nature of the offense. It will be interesting to provide tabulations of the penalties and the number penalized each month, because each type of offense mirrors the situation in the ghetto for the corresponding month as well as the work of the police in the corresponding time period—a link in the chain of police activity in the administrative area.

In the month of March 1942 were penalized:

For insulting the police	22 persons
For resisting police	22 "
For creating disturbance and commotion	2 "
For using police insignia	1 "
" escaping from jail	5 "
" going without patches	3 "
" violating orders of the authorities	35 "
" " sanitation decrees	73 "
" tearing up houses	12 "
" impeding telephone transmission	4 "

Total 179 persons

The greatest number of punished persons was for sanitary offenses, because spring was approaching and the police started a large sanitation action in the entire ghetto and, particularly, in the Brazilke, the district that had to be evacuated at that time, penalizing those who did not comply with the decrees.

In the month of April were penalized:

For insulting the police	14 persons
" resisting " "	17 "
" disturbing the public peace	5 "
" violating sanitation decrees	12 "
" for using police insignia	1 "
" blackout violations	1 "
" trading in a forbidden district	1 "
" violating orders of the authorities	1 "
" tearing up houses	1 "

Total 53 persons

In the month of May were penalized:

For insulting the police	12 persons
" resisting the police	23 "
" striking policemen	2 "
" creating disturbance and fighting	3 "
" not returning police armbands	3 "
" sanitation offenses	8 "
" escaping from jail	1 "
" trading in a forbidden district	1 "
" offenses against the authorities	5 "
" tearing up houses	3 "
" misleading the police	2 "
" not properly carrying out house manager duties	1 "
" going out after curfew	11 "
" damaging gardens	1 "

Total 76 persons

There were diverse and multifarious offenses in this month. For the first time a house manager was penalized for not properly carrying out his duties.

In the month of April there was the large reduction of the police force. In spite of all warnings, three former policemen did not return their armbands. They had to be penalized with detention and their armbands taken away.

In the month of June were penalized:

For resisting, insulting, and not complying with police orders	17 persons
" creating disturbance and fighting	9 "
" not returning police armbands	2 "
" sanitation offenses	28 "
" blackout violations	18 "
" trading in the forbidden district	3 "
" violating orders of the authorities	8 "
" tearing up houses	16 "
" not properly carrying out house manager duties	1 "
" damaging gardens	12 "
" going out after curfew	42 "
Total	156 persons

During this month the greatest number of penalties was for going out during the forbidden time. In spite of the prohibition of going out after ten o'clock, many did not observe this prohibition. The police would make raids in the streets after ten o'clock, detain those walking around, and penalize them.

In the month of July were penalized:

For insulting, resisting and not obeying the police	9 persons
" disturbing the public peace	28 "
" sanitation offenses	166 "
" escaping from jail	3 "
" blackout violations	28 "
" tearing up houses	10 "
" violating garden-security regulations	10 "
" going out after curfew	7 "
Total	256 [*sic*] persons

In this month the greatest number of penalties was for violations of sanitation ordinances because during the summer the police carried out strict inspections every day, every policeman checking cleanliness in the yards and streets of his district and section.

In the month of August were penalized:

For insulting, resisting, and not obeying the police	11	persons
" fighting and disturbing the public peace	44	"
" not returning police armbands	1	"
" falsifying documents	1	"
" sanitation offenses	69	"
" blackout violations	4	"
" trading in the forbidden district	2	"
" not having an identity card	7	"
" tearing up houses	9	"
" misleading the police	4	"
" violating garden-security regulations	38	"
" going out after curfew	4	"
" slandering	1	"
" swindling	2	"
Total	197	persons

It is typical for the month when there was no court that a resident should come to the police to complain that someone had slandered him. In the absence of a court, he turned for help to the police.

In this month, there are, for the first time, seven penalties for not having an identity card.

In September were penalized:

For insulting, resisting, not carrying out police orders	12	persons
" fighting (bodily injuries)	2	"
" not returning police armbands	2	"
" sanitation offenses	7	"
" going without an identity card	3	"

| " misleading the police | 3 | " |
| " violating garden-security regulations | 40 | " |

| Total | 69 persons |

The greatest number of offenses in this month is for violations of garden-security regulations.

As noted, there was a special detail in the police for guarding the gardens, called garden security, managed by Padison, officer for special matters. A group of policemen, assembled from different precincts, guarded the gardens day and night and detained any resident trying to pull out vegetables. They would later be penalized by headquarters. The Elder Council also issued a special instruction specifying the magnitude of the penalty. This is also a unique police function, conditions in the ghetto making it necessary that even this kind of work, normally carried out by watchmen, would also be incorporated into the activities of the police.

In the month of October were penalized:

For insulting, resisting, and not obeying the police	6 persons
" disturbing the public peace	1	"
" using police insignia	1	"
" sanitation offenses	10	"
" going without patches	1	"
" trading in the forbidden district	2	"
" violation of garden-security regulations	8	"
" violation of identity-card regulations	5	"

| Total | 34 persons |

There are penalties in the month of October for violations of identity-card regulations, which are penalties not for going without a card but for other types of offenses. This month the police began to carry out identity-card inspection in the entire ghetto area.

Card inspection consisted of policemen—each in his street and section—going from house to house, starting at ten o'clock in the evening, checking everyone's card.

Identity-card inspections had to be conducted for the following reasons:

After a few months of compulsory identity cards, many irregularities were observed. There were many people who lost their cards but failed to report the loss. Many moved from one dwelling to another and did not remove the registration [in their previous precinct] or reregister [in the new precinct]. It also became apparent that there were residents without any cards at all (those who had an interest in not having a card), and a variety of other irregularities that could be clarified only by an inspection on the spot. From October on inspections were therefore initiated, and various mistakes and irregularities were uncovered. There were also a few malicious cases, for which the people were punished.

In the month of November were penalized:

For resisting the police	6	persons
" disturbing the public peace	1	"
" violating sanitary regulations	3	"
" trading in a forbidden district	6	"
" violation of rules of bath regulations	1	"
Total	17	persons

In the month of December were penalized:

For resisting the police	7	persons
" misleading the police	4	"
" disturbing the public peace	2	"
" sanitation offenses	2	"
" trading in the forbidden district	1	"
" tearing up houses	1	"
" violating rules of the identity-card law	3	"
Total	20	persons

From all these tables it may be seen that the police force reacts under diverse conditions and circumstances, penalizes, and maintains peace and order in the ghetto.

Summarizing police activity over the entire year, control of work obligations is of greatest emphasis—this was the principal work of the police over the entire time period.

A large part of police activity is devoted to sanitation service.

Slobodka, particularly the old-city streets, were always "famous" for their filth—neglected old huts with trash containers between them that had not been cleaned for years. Coming into the ghetto, with its associated crowding, caused even greater dirt in the yards and, to an extent, also in the houses. From the very first days of coming into the ghetto, the police began to deal with sanitation. Later, beginning with the spring of 1942, a large sanitation action started, when it was established that every resident of the house had his assigned day when he had to sweep and clean the yard and the street; in this way a certain order was established. The policeman—the section leader—would come every day to inspect, and if things were not in order, then the one whose turn it was to clean would be punished.

In addition, the police force had its regular daily work of patrolling the streets, regular postings at a variety of locations, implementing a variety of sentences, informing the population of a variety of decrees and orders of the Elder Council and of the authorities, as well as dealing with various complaints of residents concerning disturbances, fights, quarrels, grievances—dozens and hundreds of cases when everyone turned to the nearby police precinct and the policemen had to hear things out, react, penalize, and restore order.

All of the previously listed administrative penalties, and the general administrative activity of the police, are actually assignments that do not belong directly to police functions, but, under our circumstances, it is not possible to separate administrative and police work; both, taken together, make up a single totality, representing police work covering all aspects of ghetto life.

The Police as a Social Organization
(the Swearing-in Ceremony, Police Concerts)

In the beginning of the year 1942, when, as noted, material life in the ghetto had greatly improved, when ideas of spiritual and communal activity began to circulate, there was also the attempt by the police to introduce—within the narrow limits of ghetto possibilities—some cultural activity into the police.

On the initiative of police inspector Zupovitz, the idea was floated in the administration of establishing a police association. The creation of some kind of sport building was foreseen, where policemen would exercise and do drill practice. Lecture series by experts were also foreseen, on community, administrative, and judicial issues, as well as lectures on Jewish history.

In January 1942 such a police building was acquired on Vienozinskio street, but it did not last long. Policemen showed very little interest in it. In addition, the Brazilke district was evacuated shortly afterwards, causing a housing shortage and requiring release of the building. Thus, nothing came of the whole matter.

In October 1942 police inspector Z. [Zupovitz], (now second deputy chief of police) again renewed his old idea of creating a police association. The impetus for bringing this about came from the following event in the life of the police—the solemn oath of all members of the police to the Elder Council, which took place on November 1, 1942.

Mr. Z. was the father of the idea of calling a general assembly of the police and having all policemen take a formal oath. The whole idea had the external appearance of playing soldier games—policemen assembling, lining up, standing at attention—tense as strings, delivering reports, marching back and forth—playing a game. Under our circumstances and in our condition it was more than a little comical.

But there was another aspect to it, one that could not be openly expressed: a demonstration of national unity, a display of our national feelings, of resolve, of pride and hope, and of the worthiness of our nationality.

Such a display, even a quiet one, could not be permitted under our circumstances—it could lead to deaths. But such an oath-taking ceremony, officially referred to as a loyalty oath by all members of the police to the Elder Council, could indirectly express the deeply hidden nationality feelings, the profound sadness of yesterday's and today's events, and our hope for tomorrow. That was the second reason for arranging the oath, the unofficial one, but the real one.

The Elder Council accepted this idea, and the procedure for the entire ceremony was worked out, proceeding in the following manner:

Sunday, November 1, it was announced in the order of the day that all policemen must assemble at twenty minutes past two in the premises of the former Slobodka Yeshiva for a solemn oath-taking ceremony.

Although it may have been just a coincidence, the fact that the oath-taking ceremony would take place in the famous former Slobodka Yeshive touched discerning people. The Slobodka Yeshive was famous all over the world; great personalities came from it over the decades, people who played a part in the Jewish world—to become famous doctors, professors, Jewish leaders, bearers of the culture. Many of these were former pupils of the Slobodka Yeshive.

During the year that the Russians were here, they closed the Yeshive and established an institute in the building. In the early days of the ghetto it was occupied by families, the same as all other houses of prayer. Later, when the houses of prayer were vacated by their inhabitants, this building also stayed ruined and empty. The police renovated the building somewhat, made some small repairs, cleaned it up.

Honorary guests were invited to the oath-taking ceremony, for whom special seats were reserved. In order to lend the entire ceremony a solemn character, police management organized musicians residing in the ghetto. Among the policemen themselves there were two good violinists, known throughout Lithuania, Stupel and Hoffmekler. Previously, both conducted first-class orchestras in Kovno. A fine orchestra was organized to play at the oath-taking ceremony under the leadership of Hoffmekler.

All policemen showed up at the specified time and, upon the commands of police inspector Zupovitz—which for the first time in the life of the police force were given not in Lithuanian but in clear Hebrew—they lined up in front. A short while thereafter arrived the vice-chairman of the Elder Council, L. Garfunkel (the chairman, Dr. Elkes, who was generally not in good health, was ill on that particular day), in the company of the member of the Elder Council Goldberg, general secretary Golub, and representative of the labor office, Liptzer. In fluent Hebrew, police inspector Z. [Zupovitz] announced their presence in military fashion.

Mr. Garfunkel opened the proceedings with a speech concerning matters of general interest. He was followed by the chief of police, Kopelman; then the policeman Ben Zion Kliotz spoke on behalf of the policemen.

The actual oath-taking ceremony followed. The text was written in Hebrew block letters, in Yiddish and Hebrew, on decoratively illustrated parchment paper, rolled like a scroll [*megila*] and bound with a wide white-and-blue ribbon.

Golub, the general secretary of the Elder Council, read the text first in Hebrew and then in Yiddish, and then again, word by word in Yiddish, which everyone repeated after him. The text of the oath is as follows:

November 1, 1942

PLEDGE

I, member of the Jewish ghetto police, Viliampole, in the presence of the chairman of the Elder Council and the chief of ghetto police, solemnly assume the obligations:

to conscientiously and unconditionally carry out all assignments and orders without regard to time, personal considerations, or danger;

to fulfill all duties without regard to personal benefits, kinship, friendship, or acquaintance;

to rigorously guard all service-related secrets and information;

I pledge to devote all my strength and experience to the well-being of the Jewish community in the ghetto;

I PLEDGE[2]

After reciting the entire text, everyone came in a line to the table upon which lay the written text of the oath, and everyone signed it. The orchestra played national themes throughout the entire time that the line of policemen approached the table to sign the pledge, which lent a solemn character to the entire signing ceremony.

After signing the written text, the entire staff returned to its place, the command to march out was given, and the orchestra thundered the well-known, stirring national march "Beshuv Adonai" [When the Lord brings back]. It was as though the sound of the tune touched off the police staff

2. The manuscript includes the Yiddish as well as the Hebrew texts of the oath, in side-by-side columns.

and part of the audience, awakening suppressed feelings, enflaming hearts and minds, our senses—dulled and atrophied as a result of the entire bundle of our troubles, and, as if by prearrangement, thundered from the throats of hundreds of people, together with the orchestra, *beshuv Adonai et shivas Tzi-yon hayinu k-kholmim, oz yimohle skhok pinu u-lshoneinu rinoh . . . ha-zorim b-dimoh, b-rinoh yiktzoru* [From Psalm 126: When the Lord brings the captives of Zion home, we will be as dreamers, yet our mouths will fill with laughter, our lips with song . . . those who sow in tears, will reap with song]. With tears in our eyes the entire assembly sang along the words of the prophecy of freedom and liberation, of the fulfillment of our dreamed-of and most sacred hopes, which are today only fantasies but may perhaps become a reality tomorrow.

With the orchestra playing and the policemen and the assembled people singing, moved by the profound impression made by the demonstration of national will, everyone dispersed.

After this oath-taking ceremony, the idea matured to establish a police association building with a permanent orchestra—a building for music that would serve the cultural needs of the police and of the ghetto population.

Creation of the police association quarters in the premises of the former yeshiva was announced in the order of the day of November 28. Guidelines for the operation of the police association quarters were developed and were endorsed by the chairman of the Elder Council on January 3, 1943. These guidelines defined the activities of the police association quarters. The guidelines consisted of seven paragraphs in which the following is set forth:

The police association building is being established to educate and develop the police staff, which is to function as a separate police entity and be managed by the chief of the police association.

Activities of the police association are divided into organizational and artistic sectors.

The organizational sector encompasses the theoretical lectures and drill exercises. The artistic sector encompasses musical and artistic activities.

The chief of the police association directs all the activities of the police association and, with the concurrence of police management, determines the work-plan for both sectors.

The chief of the police association routinely makes reports to the police administration and receives directions concerning the activities of the police association.

As may be seen from these guidelines, creation of the police association was for theoretical education and development purposes, as well as for artistic and musical performance purposes. In effect, however, the police association quarters became the only place where the permanent police orchestra gave concerts, which were at a high artistic level.

The police association building was rebuilt and renovated, a proper concert hall was arranged, complete with all the decorations, as in the good old days. Music concerts were given every Saturday and Sunday, attended by hundreds of people. Singers and actors were also included, to sing and give recitals.

At the time, creation of a concert hall in the ghetto provoked much commentary and criticism. It was said that the ghetto is not the place to give concerts; this is not the place to make musical presentations and to be merry. We have neither the right nor the desire to forget all that we have lived through.

On the other hand, it became evident later on that the concerts also had a positive character, in the sense that, when all is said and done, one must have in the ghetto a few hours in the week when one can forget a little, to rest up somewhat from the daily nightmare and to rise somewhat above the day-to-day grayness, into a nicer world that fills one with hope and gives courage.

The second view prevailed. The concerts continue uninterrupted and are a positive aspect of ghetto life.

Who would have believed a year ago that Jews in the ghetto would have concerts? Life, by itself, makes things happen that could normally never come about.

A normal life—given a little peace and a semblance of security, and already there is activity, enterprise, vigor, release of pent-up energy.

The police association—a product of its time, of improved living conditions in the ghetto.

Evolution of the Manuscript

SAMUEL SCHALKOWSKY

Who Authored the History of the Viliampole Jewish Ghetto Police?

At the very beginning of the manuscript, in the introduction, the authors (plural) are identified as being themselves policemen. But why the anonymity of the authors? Is it because of caution, in the event the document should fall into the hands of the Nazis and documentation of their brutal crimes lead to retaliation? (The police history carefully avoids any reference to resistance activity by policemen.) On the other hand, the names of policemen—but more frequently their initials—are often mentioned in the text. Whether using initials was considered sufficient to obscure their identity, or whether it was simply a matter of writing convenience, there is no reference whatsoever in the text, by name or by initials, to the identity of the authors. Nor is there information to shed light on them in the extensive police document collection of which this manuscript is a part. (*Surviving the Holocaust: The Kovno Ghetto Diary* by Avraham Tory, secretary of the Elder Council, and the book by Leib Garfunkel, vice-chairman of the Elder Council, also don't indicate any awareness by these members of the Elder Council of the details of the police history project.)

The question arises whether maintaining author anonymity was, perhaps, a conscious effort to direct credit for this project to the police force as a whole rather than to particular individuals. The entire leadership of the ghetto police was murdered by the Nazis in March 1944. All direct participants in the preparation of the police history have therefore, most likely, perished without providing any record of their involvement. The following summarizes the results of a detailed examination of the manuscript, including its numerous handwritten notations and markings, and of related background information, in an attempt to shed some light on some of the unanswered questions concerning the initiation of the project and evolution of the manuscript into the final, albeit incomplete, form in which it was ultimately found.

Of particular interest are the references in the text to the time when the writing took place. Some of these time markers give a specific date, for example, "when we are writing these lines (end of August 1943)." Other dates are arrived at by extrapolation, for example, "but now, a year and a quarter after the Great Action [October 28, 1941]" leads to the time of writing as being January 1943. There are a total of five such timeline markers in the text. They are plotted in Figure A1 against the corresponding running page number in which they appear, including a notation of the chapter number of which the page is a part.[1]

The first time marker shown in Figure A1 is January 1943. It is contained in running page number 79 of the manuscript, which is the last page of chapter 3 of the text. These 75 pages of text of chapters 1, 2, and 3 represent nearly one third of the total of 249 document text pages and must have been written over a period of a few months before January 1943. Initiation of the police history project must have therefore occurred sometime in the last quarter of 1942, a period of time actually covered in chapters 10 and 11 of the manuscript, when "our life [in the ghetto] had changed for the better" (running page 79). It was a time well into the middle of the "quiet period," characterized by the absence of organized Nazi actions of extermination, although not without frequent arbitrary killing of individual Jews.[2] As noted in the text (running page 226; this volume, page 333), "food products in the ghetto were in abundance, general conditions in the ghetto had more or less settled down and, besides this, the overall political-military situation had changed to the detriment of our enemies."

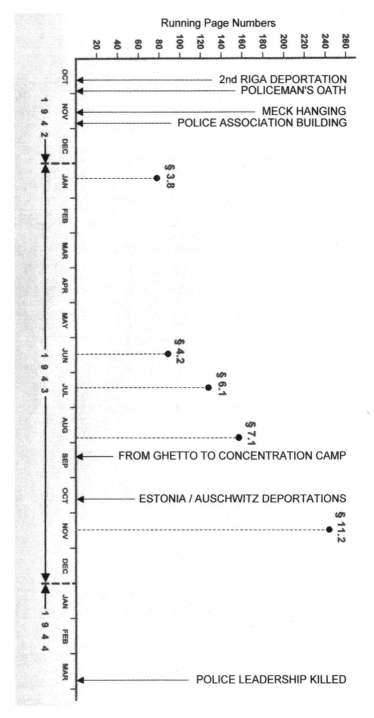

Figure A1. Timeline Markers.

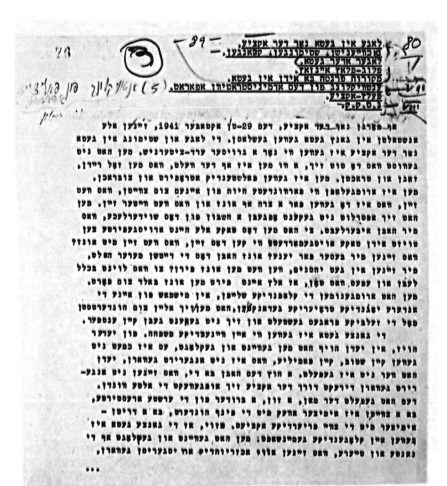

Figure A2. Topic Listings for Chapters 4, 6, 7 and 8. [Running page number 80]

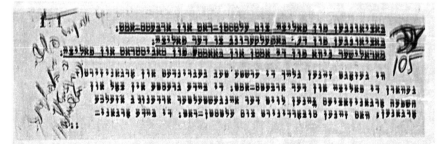

Figure A3. Topic Listing of Chapter 5. [Running page number 105]

366

5

אַרײַנפֿיר.

די געשיכטע פֿון קאָוונער אידישער געטאָ-פּאָליצײ איז אין גלײַכצײַטיק די
געשיכטע פֿון גאַנצן קאָוונער געטאָ. אַלע אומשטריסלונגען און שׂרפֿות איבער־
לעבונגען, גײִשות און, בלוטיקע רציחות, דאָס גאַנצע קאַפּיטל פֿון בלוט,
פֿײַן און טרערן – בילדן דעם שוידערלעכן באַן, האָט אַף אים האַט זיך
אָנטײַקלט די אידישע געטאָ-פּאָליצײ פֿון דעם ערשטן גרינדונגס-מאָמענט
אָן ביז זײַן הינטיקן טאָג.

עס איז אומֿמעגלעך שרײַן איצט צו שילדערן, צו מאַכן הײַסער גיט־אָיז
סך-הכלדיקע אויסמורי העבן דעם לעבן אין קאָוונער געטאָ, אונטערצוּפֿירן
אַ סך־הכל פֿון דער פּעטיקײַט פֿון די געטאָ-אײַנשטאַלטן, פֿאַרשטאָ, זהנען
מיר נאָך, לײַדער, בײַ די חורבן-צו-טאָג אין מיטן "האַנדלונגען", אין שטורם
פֿון די געשעענישן. די געשיכטע פֿון קאָוונער געטאָ איז נאָך נִיט אַבגעשלאָסען,
מעגלעכן קומען צו נײַע בלעטער, באַגאָסן מיט טרערן און בלוט, דער חשעף־
דיקער גורל פֿון דעם ביסאַלע ליטוישע אידן בכלל און פֿון קאָוונער שאֵריה
הפּליטה בפרט איז נאָך נִיט אומבאַשטימט. קאָן נאָך קריין רירי גיט הענ סך־
הכלֿן, בחשבונ, זינוגן נאָך אַ סך געשעענישן צו גאַנג, צו פֿרישן, אַז מען
זאָל זיך קאָנען אביעקטעיון אַרומזעהן העבן דער אַנגדלונג פֿון דער אַדער
יעני בערזאָן, און דעם אַרער יעניגע אינסטאַלט. מיר שטעקן צו פֿיר אין
געטאָ, אַז מיר זאָלן קאָנען זיך אומהוויגן אַף דער הירך, האָס איז גרויסיק,
כדי צו קאָנען אביעקטעיון אורטיילן העבן מעגליכן און געשעענישן.
די פֿאַראַסער פֿון דער דאָזיקער געשיכטע אַליין פֿאַליצעירן וועל
זיי אַף אַלע אַלע בפֿילע קוֿקן, אַזוי צו זאָגן, דורך פּאָליצײַשע ברילן, זו העלון
אַטאַק מיט אַלע כוחות זיך מיקן אַבזיהיון די אָביעקעיהעסען, איבעבבוגעבען
אַלע געשעענישן און מאַטידלונגען אין זייער אמת ליכֿט, אַזוי אײַ זה זאַנק
באַמת פֿאַרגעקומען, נִיט איבערסירטּאָנדיק אָ אָן און נִיט פֿאַרסיפֿערנודיק. עס
איז נאָך זיך געטראָפֿן די שתּה, חען עס זאָל מעגלעך זיין אַלֿ געוווי אַרישאו־
טאַרשן. דערײַער זינען מעגלעך אין אנדֿערע אָדער געטאָיעס אומפּאיגקפּלעקאַפּיעס,
העלכע העלן אַמٰער זין נִיט קריין באַריסנדיקע, אַלֿבֿאַלﬦ דעם דער צֹוקינפֿסינער
היסטאָריקער דע געשילדערן דאָ געבראַכע גנוגג קאַנסטאַליירטע מאַטעריאַל העבן דער געשיכטע
פֿון קאָוונער אידן בײַ די גרויליקע יאָרן 1941, 1942, ... און דאָס איז
דער היבטיקטפֿאַר ציל פֿון די חישעֿרודיקע שורות.

די פֿאַרגעשיכטע פֿון קאָוונער געטאָ.

1. די ערשטע האָבן.

דער 22-סן יוני 1941, דער טאָג, חען עס האָבן זיך אָנגעהויבֿגעפּאסטויסן
די צהי ריזן, דאָס נאַציאָנאַל-סאָציאַליסטישע דײַטשלאַנד און דער באָלשהוים־
טישער ראַטן-פֿאַראַבאַנד, איז אַ חעגד-פּונקטּ אין דער געשיכטע פֿון דער העלט־
מלחמה, העלכע דאַרף באַשטימען דעם גורל פֿון אַלע פֿעלקער און פֿון אַלע
קאָנטינענטן אַף ישׂרהונדערטערס.ﬦ דער 22-סן יוני איז אָויך דער גורל-טאָג
מאָרן ליטוישן אידנטוסּ – אין די נאָנטסטע חדשים איז אַף אײַביק ﬡ רחמאנפּטו
געהאָרן דער סיקאזאָל פֿון האָס בײַ זאָ נײַן צֹהגֵל ליטוישע אידן.
גלייך דוניסיק, דעם 22-סן יוני, אין דעם ערשטן מלחמה-טאָג, חען עס
איז קלאָר געהאָרן, אַז דאָס סאֵהױפּסישע מיליטער סיז זיך צֹויריק, אַז די
..

The last quarter of 1942 involved the Jewish police in two major ghetto events: the second transport to Riga in October 1942 and the Meck episode November 15–18 (chapter 10). But this period is also marked by initiatives by the police leadership focused on the internal life of the police institution. Thus, on November 1 took place the formal oath-taking ceremony by the entire police force, pledging to devote all their "strength and experience to the well-being of the Jewish community in the ghetto." And on November 28, creation of the newly formed police association was announced "to educate and develop the police staff." This period is characterized in the manuscript as "A normal life—given a little peace and a semblance of security, and already there is activity, enterprise, vigor, release of pent-up energy" (see last page of the manuscript). In this environment of internally directed police initiatives, it is quite likely that the preparation by policemen of the History of the Viliampole (Kovno) Jewish Ghetto Police would have been organized and set in motion by the police leadership.[3]

As stated in the introduction to the police history, "the future historian will find here sufficient verified material of the history of the Kovno Jews in the gruesome years of 1941, 1942." But to provide "verified material" required that someone other than the writer check this material. This was indeed done—at least initially by other policemen. Thus, there are numerous handwritten notes in the margins of the pages of chapter 3, mostly in the section titled "Development and Expansion of the Police Force." Some are corrections; for example, it was "Kaminski," not Jordan, who brought the certificates to the Elder Council. Others are suggested elaborations, such as the police activity being described was carried out "pursuant to an order from the commandant"; or exhortations for more detail—to give "more specific examples" of Lithuanian break-ins, raping, and killing, or of arbitrary shooting at the gate; or suggestions to provide specific dates. A number of individual policemen, familiar with the reported events, were thus involved in checking the author's text.

Another aspect of policemen participation was that of being questioned by an author about events in which they were participants or which they witnessed firsthand. For example, in the chapter 9 section dealing with the Caspi period, the author notes that were it not for the tragic ending of Caspi, who had an unusual power over the police leadership, "people around him would not be talking and authentic information would not have been available."

Support to the authors by police management is demonstrated by the access they were given to the extensive police files and archives. Chapter 11, for example, contains twelve detailed tables of data concerning the types of arrests made. Chapter 6 includes listings of police personnel categories at different times as well as detailed organizational structures and associated authority and duties.[4] Verbatim reproductions of Elder Council orders, as well as detailed instructions and decrees from the Nazi rulers transmitted to the police, can be found throughout the manuscript.

Arrangement and rearrangement of the text material can be traced through the modifications of text page numbers and through the shifting location of groupings of these page numbers. It suggests that the actual writing was done by a lead author as well as by additional contributing author(s), integration of the text into the manuscript most likely being done by the lead author.

Chapter 5 is one example of text provided by a contributing author and its integration into the manuscript. This chapter, dealing with the interrelationships of the principal ghetto institutions and the ghetto population, had to have been written by someone high in the police hierarchy. (It includes a judgment as to the "moral level" of these institutions and of their members.) Figure A2 is a copy of the first page of what was to become chapter 5, identified as text page number 71a. But page number 71, which is the last page of chapter 3, ends with a paragraph introducing the material of ultimate chapter 5; that is, it was actually at first slated to be chapter 4. Indeed, the handwritten marking to the right of the three underlined lines at the top of figure A2 shows the Roman numeral five written over a *daled*—the fourth letter of the Hebrew alphabet.

Figure A3 is the first page of chapter 4, which begins with a listing of the topics covered in the 100 pages provided by a contributing author of what was to become chapters 4, 6, 7, and 8. A translation of this topic listing is provided below (it was not included in the body of the English text):

Situation in the ghetto after the "action,"
after pains, moods, rumors.

Camp or ghetto.
Airfield work quotas.
Sources of livelihood of the Jews in the ghetto.
Development of the administrative apparatus.
Fur-"action."
NSKK.

The handwritten Roman numerals on the right of the typed topic listings indicate the chapter numbers assigned to the associated topics, enclosed in handwritten parentheses. (Handwriting to the left of the sixth line of topics reads "Development of the *police* apparatus.")

Arrangement of these 100 pages of text in the manuscript is according to the following chapter assignments:

Text page number	No. of pages	Assigned chapter No.
89–106	18	4
107–135	29	6
136–143	8	4
144–170	27	7
170–187	18	8
Total: 100		

In Figure A3, the circled Hebrew letter daled, fourth in the alphabet, marks this page as the beginning of chapter 4.

The text page numbers of 71a–89 derive from the original assignment of this material as chapter 4. These page numbers were not changed when they became chapter 5 and are therefore now out of place.

As illustrated in Figures A2 and A3, text provided by contributing authors is characterized by beginning with a listing of topics covered, without any dividing subsection titles. By contrast, writings of the lead author include typewritten section and also some subsection titles, as illustrated in Figure A4, which is the first page of manuscript text. At the top is the "Introduction" title, followed later by:

"The Prehistory of the Kovno Ghetto"
"The First Weeks"

Note that chapter number assignment is done later by placing handwritten letters of the Hebrew alphabet within the square box. Thus, the "Introduction" becomes chapter 1 and the "Prehistory . . ." chapter 2. Chapter 3 displays the same format of typewritten headings. In addition, material by the lead author also has typewritten text page numbers at the center top of the page, using the format –xx–. This is true for all of the twelve pages of chapters 1 and 2 and for the beginning pages of chapter 3. The rest of chapter 3 was apparently subjected to considerable editing, with associated modifications of text page numbers. (This also resulted in duplicate text page numbers 18–21 appearing after sequential text page number 21.)

Using the above distinguishing characteristics of the lead author's material, it can be concluded that chapters 9, 10, and 11 were also written by the lead author, possibly with the assistance of others in assembling the data tables of chapter 11. (It is likely that the sixteen pages of chapter 9 were first an integral part of chapter 10 since there is a gap of seventeen page numbers in the sequence of text page numbers of chapter 10—they run from 187 to 196, then skip to 213–216.)

The final arrangement of the manuscript text was most likely done toward the end of 1943. For, as shown in Figure A1, the latest time marker, deriving from only a few pages before the end of the manuscript, is November 1943. This is a time when conditions in the ghetto had already changed for the worse, heading to its liquidation. It started early in September 1943 with ghetto control turned over to the SS. News was received in the Kovno ghetto that the nearby Vilna ghetto was liquidated on September 23, 1943, with deportations to Estonia and Latvia. Deportations from the Kovno ghetto to nearby work camps also took place during this period. In October there were deportations from Kovno to Estonia and to Auschwitz. On November 1 the ghetto was officially reclassified as a concentration camp. With the new Nazi rulers taking over Elder Council functions, it became clear that liquidation of the ghetto was imminent.[5] Activities on the police history project became hasty, focused on arranging the material in the desired order as quickly as possible.

The table of contents served as the template for this activity. But rather than changing the text page numbers to conform to the page numbers of the table of contents, a new set of page numbers, the running page numbers, appear to have been added to identify the desired sequence of text. An attempt was also made to write in the subchapter numbers and their titles—as given in the table of contents, in the appropriate text locations. This was done up to chapter 3, then only subchapter numbers were added. In the end, in chapters 10 and 11, there are neither subchapter numbers nor titles in the text. (Their locations are readily identifiable from the subject matter of the text, and the corresponding table of contents titles are included in this English translation.)

It is noteworthy that in spite of the rush to end the project, the last few pages of the manuscript, written in November 1943, describe the more "normal life" a year earlier that led to the policemen's oath ceremony and concerts in the police association building, and—quite likely—also to the initiation of the police history project.

Notes

1. A continuous, running page number was handwritten at the top right side of every page of the manuscript, in the order in which the material was arranged in accordance with the sequence in the table of contents. Running page numbers 1–4 are of the two-page manuscript table of contents and of its two-page carbon copy. Because of these four pages, the total of 253 running page numbers exceeds by four the total of 249 manuscript text page numbers identified in the document table of contents. There are also page numbers at the top center of the page, entered by the author or editor of the material. These can appear in any one of three formats: (1) typewritten as "–xxx–," (2) handwritten, or (3) typewritten and then modified by handwriting. These manuscript page numbers, and the shifts in the placement of groups of these numbers, provide a source of information on the rearrangement of text in the evolution of the manuscript (see below).

2. See Garfunkel, *Kovna ha-yehudit be-hurbana*, 85.

3. Moshe Levin, who held top positions in the police and became its chief at the end of 1943, believed in the importance of preserving a record of Nazi crimes. On December 25, 1943, a group of Jews, who were part of the detail digging up and burning the bodies of thousands of Jews massacred at the Ninth Fort, escaped and made their way to the ghetto. Moshe Levin immediately went to them and is quoted as saying to them: "We will hide you from the Gestapo. You must remain alive in order that you may tell the whole world what you have seen with your own eyes at the Ninth Fort, what the German and Lithuanian savages were capable of doing to innocent people. I and my sons are not

as important as you!" (Z. A. Brown and D. Levin, *The Story of an Underground* [Jerusalem: Yad Vashem, 1962 (Hebrew)], 170).

Yehuda Zupovitz, who also held high positions in the police (inspector, deputy chief), was instrumental in organizing the policemen's oath ceremony and in the creation of the police association (see chapter 11, "The Police as a Social Organization"). According to Yehudit Sperling, the wife of Yehuda Zupovitz, in the ghetto, "Yehuda spoke often of the importance of collecting evidence against the Nazis and that he also encouraged his friend Kadish to take photographs of ghetto life." (Phone communication August 30, 2005.)

4. Writing about house searches and related killings, it is noted in chapter 3, under "The Personal Effects and Gold Actions," that "As can be seen now from the police archive, where accurate numbers, dates, and circumstances are recorded, the shootings proceeded as if the number of Jews to be shot daily had been specified."

5. See Garfunkel, *Kovna ha-yehudit be-hurbana*, 147.

BIBLIOGRAPHY

Adler, Stanislaw. *In the Warsaw Ghetto, 1940–1943: An Account of a Witness.* Jerusalem: Yad Vashem, 1982.

Birger, Zev. *No Time for Patience: My Road from Kaunas to Jerusalem.* New York: Newmarket Press, 1999.

Brown, Z. A., and D. Levin. *The Story of an Underground* [Hebrew]. Jerusalem: Yad Vashem, 1962.

Dieckmann, Christoph. *Deutsche Besatzungspolitik in Litauen 1941–1944.* Göttingen: Wallstein, 2011.

———. "The German Invasion and the Kaunas Pogrom." In *Shared Memory-Divided Memory: Jews and Others in Soviet-Occupied Poland, 1939–1941,* ed. Elazar Barkan, Elizabeth Cole, and Kai Struve. Leipzig: Leipziger Universitätsverlag, 2007.

Eidintas, Alfonsas. *Jews, Lithuanians and the Holocaust.* Vilnius: Versus Aureus, 2003.

Elkes, Joel. *Values, Belief and Survival: Dr. Elkhanan Elkes and the Kovno Ghetto.* London: Vale Publishing, 1997.

Faitelson, Alex. *Heroism and Bravery in Lithuania 1941–1945.* Jerusalem: Gefen Publishing House, 1996.

———. *The Truth and Nothing but the Truth.* Jerusalem: Gefen, 2006.

Gar, Yosef. *Umkum fun der Yidisher Kovne* [The destruction of Jewish Kovno]. Munich: Association of Lithuanian Jews in the American Zone in Germany, 1948.

Garfunkel, Leib. *Kovna ha-yehudit be-hurbana* [The destruction of Kovno's Jewry]. Jerusalem: Yad Vashem, 1959.

Ginaite-Rubinson, Sara. *Resistance and Survival: The Jewish Community in Kaunas, 1941–1944.* Oakville, Ont.: Mosaic Press, 2005.

Goldberg, Yakov. "Bletlekh fun Kovner Eltestenrat." *Fun letztn khurbn,* no. 7 (1948): 32.

Goldstein-Golden, Lazar. *Fun Kovner Geto biz Dachau.* New York: E. Goldstein, 1985.

Gombinski, Stanislaw [Jan Mawult]. *Wspomnienia Policjanta z Warszawskiego Getta.* Warsaw: Stowarzyszenie Centrum Badan nad Zaglada Zydow, 2010.

Gordon, Harry. *The Shadow of Death: The Holocaust in Lithuania.* Lexington: University Press of Kentucky, 1992.

Gringauz, Samuel [Shmuel]. "The Ghetto as an Experiment of Jewish Social Organization." *Jewish Social Studies* 11 (January 1949): 3–20.

———. "Dos Kulturlebn in Kovner Geto." In *Lite,* ed. Mendel Sudarsky. New York: Kultur-Gezelschaft fun Litvische Yidn, 1951.

———. "Kurbn Kovne." *Fun letztn khurbn,* no. 7 (1948): 11.

"Kamfs bavegung in Kovner Geto." *Fun letztn khurbn,* no. 10 (1948): 6–8.

Kaplan, Israel. "Di aerodrom arbet in Kovner Geto." *Fun letztn khurbn,* no. 8 (1948): 3–27.

Levin, Dov. ———. "How the Jewish Police in the Kovno Ghetto Saw Itself." *YIVO Bleter,* new series, 3 (1997): 284–290.

———. "How the Kovno Ghetto Police Saw Itself." http://yadvashem.org/odot_ pdf/Microsoft%20Word%20-%202020.pdf.

———. "Kaunas." In *The YIVO Encyclopedia of Jews in Eastern Europe,* ed. Gershon David Hundert, 1:879. New Haven, Conn.: Yale University Press, 2008.

———. *The Lesser of Two Evils: Eastern European Jewry under Soviet Rule, 1939–1941.* Philadelphia: Jewish Publication Society, 1995.

———, ed. *Pinkas Ha-kehillot: Lita.* Jerusalem: Yad Vashem, 1996.

———. "Tnuat hameri viha-partizanim shel yehudei Kovna b'milkhemet ha'olam ha'shniya." In *Yahadut Lita.* Tel Aviv: Mutual Assistance Association of Former Residents of Lithuania in Israel, 1984.

Mayerowitch-Schwarz, Esther. Foreword to "The History of the Kovno Jewish Ghetto Police (Excerpts)." *YIVO Bleter,* new series, 3 (1997): 206–207.

Mishell, William W. *Kaddish for Kovno: Life and Death in a Lithuanian Ghetto, 1941–1945.* Chicago: Chicago Review Press, 1988.

Neuberger, Hirsh. Yalkut Moreshet Archive, No. A.571.

Neuberger, Tzvi. "Be-geto Kovno." *Yalkut Moreshet* 18 (1974): 158–62.

Porat, Dina. "The Justice System and Courts of Law in the Ghettos of Lithuania." *Holocaust and Genocide Studies* 12, no. 1 (Spring 1998): 49–65.

Rabinowitz, Yitzhak. "Lishkat ha'avodah ha-germanit ba'geto." In *Yahadut Lita.* Tel Aviv: Mutual Assistance Association of Former Residents of Lithuania in Israel, 1984.

Segalson, Aryeh. *Be-lev ha-ofel: Kilyonah shel Kovna ha-Yehudit.* Jerusalem: Yad Vashem, 2003.

Segalson, Moshe. "Di groyse varshtatn in Kovner Geto." *Fun letztn khurbn,* no. 8 (1948): 50–58.

———. "Mayne Zikhroynes" (unpublished).

Tory, Avraham. *Surviving the Holocaust: The Kovno Ghetto Diary.* Cambridge, Mass.: Harvard University Press, 1990.

United States Holocaust Memorial Museum. *Hidden History of the Kovno Ghetto.* Boston: Little, Brown, 1997.

Weiss, Aharon. "Relations between the Judenrat and the Jewish Police." In *Patterns of Jewish Leadership in Nazi Europe 1933–1945,* ed. Yisrael Gutman and Cynthia J. Haft. Jerusalem: Yad Vashem, 1979.

Zupovitz-Sperling, Dita. "Gvure hot a sakh penimer." In *60 AKO: Nisht vi shof tsu der shkhite,* ed. Tzvi Hersh Smoliakov. Tel Aviv: Y. L. Peretz, 2001.

INDEX

The anonymous policemen who composed this secret history were members of a Jewish police force that served in the Kovno ghetto from August 1941 until the Nazis murdered the leadership of the force in March 1944.

Samuel Schalkowsky, a survivor of the Kovno ghetto, is a volunteer at the United States Holocaust Memorial Museum.

Samuel D. Kassow is Charles H. Northam Professor of History at Trinity College and author of *Who Will Write Our History? Emanuel Ringelblum, the Warsaw Ghetto, and the Oyneg Shabes Archive* (Indiana University Press, 2007).